Beyond Expectations

From Charcoal to Gold

Njenga Karume

with

Mutu wa Gethoi

Kenway Publications

D1218488

Published by
Kenway publications
an imprint of
East African Educational Publishers Ltd.
Brick Court, Mpaka Road/Woodvale Grove
Westlands, P.O. Box 45314
Nairobi – 00100
KENYA.

email: eaep@eastafricanpublishers.com
website: www.eastafricanpublishers.com

East African Educational Publishers Ltd.
P.O. Box 11542
Kampala
UGANDA.

Ujuzi Books Ltd.
P.O. Box 38260
Dar es Salaam
TANZANIA.

First published 2009

ISBN 978-9966-25-741-3

Printed by
English Press Ltd.,
P. O. Box 30127,
Nairobi, Kenya.

Contents

Kenway Autobiographies

1. *A Fly in Amber,* Susan Wood
2. *A Love Affair with the Sun,* Michael Blundell
3. *Facing Mount Kenya,* Jomo Kenyatta
4. *From Simple to Complex: The Journey of a Herdsboy,* Prof. Joseph Maina Mungai
5. *Illusion of Power,* G. G. Kariuki
6. *The Mediator: General Sumbeiywo and the Sudan Peace Process,* Waithaka Waihenya
7. *Madatally Manji: Memoirs of a Biscuit Baron,* Madatally Manji
8. *My Journey Through African Heritage,* Allan Donavan
9. *Nothing but the Truth,* Yusuf K. Dawood
10. *Tales from Africa,* Douglas Collins
11. *Theatre Near the Equator,* Annabel Maule
12. *The Southern Sudan: Struggle for Liberty*, Elijah Malok
13. *Wings of the Wind*, Valerie Cuthbert
14. *Tom Mboya: The Man Kenya Wanted to Forget,* David Goldsworthy
15. *No Yet Uhuru,* Jaramogi Oginga Odinga
16. *Freedom and After,* Tom Mboya

Dedication

This book is dedicated to my late wife, Maryanne Wariara,
My new-born son Emmanuel Joseph Njenga Karume,
And my entire family.
I would also like to dedicate it to all the youth of Kenya.

Acknowledgements

The following story is based on a series of extensive interviews and conversations which took place between February 2008 and October 2009. The House of History team, headed by Mutu wa Gethoi, assisted by Dorothy Holi and Wahome Karangi Karengo, have my profound thanks for arranging these memories and episodes into a coherent and readable form. Their careful translation, probing questions and accompanying research has woven a manuscript which covers many interesting and challenging events of my life.

I am especially indebted to Mutu for initiating the work. Without his constant pestering, this project may never have seen the light of day. His passionate interest, searching curiosity and analysis of cultural history have rendered a colourful and insightful backdrop to the story and I am pleased that he insisted on reflecting the cultural identity and values of my people.

I would also like to thank Professor Kibutha Kibwana, and Njoki Muhoho, for the rigorous reading and reviewing of the manuscript, their advice and many suggestions. I owe thanks to Father D. Kariuki and Dr. Wilfred Koinange for their moral support and encouragement. My deep appreciation must also go to my Personal Assistant, Lilian Wangui Gachuhi, for handling the overwhelming job of managing my schedule and my office, and James Gatheru Mukora, my driver, who has given such dedicated service for forty years.

My sincere thanks go to my publishers, East African Educational Publishers, for accepting to publish my work, and for doing such a fine job. Their team of dedicated editors and designers went out of their way to ensure this book was published within a very strict time frame.

Njenga wa Karume
October 2009

Foreword by Prof. Kivutha Kibwana

I first learned of this book in a most unlikely place. Both Mzee Njenga Karume and I had been admitted to neighbouring rooms in a hospital in Nairobi. When I found out his room was near mine, I began to visit him in the evenings and he kindly reciprocated, even bringing along a share of the fruits that his family brought him.

During my first visit to his room, I asked Karume if he had ever considered writing about his life. I knew quite a bit about Karume's background, and I was convinced that his story—the story of a brilliant, self-made man—would be a national treasure, particularly for the youth of Kenya. I tried to persuade him on the value of writing his experiences. I knew Karume's granddaughter was an award winning film-maker and I thought she could coax her grandfather to tell his history and even explore the possibilities of creating a documentary film out of the material.

I was therefore pleasantly surprised when Karume told me that his autobiography was, in fact, almost complete. He had been working with a team of writers and the story was in its final stages. I found this very intriguing, and asked if I could read the manuscript. He agreed. He actually went as far as to give me his personal draft copy and I was thrilled to learn that I would be the first 'outsider' to read the manuscript.

Even before I began to read the draft, I imagined that the book would be informative, inspirational and very interesting. From my long association with Karume from 2003 onward, I knew he was an excellent speaker, especially during political rallies. He was also an exceptionally gifted storyteller. Even during our time together in the hospital, he entertained me with many tales of Kenya's pre-independence and early post-independence eras.

As I started to read, I was pleased to see that he had maintained his creativity and his uniquely personal narrative style. Karume, the master raconteur, is revealed in each chapter of the book. In the same way I was held captive by his yarns on the *dramatis personae* of Kenya's freedom struggle while in hospital, the unfolding chapters in his book held my attention and interest to the last page.

I had first heard of Njenga Karume in the 1970s, in the context of the Gikuyu Embu Meru Association (GEMA), and had quite a few pre-conceived ideas about him. But meeting him personally made a great difference in my opinion. One thing that immediately struck me was his amazing memory. Despite the fact that his education never went beyond primary school, I found Karume's analytical skills, particularly of political, business and cultural issues, astounding. I also realised that when Karume wants something done, he will stubbornly persist until it is accomplished. I began to understand that part of his success in business and life was derived from his sheer persistence and the unrelenting pursuit of his goals. He will never postpone anything if it can be done immediately. I noticed, too, that Karume has the extraordinary gift of making friends in no time. No wonder his book contains details of so many friends, companions and lifelong relationships!

Reading the manuscript of Karume's life story revealed that he is an astute and shrewd businessman first, and a politician later. Indeed, he initially served more as a coordinator and founder of political and cultural initiatives, rather than as a politician. His personality emerges as an individual who magnetically attracts the confidence of others. Both ordinary citizens and leaders all seem to trust Karume and, on several occasions, he has served as an emissary to President Mwai Kibaki, who is his personal friend. He is a down-to-earth man, comfortable with both the wielders of power and with ordinary people.

I remember campaigning with Karume during the 2005 Referendum. We traversed many parts of the country to build up support for the proposed new Constitution. He was aware that the task at hand was not easy but he soldiered on. He was not distracted or discouraged when people commented that the "Yes Banana" campaign was led by old men. His loyalty to his friend President Kibaki and his belief in the new Constitution kept him actively in the campaign.

I became even more familiar with Karume when we visited parts of Kamba country and south eastern Kenya in order to assess the famine situation and also when I invited him to Makueni Constituency to help support religious activities. On all such occasions he has proved to be a generous and kind-hearted individual with a truly felt obligation to help those in need.

I firmly believe that the youth of Kenya, particularly those who want to excel in business will find Karume's story extremely instructive.

In each chapter they will learn that one can literally rise from rags to riches by dint of one's own hard work and sweat. They will see that a dream, whatever it is, must be pursued relentlessly, day by day. They will understand that anyone can become a consensus builder in his or her community and that any human being can be a genuine friend. They will discover that we must all respect each other, whatever station we occupy in life. For those who love to learn, Karume's life is a true education.

Karume's story is not merely about how a poor lad rose to wealth, power, fame and influence in the courts of three Presidents; Jomo Kenyatta, Daniel arap Moi and Mwai Kibaki. It is also the story of Karume the freedom fighter, the astute businessman, the cultural activist, the philanthropist, the family man, the faithful friend, the man of wise counsel, the elder, the storyteller . . . truly, Karume's story shows us he is a man of many parts. Although Karume has rubbed shoulders with the high and mighty he has clearly always been his own man, and followed his own mind and conscience.

As you will learn in the book, Mzee Njenga Karume plans to establish a Foundation for the benefit of the people in his area. I admire his dedication and hope that this institution will promote the ideals that have shaped his life, especially among the youth of Kenya. For those whom God generously blesses, He expects much in return. And indeed God has favoured Mr. Karume with a full and rich life. His is certainly a life worth learning about and an example to follow.

Prof. Kivutha Kibwana
Presidential Advisor, Constitutional Review
Republic of Kenya
October 2009

Preface

I first met Njenga Karume when, one Saturday afternoon in 1974, he was introduced to me by Jeremiah Kiereini as a guest in the Public Service Club where I was a member. He and Mr. Kiereini sat at a table with a number of friends, most of them wealthy and prominent personalities, some of whom were making their fortunes on smuggled coffee from Uganda, and I recall they were all laughing and joking, eating *nyama choma* (roast meat) and enjoying their drinks. Some of us civil servants at the bar looked on rather enviously. They all seemed so prosperous, carefree and highly confident. They spoke snidely about drinking mere beer, referring to it in Kikuyu as *munju* (filthy water) and all insisted on drinking bottles of whisky and other spirits. I especially noticed Njenga Karume because he stuck to his beer, yet he was just as jolly and exuberant as the rest.

Throughout the next two decades, Mr. Karume and I kept in touch every now and then as casual acquaintances, meeting in various *harambees[1]* (fund-raising meetings) and other functions, but became closer friends when I started working as a member with the Council of Elders of the Democratic Party of Kenya (DP), after multiple political parties were finally 'legalized' by the regime. DP's Council of Elders initially met clandestinely in Nathaniel Kangethe's office on Museum Hill in Nairobi but when our membership increased to more than could comfortably be accommodated, we changed our venue to a conference room at Jacaranda Hotel, which is owned by Mr. Karume. It was at this time that I finally got to know him more intimately, and we seemed to develop a certain rapport. Mr. Karume used to donate all the refreshments and the use of the hall for our meetings and I began to realize what a generous individual he was.

---

1   *Harambee!* was a national rallying call adopted by Kenyatta and politicians used it in political and fundraising meetings. The word had been adopted from Indian migrants who, while engaged in any strenuous group activity such as rowing their boats to the shore, would chant "Hare Ambe! Hare Ambe!" (Praise God! Praise God!) Kenyans corrupted the word to *harambee*.

Later DP faded away when it joined hands with other parties to form the National Rainbow Coalition and, since I found myself threatened and under surveillance for publishing literature critical to Moi's regime, I left for the academia in America and stayed away for ten years. Mr. Karume and I met again when I came back in 2001 and during one encounter, I proposed the possibility of assisting him to write his memoirs because I was convinced he had many fascinating stories to tell and revelations to make. Apparently, Mr. Karume had already started this project with some journalists but when they missed their 7 am appointments twice in a row, the project was abandoned. (Mr. Karume starts his business day very early, sometimes as early as 6 am!) But this meant that my prompting was perfectly timed and we began to discuss and draft an outline of the manuscript. Throughout our work together, I have got to know Mr. Karume and to admire him tremendously. My assumptions about his character drastically changed over the twenty-five months my team and I worked with him. He is an extraordinary individual, yet so humble that he is easily approachable and ready to help those in need. I would like to use the opportunity in this Preface, to amplify this aspect of Karume, the man.

Initially I was a little unsure about how many details he would recall covering the 80 years of his life, and concerned with how many specifics he would be willing to divulge. I was pleasantly surprised therefore, when he began to tell me his past with startling and vivid descriptions of events and episodes that were still fresh in his mind, even to the minute details of his childhood. His memory, coupled with his story-telling ability, made the production of this book a much simple matter than it initially appeared.

I also discovered that Karume was not just another Kenyan tycoon. Assisting a man to write his life story, merely because he is a successful businessman, might have proved somewhat bland. We all know about people who beat the odds to succeed in business. However, there is more to Karume than any ordinary business magnate. Financial acumen aside, Karume is a magnetic and outgoing personality and he has thousands of friends. Yet he lives a simple life, still enjoying the traditional foods that he ate in his childhood, taking pleasure in overseeing his cattle and talking to his friends over the ever popular *nyama choma*.

He is comfortable and at ease in all kinds of company. Whether he is with community elders, young people in the village, *jua kali* (open-air) mechanics by the roadside, top level politicians at cocktail parties, church leaders, or women picking coffee in the many estates in Kiambu, he is always the same person, engaging them with equal ebullience and magnanimity, never failing to take them seriously. He deals with everyone in an open and frank manner which is quite surprising.

Little by little, I learned the various episodes of Karume's life and then came to understand why so many people had urged him to write his life story. Here is a man who was born in poverty, received minimal education and then, through his own initiative, started doing business during one of the toughest times in Kenya's colonial history. Yet he succeeded in business beyond anyone's wildest dreams and rose to such prominence and popularity that he became a respected politician and Cabinet Minister who interacted intimately with all the first three of Kenya's Presidents.

As I assisted Mr. Karume to write his autobiography over the course of two years, I found him to be a person whose work ethic, patriotism, spirituality, knowledge of human psychology, generosity and business genius is most extraordinary. He is extraordinarily intelligent and I often wonder how far he might have gone if he had had the benefit of higher education.

I constantly found myself mesmerized by Karume's skills as a raconteur. His memory is phenomenal and I could not help being amazed when, for instance, he remembered the colour and price of the shirt he wore when he went to pay bride price in 1951, or the full names of a man he met only once and who gave him one night's accommodation in Nairobi in 1952. He tells vivid stories about the personalities that he has encountered in the past, remembering even the tiniest details of events that happened more than half a century back in his life. He even remembers the colour of the cup in which he was given tea by Mama Ngina Kenyatta, when he went to Gatundu in 1973.

This ability fits in well with his skills of oratory. Whatever the circumstances, he has a confident, husky voice and a way with words that catches his audience's attention. He is humorous without self-praise and he employs this wit equally well, whether talking to rural women or when talking to the President. In addition, he manages to keep his speeches and conversation lively with anecdotes that tickle his audience.

Probably because Karume received little formal education as a young man, he learned to overcome the deficit by using his memory to the extent that he has never needed to refer to notes. He never carries a diary, but if he sets an appointment for 2:30 pm two weeks thereon, you can be sure he will keep it. He listens to everyone's opinion, whatever age or social status they may be. He respects everyone, admires a few and fears no one.

Equally, as far as his business sense is concerned, he has often had to rely on the ability to adapt to new situations and challenges in his ventures and this has enabled him to prosper and survive seemingly insurmountable obstacles, even in a hostile environment. Due to this precocious talent, he was the first African to own a shop in the exclusive Indian Bazaar in Kiambu Town in 1958. Prominent politicians and freedom agitators were attracted by his early successes and would invite themselves to the back of his shop for informal sessions to strategize.

For this same reason, many of the foremost politicians of the day would ask him to accompany them to a variety of political activities and undertakings that might not otherwise have involved him. Very extraordinary! They were all comfortable with him around and they learned to trust him. He was talkative but also an intense listener when others were speaking, which is an attractive trait he has maintained to this day. People like Jomo Kenyatta, Mbiyu Koinange, James Gichuru and Tom Mboya trusted his instincts and consulted him on many issues despite his age and relatively low level of education. Even today, it is rare for a day to pass without ministers, politicians and others, dropping in to his office or calling over the phone to consult him for advice and assistance, long after he left the government.

When members of the GEMA proposed Karume to chair the influential organization in 1974, he was surprised, and even reluctant. He felt that others would be much more able to lead it. However, as it turned out, most leaders did not have the right qualities nor did they earn the same sort of respect that Mr. Karume commands. Yet he continues to be humble about his accomplishments in GEMA.

One of the most uncertain and turbulent periods that he ever lived through was the last ten years of the Nyayo era, that is, fifteen years after Kenyatta passed away. Because of a strong sense of his Kikuyu roots, loyalty to his old ally Mwai Kibaki, his business interests, and his conflict with President Moi, Karume underwent a tumultuous and perplexing interlude. It was during these final years of Moi's presidency and early days of Kibaki's administration, clearly mired in inter-party squabbles and an alleged Memorandum of Understanding within the ranks of National Rainbow Coalition (NARC) that a national referendum on a draft national constitution was introduced in 2005. The delegates who had come up with the document in the Bomas of Kenya constitutional review forum had virtually been hand-picked by Moi, and yet Kibaki's advisers did not see it fit to invalidate it.

Such was the resounding win for the Orange faction that Raila described it as the beginning of a "political tsunami" that would sweep away the Kibaki influence right through to the next General and Presidential Elections due in 2007. When the time came, Karume supported the belatedly registered Party of National Unity (PNU), which was no more than a loose coalition of parties under which Kibaki sought to be re-elected to the Presidency.

The two other main contenders for the top seat in 2007 were Raila Odinga and Kalonzo Musyoka. As widely forecast, Kibaki just barely skipped through to the presidency while Raila nearly triumphed. During this befuddled parliamentary election Karume was not so lucky. He lost heavily to his old nemesis Stanley Munga Githunguri. Neither the shifting sands in party affiliation nor the mismanaged 2005 referendum campaigns as well as PNU could save him.

Njenga Karume is not rich, but he is very wealthy. He insists that the customs of his people does not allow him to count his wealth because that would amount to *kuonia Ngai nda* ("showing one's full stomach to God" or "mocking providence").

He is one of the few top politicians who have never been associated with corruption. His detractors will not accept this, yet they dare not pinpoint any deal that he has won corruptly. He is convinced that some of his peers are quite jealous of his accomplishments, particularly because he is too independent and does not stand in awe of others. He has a very sharp mind and will outsmart his rivals when they least expect it; however that has never been equated with corruption.

Karume is focused and goal-oriented. He will work with a persistence and intensity that is amazing and this, more than any other factor, is the primary source of his success. Karume practises what he preaches, insisting that work ethic works, carrying on a value system inherited from his ancestors.

He has been an influential person in the corridors of power but has never taken undue advantage of his position to influence his business.

Furthermore, Mr. Karume is a most philanthropic person who has helped fund hundreds of institutions, mostly churches, hospitals and schools. His first concern has always been education. He himself internalised the limitations that were placed in his life due to lack of proper education and thus he continues to pay school fees for many of his neighbours and their children, in addition to ensuring that they have all their basic needs.

Just recently, when internally displaced women from Eldoret went to demonstrate outside Parliament, against the neglect by the Government, and were tear-gassed by the police and injured, I was present in his office when he received the information. He cancelled all engagements and went to meet the women, gave them money for food and bus fare and arranged for the injured to be taken to hospital for treatment. And he hardly knew any of them personally.

Perhaps one of the most surprising things I learned about Mr. Karume is his strong sense of spiritual justice, faith and atonement. He has no doubt that his many blessings come from God, and he feels the strong need to assure the continuity of such blessings by constantly helping others, doing what is right and proper, and fulfilling his obligation to future generations. He refuses to countenance harmful actions, or selfishness, feeling that any harm he might do, would result in the withdrawal of God's blessings that he enjoys. In short, he is very thankful to be so blessed by God and feels obliged to pass those blessings on to others.

I found the amazing story of Njenga Karume enlightening and an eye-opener, and I hope that the young and old will enjoy it and learn something from it too. I surely did.

Prof. Mutu wa Gethoi,
Independent Scholar,
Nairobi, 2009

Mutu wa Gethoi is a Professor of History and has taught at Northern Michigan University, University of Florida and Elmira College in upstate New York. Born in 1937, wa Gethoi is also a published poet and a lead researcher in Kumbuka Kalle Ltd, an initiative geared towards documentation, rehabilitation and publication of untold histories of East African historic sites. Currently, he is involved in authoring a number of biographies of various icons in Kenya.

Historical Background

Njenga Karume's lineage can be traced through the Kikuyu community. The Kikuyu are an agricultural people of Bantu origin who migrated eastwards from central Africa, and then looped up from the south into the area now known as Kenya, and settled in the uplands around one of the tallest volcanic cones in eastern Africa, known as Mount Kenya. Although in modern times the populations are mixed, the Kikuyu were originally bordered by the Embu and Meru peoples to the east and northern sides, and by the Kamba and Maasai on the southern and western sides. The Kikuyu, Embu and Meru peoples are all Bantu cousins who migrated together before dispersing around Ithanga-Thagichu, while the Maasai are Nilotics who migrated into Kenya from the north.

In early times, the Kikuyu, Embu and Meru were basically farming communities who tilled the land, grew crops and kept a few domestic animals. The Maasai, on the other hand, were pastoralist nomads with herds of cattle and goats who roamed the plains and hillsides searching for pasture. As is common when pastoralists and agriculturalists neighbour each other, there were often conflicts, especially over land and grazing rights. Both communities fought one another and carried out raiding expeditions to capture livestock. In addition, since mortality rates from common diseases were high, they also attempted to seize women in order to increase their size of their populations.[2]

The Kikuyu community first settled in the region commonly referred to as Murang'a. However, as the population gradually expanded, they needed more land and migrated farther north towards Nyeri (Gaaki) and south to Kiambu (Karura). Thus the northern Kikuyu of Nyeri had many altercations with the Purko Maasai, while the Kikuyu on the southern edge of Kiambu engaged in many battles with the Kaputei Maasai.

This fighting and raiding was not a constant phenomenon. There were often periods of negotiated reconciliation and trade during which the communities would live peaceably and barter for various goods, such as crops in exchange for livestock hides and skins.

---

2   L. S. B. Leakey: *The Southern Kikuyu before 1903*, Academic Press, London, 1972.

Although no boundaries had been agreed upon, by around the year 1500, most communities in this region had established general areas which they called their own, and this is where the first European adventurers and traders found them when they made incursions into East Africa's interior in the mid-1800s[3] which was around the time Njenga Karume's great grandfather, Njuguna, was born.

Thus the Kikuyu were relatively permanently settled in Nyeri, Murang'a and Kiambu. As stated above, they were prevented from going beyond this region by the Maasai in the northern and southwestern sides. However, even if the Kikuyu had managed to expand into the Maasai areas, the land there had low rainfall and as such was too dry for farming. It was basically range land, good for livestock but not at all suitable for crop production. On the south-eastern side, where the Kamba people had settled, the climatic conditions were similarly arid, if not more so.

From this initial settlement in Murang'a, Njenga's ancestor, Njunu, first migrated to Mang'u, near Thika. Later, Wagachire, (Njenga's grandfather) migrated from Mang'u to Kiambu around 1890, which was the time the British began to colonise what came to be known as Kenya and Uganda, in earnest.

During this time, the Kikuyu population continued to increase and the demand for arable land rose. By the second half of the 19th century, many families were living on the land of others as tenants *(ahoi)* and serfs *(ndungata)*. These two groups cultivated the landlord's farms on the understanding that they would be obliged to yield up a percentage of the produce to the landlord.

Although many people from Arabia, India and China had visited eastern Africa much earlier on trading expeditions, the first Europeans to come into the interior were missionaries and adventurers such as David Livingstone, Dr. Ludwig Krapf, Joseph Thompson and John Boyes "Karia-njahi." They, and other individuals like them, carried back reports of the wealth and fertility of the lands they visited and informed Europeans on life and conditions in East Africa.

Thompson, writing back to Britain about his journey through Kikuyuland in 1883, noted that the community was very hardworking. He wrote:

"Enormous quantities of sweet potatoes, yams, cassava, sugarcane, Indian corn, millet, etc., are raised, and the supplies seem to be quite inexhaustible . . . at Ngong, we carried away three months' provisions, yet it did not seem perceptibly to affect the supply or raise the ridiculously

---

3   Prof. Muriuki: A History of the Kikuyu Since 1500, Oxford University Press, London, 1974.

low prices. Extremely fat sheep and goats abound, while the Kikuyu have also cattle in numerous numbers."

Around this time the slave trade was a matter of great concern to Britain and other European countries. Many pressure groups felt that in order to make a halt to the slave trade, it would be necessary to 'interfere' by imposing controls in the form of instituting rules and government. Missionary societies also felt it was their duty to civilize and convert pagan Africans and wanted intervention, as well.

However the primary reason that Europeans decided to carve up Africa among themselves at the Berlin Conference of 1885, and create spheres of influence, was the extreme wealth, vast land and natural resources that the continent possessed. Greed dominated all the proceedings. Britain was allocated, among others, the region where Kenya and Uganda are now situated.

Traditional hospitality, as practiced by the Kikuyu and many other African communities, is one of the major factors that hastened colonial takeover and European dominance all over Africa. According to Kikuyu custom, travellers in need must be given accommodation and food before continuing their journey. Thus when Kikuyu leader, Waiyaki wa Hinga, gave Captain Fredrick Lugard and his men an area to construct what he thought was a temporary abode in 1890, he did not know that the visitors had no intention of leaving. The British government had sent Lugard to establish outposts which could be used as administrative centres to govern the new colony, but the local people had no idea of the purpose of his visit.

Lugard build his station in Waiyaki's compound at Kanyariri (Ndumbu-ini), about twelve kilometres from what is now Nairobi's city centre. After some time, Lugard went on to establish other outposts and stations all the way into Uganda, while his place as the British representative was taken over by Colonel Purkiss, a military man whose sole mission was to clamp down on the 'natives' and to establish the British monarchy as rulers of the land.

Shortly after settling in, Purkiss and his men, mostly mercenaries, started collecting taxes by force and demanding free labour from the Kikuyu around Dagoretti. The mercenaries also started harassing local women and by 1892 Waiyaki finally had enough of his 'guests' and rebelled. There was a physical encounter with Colonel Purkiss and Waiyaki ended up being locked up in a cell for the night. (That room is still standing today, and can be found at Ndumbu-ini just off Waiyaki way.)

The following day, the Colonel called in Kinyanjui wa Gathirimu, a man who had ambitions to take over Waiyaki's position. With other leaders of similar mind, a mock trial was held and as a result Waiyaki was banished to the coast. When the military escort arrived in Kibwezi on their way to the coast, Purkiss killed and buried Waiyaki. Legend has it that Waiyaki was buried alive, head down and legs up.

Somewhat earlier, a Giriama leader, a brave woman known as Mekatilili wa Menza, had also been banished to Kisii. She had realised the intentions of the Europeans and started a rebellion.

Although there had been many cases of European abuses against Africans throughout history, such acts as those above were among the first instances of colonial subjugation of Africans, and established the fact that the British were now the government in charge.

In terms of wealth and security, Uganda was seen as the "Pearl of Africa" while Kenya went virtually unnoticed. Uganda not only held the source of the Nile, and therefore was vital to British interests in the Gulf of Suez, it also held large and prosperous kingdoms with immense agricultural production. However, in order to properly exploit this vast wealth, the British needed some means of rapid transport to connect Mombasa to Uganda. As a result the British Government made the controversial decision to construct a railway, the so-called "Lunatic Line". This railway took five years to complete, beginning in 1896 and finished in 1901.

After undergoing a great many hardships, including the famous debacle of the "Man-Eaters of Tsavo", the railway finally arrived in the area now known as Nairobi in 1889. The coolness, the fertility of the land, the abundance of fresh water, the variety of the food, and even the availability of willing local labour convinced the Europeans that the area would make a much better base than Machakos, the previous headquarters for the colonials. The Imperial British East African Company (IBEAC) decided to shift base from Machakos to Nairobi.

There had been a devastating famine in Kikuyu land in 1888 and 1889 which left many people in a desperate state. In addition, due to the scarcity of farming land among the Kikuyu, there were many people willing to take up other occupations. Many young men were therefore willing to take up formal employment. As such, they took up manual jobs made available by the Europeans, such as being porters for caravans and expeditions. Kikuyu migration out of central Kenya thus started in earnest, and has never yet stopped.

In addition, due to the fact that the railway construction was taking place just nearby, many Kikuyus took up manual jobs with the railways or with the administration and missionaries. As the railway line advanced towards Lake Victoria, Kikuyu labourers travelled with it and many settled along the railway.

Perhaps at this point it should be briefly noted that the British ignored nearly all local names. When Speke first saw Lake Victoria (Lake Nyamlolwe or Lake Nyanza) and its surroundings, he went into a frenzy of renaming every landmark with the names of prominent British personalities he wished to honour. This trend was continued by the colonialists. Kisumu, the final Kenyan terminus of the railway, was re-named Port Florence.

As the railroad came into Nandi country, another leader, Koitalel arap Samoei, rebelled against the British and tried to stop the construction of the rail. The leader of the British colonialists murdered him without a thought.

At any rate, by the early 1900s, there were many Kikuyu living along the railway line, all the way into Kampala in Uganda. Some never came back and were gradually integrated by the peoples and customs that they found where they settled. This constituted the first batch of Kikuyu immigrants out of central Kenya and into the Rift Valley and beyond.

When the railway was complete, the British government had to justify the expense by ensuring it brought in a profit. One of the ways this was done was to bring in European settlers. However the colonials first had to ensure their safely and to this end various military "punitive expeditions" were carried out against a number of so-called troublesome and rebellious tribes. There were many such expeditions throughout Kenya and one of these expeditions, led by Richard Meinartzhagen, was carried out in central Kenya and killed thousands of Kikuyu warriors in Icha-Kahanya (Tumu Tumu) and Kihumbu-ini. Meinartzhagen was a particularly sadistic individual and was also responsible for the ambush and murder of Koitalel arap Samoei, the Nandi religious and military leader mentioned earlier.

In due course, IBEAC became bankrupt and the British government took over. As stated, the British mission was to establish white farms in order to make the colony and the railway economically viable. In 1902, the first settlers arrived in the British East African Protectorate and they arrived in their thousands, from 1902 up to the First World War (1914–1918) and continuously thereafter. The authorities forcefully annexed native land and gave it to the settlers and in the coast, Machakos, central Kenya and the Rift Valley, hundreds of thousands of acres were annexed. The Europeans called it the White Highlands and no African was ever compensated for the loss.

Among the pioneer settlers were Hugh Cholmondley Delamere and Ewart Grogan. Delamere settled on 100,000 acres of land situated between Naivasha, Elementaita and Gilgil. In central Kenya, land in Kiambu and Nyeri was taken over for settlers. Even the Maasai were pushed out of their land. This led to the displacement and landlessness of very many people and was reason behind the next Kikuyu migration.

Because the Kikuyu were agriculturalists, those who lost their land also lost their livelihood. On the other hand, settlers had land but no labour force. Thus thousands of desperate Kikuyus were willing to provide labour on settler farms. This started a wave of immigration out of central Kenya into the Rift Valley where a great many settlers had their farms.

The migration went on for decades and continued even after Kenya became Independent. Njenga Karume's grandfather, Wagachire, was one of these immigrants. In 1923, he and his family migrated to Delamere's land, and settled in a squatter village in Elementaita, deep inside the farm. Over forty years of age by that time, Wagachire spent his time herding his own animals, but his sons Karume and Kiguru were employed as casual labourers on Delamere's and other settler farms. Njenga Karume himself was thus born in a squatters' hamlet in Elementaita, (referred to as Mutaita by the Kikuyu squatters) on Lord Delamere's farm in the Rift Valley in the late 1920s.

By the 1920s, Africans continued resisting European rule and excesses even more fiercely than before. In 1922, Harry Thuku of the Kikuyu Central Association (KCA) was deported to Kismayu in Somalia after leading agitation for freedom of movement and better working conditions for Africans. Others like Jomo Kenyatta, also of KCA, were in the frontline, demanding land and better working conditions for Africans.

When Njenga Karume was born, in 1929, there were very few formally educated Africans. Missionaries had established a number of schools; however the Africans, after so much betrayal and murder, distrusted whites and not many were willing to send their children to school. In addition many had resisted Christianity as an alien religion. In fact, on Delamere's farm there were neither churches nor schools. For the Kikuyu, it was, for the most part, still the age of superstition, sorcery and witchcraft.

However, not much later, missionaries started coming in and, after discovering that formal education had its advantages and benefits, Africans started sending their children to schools. When they found that some of the missionary teaching was contrary to their own beliefs, the Kikuyu elders actually started their own independent schools.

Njenga Karume started school in 1943, while his father Karume was working at Delamere's farm. Later Karume bought land from the government and moved his extended family to Elburgon. Like many others who worked or previously lived in the settler farms, he obtained leasehold land that had been set aside by the authorities for market places and other social amenities for Africans.

However, when Karume started his first business in 1950, there were very few opportunities for Africans. Those who worked for the settlers and the government were employed in casual capacity with low wages and poor working conditions. For most Africans the highest position to aspire to was employment as a clerk in one of the farms or government offices. Some few more privileged Africans worked as *askaris*, (guards, or junior police) in the government. Furthermore Africans were banned from growing profitable crops such as coffee or tea, in order to limit their income and to force them to provide labour on European farms.

It was a tumultuous time for Karume to start his commercial enterprises. As early as 1947, the Kikuyu had already started taking oaths that committed them to fight to regain their freedom. By 1950, the oath had come to be identified with the Mau Mau, a group that was in the forefront of the agitation for independence. The oath bound one to give support, fight and even kill in order to fulfil the Mau Mau's pledge to liberate their land and people. The oath-taking was especially widespread in Olenguruone, Elburgon and other areas surrounded by settler farms in the Rift Valley.

Many of the Mau Mau leaders were men who had fought in the Second World War, Kikuyu men of the *fote* (1940s) age group, who were extremely dissatisfied with the treatment they received from the British. After many had sacrificed their lives and been injured during the war (1939–1940) the survivors received no form of compensation. While British soldiers were rewarded with land and assured employment after the war, the Africans were merely given fare to get to their homes. This embittered group of ex-soldiers formed the core of Mau Mau.

Like the majority of the Kikuyu, Karume joined the movement. When the colonial Governor declared a State of Emergency in October 1952 to deal with the Mau Mau insurgency, thousands of Kikuyus found themselves incarcerated without trial in detention camps, and Njenga was soon jailed himself. Unless they denounced the movement publicly, either in church or by joining the British authorities as home guards or loyalists (collaborators), every Kikuyu was a Mau Mau suspect. Thousands of Kikuyus were killed, either in the forests where they waged guerrilla warfare against the colonials, or in detention camps.

Karume was lucky. By using his eloquence and his knack for befriending others, he managed to avoid staying in detention for too long like some of his colleagues. However, life was very difficult during this decade, even for those who had not been imprisoned. There was constant suspicion, unremitting surveillance and persistent fear. Neighbours and families were torn apart by conflicting loyalties and movement from one area to another was severely restricted, especially for the Kikuyus. At one time there were up to five different passes required for travel. This made business and employment virtually impossible for the ordinary Kikuyu.

People were forced into guarded 'closed villages' to prevent their contact with or support to the Mau Mau. The majority of those who previously worked on settler farms and in Nairobi and other towns were detained or sent home to be locked into these villages. There was limited access to their farms. For the Africans, it was a harsh repressive period, both personally and economically.

Yet before and throughout this phase, Karume managed to start and expand his businesses despite the prevailing disadvantages for African entrepreneurs. He fought and conquered many personal and financial battles during this period, and by 1959 he had risen to become one of the leading businessmen in Kiambu district.

However, by 1960, it was clear that Kenya was on its way to gaining independence. Independence would be a new beginning for the Africans, in all spheres of life, ranging from business, education, and government. Those who were ambitious and enterprising would now be free to realise their dreams. Those who had been frustrated by colonial restrictions would soon be liberated and able to follow their beliefs.

Independence was granted in 1963 and Jomo Kenyatta became the country's Prime Minister and later President. Due to his financial successes, Karume had been befriended by many of the early politicians and Independence merely served to strengthen such ties. Karume was therefore very close to the new African government, but he himself did not join politics until many years later. His primary interests were, and still are, his commercial ventures. However, he was eventually forced into a position of accepting a political role and in due course developed a certain amount of enthusiasm for the affairs of state, which even today ensures that he keeps in touch with the prominent and powerful individuals in Kenyan society and government.

Njenga Karume's story therefore is, to a degree, a microcosm of the history of modern Kenya. Despite numerous challenges, he managed to evolve with the times and take advantage of whatever opportunities arose. His is the story of Kenya's first entrepreneur.

Mutu wa Gethoi

Chapter 1

Roots and Childhood

My earliest childhood memories are of happy days spent running and playing in the vast grasslands of Lord Delamere's[4] Elementaita Ranch in the Rift Valley dressed only in a goatskin. As a young boy, around the age of six, I would spend most of my days tending dozens of my grandfather's goats in the workers' section of the vast ranch.

According to Kikuyu customs boys had the responsibility of looking after cattle, sheep and goats, and therefore taking the goats to graze was my job since I was the oldest boy in the homestead. My grandfather regarded rearing goats as a valuable occupation because, traditionally, an abundance of goats meant prosperity and wealth. Livestock was used as the medium of exchange and for nearly all families, rearing such livestock was a customary part of Kikuyu society.[5]

The task of herding livestock educated us boys on the importance of cattle and goats and taught us the need for responsibility, teamwork and bravery. Because there were many wild animals, we also learned to look out for one another. In previous generations like those of my father and grandfather, boys in the fields also acted as scouts, watching for enemy raiders who, for those in central Kenya, were normally the Maasai.

---

4   Lord Hugh Delamere was one of the pioneer white settlers who were allocated land by the colonial government starting in 1902. He was the son of Hugh Cholmondley, the second Baron Delamere, from an aristocratic British family. He was among the most prominent settlers and he led the agitation for settler rights in the colony. Due to his prominence, a major street in Nairobi, the colony's capital city, was named Delamere Avenue. It was later changed to Kenyatta Avenue after Independence.

5   Before the emergence of a cash economy, goats, sheep and cows were the usual means of exchange among the Kikuyu, an agricultural society. Other items such as food were also used in barter. However for larger transactions such as the purchase of land, bride price and fines, animals were the preferred medium of exchange. Cowrie shells were used in a limited measure, but this was generally only with traders from outside the region, especially the coast. The more livestock one possessed, the wealthier one was considered to be and the more respected.

Goatskin and cowhide cloaks formed the attire of most common Africans earlier in the century. Few natives wore shorts, long trousers, shirts or other articles of European clothing. Such items were the privilege of colonial masters and white government administrators of the time. The only African adults who dressed in this style were domestic employees such as cooks, gardeners or other house servants who worked in *Wazungu* (European) homes. If they were lucky to find favour with their masters, the house servants would get 'hand-me-downs' when their bosses had had enough of a particular piece of clothing. However, the *Wazungu* would never give Africans long trousers. They would only give out their old shorts in case Africans forget their place in the order of things and imagined they had the same status as the masters. Those who did farm labour for the colonialists or who were unemployed would view the domestic staff with awe as they strutted around the village showing off their cast-off European clothes. An additional small minority of other Africans also wore such western clothing. These were those who lived, worked or had been schooled in the Christian missions.

By the time I was growing up, imported clothing—Indian, Arabic and European—was slowly becoming more widespread among the African population. However for children, such foreign wear was not yet common.

Almost every African child was dressed in his or her traditional cloak. It was not a matter of fashion or status to be dressed in skin; it was a normal, everyday habit, just as was the carrying of clubs and sticks by boys, and spears by herdsmen as protection against wild animals. The skin cloaks were easy to acquire and in most cases the only clothing material available.

Children were occupied with family chores and did not go to school. At that time, the missionaries were the only ones educating 'natives'. The missionaries' activities were concentrated in very few areas in the colony. The Church of Scotland Missionary Society worked in Thogoto in Kiambu, Chogoria in Meru and Tumutumu in Nyeri. The Catholic Missionary Society functioned in Msongari in Nairobi, Mang'u in Kiambu, Mathari (Nyeri), Tuthu in Murang'a and other areas. The African Inland Mission was located in Kijabe and the Orthodox Church Missionaries worked in the Rift Valley.

In fact, the first person I saw in a complete set of western clothing was Arthur Gatung'u, a preacher in the Orthodox Church. In 1939, he was one of the first Africans who owned a car. In 1942 he came to see us in the squatter village of Kagaa in Ndunyu-Buru where we lived on

Delemare's farm, with the intention of converting the people there to Christianity. Quite a few of my family members were converted. He baptised my uncles, Samuel Wanjema, Silas Kiguru, Benson Munge, and Wanjema's wife, Naomi and Kiguru's wife, Rakeli. So my grandfather's home produced five Christians.

While preaching and teaching to the new converts Arthur explained that many Kikuyu customs were sinful and not acceptable to Christianity, and one point he was quite strict about was traditional dances. Now it so happened that my uncle Munge was a great dancer, and he was extremely fond of dancing whenever he had the opportunity, but he tried his best to avoid the temptation. One time however, he found one of his most favourite dances taking place by the path just near the church. His favourite dance was the *Gīchukia*, which was performed by young unmarried men and women. This dance gave the men and women a chance to get to know each other and flirt. He felt terrible that he could not join them but he was reminded that he now had "God's name" (that is, he had accepted Christianity) and that such dances were sinful.

Munge was not happy at all. He wondered about how to get rid of the "God's name" and began trying to find a method of doing so. One day he was informed that there was a witchdoctor in Kisumu who would be able to remove this baptismal name for him and so he sold some chickens in order to get the train fare to Kisumu. He did the rounds in Nyanza looking for the witchdoctor but did not find what he was looking for. However, when he came back, he bought himself a beautiful deep red sheet in Elementaita and wore it round his body, and abandoned the church. Everyone, especially those in the dance troupe, was very happy to see him back, but they were not sure he had been wise in reverting to his non-Christian status.

A few years later, in 1945, while walking in the fields, looking after Delamere's cattle, Munge saw something on the ground. It was an interesting shaped smooth shiny object and Munge thought it would make a lovely snuff box for his mother. So he picked it up and looked at it more closely. It was quite unusual. He tried to open it but it just didn't budge. Then he placed it on a flat stone and tried to hammer it with a wooden club. Suddenly there was a huge explosion and he was stunned. He was bleeding and drops of blood were dripping from his forehead into his eyes. It was only when he tried to wipe the blood from his face that he realised his arm was gone, severed at the elbow. His left eye was also damaged. That interesting little object was apparently some sort of bomb or grenade that had been left behind by military troops on field exercises in preparation for World War II.

One way or another, the Christians seemed to feel that this misfortune had happened because he had left the church. People were convinced that God had punished him for abandoning his Christianity.

"Take care! If you go for those dances you may end up like Munge!" the newly converted Christians warned each other.

As a child, I normally wore a skin cloak referred to as *karūa,* and it was also intended to be used as a blanket during the night. For an older person such a garment was referred to as *gīthii.* A *gīthii* would last for years and a new one was only made when the old was worn out. Children's garb was usually made of the softer goat or sheepskin while adults made theirs from cowhide. Such leather pieces were larger and tougher therefore softening them required arduous labour.

However, on Delamere's ranch, Africans were not allowed to keep cattle so the adults wore sheepskin as well. Such a sheepskin would have to come from native sheep. If any African was caught with the skin of a Merino sheep (the breed favoured by the settlers), he could be put in prison. Women would remove the hair from the hides they wore as their clothing, while men would wear the hides with hair.

Wealthy men would wear the same style, but their cloaks were made of hyrax hide, which was naturally more beautiful and softer. It was difficult to acquire hyrax skins and for this kind of cloak several would have to be treated and then stitched together. The wearer of such a garment would most likely be a respected man in the society. The headgear that went with this outfit was made from goatskins, though the rich and powerful would wear *gītukū,* hats made of ostrich feathers.

Many older men wore such traditional types of clothing made of hyrax skin. I remember my grandfather wearing it occasionally. I recall that my grandfather was honoured on one particular occasion and he wore the full costume, including the pointed hat.

The method of preparation of these hides was fairly simple. After slaughtering an animal, the skin would be stretched in the sun until it was dry. Afterwards it would then be thoroughly flayed with sticks to soften it. Next, animal or castor oil would be applied to make the skin even softer and at that stage it was regarded as ready for use. Clothing was never regarded as an issue of style, its purpose was merely to cover nakedness and protect against the cold, especially July's *gathaano* or August's misty *mworia-nyoni* which was so cold that some tropical birds dropped dead from the bushes.

There were specialists who prepared these traditional garments, and men's garments would be made by men, and women's garments by women. Women were generally responsible for making garments for the children, too. As I said, we would wear these garments without changing them, for as long as they lasted, but animals were never slaughtered just for the purpose of making clothing. We had to wait until a goat or sheep was slaughtered, or died, before we would get fresh clothes.

Some time after I was born, cotton clothes became much more common and my father and uncles started buying shirts and shorts. However, they would make an effort to find dark coloured shirts which would not show dirt. They would wear these shirts every day until they were in tatters. Sometimes it would be more than a year before they bought another one. In some instances, the shirts would be so ragged, torn and filthy that they would just throw them away after buying a new one.

There was a time my uncle Wanjema bought a shirt. I remember that the shirt was a very bright colour. After my father saw it, he started teasing him.

"You must have grown quite rich!" my father exclaimed.

My uncle frowned, "What do you mean? It's just a nice, regular shirt."

"But where will money for the soap come from?" my father asked.

Soap was a luxury. We bathed with water every few weeks and considered ourselves clean enough.

To this day I have fond memories of my old clothes but I cannot imagine how my childhood friends and I ever survived the chilly months of July and August with just these little skins to cover us. Within my lifetime, things have changed so much that I remember with nostalgia that I never had a shirt or a pair of shorts until I was fifteen years old. How different life was in Lord Delamere's farm from modern Kenya today!

While my friends and I went to tend the animals, we would carry a bundle of food, known as *rũgu*, which was usually *gĩtheri* (boiled maize and beans) wrapped in leaves or fibre. We would eat the food at midday or earlier, if we felt hungry, and we would share whatever we had amongst ourselves. We rarely carried roasted or boiled meat since it was a rare delicacy. Out in the bush, there were also many fruits and berries and we boys would devour these with relish. Once in a while we would cut a bit of young maize and chew on the stalk. It was quite sweet, like sugarcane. However, we had to be careful about cutting it because if we were ever caught chopping down some other family's crop, we would be in trouble.

I never had real sugarcane till I went to school much later and as for bananas, which my mother occasionally bought in the market, I always imagined they grew close to the ground like beans. After all, the shape of a banana is like that of a giant bean pod. I was really surprised when I actually saw banana plants later in Kiambu!

In short, my age mates and I had a reasonably varied and well-balanced diet and more than enough to eat except in times of famine. I thoroughly enjoyed those daily trips to herd the livestock and understood it as the beginning of a traditional education. By the age of five or six, I was already skilled at herding my family's domestic animals. Obviously everyone in the homestead was expected to contribute to the welfare of the family, including the children.

My grandfather and a handful of other landless Kikuyu had migrated from Limuru down to Lord Delamere's vast estate in Naivasha/Elementaita area. Before the advent of colonialism, the area was used as grazing land by the Maasai. To us, the area was known as *Mūtaita*, a Kikuyu version of the Maasai word Elementaita. Many of us who were born there still refer to it as such.

My grandfather and the other men had made an agreement with the white settler, pledging to work on his sprawling farm on the condition that they were allowed to keep a specific number of goats and grow some food crops on one acre of land per household. Rearing traditional sheep and cattle was completely prohibited, lest they contaminate the *Wazungu's* imported pedigrees.

I was born in 1929, on Lord Delamere's estate, in the squatter village called Kagaa in Ndunyu-Buru. I do not know the exact date, but from casual investigations I undertook later while I was at school, I reckoned that September was most likely the month of my birth because, according to my parents, I was born at the onset of the short rainy season which normally falls in October. In those days, very few people bothered about dates or months. The concept of dates or the calendar was alien to many Africans since they had never stepped into a classroom. No one in the village noted the date of my birth; in fact it is most probable that no one cared. Much later I tried to track down any possible indication of my birth in Lord Delamaere's old registry and record office but was unable to find any trace. Perhaps the ranch management did not care either.

Rites of passage such as initiations were regarded as significant but birthdays were irrelevant.[6] People noted the passage of time by seasons, such as the rainy, dry, or cold season, in addition to any significant events that occurred. Thus when I was born, in the usual Kikuyu tradition, the village women gave voice to five *ngemi* (ululations) to announce the birth of a boy. In the case of a girl it would have been four *ngemi*. Of course, a midwife and women from the neighbourhood oversaw the birth. Hospitals were relatively new phenomena in Kenya but in the middle of a hundred thousand acre ranch, a medically assisted birth simply wasn't feasible. Consequently, without a real birth date, I decided on my probable date of birth as 4 September 1929. However, 4th is entirely my invention for purposes of correspondence and records, and also for the marking of my birthday, which, despite the fact that I am not particularly keen on it myself, my family insists on celebrating.

I was lucky to survive my birth and toddler years. In those days, the mortality rate was high, owing to a limited knowledge of science, ignorance about viruses, germs and bacteria and the presence of traditions which we would today regard as questionable. Epidemics would ravage villages and wipe out significant portions of the communities. For example, an outbreak of the bubonic plague in the 1890s killed a large percentage of the communities in East Africa. Rats escaping from trading ships in Mombasa had spread the scourge through the various communities until the plague reached central Kenya. Outbreaks of this sort would erase masses of the people and there was no escape, nor any known cure. Diseases such as small pox, polio, mumps and others would cause the death of the majority of the children in any particular area and at some homes only one or two children out of ten would survive. Herbal medicine was ineffectual or hopelessly inadequate and in many cases, illnesses were blamed on witchcraft and sorcery.

I remember that, after we moved to Elburgon, a witchdoctor would come and cast spells on people who were suspected of wrongdoing. The witchdoctor, Karigithu, was quite scary-looking and held in awe, especially by us children. One of the grossest things he did, in trying to

---

6   Because of the high mortality rate among children, the Kikuyu system involved naming age-groups (*Mariika* – singular *Riika*) – after the time that a person underwent the initiation rite of circumcision around the ages of 16 to 20. This was because many children used to die quite young and did not reach adolescence. These initiation age-sets should not be confused with the warrior regimental age-sets or the elder ruling age group that governed the community.

impress us with his powers, was to bite off the head of a live chameleon during one of his ceremonies. It was still an age where such acts were regarded as magic and superstition was common.

Children were especially vulnerable to these diseases. In addition, whereas a simple case of breech birth can today be sorted out through a caesarean delivery, in those days, unless the traditional midwife was able to turn the infant into position, it meant severe complications or death for mother and child. Whooping cough, measles, diphtheria and countless other diseases which are today prevented by vaccination, killed thousands of children at that time.

My brother, Njoroge, died of one of these childhood diseases. After all, the only option open to parents with a sick child was to go see a witchdoctor, a futile exercise, but then nothing else was known or available. Furthermore, I was born in a place teeming with wild animals and I was exposed to them daily as I went about my chores of tending the livestock.

I was lucky that I was never attacked by any wild animals while herding or while in the forests, but once in a while we would find one or two of the goats killed by leopards or lions. Although we were not happy when an animal was killed, we benefited in a way, since a leopard kill would always mean extra meat for us. After killing a goat or sheep, the leopard would suck out the blood, eat the heart and some of the internal organs like the liver, and leave nearly all the meat behind. Strangely enough, leopards seemed to avoid human beings. Perhaps they had learned that humans were more dangerous than themselves!

There were also droughts and famines that would occasionally devastate our lands. In those years, our people were often badly prepared for these seasonal variations. Although there were always seers and medicine men who could recognise and recall the various weather patterns that occurred over some decades, every now and then some meteorological anomaly would occur and disaster would follow.

There were also men known as "rain makers" but their abilities were often more myth than reality. So when the famines came, it was nearly always a catastrophe since people could not store more than a limited amount of food. One such famine occurred in eastern Africa in 1888–1889 and wiped out such a huge part of the population that when Europeans invaded they faced very little resistance from the inhabitants.

❖   ❖   ❖

But to get back to my early days, I should explain that Delamere had hived off a portion of his ranch for construction of a workers' village with sufficient space around it for subsistence farming. The men who worked for Delamere, together with their families, lived in small grass-thatched huts in this village and when the men went off to work, the women and children busied themselves in their homesteads, on the small patches of land, or tended the family's livestock. The women cultivated crops and the children looked after the goats while the men worked many kilometres further out in the ranch.

In this village of Kagaa where I was born, Delamere set up regulations, as mentioned earlier, that Africans could neither keep cattle nor pedigree sheep as domesticated farm animals. The labourers and their families were barred from raising these two animals because, firstly, the Europeans had brought pure breed merino sheep into the country. Once the merino mixed with inferior native breeds, a half-breed called *nuthu* was produced, something very undesirable in European eyes, and, of course, the pedigree was degraded. In addition, white settlers were afraid that native livestock had diseases which could infect grade cattle and finally, Delamere and his fellow settlers knew that cattle were a medium of exchange among the Kikuyu and many other tribes. If he were to allow his workers to rear cattle they would accumulate wealth and this in turn would lead to desertion of his labour force. The possession of cattle might also give his workers a sense of independence and this would not do for the settler, either. Cheap or virtually free labour was vital for European dominance. Therefore only goats were permitted for the Africans on the Delamere ranch.

I think that Delamere's line of thinking was probably something along the lines of, "Pacify the Africans, give them just a little leeway, and there will be peace since they will have their goats but they will still work for me." It was quite effective most of the time. Essentially, Europeans insisted on the myth of white superiority.

My father was called Karume. Since I was the first born son, I was named after my grandfather, Wagachire, and also named *Njenga* after my grandfather's *riika* (age group).[7] In those days, age was calculated by initiation age group, that is, the time a group of those boys of roughly the same age underwent the rite of passage into adulthood. At that time this usually occurred when boys were roughly between the

---

7   Kikuyu families traditionally name the first children after the paternal grandfather or grandmother. The next two children would be named after the maternal grandfather and grandmother. Thereafter the names would be those of the father's siblings, and then the mother's siblings. However with Westernisation these customs are slowly disappearing.

ages of 16 to 20. Once circumcised, they were recognized as adults and warriors who would protect the community in case of war or aggression from enemies. Because it was believed that bad luck might come into a home where the daughters were not circumcised, girls were usually circumcised somewhat earlier, just before puberty.

A *riika* would be named after a singularity which was prevalent at the time of initiation, say some climatic condition or social issue. As a matter of fact, every Kikuyu man who is named Njenga has another 'real' name, or is supposed to have one, according to tradition. It is not clear what phenomenon gave rise to the name *Njenga*. I personally believe it was because the young people of the *Njenga* age group had vowed to *gūchenga* (cut up) the European invaders. But then again, armed resistance against the Europeans was rare at that time. Perhaps it may have to do with '*njenga*' (semi-crushed maize grains) which were cooked into a rough porridge. Initiates used to feast on this meal as they were recovering from circumcision.

As for my father, Karume, he was circumcised in 1922 in the *riika rīa Ciringi* which is in reference to "Shillings". Shillings first appeared in the area at about this time. Whatever the case, I was nevertheless named after my grandfather but Njenga is the name that I have been known by since birth.

However, my roots were not in the Rift Valley where I was born. In fact, I was the first of the family to be born away from home in the Rift Valley. Some five generations back, my ancestor, Njunu, came into Mang'u in Thika from as far a field as Gaaki in present day Nyeri at the foot of Mount Kenya. My clan, in fact, is named after Njunu, thus I belong to the *Agacikū a mbarī ya Njūnū*, that is, the Agaciku clan of Njunu's extraction.[8]

According to the Kikuyu creation myth, all clans are named after the nine mythical daughters that *Mūrungu* or *Mwenenyaga* (God) gave to Gīkūyū (the first man) when he created him along with his wife, Mūmbi. Some legends actually tell of ten daughters. One of these daughters was called Wanjiku, as the myth has it, and the *Agacikū* part of the clan name is a derivative. The word Ngai was later adopted from the Maa language of the Maasai to refer to God.

---

8 The Kikuyu named their family units through the *Mbarī* system. When land was demarcated by the clan elders, it would be given to each clan family, according to the amount they could farm. Directed outward from a central point, most likely the patriarch's hut, each wife and family would be allocated a stretch of land *(mbarī)* and for purposes of identification the family would be known as the Mbari of "so and so", the name of the head of the household. Thus, I belong to the Agaciku clan and to Njunu's family *(mbarī)*.

I am not sure why my ancestors decided to go south, but the historical explanation for migration in the mid 18th century usually involved the search for more land for pasture or for farming. The area surrounding Nyeri and Murang'a was becoming quite populated around that time, and there was considerable warfare among the Kikuyu and Kwavi (northern and Purko Maasai) over cattle and grazing land. Therefore many people migrated from the area, with some settling in southern Murang'a and others going even further to settle in present day Kiambu. They did not realize until much later that there were more Maasai on the southern flank of Kikuyu territory as well.

I have learned some of the history of my clan from others. Shadrack Githua Githegi of Mang'u, was circumcised in 1925 in the *Munai riika*. At the age of 103, he is still in command of all his faculties, in addition to possessing a wonderful sense of humour, and he was able to give me some interesting information. Apparently, after leaving Gaaki/Metumi region, Njunu settled in Mang'u. He had a son named Wagathanji and, according to oral history,[9] he in turn had three sons namely Munene, Kairu and Njuguna Karume. Njuguna Karume, (who thus was my great grandfather) in turn sired my grandfather, Wagachire.

Wagachire was not a wealthy man when he later moved on from Mang'u. At first, he settled at Ikinu in Githunguri before moving shortly thereafter to Kiambaa. His first wife was Kaheti and his second wife was Watoro.

In 1923, Wagachire and his wives and children moved to the Rift Valley. As with many others, he was an economic migrant in search of employment and pasture for his livestock. A friend had informed him that Lord Delamere, a settler with expansive land in Elementaita in the Rift Valley, was looking for labourers to herd and milk his cattle along with other farm duties. His son, Karume, (my father) had just undergone the rite of circumcision, so Wagachire took his family, consisting of his wives and children, and moved onward.

He was not the only one from Kiambu immigrating to the Rift Valley and beyond. Since the population was growing, many people with ambition were moving to new areas. This move had two main reasons behind it. Firstly, the Europeans had already alienated most of the traditional land in the southern areas of Kikuyu for farming purposes and secondly, the

---

9   Oral history (through memory and recitation) was used by many tribes to convey their history up to the mid 1850s. Written history starting from the latter part of the 19th century was recorded by Europeans who often skewed or misrepresented the facts as they did not understand the full picture or the ways of the people they were describing.

farmers in the Rift Valley gave the labourers some pieces of land on which to herd their animals.

Settlers in the Rift Valley paid their labourers very poor wages compared to those in Kiambu. They were paid three shillings per month but could sometimes stay up to six months without being paid. If they happened to ask for their wages, they would even be beaten. Therefore the most tempting condition which attracted African labour was the fact that they were allowed to raise sheep and goats.

However, even in Kiambu, many young men felt insulted by the humiliating wages paid in the farms that had once actually belonged to them and their parents before the European invasion. Dispossession had left them bitter and many felt it was better to work as labourers in new lands. So away they went.[10]

My grandfather Wagachire with his family, including his son Karume, took off for the Delamere ranch. Wagachire's brother, Riitho (my grand uncle) went to work on a settler's farm in Subukia and his other brother Munge was left behind in Kiambaa.

Although Wagachire had initiated the move to the Rift Valley, he did not seek employment at Delamere's ranch. He was getting old and could no longer keep pace with the young men who were working in the ranch. He was more interested in the fact that he would have pasture for his goats. However his sons Karume and Kiguru were employed as labourers.

My mother, Teresia Njeri, was originally from Ndeiya in Limuru where she had met my father, before my grandfather moved his family to Elementaita. On the days he was free, my father would make the journey all the way from Delamere's ranch up to Limuru to visit her. After a period of this long-distance romance, the two finally got married in 1928, with all the customary rituals and my father brought his new bride to Kagaa, Delamere's squatter village. As was customary, my grandfather made the dowry payments on behalf of my father, by donating a number of the animals. This was the normal tradition for marriage of the first wife. If a man wished to marry additional wives, he would have to make the dowry payments himself.

---

10 Work crews arrived in Nairobi in 1889 during the construction of the Kenya Uganda Railway (1897–1901). Because of the famine in central Kenya, many Kikuyu men saw this as an opportunity and took up employment with the railway. The track was built up to Port Florence (later Kisumu) and then into Uganda and the workers followed the rails. As a result there are many people with Kikuyu blood along the whole length of the line. This migration of Kikuyu in 1890s, the first out of central Kenya, has not been recorded properly. It was the precursor to many other such migrations.

My father, of course, already had a small bachelor hut which he had built for himself when he was initiated into adulthood, behind my grandfather's *thingira* (elder's hut), but now, as a married man, he was given a proper place to construct a house of his own. He was now a man like his father and could have a *thingira* (elder's hut) in the centre of his compound, which would be surrounded by huts for his wife, or wives, if he married more.

While they were on duty, my father and other labourers lived in separate quarters nearer to the cattle. They would work in a place about 16 kilometres from our little village, at a place called Ngambu. I am not sure why this particular arrangement was made, but I think it was because the *Wazungu* hated to see African families around. Karume's chief duty was to take care of the cows and milk them and therefore he would only come to see us, his family, when he was off-duty.

As stated earlier, my grandfather was very fond of goats and his main ambition in life was to acquire as many as possible. For him, one reason to keep livestock was to see the evidence of wealth. Wealth was respected. However, those who boasted that they had money in the bank, had nothing to show.[11]

"They tell us they have money in the bank," he would say, when drinking with his similar-minded friends, "but how shall we know? Probably they never had it in the first place. If they are wealthy, they should buy goats that we can see. Then the one with the bigger herd can boast."

One of the reasons behind this contempt for those without livestock was the custom of segregating the poor or lazy. In the past, rich men would gather in a hut and drink as much *mūratina* (traditional beer) as they wished, in large drinking horns, and feast on roasted meat. Meanwhile the poor men would be forced to sit outside, sharing just one guord of beer between them. (Perhaps this custom was a way of encouraging men to be ambitious and hard-working.)

But without livestock, how was one to know if a man was rich or poor? Money in the bank was not something one could see.

Certainly my grandfather's concept of wealth was centred on livestock and this was common with others of his age. It was these goats, which numbered about fifty at any one time, which my grandfather and I would tend. It was an easy job since neither of us had other commitments. Thus most of my early life was spent in the company of my grandfather, with the exception of the times I would play games with the other children or when the old man was talking with other elders or having a drink. I was

---

11   The Bank of India and the Bank of South Africa were in Kenya in the early 1900s.

generally a healthy boy and although my parents were not wealthy, they were not poverty-stricken either.

I credit my love and knowledge of Kikuyu culture to my grandfather. He had a deep and powerful informal education. Wagachire taught me that I belonged to the Kikuyu nation.

I remember that my grandfather was so fond of me that we would share secrets just between the two of us. I sometimes slept in my grandfather's *thingira*. Sometimes he would wake me up when everyone else was asleep and we would have a hearty meal of *rūkūri*. The Kikuyu regarded *rūkūri* as one of their most delicious traditional delicacies. A goat from the herd would be slaughtered on various celebratory occasions and guests and family members would be treated to the feast. The prime cuts of the animal were kept for the old man of the homestead. These cuts would be cooked or roasted and then marinated in honey to form *rūkūri*. I am sure that anyone who has ever tasted this dish will testify to its more than delectable flavour.

But *rūkūri* was not for women or children. Traditionally it was reserved for elders only.[12] Even men who were considered lazy or weak would not be invited to share it, just as they would never be invited to share a gourd of *mūratina*. My grandfather was defying tradition by inviting me for these midnight feasts. I would sneak out of my mother's hut, gorge myself on these delicacies and then slink back to bed. When I was served 'ordinary' food such as sweet potatoes or bananas the following morning, I would excuse myself by saying I had a stomachache. But my mother, Teresia Njeri, was never overly worried about such illnesses, because by lunchtime I would be ravenously hungry again. I am certain she knew about my midnight escapades with my grandfather. At any rate, she chose not to talk about it. After all, the old man was her father-in-law.

Another memory that I retain of my early years on Delamere's farm, was the provisions shop. There was only one shop on the estate where all the workers and their families bought their groceries. It was located near the railway station and was owned by an Indian, a cheery chap named Moraj who might have been a member of one of the Indian trader

---

12 According to Kikuyu tradition, every part of the carcass was designated for a particular age group or for men or women. For example, the head was for the old men. The skin would be charred off, and then it would be made into a delicious soup. The head was then divided into three pieces and these would be reserved for the special friends of the head of the household. Mature girls would eat the forelegs, ribs were for the men, the hind legs for wives, the neck for uncircumcised boys, liver for men, kidneys and ears for little girls, the intestines were for women, the chest for circumcised young men and lungs for the old men.

families who had come into the country during the construction of the Kenya-Uganda railway. This was the first time I noticed people buying and selling goods. At that age, of course, I did not give it much thought. In fact I remember that I believed that such activities were reserved for foreigners.

Africans were not allowed to have businesses especially on settlers' farms. Delamere and his class of aristocratic settlers were of the opinion that giving any kind of power to the 'natives' was asking for trouble. Therefore, the employers tried to frustrate African businessmen as much as possible. In some cases, the conditions of employment for their workers were just like slave labour and workers were forced to sign (or rather press their fingerprints) to letters of agreement, which of course, they could not read. Most such documents barred Africans from engaging in any other business while in the employ of the settlers, in addition to forcing them to accept poor wages and corporal punishment and furthermore, any absence from duty was regarded as desertion. Such contracts were just a fraud. Under such conditions, my father earned three shillings per month, though his wages were later raised to eight shillings.

While in Elementaita on Delamere's ranch, the family expanded. My father married another wife, Mugure. After all, according to traditional Kikuyu beliefs and customs, a big family brought prestige and added to the family's labour force. This time my father paid the bride price by himself. The dowry, usually in the form of livestock, was usually agreed upon between the elders of the two families. Essentially bride price confirmed the bridegroom's commitment to his bride and also symbolised the exchange of one life, the girl's, for another, the animals given.

Polygamous families were considered normal in those days, and my family was no different. The family bonds between all of us brothers and sisters were considered important and we were taught that we were all equal and should live in harmony. Later, when we moved to Elburgon, my father married a third wife called Waceke.

During the years on Delamere's ranch in Elementaita, my mother had more children. She gave birth to my brothers Njoroge, Munge, Njoroge, Gathecere, Kamonyo and Wanjema in that order. I also have two sisters, named Muciri and Nditi. It can be noted that there are two Njoroges in my family, a matter that could be very confusing. There is a simple explanation. In those days, it was very important to name children after both parents' relatives, to perpetuate the family identity and roots, or, in the case of dead relatives, something vaguely like reincarnation, if one could call it so. Njoroge, the second born in the family, died in his infancy from one of those maladies mentioned earlier. My parents decided there must be a Njoroge in the family since Njoroge was the name of my mother's father. And so when they were blessed with another baby boy, they named him Njoroge once again. That is to say the Njoroge who had died was 'replaced'—*gūcokio*[13].

During my childhood, I did not have much of a chance to interact with my siblings. This is because I was the eldest and carried more responsibilities, particularly looking after my grandfather's goats. Furthermore, as the others were growing up, I moved from Elementaita in order to go to school in Kiambu. However, my brothers and sisters and I kept in close touch as we grew into adulthood and we helped one another whenever possible. Those of us who are alive still meet. Now most of my siblings have passed away, with two dying in road accidents and others of natural causes. My younger brother, Wanjema, and my sister Nditi are the only ones who are alive and the three of us occasionally meet to reminisce during family functions.

During these years, my father was normally in the labourer's quarters and the only time I saw him was when he visited our family in Kagaa village. My father usually came at the end of the month to shop for us, though at times he would come for a day or two in the middle of the month. He would take me along with him to Moraj's shop where we would buy household necessities such as sugar, tea and salt. He would then give my mother the rest of his earnings for safe-keeping. Like any child, I loved my mother dearly, but because of my father's long absence from our home, I was closer to my grandfather, rather than my father, during my childhood.

I remember one incident between my father and grandfather that really amazed me when it happened.

There was a time when my father bought two goats and brought them home. Naturally they joined the rest of the herd and my grandfather and I would take them out to graze.

---

13 *Gūcokia* was a traditional Kikuyu practice that took place after a child had died. When another of the same sex was born, he or she was named after the deceased so that the name might be perpetuated in the family. So if a boy named Maina died and the parents later had a boy, they would again name him Maina or Mucoki (the one who came back), or Kariūki (the one who has resurrected) to 'replace' the dead one. In the case of a girl, she would be named Njoki or Gacoki.

One evening my father came home, just as I was bringing in the animals. The enclosure for the animals was near my grandfather's hut, and he had already gone inside to relax while I finished up. My father watched as the goats came forward and looked for the two he had bought.

"How are my goats, Njenga?" my father asked me.

Before I could answer, I saw my grandfather storm out of his hut with a walking stick in his hand. My father had his back turned to the hut so he did not see the old man charging.

Thwack! Grandfather hit my father on the back with the stick! My father yelped in pain and surprise.

"What do you mean *your* goats?" the old man demanded. "This is my flock! Which goats are you talking about? This is my home and I am the owner of its goats!"

I will never forget the look on my father's face!

As a child, of course, I loved having adventures. Although non-labourers were banned from visiting the workers' quarters or going near Delamere's or his managers' houses, I was interested to see how the people on the other side lived. Perhaps I felt stifled in the squatter village or perhaps it was just my natural curiosity as a child.

Since I was the first born in my family, according to our culture, I was removed from the "evil eye" of any jealous person. So, as a young toddler, long before I started herding goats, I was sent to stay with my uncle, Silas Kiguru, in Ngambo, which was, as I mentioned, about sixteen kilometres away from home and it was there that I noticed the general manager, a white man whose name I cannot recall, but who was nicknamed *Mūrunyu*. He was the first white person I ever saw. Kiguru would warn me to hide when a car was coming, or even if one of the supervisors came around.

Although I never saw any other whites as a young child, as I grew older, I was mesmerized by the ways of the white people and did not understand how they could manage to have such authority over Africans. When I asked my father and uncles what made the *Wazungu* so powerful, I was told that it was due to their education. I could not understand but was nevertheless fascinated.

I heard about all the restrictions and rules that the *Wazungu* imposed on Africans and was very disturbed. I could not understand why, for example, my father and the other men were not allowed to live with their families yet they were in the same general area. After all, they did not work at night. I was also puzzled by the fact that African adults seemed so frightened of encountering a white person. Why did I have to hide when my uncle smuggled me into the workers' quarters? What was it that everyone was trying to conceal?

One particular issue troubled me more that all the others. I was stunned when I learned that whites and the supervisors under them would cane any native for whatever offence. The concept of adults being whipped, not only by the whites, but also by their black underlings was beyond my comprehension. I never witnessed this whipping myself, but I had always believed that my father, uncles and adult neighbours were fearless and were the protectors of the community, and just the thought of them being whipped was horrible.

I also wondered about the white children. I could somehow understand that the workers were supposed to address the white men as *Bwana* and the women as *Memsahib.[14]* But they were also supposed to address white boys as *Bwana Mdogo* (little master) and white girls as *Memsahib Mdogo* (little mistress). I heard that failure to address them in this manner could lead to whipping and harsh recrimination. I was really disturbed by this phenomenon. I had been brought up to believe that children should respect adults, not the other way around.

When supernatural assistance was required, witchdoctors and sorcerers were widely consulted and Kikuyu rituals were practised with religious zeal.

I remember one particularly interesting custom that my people held in reverence. As earlier stated, livestock was highly valued and my grandfather, Wagachire, would occasionally get me and one of my sisters to participate in a ritual to 'bless' his goats and the clan in general. This ceremony, known as *gūthiūrūra mbūri* (blessing the goats) was a prayer to *Ngai* or *Mūrungu* to bless the home, the family and the livestock.

First the elders would slaughter a goat and remove the stomach and place the contents *(tatha)* into a container. The rest of the goats would then be herded together and a boy and girl would go round them for a specified number of times. It was believed that if young children

---

14 *Bwana* is from Kiswahili and *Memsahib* is a combination of *Mem* – a corruption of Madam, and *Sahib*, a Hindi word meaning "boss". The lingua franca of East Africa is Kiswahili, which, although based on Bantu languages in general, has absorbed other languages from all countries surrounding the Indian Ocean area. Europeans, Arabs, Indians and all visitors to Eastern Africa used Kiswahili, the traders' language. As for the labourers, they could understand Kiswahili far more quickly than English because Kikuyu is a Bantu language.

(signifying innocence and purity) went round the herd and homestead several times, God would bless the herd, the offspring would multiply and the family would be safe from any misfortune. Elders would accompany the children, splashing the *tatha* around the compound. This ceremony was taken so seriously that plans were made more than a week in advance.

Not just any child could perform this ceremony. For some reason, which was never revealed to me, I was considered a 'charmed' boy and thus I was chosen for this task. I would head the procession and one of my sisters, either Muciri or Kaheti, would be directly behind me. It was a special privilege for a child to be chosen to lead this ceremony as a symbol of purity in both mind and soul, and many children envied me. It was regarded as such a solemn occasion that my grandfather would slaughter an extra goat each time his herd was 'blessed', for our family to feast on. I can remember the ceremony fairly well. I would be first in the line carrying the *tatha*. Next came my sister and the elder conducting the ceremony would follow. As the contents of the goat's intestines dripped out on the ground, the leading elder would chant and those behind him would repeat each line.

1ˢᵗ Elder: Twahoya mbura! (We beg for rain)
Elders: Twahoya mbura!
1ˢᵗ Elder: Twahoya ciana! (We pray for more children)
Elders: Twahoya ciana!
1ˢᵗ Elder: Tũgĩe tũhĩĩ! (May we beget boys)
Elders: Tũgĩe tũhĩĩ!
1ˢᵗ Elder: Tũgĩe tũirĩtu! (May we beget girls)
Elders: Tũgĩe tũirĩtu!
1ˢᵗ Elder: Tũgĩe mbũri! (May we get more goats)
Elders: Tũgĩe mbũri
1ˢᵗ Elder: Tũgĩe ng'ondu (May we get more sheep)
Elders: Tũgĩe ng'ondu
1ˢᵗ Elder: Tũgĩe ng'ombe (May we get more cows)
Elders: Tũgĩe ng'ombe
1ˢᵗ Elder: Tũgĩe imera (May we get a good crop)
Elders: Tũgĩe imera
1ˢᵗ Elder: Tũgĩe magetha (May we get more harvests)
Elders: Tũgĩe magetha
1ˢᵗ Elder: Tũgĩe thaayũ (May there be peace)
Elders: Tũgĩe thaayũ

*1ˢᵗ Elder: Thaai thathaiya Ngai thaai**
Elders: Thaai thathaiya Ngai thaai
1ˢᵗ Elder: Thaai thathaiya Ngai thaai
Elders: Thaai thathaiya Ngai thaai
1ˢᵗ Elder: Thaai thathaiya Ngai thaai
Elders: Thaai thathaiya Ngai thaai

The elders prayed for blessings on the home and the whole community, and this way they paid homage to God.

Another spiritual matter concerned the customs surrounding death. In those days, burials did not take place unless the dead person was wealthy, was a clan leader, a seer or a respected medicine man. Ordinary people, when they died or were terminally ill, were merely thrown into the bush to be eaten by hyenas and other wild animals. The removal of such a sick person was conducted at dawn before the children woke up. If they happened to enquire about the whereabouts of that individual, they would be told that he or she had gone on a long journey and would be returning later, and, naturally, as the days passed they would forget the matter. The adults did not want to expose us, as children, to the traumatic reality of a beloved relative literally being thrown away.

It was considered bad luck for a person to die inside the house and in such cases, a ram was slaughtered to cleanse the homestead where this occurred and the hut would thereafter be burned down.

One day, as I was strolling in the bush hunting for rabbits and other small animals, I came across my great grandmother, who had been abandoned there because she had shown signs of a serious illness. I loved this great grandmother, who was Wagachire's mother, quite dearly. According to Kikuyu custom, I had a joking relationship with her and referred to her as my "wife" since she was married to Njenga, and I was named after him.[15] She was a generous woman and a talented cook.

I helped her to her feet and walked her back to the homestead and into her hut. The adults did not explain the matter to me, but they were not happy and pretended to be busy with other matters when I started asking why my grandmother was in the forest. After all children were supposed to be ignorant of such things and although I did not fully understand what was happening, I kept an eye on her. And perhaps I had sensed something

---

15 In Kikuyu culture, the spouse of the person you are named after was referred to as your 'wife' or 'husband'. All your father's wives were your 'mother' and all your father's brothers were your 'fathers'.

* This was a religious chant to God beseeching Him to hear their petitions.

which the adults had not, because the old lady was nursed back to health and lived for at least a year in perfect health. *Ngwĩciria irathimo ciakwa ciumaga kũu.* (Perhaps my blessings are a result of these little things.)

After about a year, my great grandmother started being sickly once again. When her relatives saw that the old lady was, once more, about to die, they constructed a *gĩthũnũ* (a rough shelter) a little distance from the homestead and led her there. A separate one, (near the hut where my great grandfather spent his last days), was constructed for Munge, since he was given the responsibility of looking after her.

Munge would get food from my grandfather's homestead and take it to her. But one morning when he went to take her some porridge, he found that she had died. He informed the family that the old lady had passed away.

Around this time, burials had started to become more common and the family decided to bury her. She was the first member of the family to be given a burial at Elementaita. All other members of the family who had died previously had been disposed of in the more traditional manner, that is, thrown away in the bush. Since I was a child at the time, and children were kept out of such ceremonies, I did not understand the intricate ceremonies that went with the burial, but my uncle Munge told me all about it afterwards.

I would like to explain this in detail because it was not the kind of burial we have these days.

A special elder was called in for the occasion. He had generally overseen other burial ceremonies in the area and presided over the burial of my great grandmother, as well. Munge and another male relative were given the responsibility of digging the grave. The presiding elder escorted them to a spot and pointed it out to them. He did not utter a word and used gestures to communicate with them throughout the ceremonies.

Through these gestures, Munge and his helper were instructed to dig out the soil and put it next to the hole. The soil was not supposed to be thrown behind them as this was taken as "besmirching" the ceremony. The digging process was therefore very slow. According to Munge, the elder signalled them to stop digging when the grave was about three feet deep.

The elder then instructed Munge and his assistant to bring the body. One of them held the corpse by the neck and the other by the legs. The elder then indicated how the body was to be placed inside the grave. The body was to lie on its side and the head was to face to the east, where the sun rises and which (in that area) was towards Mount Kenya. The elder showed them how to arrange the limbs with the left hand down and the right hand up. The right hand was respected in Kikuyu mythology since it was believed to be the 'working' hand. Left-handed people were generally stigmatised and parents tried their best to discipline their children to use the right hand, no matter what their natural inclination was. Placing the right hand up symbolised that the person would work if they rose as a spirit. It was quite complicated.

After placing her in this position, Munge and his helper took my great grandmother's other clothing and laid them over her. Then the skins that she had used as bedding were placed on top of the pile. This, I was later told, was just in case she might need them in 'the next world.'

Next, the two gravediggers were given a signal to put back the soil over the body. After this, a pile of thorns was placed over the mound, to keep any animals away. All this was done in silence, with the use of gestures, throughout. No words were used as a mark of reverence to the spirits and the solemnity of the occasion.

After the burial, my uncle and his assistant had to stay in a shelter some distance from the homestead for four days. This was because it was felt that they had the 'spectre' or 'shadow of death' on them. During those four days, a particular person would bring them food. He would hang it on a tree near the shelter and knock on the tree to let Munge and his helper know that food had been delivered.

After the four days had passed, a medicine man was called to cleanse the homestead. A ram was slaughtered for this occasion, and the two gravediggers were cleansed with *tatha* and were given some nauseous stuff, a mixture of blood, *tatha* and bitter herbs, to make them vomit. This vomiting was symbolical — to show that they had got rid of any unknown spirits that might have contaminated them. This symbolic vomiting was called *gūtahīkio wariga* (vomiting the evil unknown, or the mysterious).

Munge then told me that once this was done, he and his helper had to shave off all their hair to rid them of the 'death spirit', and then the ceremony was completed.

However, after about two seasons, another ceremony was performed. A ram was slaughtered and the final cleansing was done. This was referred to as *kūhukūrwo* (restoration). After that, the two could once more associate with other people since the blemish of death had been removed. My uncle Munge, who lives in Kiambaa, still remembers all the details vividly.

❖ ❖ ❖

Another incident that demonstrates the people's deep belief in witchcraft and superstition happened in 1937, just before my grandfather died. Over the years the old man had grown frail with sickness and eventually neared the end of his days. I now went to look after the goat by myself, but I had checked in on my grandfather that morning, before I left, and then went out to look after the goats as usual. As I was told when I returned that evening, when he felt his time had come, he called all his wives and daughters-in-law together in order to tell them his dying wishes.

My grandfather had previously shared out his other wealth among his sons, and then he wanted to have a word with the women of the homestead and the men who were present. He spoke in metaphors and told the women that "when one goes on a journey, one never knows when or whether one would return." He said that although he was not going on a journey, it was always better to be prepared lest he did not return. The women listened in silence, but of course, they understood.

Then my grandfather shocked them by saying that he wished to bequeath his herd of goats to his favourite grandson, that is, me, whom he fondly referred to as *guuka* (grandfather), since I was named after him. The women found this incomprehensible. The old man had many sons, including Karume, my father, who would normally inherit the livestock. Yet he insisted that I, a mere boy, who was then away herding his goats, should be the heir.

Respectfully, my mother told the old man that such an arrangement was bound to cause friction in the home. Many of the old man's sons were not yet married, she pointed out. Would they be expected to ask me, a boy, barely into puberty, for goats to pay bride price? The goats should be inherited by the whole family, she suggested, so that there would be no resentment against me, or even attempts to bewitch me in order to get the property. She thought that the herd should be allocated equally to all families in the homestead.

The old man thought for some moments and then made a decision. He agreed that leaving all the goats under my guardianship might be awkward. He also agreed that the whole family should inherit the herd. But he set one condition to these concessions. He was adamant that his favourite and largest nanny goat, nicknamed *Mbarathi* (horse), because of her size and colour, must become my inheritance. *Mbarathi* had a black mane and white hide, just like many of the horses which the settlers rode. She was an extraordinary goat not only because she was so large, but also because she constantly gave birth to twins and produced more milk than any other goat in the herd. She was a legend throughout Elburgon and was admired by all. All Africans compared her to the graceful horses they saw ridden by the *Wazungu*.

The women agreed that this decision was reasonable. My grandfather then removed from his neck a ceremonial necklace made of heavy ceramic beads, licked it (as a sign of blessing) and said, "May the boy live to raise many goats and cattle that he will have to summon them by blowing the *coro* (a trumpet made from the horn of an animal). As for the rest of you," he added, "pay his dowry with my goats when the time comes."

I have never forgotten this and, although I was not present when it happened, the story remains ingrained in my mind.

From many generations past, the *coro* had been the instrument that the Kikuyu used to broadcast messages across the valleys and hills. Whether it was good tidings or an enemy tribe (usually the Maasai) approaching, people would deliver the news to the next village by blowing the *coro*. There were different tunes for every type of message, whether good or bad. Therefore my grandfather wished that I, as his favourite grandson, would acquire such large herds that a *coro* would be required because a mere human whistle would not be sufficient to reach and control the livestock.

Everyone agreed with my grandfather's decision and they left the *thingira*. He asked that I be brought to his deathbed, but I was away in the fields. That same evening, before I returned, Wagachire passed away and a little later, since he was a prominent person, he was properly buried in the traditional manner. Sheep were slaughtered and his body was wrapped in their hides before being put into the ground. Soon life went back to normal.

The goats were allocated to each of his wives and their sons, as they had agreed, but everyone knew that the queen of the herd, Mbarathi, belonged to me, the old man's favourite grandson. Today I own hundreds of goats, sheep and cattle in my Cianda Estate, and perhaps I should attribute this to the blessings of Wagachire Njenga, my grandfather.

However a problem came up a short while after the old man died. One of my uncles, Daniel Wanjema, decided to get married to a woman named Wangui Murungaru. As was the custom, the family had to pay bride price in terms of a sizeable number of goats. This was normal and expected and the old man had left them plenty of animals for such requirements. However Wangui's family, who lived in the neighbourhood, knew about Mbarathi's exceptional gift of producing twins. They demanded that the nanny goat be included in the bride price, otherwise, if she was not part of the dowry, they would not permit Wangui to marry. I suppose in-laws have always been difficult and demanding people throughout history!

My family gathered and discussed the matter, considering what actions they would take. What was to be done? The old man's dying wishes had to be respected and the nanny goat definitely belonged to me. All the same, the in-laws stood firm in their demands and reiterated that Mbarathi must be part of the dowry. At last our family reached a decision. They concluded that my own needs could not surpass those of the entire extended family, and therefore they decided to give away the goat. Wanjema got married, and everyone was happy.

Everyone, that is, apart from me. When I discovered that Mbarathi had been given away, I was filled with sorrow. But I had to accept the loss since the adults had made the decision.

A month after the marriage, my step-sister, Kaheti, Mugure's daughter, fell seriously ill. No one could identify exactly what was wrong with her, but we could all see she was dying. All types of herbal concoctions were tried but nothing worked. Neither did prayers or charms. As was the usual custom when all else failed, the family decided to consult a seer, or prophet, in case they had wronged the gods in some way. As I was later informed by the family, the woman, a respected female figure of the Elburgon community who was known as Njikuru, cast her *mbūgū* (charms), studied them, mumbled some incantations and then delivered her solemn appraisal of the situation. She said there was a special she-goat missing in the homestead and it was still alive. Unless the goat was returned to the home, Kaheti would die, and so would many other members of my family.

The family was dumbfounded and anxious. Since, as stated earlier, it was an age of superstition, they all believed in the seer's prediction that they would die, one by one, if the goat was not returned. Furthermore they all knew which goat was missing. Therefore, they approached the in-laws and informed them of their plight. Luckily enough the in-laws were understanding and gave back the goat the same day. I later learned that Kaheti was cured and working on the farm one week later. Our whole family was relieved that we had averted a catastrophe.

In retrospect, however, I do not believe that Kaheti actually had a terminal disease, or that a 'missing' goat could cause a family to die. Perhaps Njikuru had heard the story of Mbarathi and saw the opportunity to collect her fee as a seer. After all she was the mother to the wife of my uncle Kiguru. Most likely one or two family members conveniently arranged the whole matter in order to get back my nanny goat.

However the belief in witchcraft, sorcery, curses and other such things was so deep that people could not ignore the customary traditions concerning them. Witchcraft and sorcery were an important part of the rituals, and Christianity was a remote and suspicious concept to the people in my community. When an individual was suspected of theft or other crimes, he or she would be taken to a witchdoctor and various mystic rituals would be performed. The individual would then be given a choice, either confess or die. Those who were guilty readily returned whatever they had stolen or paid the fine imposed by the elders. This atmosphere of fear and uncertainty is something difficult to overcome and despite modern enlightenment I often wonder how much of these traditional superstitions still influence me.

These days it might be considered strange, but in my community, stealing was considered a more serious crime than murder. If a person was killed accidentally during a squabble, the elders would meet and discuss reparations. The family of the killer might be fined a certain number of cattle or, in some cases, be forced to give a child to the victim's family in order to 'replace' the person who had died. In cases where malice was determined to have been a factor, the killer would be banished and was no longer considered a member of the community.

Theft and sorcery had more severe consequences. In such cases, elders held grim sessions to determine the guilt and punishment of the suspect. For example, a process called *kũringa thenge* (hitting the he goat) was only undertaken in extremely grave cases including the theft of valuable property, such as the theft of a neighbour's beehive.

Let me briefly explain this process. When a suspect was accused of theft or sorcery and he denied his guilt, a he goat, symbolising life, would be slaughtered in front of a council of elders and witnessed by the members of the clan or clans that were involved. The accused was supposed to stab the dead animal repeatedly with a stick and take an oath, which was supposed to kill him if he was indeed guilty and was lying about it. He reiterated his innocence with every stab, saying, if he was accused of stealing someone else's beehive, for example:

Thenge ĩno ĩrondĩa akorwo nĩ nĩĩ ndĩraiire mwatũ wa Mwangi. (May the spirit of this billy goat kill me if I am the one who stole Mwangi's beehive.)

By taking such an oath, it was believed that the accused person's family and his clan would suffer dreadful misfortunes if he was actually guilty. Thus the destiny of the family or clan was important in determining the guilt or innocence of the accused person. This particular oath was used for serious matters only, such as land disputes. The clan would therefore do everything possible to influence, persuade or coerce the suspect to confess. Even hardened criminals seemed unable to bear condemning their families to suffering and death.

Whatever opinion one might hold about such customs in terms of morality or religion, the fact remains that it functioned well in terms of maintaining order in the society and preventing wrongdoing through a form of psychological pressure. Traditional societies had few alternative methods of dealing with these matters as they had no written laws. In fact, I believe that society was very orderly and the community generally peaceful. People respected their neighbours and crime was minimal. The village elders and the chiefs would sit and solve all differences and impose fines if they deemed it fit, and that would be final. The environment in which I was brought up had a sort of universal belief in social justice whereby everyone was answerable to the society, was part of it and had responsibilities to it.

But written laws were soon introduced by the colonial masters and they were often inappropriate or arbitrary in the context of the traditional society. Africans took quite some time to adjust to such laws. Perhaps Kenyans are still grappling with them even today.

By 1945, my father managed to move to Elburgon, somewhat farther into the Rift Valley, past Elementaita. My uncles also moved. Kiguru went to Kericho and Wanjema went back to Ikinu in Kiambu.

My father had never been comfortable on Delemare's ranch and had always wanted to live independently. Luckily, he got a job with the forestry department and was given a little allotment for a house and space for his animals. Limited grazing for cattle and sheep were permitted, but goats were not, as they were considered too destructive.

At that time, the government would allow the families of the forest workers to cultivate land while at the same time, interplanting and tending to the tree seedlings. Once the seedlings grew too large, the families would be moved to other parts of the forest to start all over again. If even one seedling died, the families would be required to replant. This strict system ensured that there was plenty of food for the people, while maintaining a self-sustaining system of forest management. The forests at the time, were very carefully tended.

So, although my father did not own the land he settled on, he was happy that he could now rear his sheep and cattle, outside the stifling environment of Delamere's ranch. One of my father's friends had a licence to cut timber, and so my father would also help out in this regard as well.

Before we moved to Elburgon, my childhood was quite happy and I had lots of fun in between doing my chores. I used to play with a boy called Waronja Gachunga, and he is the one who took over as leader of the age group when I went on to the next.

Each age group is generally led by the oldest boy within the group. Perhaps I impressed the age group which was senior to ours, because I was promoted to this set even before I was circumcised. This 'promotion' meant that I stopped interacting with the younger uncircumcised boys and perhaps I was also exposed to the responsibilities of adult life somewhat earlier than my age mates.

Elementaita had lots of snakes. Sometimes, when I was out in the fields herding the goats, I would take a nap at midday, when the sun was hot and blazing down. Once in a while I would wake up and find a snake basking in the sun next to me. I know most people would be afraid of such a situation, but I have never been frightened of snakes at all. However, I am scared to death of chameleons!

I loved to hunt and to practise games which were meant to improve one's aim. There was one game in which the boys would make hoops out of green branches and then roll them along the ground. As the hoops rolled, we would try to put our *mīnyago* (sharpened sticks) through. I got very good at this and consequently was able to bring down quite a bit of small game using spears and arrows.

When we moved to Elburgon, I used to kill impala, dikdik and hares. Our family *shamba* (farm) was fenced with interlaced wooden stakes and I would sometimes lower the fence in one section so that gazelles would be tempted to jump over the barrier and come in to eat the crops. After I lowered the fence, I would place a wooden stake just behind the hole, so that when a gazelle jumped over it would be impaled on the stake.

I also learned how to make little traps for game birds and managed to get some partridges and guinea fowl every now and again.

This game meat never made it home, though. Such things were for uncircumcised boys, and adults would never consider eating such meat. So we would light a campfire out in the bush, roast the meat and eat it ourselves. If any of us dared to bring game meat home and use a family pot to cook it, we would be in big trouble, and the pot would never be used again.

Chapter 2

The Quest for Knowledge

The concept of education and school continued to fascinate me. I had always wondered why Europeans and their children were so different from us Africans, and I marvelled at how such few whites could control and subdue so many Africans. The Kikuyu called the whites *Athūngū*, that is English people, and the strange tongue they spoke, was called *Gīthūngū* (English). People who spoke English were held in high esteem. I longed to get an education. I wanted to speak English and get a good job, perhaps as a farm clerk. The African clerks were smart, well paid and, to my own perception, seemed to be the cream of African society. They did not herd or milk cattle, nor did they dress in skins or live in shacks. Their occupation was to supervise the milking and weighing of milk, to pay their fellow Africans their tiny salaries and, seemingly, to look down on those who had no education.

I dreamed of getting a well-paying job. Little by little I became dissatisfied with the conditions we were living in. I did not want to be just another labourer and I did not want to live in the same squalid conditions as my father and his colleagues.

Two separate factors encouraged me to get an education.

The first was a boy in the village who used to go to school in Kiambu and come home to Elementaita for the holidays. The rest of us would play, sing and run about whenever we were free of domestic chores but this boy would sulk and shake his head back and forth, jerk about, and would generally keep away from us other children. When one of us asked him why he was acting so strangely, he said it was the English in his head that was bothering him. The English needed to come out, he would tell us, but there was no one with whom he could converse. Since we were young and inexperienced, we were quite impressed with this explanation and thought very highly of him. It may be that he suffered from some nervous disease, but we children were awed by the fact that he could speak English like the white people.

I remember that the boy's father eventually became concerned with his son's behaviour and called the elders together to discuss the matter. As I recall, I escorted my grandfather, as one of the elders, to the meeting, and I listened intently to each speaker.

The boy's father explained that the English language bottled up in his son's head was the source of the problem, but there was nothing he could do. No one else in the village could speak the language and thus there was no way the English could come out. As he spoke, the elders nodded their understanding.

"Why don't we take him to *Mūrunyu?* They can speak English together and he will be cured," suggested one of them. *'Mūrunyu'* was the mispronounced English name of one of Delamere's white managers.

The elders discussed it further. If speaking to a *Mzungu* would cure their son, why not attempt it?

But after consideration, one of the wiser men pointed out a difficulty.

"There are no schools on the farm. The whites will want to know where the boy learned English," he explained.

This was definitely a puzzling issue because white people were quite happy that the labourers had no education. In fact learning was never encouraged by the settlers at all. If the elders took the boy to speak with the manager, the whites would become aware that their children had been secretly educated and they would be in trouble.

"If they know that we have educated our son to the point where he can actually speak with Murunyu, we will definitely be sacked," stated another.

To the disappointment of the boy's father, the other elders agreed with this observation. They came to no other possible solutions and eventually the matter had to be dropped.

I never learned what happened to the boy after that because a short while later I went off to school in Kiambu. But when I look back at the whole episode, I realise that our fathers and grandfathers saw Europeans as people with whom they had to watch their every little step. In addition they seemed to believe that the English language was magical to the extent that it could make a person sick if he did not have an outlet for it.

The second factor that increased my craving for education was my uncle, Gatenjwa, who lived in Kiambu and would visit our family in Elementaita. He harped on the advantages of education and was quite proud that he had enrolled all his children in school. After such a visit, I would plead with my father to pay fees so that I could join a school, but my requests were always turned down. Every time my uncle visited, I would pester him with questions about school. I would then plead with my father yet again, and cry myself to sleep after another rejection.

But apparently my father had reasons for rejecting my appeals. Primarily, many people of my father's generation did not value formal education because they did not understand what it was all about. Many were suspicious of the white man's religion and education, and could hardly differentiate between the two. In addition, they were contemptuous of the European attitude towards Africans.

Furthermore, the whites wished to abolish age-old customs such as female circumcision. The missionaries who educated girls urged them not to get circumcised and this, of course, was anathema to the Kikuyu traditionalists who had inherited the custom from their ancestors. The majority of the people differed from the missionaries' point of view on many aspects in life. Missionaries, settlers and colonial administrators were all seen as the enemy.

To the traditionalists, anyone associating with the *Wazungu* was treated as an outcast who had betrayed the community. Europeans had invaded the country, made all the land their own and forced Africans to become servants on what had been their own property. Indeed, Kikuyu traditions revered land as being under the custody of ancestral spirits and for the purpose of economic sustenance. But the Europeans destroyed centuries-old traditions and killed Africans for strange and arbitrary reasons that the African did not even understand. In short, the traditionalists considered European economic and cultural activities evil and therefore a great many parents forbid their children to have association with anything European. European education was seen as a form of indoctrinating African children against their own culture and traditions.

In the few cases in which parents allowed their children to go to *Wazungu* schools, this rarely included girls. This was because girls who went to school seemed to become disobedient, defied such customs as circumcision and were generally seen as rebellious and a little too independent, especially in the concept of a male-dominated society. At the time, girls were considered a family asset that would bring wealth in terms of dowry when they married. Most men of that day would never consider marriage with a *kĩrĩĩgũ* (uncircumcised girl) who had independent ideas of her own. These factors, in addition to the harsh governance that included heavy taxation and poor wages did nothing to endear the Europeans to the Africans.[16]

Although labourers on the settler farms did not pay any taxes, they would have to carry identification papers when they travelled outside the farms. Because one would have to show proof that these taxes had been paid, I remember that when adult men travelled from the settler farms to Central Province or Nairobi, they would borrow one another's identification documents. The *"kipande"* was a small piece of folded metal. Inside was a paper which contained the name and home of origin of the individual, where he worked, where he was travelling to, among other details. Since there was no photo included, anyone could easily claim to be the owner. When tax was paid, a piece of paper certified with a stamp would be included in the *kipande*, and this would allow the traveller to proceed without harassment to wherever he was going. Since the early 1920's[17] the *kipande* was one of the most demeaning impositions of the colonialists. It was meant to be hung around the neck and people thought this was even worse than being branded like animals.

Before he moved to Elburgon, my father worked for the whites because he had no alternative. He often told my mother that if he had had a choice, he would never have worked for Europeans. Nevertheless, he was a young man with a family to support and he wanted to make something out of himself, so being a labourer on a settler's farm was the best option available. As mentioned earlier, he and the other labourers were forced to sign contracts which bound them to various dubious conditions. At any rate, Karume hated the Europeans and their ways with all his heart. By refusing to allow me to go to school he saw himself as protecting me from what he believed were harmful and sinister influences.

The second reason he opposed my appeals for education was that, like most communities of the time, he depended on his sons to herd the livestock and do other chores around the homestead. If a man talked about taking his sons to school, his drinking companions would tease him.

---

16 The European colonialists first imposed a hut tax. The man of the homestead was deemed to pay the tax equivalent to the number of huts in his compound. The more the huts, the richer the owner was supposed to be since this showed he had more wives and only well-off men were able to afford more than one wife.

17 In 1922, Harry Thuku was imprisoned in Nairobi for leading a protest in which workers in the town demanded an end to the practice of being forced to wear the *kipande* around the neck. During a protest outside the police station next to Norfolk Hotel, which settlers and colonial administrators patronized, dozens of Africans were shot dead. Harry Thuku was subsequently imprisoned for seven years in Somalia. The station is today referred to as Central Police Station and the road along it is named after Harry Thuku.

"Have you grown so poor that you don't even have a single sheep for your son to look after? Have you lost all your livestock?" they would ask. "If you don't have any animals, tell us so. We will give you some, you poor man!"

Along this same line, something else which put western education in bad light was the fact that when my father's generation was young, some lucky few children were actually paid to go to school. They would be given something like twenty or twenty five cents, and this made it seem like education was something unpleasant, something you had to be paid to endure.

But as I said earlier, labour was shared out and everyone's role was well-defined. While the men worked in the ranches, the women would cook, clean, look after the children, cultivate the family holding, fetch water and firewood and do other domestic duties. Girls would assist their mothers and boys would herd the family's livestock. If the older children went to mission schools, there would be no one to perform the chores.

It is interesting that in many African homes, it was mainly boys who were disobedient or physically weak and unable to perform domestic tasks, who were sent to school. Basically it was seen as an opportunity to get rid of stubborn boys who would refuse to herd the goats, or weaklings. Thus it was thought that the strong children would perform their chores without hindrance. Girls, at the time, were not allowed to go to school at all. I think it is ironic, that the weak children were the first to get an education, and later, well paying jobs.

However, an incident occurred that led many of the adults in Elburgon to change their minds; an event that finally persuaded my father to allow me to go to school. According to the way I heard the tale, it was all about water pipes.

One of the more wealthy men in Elburgon was a man called Karanja wa Maara. Although he was a squatter just like the rest of us, Karanja was the most prosperous man in the area and had large herds of livestock. He was married to ten wives with many children and had a sizeable house in a very conspicuous location on the slope of a hill overlooking the valley where Elburgon Township was located.

Karanja was a generous man, a pillar of the society, and the community had a great deal of respect for him. I saw him on a number of occasions and I was always impressed. He had this beautiful red *shuka*, made of brocade silk, I believe, and a thick wool blanket that he wore as a cloak. However he had no admiration for Europeans and was contemptuous of their domination. Those who were similarly opposed to white rule formed a group with him as their unofficial leader

Karanja was also a proud man. One day, as he took a walk to stretch his legs, he came upon the village spring high up the slope where everyone in the surrounding area fetched water. When he inquired whether the spring was the source of his household water as well, he was told that, indeed it was. His family drew water from the spring just as everyone else did. He found this notion quite depressing. He did not like the idea of getting water from the same stream as the common villagers.

"*Ndingīnyuithania iriūko rīmwe na ngīa,*" he declared, meaning, "I can't drink from the same source with the poverty stricken."

Being a wealthy man, he decided to buy some water pipes from Nakuru. His sons contributed funds to assist in the purchase and then he hired some plumbers to install them. He found a spring among the rocks higher up the slope inside a *Mzungu* farm which he decided to use as his source of water, and had the piping run down to his *thingira*. He was extremely pleased with accomplishing this arrangement as he was the first to have piped water coming into his home. The other villagers marvelled at this novelty.

One day the *Mzungu* settler happened to chance upon the pipeline leading to Karanja's house. He knew there was no other settler in that area so, being of a curious turn of mind, he decided to follow the pipes to their end. The pipeline, of course, took him up to Karanja's home, and, as he entered the gate, he found some children playing and asked them to direct him to the head of the house. The children ran off and informed their father, Karanja, that he had a *Mzungu* visitor outside in his yard. Karanja, with his hatred of whites, boldly walked out of his *thingira* into the yard and confronted the visitor with defiance. In Kiswahili he sarcastically asked the settler why he had honoured him with this visit.

But the *Mzungu* ignored the question and demanded, "*Nani nakwambia wewe weka pipe kwa nyumba yako wewe niga?*" (Who gave you permission to have piped water in your house, you nigger?)

Karanja answered with words to the effect that the *Mzungu* could go roast in hell but then, in anger, the settler made an error of judgement. He made the big mistake of insulting and slapping Karanja.

Karanja, the son of Maara, a brave warrior who could not bear humiliation, especially in front of his wives and children, immediately retaliated by striking out with his walking stick and beat the man thoroughly until the settler finally found his feet and ran away.

Karanja made history that day. Hitting or even rudely answering a white person was an extraordinary matter and the people of Elburgon had never seen it happen before. But Karanja had done it, and word spread throughout the town like wildfire.

"Karanja nĩ ahũra mũthũngũ!" (Karanja has beaten a white person).

The people joked and laughed over the beating. However all the hilarity and triumphant sense of settling of scores was bound to have repercussions, and these started the same day around mid-afternoon.

The settler had gone straight to the police in Nakuru. In the mid-afternoon, the police came looking for Karanja and he was arrested and hauled to Nakuru Police Station where he was locked in a cell overnight. The following morning he was charged in court with assault. Of course the police, the prosecutor and the judge were all whites. In fact the judge was the Nakuru District Commissioner, who in those days also acted as magistrates, and he sentenced Karanja to two years in jail without the option of a fine.

Elburgon elders were shocked when they received the news. Not only was Karanja a role model in the society, he also employed many of them and their adult children and was a philanthropist. They could not imagine that a distinguished person of Karanja's status could be arrested. The elders decided to send a delegation of the most respected old men the following day to reason with the judge so that he could affect Karanja's release. But they were in for a rude shock.

"Doesn't the DC know that he has arrested Karanja, *the Karanja*, the son of Maara?" they asked a court orderly. "Tell him that the son of Maara cannot stay in prison. What is wrong with the DC?"

When a court orderly informed the judge that a delegation wished to discuss Karanja's case, he laughed them off and told them to go away. British law did not recognize delegations of elders, he said. At any rate, to the European mind, Karanja had committed the ultimate sin, beating and humiliating a white man.

The elders deliberated and came up with an alternative. They proposed to bring one of Karanja's eldest sons to take his place and serve the sentence on behalf of his father.

The judge again turned down their proposal. No one could serve time in prison for the offence of another.

In that case, the elders told him, they would bring two sons who could both serve the sentence so long as Karanja was released. After all, they reasoned, this would be even more beneficial for the court because if prisoners were sentenced to a period of time with labour, two would definitely be able to accomplish more work than one.

This was not possible, the judge informed them.

But the old men were insistent. Would the court then take three sons in return for Karanja? Four? Five?

Not even ten, the judge informed them with increasing anger. And what is more, he warned them that if they continued being a nuisance, they would soon join Karanja in prison.

The elders went back to Elburgon, dejected with their defeat. They discussed the issue and deliberated at length over all the possible consequences and repercussions of the Europeans' actions. They realized that none of them was safe from the white man's law. If Karanja could be jailed, then anyone, no matter who they were, could be jailed. They thought of Karanja as a village leader, a respected elder who was beyond reproach. Now it dawned on them that not a single one of them was beyond the reach of the white man.

One of the things they realised as their discussions proceeded was that Karanja had been handicapped by the lack of a lawyer. They knew what lawyers did, and knew how they operated, but no lawyer had represented Karanja during the trial. They had not bothered to look for one. They had believed that no judge in his right senses would imprison the great Karanja wa Maara. The only measure the elders could now take, they decided, was to give their children a European education. If they allowed their children to go to school, they would be better able to protect themselves and the community.

Some of them came to understand that the only way they could have effective ammunition against the white man would be by knowing his secrets from within. They were following the precepts of that well known adage—know your enemy.

Consequently, in 1942, while we were still living in Elementaita, my father agreed, albeit reluctantly, that I could join primary school. However there was no school anywhere nearby so they decided to send me to my aunt's home in Kiambu[18] where there were many schools. It was arranged that I would live with relatives of my maternal grandparents in Ndeiya and attend Kahuho Karing'a[19] Primary School.

18 Kiambu– the origin of the word is "Kia-mbu" the place of *Mbu* (screams). The place bordered the Maasai to the south and so, when the Maasai went for animal raiding expeditions, people would scream to alert their neighbours of the arrival of enemy raiders.

19 Karing'a was the name of the movement that started independent schools outside the missionaries' system. The schools, while aiming to teach formal education, also meant to uphold Gĩkũyũ traditions such as female circumcision which the missionary schools opposed vehemently.

Fortunately, there was enough money to pay school fees. My father's salary at Delamere's had increased to eight shillings per month, so life was a little easier for our family. In addition, my goat, Mbarathi, was sold for eleven shillings to add to the funds I needed for school. But before I boarded the train to Limuru, which was the nearest station to Ndeiya, a few preliminaries had to be undertaken. First, my father loved me very much, and he had a goat slaughtered for a family feast as a sign of farewell. Second, I had to discard my goatskin and get some sort of European attire in order to join school. My father decided to buy me a *shuka*, that is, a cotton cloth, to wrap around myself and knot at my shoulders, something like a toga. This was the attire that most school-going children wore at the time.

The only shop in the area that had a variety of supplies including clothing material was the one previously mentioned, which belonged Moraj.

At the time length was not measured in centimetres or inches. The unit of measurement used was the *dhiraa*, commonly known as *mkono*, that is, the length from the tip of the fingers to the elbow—a cubit, in other words. One could buy as many *dhiraa* as they wanted, but each adult was supposed to measure the length for himself or herself.

Moraj was a successful shopkeeper because he was clever. He well knew that the lengths of people's forearms were different. The shorter the forearm, the less material would make up the measurement. Naturally, therefore, he disliked customers with long forearms since this meant less profit. However, it just so happened that in Elementaita, there was one giant of a fellow called Gachungui who was not only large and strong, but was also blessed with quite long arms. Due to this attribute, villagers who wanted to buy cloth would send him to Moraj's shop on their behalf. This way, even undersized villagers were guaranteed of getting the maximum measure of material. A person who made use of Gachungui's services would afterwards take him a *gītumbī* (large gourd) of *mūratina* as a sign of gratitude. I remember that, as a result, Gachungui was quite inebriated most of the time.

So when I needed my *shuka*, Gachungui, my father and I went to Moraj's shop and I acquired new clothing, a white cotton sheet worth a shilling and fifty cents. Some parents bought shorts for their school-going children, but my father just could not afford it.

But I did not mind. I was over the moon. A *shuka* in itself was more than many other children could dream of. The cloth, due to the dimensions of Gachungui's long arms, was quite big, and I remember I had to fold it in the middle so that it could cover me without dragging on the ground.

My mother and my uncle Munge walked with me up to the train station at Eburu. It was the first time I had ever got a chance to sit and ride on a train and, since I was alone, it was a big ordeal, but I loved it all the same. I was especially impressed with the Asian ticket collectors who came along to check and punch each person's ticket. They were dressed in sharp khaki uniforms with badges and shiny buttons and looked totally unlike anyone I had seen before. They were helpful too, and would inform those who were uncertain, exactly where they should alight. I immediately decided that, when I grew up, I would be a train conductor.

All of us sat on hard wooden benches but I never noticed any discomfort because it was so exciting. The train rolled through hills and valleys and I had few regrets apart from feeling homesick. I knew I would miss my family, of course, but I would finally be starting school, which was a dream come true for me. I would learn to read and write and to speak English like the white people and their African clerks. I would even be able to speak to the boy who was troubled by the English in his head and make him feel better. All the possibilities of what I could do with an education seemed infinite.

I was fascinated with every scene I viewed along the way and longed to discover new places since I had spent all my childhood in Delamere's ranch. I was entering a new world and I was eager to meet my future. Wanja, my maternal aunt, met me in Limuru at the train station, and I started my new life at her home.

I started school in the beginning of 1942. I was about thirteen years old, which, in that day, was quite an ordinary age to begin school. It was not unheard of for some people to start school at seventeen. I gave my aunt Wanja the money for my fees and upkeep and I was enrolled in Kahuho Primary School where the fees was one shilling and fifty cents per term.

The Kahuho Primary School was made up of a few classrooms. Some were built of bamboo and others of clay and wattle, and were roofed with thatch or corrugated iron sheets. Altogether there may have been over seventy children, but there were just a few desks, up in front of the class. The rest of us had to make do with stones or logs to sit on. I was overjoyed and I fitted into school life with ease. Although the teachers enforced a very strict code of discipline, I never had a problem with any of them since I was a punctual and obedient boy.

I was enrolled in the Beginners' Class 1 (Sub A) where the pupils were taught how to write numbers and letters on the dusty ground because there was a shortage of paper and learning materials such as exercise books. We were also taught vernacular. At this level, we would often spend our day out in the sun or under the trees as we studied. After learning the alphabet and some words and sums, we moved on to Class 2 (Sub B) and used chalk and a black cardboard slate to practise our writing and math. Graduation from these 'Sub' classes was a major cause for celebration and I remember I was so excited to actually get my own slate that I could not sleep the night before.

The teachers coached and supervised us, and when I graduated from this class and was ready to join Standard One, each of us was finally given an exercise book and a pen. At this point we already considered ourselves 'educated'.

I remember one of the teachers, Dedan Macharia. When the weather got really cold, he would arrange for a big log fire in the middle of the classroom and we would all huddle around it as we learned.

I still had not acquired a pair of shorts, but this was not so very important. Not many boys had them, anyway. As for shoes, we did not even dream of them. In fact, even if we had owned a pair, we might have never dared to wear them. Teachers, some of whom wore shorts as well, understandably developed a very negative and sarcastic attitude toward pupils who were dressed smartly than themselves. Many teachers did not even own shoes at all and I am sure any student who would have dared come to school wearing a pair would have been kicked out of school.

This transition to Standard One was viewed as very important. It demonstrated that a pupil was mature enough to sit in class and handle books, and it also signified that the student had the resilience to sit through a class, stay in school and continue learning. Many pupils dropped out after the first two levels and only those who were serious, or whose parents or guardians were determined to see their children educated, managed to get past the beginners' classes. Luckily, I had completed the beginner classes in less than a year, and was among the best pupils to do so.

When we joined Standard One, we were taught basic literacy. The teachers concentrated on the three Rs, that is, Reading, Writing and Arithmetic. I had a natural talent for numbers and felt at ease with the subject, but I was not as confident with language and history. However I was determined and struggled with the difficult subjects and through my efforts I managed to obtain above average results. I was always among the top three in class. Furthermore, I maintained a good standard of cleanliness. I took very good care of myself and my clothing, washing whenever necessary, and, when we were inspected I enjoyed being able to be proud of my appearance and usually came first.

Another favourite of mine was "Drill", something like physical exercises done with a group of students in unison.

While I was at Kahuho Primary School, I remember getting into trouble once, just because I was too hungry. Since we lived in an agricultural society, nearly all schools taught the basics of agriculture to the students and we had a school farm where we practised growing various crops. One day our class was directed to dig a portion of the land to get ready for the planting season. We arrived on the farm early in the morning and our teacher, Andrew Gathia, said we should work quickly because we would not be allowed to leave until we had finished. By around two in the afternoon, we still had not completed the task, and we were all very exhausted and hungry.

It so happened that the previous year the farm had been planted with sweet potatoes. It is never possible to get every single potato out of the ground; there are always a few left. So while we were digging we found the occasional tuber and since we were so hungry, we just ate them raw. Raw sweet potatoes are crunchy and taste fairly nice. It is a bit like eating carrots straight from the ground.

One student dug up a large sweet potato which was smooth and round. It happened to catch the attention of the teacher and who asked the student to take it over to him. I guess he was hungry as well, because he called me over, gave me the potato and a matchbox, and asked me to roast it for him. He said I could go over to an abandoned shelter on the borders of the farm and roast it there.

I gathered some twigs, went inside the hut and made a fire. As the sweet potato began to roast, the delicious smell was overwhelming. At this time it was nearly three in the afternoon and I was starving. Without even realizing what I was doing, I cut a tiny piece of the tuber, just to taste it. It was incredibly sweet! I cut another little piece and ate it. I am not sure how it happened, but before I understood what I was doing, half the sweet potato was gone. Hunger had somehow triumphed over my common sense and my fear of the teacher.

When I came to my senses, three quarters of the sweet potato was gone and I realized I was going to be in trouble. I had eaten the teacher's sweet potato! I tried to think what I should do but could not come up with any sort of excuse, so I just resigned myself to the fact that I was going to be punished. And if I was going to be punished anyway, I decided I may as well eat the rest of it.

I stayed in the hut a little while, waiting to see what was going to happen. I guess the teacher was mentally calculating the amount of time it would take for the potato to be ready. When it seemed to him that I was taking too much time, he sent another pupil to come and fetch me. I knew I was in deep trouble, and I told this pupil to tell the teacher I needed a little more time for the sweet potato to cook properly.

About ten minutes after that, the teacher, who must have been starving, sent another pupil to tell me that I should bring the sweet potato whether it was done or not.

Fearfully, but with resignation, I left the hut and walked over the fields to the teacher.

"Njenga," he asked, looking at my empty hands, "where is my sweet potato?"

"I have eaten it, Sir," I replied, shaking like a leaf.

"Why?"

"*Nĩ mara ma ũtũmwo,*" I blurted out, which literally translates to, "It's the intestines for the messenger."

To clarify this statement, I have to explain that in traditional Gikuyu culture, when a person was sent on a mission, he would be given a token of appreciation for his effort. If a goat or sheep had been slaughtered, the messenger was given the *mara*, the intestines. This part of the carcass was normally eaten, but was not regarded as particularly tempting. In any such case, it was always expected that the messenger got some sort of small reward or gift. In modern times it would be regarded as a tip.

"You have not eaten the intestines, you naughty boy," said the furious teacher. "You have eaten the whole animal!"

Well, if you cannot imagine what happened next, let me just say that I found it difficult to sit for the next full week! If I blame my hunger for my own silly behaviour, I guess I should blame teacher Githia's severity on his!

On weekends, while in Ndeiya, I used to do the usual chores assigned to boys of the homestead. These involved a little farming and herding the goats and calves. Ndeiya is a dry area, just on the precipice before the escarpment into the Rift Valley.

At the end of every term I would go home for the holidays. My aunt would escort me to the train station at Muguga where I would board the train down to Eburu station, and all through the journey I would be excited at the thought of returning home to my family and seeing all my friends, once again. I remember that the first time I came home on holiday, all my mates in my *riika* came to see me. They were full of questions about the train, the school and the sights along the way. It was flattering to be the centre of attention.

Before I returned to school to begin Standard Two in 1944, I had a long talk with my father. I told him that although I enjoyed my school life and obtaining an education, living with my aunt Wanja and the in-laws presented some difficulties. Although they were kind people and treated me well, I found life in Ndeiya somewhat gruelling. My aunt's family simply did not have much in terms of money or material comfort. I had to do farm work during the times I was not in school and I did not really enjoy this. Life in Elementaita had been much better.

By this time my father had realised that I actually needed an education if my life was to be any different from his own or that of other villagers. He thought long and hard about the situation and finally came up with a solution. My paternal relatives (those my grandfather Wagachire had left behind when he moved to Delamere's) were doing quite well in Kiambaa, and since there were schools there, too, I could go and join them, instead. After all, it was traditionally believed that it was better for a family to receive help from the paternal side of the family than from the maternal side. Receiving help from the maternal side was considered less dignified. In those days, after all, a child belonged to the father's clan, not the mother's.

My father consulted his step-brother, my uncle Gatenjwa Munge, the same man who used to boast about having all his children in school during his visits to us. Gatenjwa and his brother, Paul Mwobi, were astute businessmen who were doing quite well in Kiambaa. They owned general shops at Karuri market in Kiambaa and welcomed the idea of allowing me to board with them as I pursued my ambitions of acquiring an education. And so when I went back to school, I found a new home, about thirty kilometres from where I had lived with my aunt Wanja in Ndeiya.[20]

---

20   It is important to note the importance of the family institution in the advancement of education in those days. Many people born in places where there were no schools went to live with relatives who lived where formal learning was available. For this reason many people born in the Rift Valley farms returned to their homeland in Kiambu and other places in central Kenya.

In addition to this change, I now joined a Catholic School, Riara Primary, which was 11 kilometres away from my uncle's house in Kiambaa. The year was 1944 and I was fifteen years old and just starting Standard Two. On the face of it, this might be hard to believe since today, a fifteen year old would be in Secondary School. In those days, however, there were many others who were even older than me. And, for those who find it confusing, we pupils were able to progress according to our abilities, so I had managed to complete Sub A, Sub B and Standard One, all within a year.

Riara Primary was much larger than Kahuho and many of the teachers were white missionaries. The school was headed by an Irish priest called Father John Doody. Apart from the three Rs, I now started studying Christian Education. After all, the missionaries had come to Africa with evangelization as their main purpose. Education was a tool they used to create an understanding of their religion among Africans and to make it easier to work together with them. Since a number of my family members had already been baptised, I found it quite interesting and studied the ideals and mechanisms of Christianity. My curiosity in the white man's religion was deeply aroused.

For example, I wondered why the teachers and priests were referred to as Brothers when it was obvious that the colour of their skin, language and background eliminated the remotest possibility that they were related to any African. Another puzzling feature was that the Brothers were not married and I could not understand the reason behind this since a number of them were well past the age of acquiring spouses. Furthermore, unlike other Europeans I had known, the missionaries were kind and they seemed to genuinely care for the pupils and the community. They went out of their way to interact with Africans, a factor that I initially thought quite odd judging from what I had heard about them. And of course, at the time I did not realise that the leadership of the Catholic Church was distinctly separate from the British who headed the colonial government.

In terms of status, I felt I had risen several ranks because my uncle bought me a shirt and a pair of shorts for school. This was a significant step upward for a boy like me who had previously considered my cotton quite *shuka* impressive, after having worn goatskins since birth. After all many adults were still quite contented wearing *shukas* and blankets. Furthermore, children who wore these items were a small minority, and I considered it a privilege to wear them; to be one of the small minority!

At any rate, Gatenjwa had insisted I wear them. After all, his own children wore them to school, even while playing, and he did not want me to feel like the odd one out in my *shuka*. I marvelled at my new clothes and thought things could not have been better. I never imagined wearing shoes and, as for underpants, I did not even know about them.

In 1945 my father moved to Elburgon so when I went home for my holidays, my new clothes caused quite a bit of interest among my friends. Many of the boys, especially those coming from families who were even unable to buy *shukas*, admired my outfit. One of my friends, a boy called Migwi Kariuki, asked me to loan him the pair of shorts, just for a day, so that he could experience wearing the garment for himself. I obliged and the boy went home to change.

A few hours later, Migwi came back. He was furious with me and close to tears. With bitterness, he explained that the shorts had made him look ridiculous in front of the whole village and he would never wear them again. He said that all the boys and girls he met on his walk had laughed at him. I could not quite understand what had made everyone laugh at Migwi, but when I looked at the shorts closely I also burst into laughter. Migwi had put on the shorts back to front and the buttons were at the back.[21] Therefore, while Migwi had been strutting around the village like a peacock, he had actually made an idiot of himself.

Amid more hilarity, I explained the problem to Migwi. After that it was many more years before Migwi tried on a pair of shorts again. We remained friends for life and until his death a few years ago, we used to laugh over this childhood incident. He became a rich businessman and although he never went to school, he was quite successful. He started out with a lorry and later bought a farm, the land currently opposite Stem Hotel in Nakuru.

After the holidays I went back to my new life in Kiambaa and adapted well. Other than Sunday mornings when I went to church, I spent my free time helping my uncles in the shops, doing chores and cleaning up. Here I first experienced the mechanics of commerce. I watched while my uncle.bought goods and then resold them at a profit. This was an exciting revelation for me and later inspired me in my first commercial enterprise.

During my first three years at Riara School, I was a good student and I easily gelled into the school system and had no learning or behavioural difficulties. I was made a Class Prefect in Standard three, and was given the responsibility of monitoring the behaviour of my fellow pupils.

Perhaps one of the reasons I was popular was because I was talented in telling stories. In my younger days, as I sat at my grandmother's fireside in Elementaita, she had told me and my siblings an incredible

---

21   At this time zippers were unknown in rural Kenya.

amount of folk tales and traditional legends which were full of interesting characters, adventures, poetry and music. As we children sat in her hut, waiting for her or for our mothers to prepare food for us, I absorbed the art of story-telling from her. My grandfather also told me many stories, although his were more to do with wisdom and customs.

When I went to school I passed on these stories to my friends, and whatever details I could no longer recall, I made up along the way. My schoolmates nicknamed me *Wamūcema* (loosely translated as 'the Stalker') after one of the characters in my narratives.

Although the origin of the *Wamūcema* character is hazy, I remember that he was a naughty fellow who had gone missing for some reason. But the name *Wamūcema* came from a song that accompanied the story. As far as I can recall, the lines used to go something like this:

Wamūcema, Wamūcema ndarī kuo ĩĩ
Wamūcema, Wamūcema is not at home
Athire kū, Athire kū?
Where did he go? Where did he go?
Ĩ gūcera ĩĩ gūcera ĩĩ
He went to visit, he went to visit
Kwa arata na ndūgū ciao ĩĩ
To friends and clansmen
E njĩra akĩona mūthige ĩĩ
On the way he saw a jackal
Ĩingatanĩte na mbūkū ĩĩ
Chasing a hare.

I cannot now remember the particular story that featured *Wamūcema*. I think I probably made up the character's name on the spot. At any rate, Friday afternoons at school were story telling times, and I was always thrilled to be able to tell one of mine. I also enjoyed relating these during break and after class because my friends, and the other children would mill around me, urging me to tell "just one more" as I entertained them with one folk tale after another. It was quite an amusing and educational way to pass time. All the stories had moral lessons and I would get my spectators to be involved in singing the songs, quoting proverbs and responding to questions. This was the way African folk tales were traditionally told, with a great deal of audience participation.

I have always been thankful to my grandmother and my grandfather, too, for teaching me all these stories that actually made up a part of our typical traditional education. I consider proverbs, known as *thimo* in Gĩkũyũ (which literally translates as 'weighing up the language', or 'summing up the essence of language'), to be one of the richest modes of conveying knowledge and cultural heritage in pre-literate days.

Not many people are aware of it, but I have a baptismal name which I acquired in 1946. After conversion to the Catholic faith, the Brothers who taught and ministered over the school's religious classes advised me to be baptized.

Being born again, they told me, would mean I was a new person who was closer to God. It was a symbolic way of accepting Christ as the guiding light of one's soul, they informed me. Since I had already accepted Catholicism, I readily agreed. After all it was mandatory for the pupils of Riara Catholic to be baptized. I chose the name James, a name I liked and which I had come across in my Bible lessons. Nearly all the baptismal names of students in the missionary schools were derived from the Bible.

In 1947, I received my Christian confirmation. I recall the humorous fiasco that surrounded choosing a name for this ritual. Everyone had been instructed to select a suitable name but I had forgotten all about this requirement.

We were all standing in line waiting to be confirmed. Suddenly the boy behind me, Josephat Kimani Njoroge, gave me a nudge. I bent my head near to his to hear what he was whispering.

"I forgot to choose a name!" he explained in a panic.

I was shocked. I had forgotten to select a name, too!

I looked ahead and saw I was about third in line from the Bishop, a man called McCarthy. I panicked and knew I would be admonished or even punished by the school authorities for my lack of seriousness if I did not come up with something.

Unable to think of anything else, Kimani suddenly whispered, "Maybe we can exchange names," he said.

I digested this quickly, and thought it was a brilliant solution— exchanging our baptismal names! I, as James Njenga, could therefore become James Josephat Njenga, and Josephat Kimani could become Josephat James Kimani. With little time to think of an alternative plan, that is exactly what happened. We put on straight faces and the priest never thought anything about the coincidence.

Kimani, by the way, lives in Ndumberi near my home and we still laugh over our close escape.

I no longer use those names. Although I am a staunch Catholic, go to church every Sunday and have supported the work of dozens of churches, I feel comfortable being referred to as just Njenga Karume. I do not understand the logic behind adopting foreign names instead of local ones for baptism.

Another important milestone in my life was my circumcision. I nearly got into a great deal of trouble over this matter, too.

When I went for my school holidays in Elburgon, I found that all the boys in my age group had been circumcised. Unfortunately for me I had not yet gone through the ceremony since I had been away at school. In other words, I was still a 'child', while the others were now 'men.'

No one seemed to realise that I had not yet been circumcised and I did not tell anyone except my friend Gathigi Njoroge. He promised to keep it a secret. So I joined my friends in their daily activities and joined the occasional dances. We would walk together, visit our age mates and talk to girls.

One day my friends and I were sitting by the fire inside a hut. We were warming ourselves against the evening chill, and when some girls came along, some of my age mates went out to talk to them.

One of the girls was my sister, Kaheti.

The boys, those who were standing outside, invited the girls to come in and join us in the hut. They suggested that the girls sleep overnight.

My sister, quite innocently, asked what the sleeping arrangements would be since there was an a *kĩhĩĩ* (uncircumcised person), among them.

Everyone standing there was shocked.

"Who is it? Who is this uncircumcised person?" they asked.

"My brother, Njenga," she said.

All the boys and girls were livid with anger. I had been pretending that I was circumcised all this time. The group had treated me as one of their own and had even shared 'adult' secrets with me.

Realizing that she had made a blunder, my sister quietly sneaked into the hut and told Gathigi and me to hide quickly. Both of us left as unobtrusively and swiftly as we could. As we rushed off, I instructed Gathigi that, if he was questioned, he should say that I lied to him. Gathigi then went home while I ran to my father's compound and locked myself in my mother's granary. I knew I would be in serious trouble if the group caught up with me.

Soon they came, dozens of boys belonging to my age group. They searched all the houses on the compound but they could not find me.

The following day, a Sunday, there was a big meeting held in Rongai, a few kilometres away from Elburgon. Gathigi was asked why he had kept company with a *kīhīī* and why he had tried to fool the *riika*.

As I had suggested, Gathigi told them he had not known that I was not yet circumcised and said I had lied to him. The group forgave him, but warned him not to be taken in so easily in future.

If they had not excused him for the lapse, he could have been punished by *kūhingwo* (to be shunned or isolated). No member of his age group would have talked or interacted with him in any way. And because of the closeness of society, such isolation was devastating. Some people who were treated like this migrated or got severely depressed.

The group resolved to hunt me down and 'discipline' me. Fortunately, a cousin of mine was in the meeting and rushed home to tell me the *riika's* decision. So I immediately took off for Kiambu and did not go back to Elburgon until the following year, when I was already circumcised, and it seemed the issue was no longer regarded as important and I was accepted as one of them.

For most children in school the holiday break was the time to undergo this traditional ceremony which marked the passage of a person from childhood to adulthood. It was—and still is—an important rite in Kikuyu traditions, and when boys and girls underwent the ritual they were initiated into adulthood and were then considered to be men and women. Young women were considered ready for marriage after this ceremony while the young men were considered warriors and the protectors of the community. They could also begin courting young women at this age.

While missionaries had no problem with the circumcision of boys, since it was an ancient biblical custom, the circumcision of girls was another matter altogether. Missionaries felt that it was a brutal mutilation, but the traditionalists maintained that it was a Kikuyu custom practised since time immemorial. Girls who followed Christian doctrine and did not undergo the ritual were referred to as *irīīgū* and were treated as immature. Many of them took refuge in the Christian missions when Kikuyu society became hostile to them and they managed to get suitors from among male converts to Christianity. In general, great pressure was put on all Christians to shun female circumcision.

So I was circumcised together with about twenty other boys in Kiambaa at the Giichi River. We were counselled in *mītugo* (morals), warriorship, marriage and our role and duty in society and the clan, and the survival of "*būrūri*", i.e. the Gĩkũyũ nation. All the boys stayed at the home of my uncle, Gatenjwa, for recuperation and the post-initiation rites since he, with his two shops, was considered well-off. In those days, initiates would stay at one homestead and receive counselling and guidance from the elders there. Usually, the home that was chosen for these ceremonies belonged to a wealthy man, and the parents of the other initiates were supposed to donate a goat as part of their food supply. This made the exercise easy because all the initiates would be well fed, given medicine if necessary, and educated together on what was expected of them henceforth.

People's ages were determined by their *riika*, which was named after the season, or a significant occurrence happening in the year in which they were circumcised. Since I was circumcised in 1947, my age group was named *Njata* (Star). That year, a meteorite or some such phenomena fell to earth and landed somewhere in Meru. This starry spectacle was the subject of talk for many seasons thereafter.

After my initiation, I returned to school at Riara in 1948 at the age of 19, to continue with my education and now proudly regarded myself as an adult. We could court young women at this age, but most of us were still a bit shy. It seemed impossible to befriend girls at school. When I went on holidays to Elburgon, we would talk to the girls there, but it always seemed to be that the girls around Kiambu were more beautiful, simply because those in Elburgon could not get nice dresses and so did not impress us as much. Many of them were uneducated, too.

My outlook to life had now changed because I had realised that I was the only one who could chart my own destiny. I took my studies seriously and excelled especially in mathematics. In addition, I was still a Prefect, and on Sundays I was given the extra duty of waking and shepherding the other pupils to church for mass. This made me feel rather important.

Final year students used to board at the school. We used to prepare our own breakfast, which was usually porridge made from flour provided by the priests. I remember the dormitory well. It was made of timber and we had nicknamed it *iherero* (hell) because it was terribly unpleasant and it was tedious to cook our meals.

It was during this time that I made my first venture into business. Whether I had an inborn talent or was driven by financial need is not quite clear to me now, but nevertheless, I saw an opportunity and took advantage of it. I discovered that exercise books cost fifteen cents in an Indian's shop in Kiambu Town. The Catholic bookshop sold the same books for thirty cents, which was double the price. I realised that the missionaries were making a large profit by selling books to pupils at such exorbitant prices. And if the missionaries could make money, why shouldn't I?

I decided to buy exercise books and sell them to my fellow pupils. However I had no starting capital and wracked my brains for a solution. Finally I decided to delay paying my school fees at the beginning of the term and used the money to buy exercise books. I could then pay the fees a week or so later and still retain my profit. From then on, the concept of profit and loss became part of my central motivation.

My first business venture was very successful. I bought the exercise books at the cost of fifteen cents from the Indian's shop in Riara, and sold them for twenty-five cents apiece to my fellow pupils who took advantage of the lower prices and still got me ten cents profit. They would have bought the same book for thirty cents at the Catholic bookshop. When they bought from me, they saved a few cents which they felt they could better use to buy *mandazi* (doughnuts) and other snacks such as sugarcane and bananas. This business was carried out clandestinely since I did not want to seem to be competing with the authorities. My customers understood that if the Brothers got to know about the business, I would be stopped, and the church bookshop would continue exploiting us.

I remember that I had to wake up very early, wash, dress and generally prepare myself. I would then rouse the other pupils so that they could prepare porridge for their breakfast and get ready for morning mass. While the others were occupied with preparing themselves, I would carefully sneak out of school, run all the way to Kiambu, breathlessly buy the books in a rush from the Indian shop and then run back to school barely in time for the mass, where I had a hard time disguising my exhaustion. I ran this scheme on my own, not because I did not trust others, but more because I could not find anyone who shared my ambitions. Without a doubt, doing business and making a profit started to fascinate me, and I understood that it took a lot of work, as well.

Like all children, we were also naughty on some occasions. It was common practice that when a pupil's exercise book was filled up while taking notes during class time, he or she would put their hand up and report to the teacher who would then give them permission to go and buy a blank book from the school bookshop. However, instead of heading for the bookshop, my clients would give me a wink and I would secretly pass over one of my exercise books under the desks, certain that I would receive the payment later.

One day Father Doody gave me a scare during the morning parade when he wondered aloud why the sales of exercise books in the church bookshop had declined. My heart started beating rather frantically. Thankfully, none of my customers gave any indication that they knew anything about the matter. In any case, through this insignificant beginning, I became the wealthiest pupil in the school for the remainder of my stay.

Although I had observed the commercial gains to be made in business while working in my uncles' shops, this little exercise book enterprise truly opened my eyes to the infinite possibilities of making money in commerce. I believe that my experiences in Kiambaa and Riara led to everything that followed. These events without a doubt, started up the initial foundation of my core business sense.

I used the money I made from this venture to make my life more comfortable. I was now able to afford snacks and other simple luxuries that were out of reach for most of my fellow pupils. I actually had so much pocket money compared to them that they often wondered at the extent of my father's riches back in the Rift Valley. Little did they know that my father was not wealthy at all and that all the money I had was from my own initiative. I learned that in the world of business there is no need to give away any secrets.

Once in a while I would go to eat at a kiosk near the school, at a market centre called Tugitu. The centre was frequented by teachers, mainly because teachers were the only ones who could afford the prices charged in such a place. The kiosk was owned by Modest Wakogi who taught at our school, and it was managed by his sister Beatrice. I would come up quite unobtrusively, trying to arrive at times when there were no teachers in sight and buy a half loaf of plain bread. Despite the fact that I could have easily afforded to have a little butter with it, I did not dare ask for it. I knew that if any teacher came and found me eating a luxury like buttered bread he might turn against me and I might earn his antagonism.

I remember one day when I was eating at the kiosk and two of my teachers, Phillip Kamau and another called Ngugi, came in for lunch. I was sitting at a corner several metres across from them but they did not talk to me. I recall that they asked for a meal which included beef. When their food was brought to their table, they realized that the meat was stale. Nevertheless they still ate it, albeit grudgingly.

Another teacher, Peter Muhoho, who was their senior, joined them for lunch. He saw what they were eating and asked for a similar meal.

Before he started eating, the other two teachers warned him that the meat had a bad smell.

"Oh, I see," he said. "And where did you throw your rotten meat?"

The teachers did not answer. They had eaten every bit.

"Tell me where, so that I can throw mine in the same place."

The teachers mumbled in embarrassment and I sneaked out. *Mwalimu* (teacher) Muhoho could be very sarcastic if he wanted to.

It must be noted that the exercise book business did not interfere with my education and I was still dedicating most of my time to my studies, and continued getting good marks.

Just recently, after a church service in Riara, I had a cup of tea with Father Gathongo, a former schoolmate of mine who was a few years behind me at Riara School and who is now retired. As we and some of the younger priests in the diocese enjoyed our refreshments, Father Gathongo related amusing stories about my antics in school. One of the things he recalled is that I had jokingly given him some interesting advice. You can imagine two young boys, one a few years older than the other, and I as the older of the two, advising the smaller one that he would never learn English or Mathematics if he did not stop buying books in the church bookshop and start buying from me. Of course I was just teasing him but I had already learned the value of advertising!

When I was in Standard Two, there was a time that the school became congested. There were just too many students and we were told that some of us would go to Kanunga, which was a boys' only school. Those of us who were from the Kiambaa side, near Kanunga, were sent there, only to come back to Riara in Standard Three after more classrooms had been constructed. It was wonderful to see how the hunger for education had caught on.

One of my favourite teachers was Peter Muhoho. Muhoho taught us history and geography and I was impressed by how much he knew about far-off lands. I used to marvel at the exotic empires he introduced to us. However, he was a strict disciplinarian who insisted on punctuality and good behaviour.

I remember one incident where I got into trouble with him. One day, my uncle had some tasks for me at home and he told me to go and ask for permission to be absent for the day, from my class teacher, Mr. Muhoho. I walked all 11 kilometres to the school and found the teacher busy in class. When I got a chance, I told him that I had come to ask for permission to be absent. He gave me his permission but then noticed that I did not have my school bag with me.

"Come back here," he told me. "Where is your school bag?"

"I left it at home, Sir," I told him.

"I see. So you had already given yourself leave, eh? Now go home and get your books and come here at once. Your leave is cancelled," he snapped.

I walked back home and picked up my books. It had rained the night before and by then, all the walking back and forth in the mud had made me quite dirty so I stopped at a stream to clean up. When I arrived back at the school, I found Mr. Muhoho busy writing on the chalkboard, so I just sneaked in and sat at my desk.

"And who is that who just walked in?" he asked without turning away from the board.

"It is me, Njenga Karume, Sir," I said timidly.

"This is not your father's *thingira*. Can you go out and come in in a civilized manner?"

As I walked out, he noticed that I had left my bag behind. "And where is your school bag?" he asked.

"It's on my desk, Sir," I replied.

"Get it, then, go out and come in like a person who was late for school. I did as the teacher asked. I went out, knocked on the door and was told to enter.

"Why are you so late?" he asked.

I explained that I had stopped by the stream to wash.

"What! Were you washing in the river to get circumcised?" He was referring to the traditional ice-cold dip to numb the nerves before circumcision.

At the end of it all, I received a thorough caning, and was never late for school again. I still try my best to be punctual for my appointments and I have little time for people who are late. Anyway, Muhoho eventually became a very good friend of mine and I often go to visit him in Kiambaa.

At school, I was quite good at maths, especially when it came to calculating sums involving money, and there came a time when I was able to use this skill to help my uncle.

Around 1948 or 1949, one year before I left school, my uncle Gatenjwa went to buy beer from the East African Breweries depot in Nairobi. He had opened an off-licence bar behind his shop at Karuri centre and would replenish his supplies from this depot which was housed in a wooden building located along Victoria Street (what is today Tom Mboya Street), in the vicinity of today's Gill House. One day, after he completed his purchases in Nairobi, my uncle discovered that he had either misplaced or left a number of crates behind. The following day, he returned and complained to Bryan Hobson, the affable depot manager. Hobson in turn referred him to Sultan, a sales clerk, who denied that any extra crates had been forgotten and accused my uncle of making false claims.

My uncle became furious and reported the matter to Hobson. He said that he would come with his own accountant the following Saturday in order to prove that he had lost some crates and Hobson agreed to see them both.

The reason my uncle settled on Saturday was because he actually had no personal accountant at all, but he believed that I, who was in school during the week, had the mathematical skills to settle the matter. That Saturday, my uncle and I went down to Nairobi and reported to Hobson's office. Naturally Hobson was surprised at my youthfulness but my uncle had confidence in me. While Hobson and my uncle, who knew each other fairly well, continued to converse, I was sent to Sultan's office to look into the problem.

Sultan and I checked and cross-checked the records for about twenty minutes and by the end of the period I had proved that indeed some crates had been paid for but had not been received by my uncle. Sultan realised he had made a mistake and we reported the matter to Hobson who was immensely impressed by my mathematical skills. He presented me with a reward of five shillings, a rather large sum in those days, and asked me to stop in at his office whenever I was in Nairobi. My uncle, highly pleased with the outcome, treated me to a sumptuous lunch at the Green Hotel, which was once the most prestigious hotel for Africans in Nairobi. The hotel is still located on Latema Road and currently goes by the name Modern Green.

That meeting with Bryan Hobson would form one of the most significant encounters in my business life.

To get back to my school life, however, Father John Doody was the school's Principal and Head of the Mission. We secretly referred to him as "Ndūti", meaning "ugly" because he was such a sulky and ugly looking fellow.

One day he made a speech to the pupils. He explained that whatever the colony might undergo in the future, it was a foregone conclusion that European missionaries would not be around forever. Moreover, given that European missionaries were so few, the task of evangelizing the African population was unachievable. Africans themselves had to become involved in converting their compatriots to Christianity if the mission of spreading the gospel was to succeed. The most obvious choices for such evangelists were students like ourselves, he told us, because we were converted and educated. He asked the pupils to select, by secret ballot, one among us who would receive the honour of being the first student from Riara who would be trained for the priesthood. This was my first exposure to the concept of a 'secret ballot'. He explained that we should choose someone we trusted, of outstanding character and moral behaviour, and one who had leadership qualities.

We were each given a piece of paper to write down our selection, and when the votes were tallied, I emerged winner with a landslide. I was overjoyed at the prospect of travelling to one of the centres where Africans went to train for priesthood. At the time these institutions were in Kilimambogo in Ukambani, Morogoro in Tanzania, and Gulu in Northern Uganda. I readily accepted the invitation with enthusiasm, but Father Doody quickly reminded me that the final decision on this rare opportunity did not lie with me. My parents, or guardians, would make the crucial decision, and in this case it meant that my uncle Gatenjwa would make that decision, since my father was too far away to be consulted.

That evening after classes, I got the thrill of my life when I rode in Father Doody's car for a ride to my uncle's house in Kiambaa, about eleven kilometres away. Riding in the car was so exhilarating that I wished the journey would never come to an end. Nowadays, of course, babies and children ride in cars all the time, even before they are fully aware of it, so they never experience the delight and adventure that we did in those days.

My mind was in a whirl. Here I was riding in a car for the first time, a privilege that was only a dream to most other black children. My future prospects suddenly seemed overwhelming and I was really excited by the time we arrived at my uncle's shop. The priest and my uncle conversed casually before Father Doody came round to the subject of his unexpected visit. He explained that I had been honoured by being selected to be trained for the priesthood. If all went well, I would work alongside the missionaries. As my guardian, Father Doody explained, my uncle's approval was necessary beforehand. Father Doody must have been surprised when my uncle did not seem to be much in favour of the idea. After considering the issue for some time he asked Father Doody to return after one month. This would give him time to "consult clan members and come to a decision". Father Doody seemed to understand. This was a reasonable request, after all. I, and by extension, my family, would be deliberating over a move that was totally new and foreign to us.

The month passed, and time dragged for me because I was eager to start my training. I tried to convince my uncle to see my point of view but he was non-committal. He refused to discuss the issue and I became anxious and worried. Eventually the day came when Father Doody was to call on my uncle for his decision. After class the priest found me waiting patiently by his car and we again made the journey to Kiambaa. But when we arrived at my uncle's home, he was reluctant and asked for another two weeks to make the decision. Finally, after these delays, at the end of it all he told Father Doody that the clan had decided against allowing me to train for the priesthood. He said that the family and relatives had been consulted and they felt it was neither an advisable nor appropriate course for me to pursue. Furthermore, my uncle said, he had a personal reason of his own. After considerable soul searching, he had decided that he wanted me to name a son after him. The Kikuyu named their children after relatives, but since Catholic priests remain celibate and never marry, I would never have been able to perpetuate the name of Gatenjwa, and there was nothing as unfathomable to someone like my uncle as the idea of a man growing old without siring children.

Father Doody was quite disappointed and unhappy about the decision but there was nothing he could do, so we just drove back to the mission. As for me, I cried myself to sleep and it was only many years later that I discovered the deeper reason that my uncle had turned down the opportunity.

The fact was that although my uncle believed in the necessity of education, he saw the acquisition of knowledge as useful for only two specific purposes. Firstly, he believed that the younger generation needed formal education in order to better their own lot in life, and secondly, he was convinced that education would help them understand the ways of Europeans so that Africans would eventually liberate themselves from the colonial yoke of oppression. While education was valuable if used in the achievement of these particular goals, my uncle saw nothing to be gained in letting me become a priest. It would defeat the whole purpose of enrolling me in school in the first place. He and many others of his generation wanted their children to understand the ways of the whites, but not to be like them. They wanted their children to gain knowledge for their own sake and the sake of the community, not to become carbon copies of the Europeans. This missed chance at the priesthood is something I often wonder about.

But life went on and I soon got over my disappointment and continued with my education. I studied hard and began thinking about secondary school. Those who passed their exams in mission schools usually found it an easy matter to join secondary schools associated with the same missions. In the case of Catholics, they would join Mang'u High School in Thika, Nyeri High School in Nyeri or others, while those from Protestant mission schools would join Alliance High School in Kikuyu. I was determined to pass the primary school examinations and continue my education in order to be employed in some prestigious position. At that time educated Africans were in big demand by the colonial establishment since there were not sufficient numbers of Europeans to fill posts such as clerks, assistants, and other mid-level ranks. Even subordinate posts in government offices required at least some basic education.

In December 1949, at the age of 20, I received the results of my final primary school examination, which was known as the Common Entrance Exam, and no one was surprised that I passed with distinction. I was ecstatic and I eagerly anticipated joining a high school.

Only two others in my class had passed with such high grades. These were Kimani Ndung'u and Hannah Nyagicuhi. We had all constantly maintained the top three positions in class, year after year. I maintained contact with them and we stayed friends after we left school. Kimani, who had been working for the Post Office, died in 2007, but Nyagicuhi is a farmer and a staunch member of her church.

I had taken only five years to acquire sufficient education to pass my Common Entrance Examination, but for others it often took seven years or more.

There are moments when one's life is at a crossroads, moments of joy, excitement and anxiety that play a decisive role in defining one's destiny and the future. For me, passing the Common Entrance Examination was one of those moments, but it all unravelled after I rushed to my father to tell him that I had passed. I feel that this one incident changed the course of my life forever.

I expected my father to be overjoyed that I had achieved such excellent results, and that I could now proceed on to secondary school. After all I was making a name for myself in Elburgon. But instead, my father brought me back to reality with a shock. My father said he had no money for me to join Mang'u or any other secondary school. The money he earned on his farm in Elburgon was just adequate for our family's basic needs. And now that he had understood the advantages of having some schooling, he wanted to give my siblings a chance to get a few years of education as well. His money could not be stretched to include fees for high school. Another reason for the tight budget was that, by this time, as I stated earlier, my father had married two more wives and there were new more mouths to feed.

I was at a loss. Unhappy and dispirited, I went back to Father Doody and informed him of my predicament. The priest was sympathetic but there was little he could do. The only scholarship made available by the church was exclusively for those studying for the priesthood. Father Doody finally advised me to join Kilimambogo and train as a catechist and a teacher.

However by that time, I had higher ambitions. I did not know exactly what I would do or where I was going to start, but I was no longer willing to be a mere teacher. I decided to go back home to Elburgon and weigh my options.

And so my formal education came to a halt for some time.

Around six years after I left formal education, the DO1 in Kiambu District advised me that if I really wanted to go into business seriously, I should enrol in a business course at Jeans School present day Kenya Institute of Administration. At the time, J.S. Smith was the Vice Principal of Jeans school, and I met many people such as the late Dr. Taita Towett who was later to become the clerk of Kipsigis County Council before he went on to become a cabinet minister. We had many lecturers, including Duncan Erskine, Titus Mbathi (who later became a Cabinet Minister and Chairman of KenGen) and Charles Kabetu.

By that time I had married, and I was happy that my wife, Wariara, was managing our shop, so I had no need to worry about my businesses back home. The courses I attended at Jeans School lasted for six months and we stayed in the dormitories. We took courses in bookkeeping, accounts, business management and others, and even went on tour to view the operations of large companies. At the end of it all, we were awarded Certificates in Business.

Like many of the stories surrounding my life, the myth concerning my education is perhaps the most distorted by observers. Many people are amazed that I, a presumably illiterate poor boy, made it to where I am today. Many more are amazed when they hear me speak English. But the truth is that I had an excellent, although basic, education up to Class Four and passed the Common Entrance Examination, which is more schooling than most of my age mates. Naturally I would have liked to acquire further formal learning. There may perhaps have been more opportunities for me if I had managed to do so, but that is now all water under the bridge.

Chapter 3

The Rise of a Charcoal Burner

As was true with many other market centres in the 1940s, Elburgon was a dusty little commercial location that drew residents because of its position along the railway. Most of the newly arrived residents were either working in or had retired from the white settler farms in the area. And of these, most were Kikuyu from Central Province. Other than those who worked for the settlers, there were also people who had come to the area with the building of the Uganda Railway. Since farming land was so scarce in Kikuyuland, very few of them had plans to return to their motherland.

Technically, the land they were occupying did not belong to them. It actually was the property of the government or the Railways. Such land was referred to as *Lhandies* by the Indian railway workers and the word was subsequently used by Africans.

Most African residents were squatters who had a member of the family working for white settlers. They farmed subsistence crops such as maize and beans on the outskirts of Elburgon while others engaged in small trading enterprises. Still others raised livestock such as cows, goats and sheep. However, raising cattle was highly discouraged because the white settlers feared that native cattle would spread diseases to their imported animals.

It was not a particularly prosperous area in terms of wealth. Elburgon centre was just a rural marketplace similar to many others in those days. All the same, the forests surrounding it did well because the land was fertile and the climate was favourable.

The oppressive rule of the colonialists caused extreme resentment. The Kikuyu, especially the landless Kikuyu whose farming lands had been taken by colonial forces in Kiambu, Thika and Nyeri, were full of bitterness and anger. Further agitated by the return of highly disgruntled soldiers at the end of World War II, Kikuyu adults had already started taking secret loyalty oaths as early as 1947 in Olenguruone. Their central aim was to bind themselves together in the fight against white rule and to recover their stolen lands.[22]

At the same time, there were many, especially the wealthier, land-owning Kikuyu in central Kenya, who were loyal to the colonial government. These Africans chose to collaborate with the colonial authorities and served as headmen, chiefs and *askaris*. These landowners were hated by the majority of the people as they were considered traitors.

However, not all chiefs were collaborators. Some, such as Senior Chief Koinange wa Mbiyu rebelled against their masters. Mbiyu was so pro-Mau Mau that the Mau Mau oath was administered in his home and he was even detained by his former employers.

Beneath the veneer of business as usual, most people went about their lives with uncertainty, not knowing what the next day would bring. The average person was not only in danger from those who collaborated with the British, who might denounce him or her as Mau Mau, but was also in danger from the Mau Mau if he or she did not agree to join them. This later caused a situation similar to a civil war to the extent that it split the Kikuyu community into two, despite the fact that everyone was opposed to colonial rule. But at this time the freedom struggle was just about to reach its apex.

On its part, the colonial administration was cracking the whip on those they considered dissenters or trouble-makers. There was widespread fear, intimidation and suspicion all over the land. The country was at a crossroads. The imperial mind and the white settlers had not realised or even contemplated the possibility that the British Empire was coming to an end. They assumed they would hold on forever. Meanwhile, Africans had reached their limits and the spirit of rebellion was rising by the day. Politically conscious Africans had rejected the notion that they were destined to remain British subjects forever. They decided to act. Although I was still relatively young, I was fully aware of the mood and activities going on around me.

---

22   The first Mau Mau oaths started in Olenguruone before spreading to Kiambu and other areas of Central Kenya. Perhaps they started in Olenguruone and other squatter villages among settler farms in the Rift Valley because the people there felt, even more that their kin in Central Kenya, the subjugation by the colonialists and the abject poverty brought about by landlessness and poor working conditions. In Kiambu, a lot of oathing was done in Senior Chief Koinange's home.

This new awareness was spearheaded by ex-World War II soldiers and the urban unemployed—a distressing reality that had taken a life of its own. There was a group of disgruntled youth known as *Anake a fote* (young men of the 1940s). These were young men who had been initiated around 1940, after World War II had broken out, and their age group was therefore known as *Fote Riika*. Along with Europeans, they had fought with British forces in the war overseas and afterwards felt they faced discrimination and neglect by the *Wazungu*. They had expected some compensation after helping the Allies win the war. They saw their European counterparts being generously rewarded with government loans to start businesses or to buy land in the White Highlands, yet they received nothing. During the war they had also realised that white men were just as vulnerable as anyone else in the battlefield and were in no way superior beings. I met with and listened to a few of these ex-World War II soldiers as they narrated their fascinating experiences in Burma, Abyssinia and other far-away places.

These young men spread the message of discontent and it was they who became the core members of the Mau Mau movement. The Mau Mau administered loyalty oaths to both men and women, binding them together in their struggle against the colonialists. The oath was profoundly serious business—once a person had taken the oath, he or she was bound as a member of the Mau Mau to help the freedom struggle in any way without question.

There were also the nationalists, such as the moderates Mbiyu Koinange and Jomo Kenyatta, and the fiery Achieng' Oneko, and others who went around the country lighting the flames of liberation. These nationalists were a widely travelled, cosmopolitan and educated group and they boldly demonstrated to the ordinary people that the white rulers could be defied. These nationalists were bent on convincing the people that the land was their own and that the days of the Europeans were numbered. Without calling it by name, they spread human rights awareness among the African people.

This is the situation that I found myself in during 1949 in Elburgon, after my education in Kiambu was cut short. But I was not desperate at the time. I knew that anyone with an iota of formal education would be quickly snapped up in the job market. So I expected to land a good job at one of the many settler farms in the Rift Valley. In those days most of us considered a good position to be a clerical or supervisory job in the European farms. Compared to the physical work in the farmyards or herding and milking cows, clerical work was better paid and definitely a 'white collar' job.

As far as finding clerical work was concerned, I was in luck because, as one of the small, educated elite in the region, I was sure I would find myself in demand. A friend of my father, Willie Mwangi Michuki, who owned a dairy, told me there was a job opening in a farm nearby. Willie bought milk from one of the settlers in order to sell it to the residents of Elburgon and it just happened that this settler was looking for an educated clerk. Willie advised me to go to the settler's place, called Elvance farm, on the following morning and tell the *Mzungu* that he had recommended me for the job.

The same morning, I walked about 16 kilometres to the farm office but found the settler absent. He had gone to attend a *baraza* (public meeting) held by the Labour Officer, somewhere on the farm. I looked for the manager but he was away, too. Apparently everyone from the surrounding area was at the *baraza* because colonial administrators and labour officials were to address the people on African labour issues, a hot and controversial topic. The administration had heard African complaints of mistreatment and poor working conditions on white-owned farms, and wanted to address the complaints and pacify the Africans whose labour was a necessity the settlers could not do without.

So I walked back out to the fields and found a large crowd of Africans in attendance. Most of the white farmers in the area were there, as well. Various administrators addressed the gathering in Kiswahili, a language which was understood reasonably well by both the Africans and the white farm owners. They promised to look into the complaints and find solutions to the problems. The Nakuru Labour Officer told the meeting that it would be a disaster if African labourers rebelled since the settlers had bought the land for a great deal of money and invested heavily in developing their farms.

Then it was question time, and those in the crowd asked for clarification or redress on the subjects that concerned them. There was a Kisii translator who spoke Kikuyu, Kiswahili and English, and he interpreted for those who needed assistance. He would listen to the labour officer speak in English and translate into Kiswahili for the crowd. When a labourer spoke in Gikuyu he would translate for the *Wazungu* into English. Many of the questions raised were to do with wages, allowances and working conditions.

I listened carefully. It was interesting to hear about the various complaints the workers' had. I recall that one of the farm hands talked about all the labour they were forced to undertake and how difficult it was to accomplish their duties properly and in good time. He felt that the wages he and the others were getting were far too little and asked the Labour Officer to see if anything could be done. Specifically, he wanted the Labour Officer to ask the *Bwana,* that is, the settlers, to raise the farm workers' wages.

The Labour officer briefly considered the matter and then, turning to the settler, asked him to look into it. That naturally raised the hopes of the farm hands, but the Labour Officer then dashed their momentary happiness by telling the workers that if their wages were raised, they would have to work even harder in order to ensure that the farm owners realised a profit.

I thought I could ask a question, too. After a while, I raised my hand and was given the chance to ask a question. I do not remember now what exactly prompted me to do so at the time; perhaps the chance to show off a little, perhaps genuine curiosity or perhaps I wanted to be a bit sarcastic and critical. Whatever the case, I stood up and addressed the Labour Officer who had previously stated that settlers had spent a lot of money in acquiring their land.

Looking directly at the interpreter, I asked in Gikuyu, *"Bwana* has said that the settlers bought their land for a lot of money. My question is, from whom did they buy the land, and for how much?"

There were gasps of shock from the Africans in the crowd and the whites waited and looked towards the interpreter to translate my question. The interpreter hesitated for a moment. He knew my enquiry would offend and upset the *wazungu,* but then he shrugged and translated my words into English anyway. The Europeans sneered and began to grumble furiously among themselves.

"Wewe!" the labour officer exclaimed. *"Wewe mtoto! Simama!"* (Stand up, you child!) What's your name? Where are your parents?"

"My name is Njenga Karume, *Bwana."*

"Where do you come from?" he demanded.

"I am from Kiambu, *Bwana."*

"Where do your parents live?"

As you can imagine, I was getting more and more nervous and anxious as the Labour Officer continued to question me. I could see the outraged Europeans staring at me and muttering angrily. All around me the Africans in the crowd hissed with whispers.

Full of fear, thinking the Officer might even trace my family and punish them in some way, I murmured apprehensively in Kiswahili, "They live near the forest, Sir."

"Listen carefully! You are young and stupid and should not ask about things you do not understand. Do you know you can be deported back to Kiambu?"

I was now completely alarmed and frantic that things had gone further than I anticipated and I turned to English and apologised.

"Sorry if I made a mistake, Sir."

"Na nani alipatia wewe ruhusa ya kuongelesha Bwana kwa Kiingereza? Kaa chini! Jinga!" (And who gave you permission to speak to *Bwana* in English? Sit down, you idiot!)

When I look back at the incident, I guess he was seriously offended by my English because no doubt he assumed he was dealing with illiterate labourers who could easily be manipulated and confounded. I am sure my English words gave him something of a startling shock. Perhaps I misjudged the intensity of the racial and economic barriers between white employers and the African labourers.

As you can imagine, that put paid to my chances of employment in the area. It was almost unheard of for a black worker to question a European, especially in what might be deemed a disrespectful manner.

The Africans attending the meeting were apparently just as shocked by my behaviour as the obviously incensed Europeans. The Africans, noticeably uneasy about disturbing the *status quo*, could not understand how a boy like me, who just came from school the other day, could ask *Bwana* such a silly question.

I cannot claim I was totally innocent in my motives, but I could not understand the hostility that was in the eyes of my fellow Africans. I had only asked the question out of a sort of boyish critical curiosity.

As the meeting continued on to other issues, some men standing next to me called me aside and one of them started questioning me in a soft whisper.

"Who are you? Who is your father?"

I was really on edge at this point but told him I was Karume's son.

"I know him. But what are you doing here?"

"I came looking for a job. I was supposed to meet a farm manager who needed a clerk," I explained nervously.

The man shook his head and gave an unhappy laugh.

"Forget all that now. You have to get out of here otherwise you can be arrested as an agitator after the meeting is over."

In a whisper, he advised me to leave the area immediately for the sake of my own safety. If I did not, I could be arrested after the meeting and might even spend time in jail because the settlers could bring some sort of charges, like incitement, against me. He told me to pretend to go into the bush to answer a call of nature and then take off.

I did not need to be told twice. I had already seen what happened to those who were labelled dissenters. In addition, I remembered the story of the respected elder, Karanja wa Maara, who had been jailed for two years despite the community's plea for amnesty. So I discreetly got up, walked to some nearby bushes and then swiftly and silently disappeared. I had just graduated from primary school and had no intention of graduating from His Majesty's prisons.

I went through a roundabout route and when I arrived back in Elburgon Township, I found Willie Mwangi enjoying a cup of tea with others in his restaurant. He was happy to see me, and gave me a slap on the shoulder.

"So, did you get the job?" he asked enthusiastically.

When I did not answer straightaway, he began to look concerned.

"What happened? Surely your education was enough for him, wasn't it?"

I gulped down my nervousness and told him I had not even managed to talk to the manager. Then I related the whole story of the *baraza* and what I had done.

Obviously Willie Mwangi became furious. He told me that I was incredibly naïve and called me a fool; that I had not yet learned how to step carefully around Europeans. He scolded me strongly and told me that he wanted nothing to do with me.

"Did you come from that school in Kiambu to get land for the people of Elburgon?" Willie asked me. "Has any of your land been taken? We have been here with Europeans all the time and you come to mess everything up."

Impatiently he directed me to get away from the restaurant and away from him, too, adding that I had probably messed up his business relations with the settlers who sold him milk.

Much later, Willie told me that on the following morning when he went to buy milk at the settler's farm, he was called aside.

The *Mzungu* looked at him critically and then asked, "Look, Willie, you've always struck me as a good man. Why did you recommend that cheeky, rebellious boy to work on my farm?"

Not knowing what to say, Willie just stood there.

"That silly boy could have incited my workers! He could have ruined my business!"

"Sorry, *Bwana,* but I didn't know he was so bad," Willie replied. "In fact, I'm shocked. I've now learned that even his father chased him away from home when he learned about his son's wicked behaviour in the meeting."

The settler seemed to find that explanation satisfactory and he continued doing business with Willie. Nevertheless, for some time after that, people in the shops and restaurants avoided conversing with me.

One day, shortly after I was snubbed over this incident, I heard that the people around had started taking the Mau Mau oath and that a group of young men were arming themselves and going to the forest in order to wage guerrilla warfare. This was in early 1952 and Mau Mau oathing was at its peak.

I recall that I joined a meeting in the forest where elders were consulting a mystic. They wanted him to divine the future in order to tell them if their young men would be safe.

As is usual in such events, the mystic mumbled some incomprehensible incantations, threw his magic charms out of a polished gourd to the ground before him, and then solemnly interpreted whatever symbols he seemed to find in their placement and position.

He told the elders that the young men should not travel to the forest on that day. They should travel on the following day, and then they would be safe.

As I was watching, I concluded that all these ceremonies and even the dangerous missions were unnecessary. I was struck by a bright idea and could not keep it to myself.

I blurted out my solution: If Europeans are a problem, I asked the elders, why not bewitch all of them? Instead of risking our lives against the *Wazungu,* with their guns and bombs, why not take the easy way out through magic?

After all, witchdoctors were considered fearfully powerful and were believed to be able to cure any malaise in society. Instead of consulting on the efficacy of various oaths why not just curse them and kill them all? In this way, no African would suffer or get hurt and the *Wazungu* would be eliminated.

I even went so far as to suggest a better solution. I thought the elders should gather all the witchdoctors in the country, even the famous ones from as far away as the coast, and have them all combine their skills to bewitch the enemy. I gave them instances to support my idea, reminding them of people who had been killed by means of witchcraft, and that on occasion, witchdoctors from Tanganyika had been contracted when local ones were unable to deal with a particular crisis. If a witchdoctor in Elburgon could manage to curse and kill a person in Mombasa, why not kill all the *Wazungu*?

"Why shed the blood of our people in war when witchdoctors can easily eliminate all whites?" I posed, feeling very wise.

My argument irritated and angered the mystic, who felt that I was challenging him, as though he did not know what he was doing.

"Do you not know," the seer asked me, "that *Wazungu* eat pork every day and they are invincible as far as *ūrogi* (witchcraft) is concerned?"

Pork, for whatever reason, was supposed to make one immune to *ūrogi*. Due to this superstition, children were occasionally smeared with fat from pigs while elders sometimes carried small pieces of pig bone, or put them in their houses to ward off the evil eye. At that time, pigs were slaughtered for ceremonial purposes only, and were not eaten.

However, the *Wazungu* ate pork just like any other meat, and, the mystic informed me, for this reason the Europeans were regarded with fear. At the end of his explanation, I was hurled out of the meeting. I had never meant to belittle the seer or interfere with his job—it was just another case of my youthful exuberance overcoming my discretion.

Looking back on it now, it seems rather odd, but the minor incident which caused me to lose my clerical position even before I had got it, led to factors that would affect my future immensely. First, I would be unable to acquire the clerical job I wanted in any of the farms around Elburgon. I had become an untouchable after my behaviour at the meeting. None of the middlemen or supervisors who dealt with the white farmers and administrators wanted to have anything to do with me.

Second, on understanding how the position of things had changed, I made a decision that I do not think I have ever regretted and which ultimately shaped my future. I decided I would never be employed by anyone, and that I would be my own boss and go into business.

Although I found myself in difficult circumstances, I was not one to despair under pressure. Nevertheless, my decision to go into business was not an easy one. I had been educated to basic primary level and my parents, age mates and society expected me to take up a 'good' job with a European. I had ruined this chance, but decided to treat it as a potential test of my personality. I would transform this negative experience into an opportunity.

Over the years I have learned to treat challenges and barriers as occasions to improve myself. Some people will despair or go into depression when they are faced with big challenges, but this outlook on life is defeatist and should be shunned by anyone who wants to get on with his or her life.

So I mulled over my decision for a week or so and in the end, the business that I chose, shocked many people in the community. After looking at the potential of various endeavours and the profits that were coming in, I chose to go into charcoal burning and cutting fencing posts from the bush. Many were stunned and astonished by this choice of business because despite the fact that I had an education, I chose an enterprise regarded as 'dirty' or 'low', one that was reserved for the illiterate in society. People felt that a person of my background and education was lowering himself by going into that sort of demeaning trade.

But I did not care about public opinion. On the contrary, I searched for others who might be interested in taking up the opportunity with me. In this regard, therefore I approached some of my old school friends to join me in the trade but they laughed me off. One of them, John Murunga, said that I must be out of my mind to consider burning charcoal when I had had an education. John said that he himself would never waste his education on burning and selling charcoal, and that if it had ever been his ambition, he would never have gone to school at all. Funny enough, John later, joined me in my business, but as an employee, not a partner!

There was another friend of mine, John Njenga Kimani, who did not have any reservations about 'dirty' work. I asked him to join me in the trade and he started burning charcoal and cutting cedar posts, and before long, he had a small sawmill in Njoro.

As mentioned earlier, my first experiences in making a profit and guarding my capital had started in Riara School, selling exercise books to my fellow pupils. Now I was ready to expand my ambition and develop it into something worthwhile.

So I went to the bush and started burning charcoal and cutting cedar posts. I would sell the charcoal to my fellow Africans and the cedar posts would be bought by the settlers for fencing. A sack of charcoal sold for 25 cents and each post cost a shilling. Since at the beginning I had no costs other than my own physical energy, this was quite a good profit. Later I started hiring others to do the more strenuous labour. Every now and again I would climb up the top of the trees we were harvesting, but most of the time we would hire some people who specialized in this type of risky work.

Burning charcoal is hard work but requires virtually no capital. All that is required is the raw material, namely trees, an axe, a *panga* (machete), a hoe and a spade. And, of course, energy, patience and determination. In my case, I also required luck, since I was burning my charcoal deep in the bush and thieves could steal it!

After cutting down a tree, I would cut the trunk into short logs. I would also cut the big branches into similar lengths. Then I would dig a hole in the ground, lay the big logs on top of each other and place the smaller dry branches in between the big ones, ensuring that there were enough gaps between the wood for ventilation.

Next I would lay green twigs on top and then cover the whole pile with a layer of soil. By this time the whole thing would look like a big mound of dirt. I would leave a small hole on the edge of the mound at ground level and then light a fire through this point. The dry branches would smoulder and spread the fire throughout the pile. At the end of three to four days, this method of burning with a limited supply of oxygen would turn all the wood into charcoal.

However, I constantly had to check the process. If the top soil layer was not adequate, the wood might simply burst into flame and be reduced to ashes. On the other hand, if the dry twigs did not catch and spread the fire, the pile would not burn and I wouldd either have to re-light it, or take the whole pile apart and reconstruct it.

I had also to avoid thieves and forest wardens. In this respect I was somewhat protected by one of the forest rangers, Jackson Mwangi, who became my friend and kept an eye on the proceedings.

If I was lucky, the whole pile was done and I would then break up any pieces which were too large and then put the charcoal in sacks ready for sale. It was dirty work, but that was the least of my worries. I was determined to succeed.

As for making posts, it was not an easy job, either. There were quite a few different steps involved.

First we had to cut down a huge tree, usually cedar we had to do the cutting with an axe. We would chop away at the trunk until the blade was blunt and then stop to grind the axe with a file to sharpen it before resuming the hard task. When finally the big tree fell, we had to trim off all the branches and then hammer in wedges, all in a straight line, into the main trunk to split it up. We would split the trunk into halves, then quarters and further fractions, until we had as many posts as we could get.

We would also use a two man saw, one which had handles at both ends, when we were cutting lumber. This was quite a different procedure. The log would be placed up on two forked posts about a metre and a half above the ground. One of us would climb up and the other would be on the ground. We would each hold an end of the saw and cut straight planks of wood from the log. It took a lot of coordination and strength, and in order to keep the rhythm going we would sing verses of songs which had a steady beat. In Elburgon, one of the songs used during this type of work was the one below. This was a song which was meant to tease the women in the community into giving the lumber workers some food after their heavy labour.

Mūtumia ūrīa ūkaima mabundi irio,
Aroitīka ta mūtu ūyū wa kīgecha.
(May the woman who denies loggers food
Scatter with the wind like this sawdust.)

All this work took enormous energy, but I was young, quite strong and driven by my ambition. And I have to admit, I had a bit of luck—I had made friends with the African forest wardens so I got the trees for free.[23]

At that time there was strict control over the forests. Under the "Shamba" system, the European Forest Officer would give the forest workers one or two acres to look after. The workers were responsible for branding the trees, and planting the seedlings. The workers would interplant their crops and as they cultivated their farms, they would look after the young trees as well. Once the trees reached a certain level of maturity, the workers would be moved to other areas. Then, when a mature set of trees were cut and sold, the wardens would come in again and plant more seedlings. People at that time were very honest and cared for the trees with dedication. In fact, if a seedling dried up for any reason, it was immediately replaced. Unfortunately, today people just cut trees without a thought to the future.

Speculation on the origin of my businesses has centred on this timber trade, especially on my charcoal business. I would like to put the record straight and confirm that this indeed was my first business apart from the minor sales I made from exercise books at Riara Catholic School.

---

23 At the time, forests were not threatened with destruction. The population was low and the demand for timber and charcoal was minimal. With the population explosion, logging grew ever more destructive to the environment and it is not a business I would go into, today.

After some time, I found that my profits had grown to such a level that I was able to expand and employ a number of people on a casual basis. In addition, I started trading in red potatoes. Many forest workers and their families cultivated potatoes in the very fertile land in the forest and often produced sacks upon sacks of these potatoes. However, many of them did not know how to market their produce, so I saw an opportunity to venture into potato trade. I would buy a sack for a shilling and then sell the same at the market, or to European pig farmers, for as much as two shillings, making myself a 100% profit!

Next, I started selling timber, which I would send by train to Nairobi. The saw millers got to know me as an honest and reliable person, and since I always paid my debts on time, they got to trust me. Thus, when I had a big order, I would get timber on credit from sawmills in Elburgon and then pay after selling it to Indians in Nairobi. In a fairly short time I was doing quite well and I was aware that I was the subject of gossip and amazement in Elburgon.

But I did not care much for other people's approval or admiration. I had never bothered about the approval of others and this success did not change my nature. I continued my business as usual, always looking for more opportunities to exploit and expand my trade.

As I went about my enterprises, I later learned that a number of important people noticed my industriousness and were apparently impressed. Such people included a group of five of my father's friends who carried out various small businesses in the area. The quintet, led by a forest warder, Reuben Kiriri, invited me for a meeting. They explained that they had heard I was honest and had a sharp eye for business, so they had an idea which they wanted me to consider. They said they wanted to start trading in timber and if the arrangement was suitable to me, we could all be partners. They wanted to make use of my experience in the timber trade while I benefitted from using their capital to expand my own business.

It was proposed that Kiriri would be the chairman, his four friends the other directors and I would be the secretary, since I was educated. Naturally we did not actually use these official titles since the old men were illiterate, but I thought of the arrangement in such terms. The old men would trust me to ferry timber to Nairobi, sell it and then we would all share in the profits.

The proposal was quite interesting to me and it was decided that each of the six of us would have to raise three hundred shillings. In order to make me a partner, these friends loaned me the three hundred shillings.

The total investment was one thousand eight hundred shillings, which was a massive sum to advance in those days. The old men bought an exercise book and gave it to me for keeping the records of the business. They gave me very precise instructions and I was to use a particular format when recording my notes. Once I sold a consignment of timber, I was to report back to them as soon as I returned to Elburgon. I was not to buy more timber, no matter what the demand, without informing the whole group. I saw this as a golden opportunity. It was not every day that one had such a large sum to invest.

And so the six-man partnership started to trade. With the one thousand eight hundred shillings advance, I bought timber and shipped it to Nairobi. After all expenses such as rail fare, food and other allowances had been deducted, the income was two thousand four hundred shillings. Thus the first transaction that the partnership undertook resulted in six hundred shillings profit. I called a meeting with the group of friends and informed them of the details and was told to record it all in the exercise book and then give the cash to the group's treasurer. Once I had written it all down, those who could write signed their names while the others imprinted their thumbprints on the page. Then we would start a new page, and I was told to write down that this was a "New Business", with a capital of two thousand four hundred shillings and the men would put on their thumb prints. I was the given back the two thousand four hundred shillings with the directions to buy more timber. I successfully sold this second lot at two thousand eight hundred shillings, which was a good profit and naturally pleased the partners. Then a new page and a "New Business" would be started all over again.

The process of receiving my report and writing down the state of the account was repeated every time I came back from Nairobi. Perhaps starting a "New Business" each time was to show me that the money belonged to the partnership, or perhaps because the men were illiterate and this arrangement made it easier for them to understand. This procedure of buying, selling and presenting a report continued for a year, when my partners decided to pull out.

One day, when I returned to Elburgon after one of my trading trips, I reported to my partners as usual. I reported that the account stood at seven thousand two hundred shillings. Business had been good and my partners were very pleased. However, Kiriri said, it was time to dissolve the company while the going was good. Rebellion and conflict was on the horizon and there was considerable speculation, hostility and suspicion among many groups of people in the land. There were the colonialists and their collaborators on the one hand, and the Mau Mau[24] members and their supporters on the other. The ordinary man was forced to live and survive in the grey area between these two opposing groups. It was a time of uncertainty.

Quite unexpectedly for me, Kiriri stated that the partnership should be dissolved. Each partner received one thousand two hundred shillings from their initial investment of three hundred shillings each. The elders deducted the three hundred shilling they had loaned to me and I was left with nine hundred shillings. These amounts may sound like nothing today, but at the time nine hundred shillings was a great deal of money.

I felt that my first partnership had been successful and I was not as pessimistic or cautious as the older men and was still ready to continue investing. By this time I felt I had learned the ropes of the timber business and was now even more enthusiastic to go into business on my own. So, while the old men dropped out, I continued buying and selling timber, with a fair amount of success. Not long afterwards, in 1951, I opened my first bank account with the Standard Bank of South Africa in their Nakuru Branch.

Eventually I expanded my timber business, and in time called my old friend John Murunga, who had previously turned down a partnership, and employed him as a clerk. I wanted someone on the ground coordinating the various activities while I was away in Nairobi or elsewhere. Since I knew he had no desire to do manual labour, I assigned him the accounts. I suppose that some people are like that—they believe that certain jobs are beneath their education and status. Fortunately I have never had that attitude and I am always willing to do any type of work.

While in Nairobi going about the business of looking for buyers, a friendly character from Murang'a, who owned a little restaurant along what is now Racecourse Road, where a petrol station stands today, Mwangi Chege would give me a spot on the floor where I would spend the night.

Another young trader from Elburgon, Muiruri Laban, was given the same privilege and we became friends. We would lie on some sacks on the floor for the night. We were both young and adventurous and this

---

24 By mid 1952 high discontent and political agitation precipitated an uprising of Africans (mainly Kikuyu) and was curiously labelled "Mau Mau," a term that was very alien. A number of theories purport to explain its origin and meaning, including one theory that a government intelligence agent is said to have overheard, *"Mau maũndũ ni mau mau,"* (Those things are as they are) in a hut occupied by oath administrators.

sleeping arrangement did not bother us. Although Mwangi Chege did not know us, he nevertheless trusted us enough to let us sleep near his cafe, treating us like his own sons. This sort of hospitality was tradition among the Kikuyu and most African tribes, but there is too much distrust these days, so it has died out.

Shortly afterwards, I got into a partnership with Muiruri Laban. Muiruri was just as ambitious as I was and we travelled, dined and shared sleeping quarters. We were both determined and motivated and we had money to invest in projects. After some discussions, we decided to venture in the profitable timber trade once more. One of our major clients was Mowlem Construction Company.

The business prospered, and at one time each of us had as much as ten thousand shillings in our pockets after selling a consignment in Nairobi.

After getting our payment, we both travelled home by bus from Nairobi. As was the custom, when some elderly people boarded, the conductor would ask usto surremder our seats to the old people. As Muiruri and myself stood there, swaying and trying to keep our balance as the bus bounced over the rough road, we would looked at each other and could not help but laugh. Little did the conductor know, but we had more than enough money in our pockets that could buy such a bus outright, if we had so wished. A bus cost just four thousand shillings!

After one such trip we decided to spend the night in Nakuru and proceed to Elburgon the following morning. There was a new lodging house in the town, Ngamini Boarding and Lodging, which had been built by James Gichuru, and his partners, Simon Mbacia and Evan Ngigi, and we were curious to see what it would be like. Although we were normally careful with our money, we decided to take some rooms.

From the bus stage, we hired bicycle taxis at thirty cents each and were dropped off at the hotel. We arranged our stay and since each room had one bed only, we asked the receptionist to arrange to move an extra bed into one of the rooms. We often talked late into the night, so we found it more pleasant to share rooms. We then went out to eat and have a few drinks.

When we got back to the hotel, we had to find a safe place to keep the huge amounts of totalling twenty thousand shillings, that we were carrying in cash. Muiruri suggested that we should use the money as our pillows and this is exactly what we did.

The following morning a hotel maid brought tea to the door of our room and knocked. Often, the tea would be placed just outside the room for the boarder to take at his own convenience, but since we were already awake, we asked the girl to bring the tea in.

At the moment she entered the room, I was sitting on my bed counting my money. The largest denomination at the time was a twenty-shilling note, so the bundles were quite bulky. Muiruri was still stretched out on his bed relaxing, his hands behind his head. Scattered under his head and hands, were bundles of cash.

The girl almost dropped her tray in astonishment.

I smiled and almost laughed, but Muriuri kept a straight face.

"You see madam," he said solemnly, "your pillows are too hard!"

The girl was speechless and with shaking hands set the tea on a little table. I wondered what was going through her mind.

"If your pillows were not so hard," Muriuri continued, "we would not have to use our money to cushion our heads."

Well, we had a good laugh over that incident. We were quite young, we had the energy to work incredibly hard, life was good and we had plenty of money. Anyway, we then took a taxi up to Elburgon.

Muiruri and I were also doing business in hides and skins, buying them from the country people and selling them for a profit to traders in Nairobi. One day we were told that there was a certain *Mzungu* who had many hides and skins for sale near Rongai, about 48 kilometres away.

We hired two bicycles from a garage owned by Patrick Mwaniki and Mukuria Karoki. Each bike cost us a shilling and fifty cents a day and we planned to return the same evening.

We rode to Rongai, and spent the day fruitlessly looking for the *Mzungu*. It was quite late by the time we gave up our search and then we realised it was too late to ride back to Elburgon. So we looked for lodgings in Rongai but could not find any rooms available, either. It seemed like we were out of luck and Muiruri and I wondered what to do next.

Finally, we approached two people who had a small hut near the railway station and told them about our predicament. After hearing about our problem, the men politely offered to give us shelter for the night. That is what it was like during those days. People trusted one another and strangers would be assisted and accommodated without suspicion.

Our hosts were in the process of preparing their dinner and Muiruri and I watched as they cooked. It was an unusual process.

The two men apparently had only one pot and not a single plate. First they cooked the *ugali*, which is a very stiff maize meal porridge. After it was done, they placed the *ugali* onto a battered tin sheet and, without bothering to wash the pot, they put in some *terere* (amaranth greens). The greens in turn were cooked and when they were ready, one of the men pounded a hole into the mound of ugali with his fist and then poured the vegetables into the hollow.

Muiruri and I were amused and fascinated with the process and, funny enough, when the four of us gathered around to eat, we found it absolutely delicious. There was not a crumb left over.

Kuumagara nĩ kũũhĩga! (Travelling enriches one!), as we say. Travel is certainly enriching.

That night Muiruri and I talked it over and decided that we might as well try to see if there were any business opportunities upcountry. We decided that Muiruri would take a train the following morning and go up to Karuna forest, near Kitale. He would investigate the possibilities of acquiring a license to cut timber there.

So the following morning, Muiruri took the train to Kitale, and I was left with the headache of getting his bicycles back to the owner. I went to the railway station and arranged to have the bicycle transported to Elburgon. When I had finished, I headed back to Elburgon on my own.

What Muiruri and I did not know was that Patrick Mwaniki and Mukuria Karoki, the owners of the garage where we had hired the bikes, had reported us to the police. Since we had not returned the bikes in the evening of the previous day, as we had planned, the garage owners assumed we had stolen them. When I arrived in Elburgon, I learned that the police were looking for me. And when I went to return the bicycle, the owners were very hostile. They refused to listen when I informed them that the other bicycle would be coming on the midday train, and they insisted that we all go down to the police station.

I showed the police officers the receipt I had, which clearly indicated that I had paid to have the bicycle brought by train, but the police did not believe me either. They said the receipt was a forgery. I was then detained at the station until the midday train arrived.

When it finally pulled into the station, the bicycle was found to be on it. I was quite relieved. But the owners then made me anxious again and demanded that I add an extra shilling for the hire charges to cover the additional hours. I did not mind paying the extra money but it was stressful to be suspected of stealing. None of it made me happy.

So the Rongai mission had been a total failure. We did not get the skins we wanted and after spending three days in Kitale, Muiruri did not acquire the licence. We were quite disappointed. But at least I had discovered a new way to serve *ugali* if I ever ran short of pots and plates!

When not working on his timber business, Muiruri used to moonlight as a sales clerk in his Uncle Benjamin's hardware shop. However, the more money he and I made, the more inconvenient it became for him to spend time working in the shop.

One day, he went to the shop and asked his uncle to let him resign since he wanted to concentrate on his own business. In addition, Muiruri asked his uncle if he would consider selling one of his two lorries so that Muiruri could ferry timber with it. The old man was shocked. He had not imagined that the two of us, as young as we were, had been making such huge sums of money to enable us purchase a lorry.

All the same, he agreed to sell the lorry to Muiruri at six thousand shillings. No problem, Muiruri said, although the lorry was vastly over-priced. Without batting an eyelid, he removed a bundle of notes from his pocket, counted out six thousand shillings and gave it to his uncle who became suspicious and astonished that his nephew had so much cash.

The following morning, the uncle hired accountants to go through his books and find out whether Muiruri had been siphoning money from his shop. When Muiruri and I heard this, we laughed to no end.

"Even if I sold every single thing in my Uncle Benjamin's shop at one go," said Muiruri, "it would be nowhere near two thousand shillings, leave alone six!"

I still laugh when I remember this, and find it very droll. The two of us were doing quite a roaring business.

In fact our business was doing so well that we decided that Muiruri should coordinate the business in Nairobi while I ran things in Elburgon. I bought timber and sent it to Muiruri who, in turn, would look for customers. In Elburgon, I retained one of Muiruri's signed chequebooks while Muiruri had one of mine in Nairobi. The two of us trusted each other deeply and we each could easily complete business transaction without the presence of the other. Despite the political storm that was reaching tumultuous proportions in the rest of the world, business was good for us.

As young men, naturally, we also made time to enjoy ourselves and have some fun. We would hire a taxi and ride out to Githunguri in Kiambu, which was the original home of Muiruri's parents. We would drink beer, eat roasted meat, flirt with the girls, and generally have a great time. I recall that we would hire the driver and vehicle for the whole day and it would cost us only eight shillings.

However, the time had come for me to undergo another rite of passage. I was a young man in my early twenties, doing quite well, and the one thing conspicuously missing in my life was a wife. I had actually already made my choice, but there were some complications in my way. The girl I had chosen had no opposition to marriage. She was called Maryanne Wariara[25] and she was the first born of Wairiri Kigera, one of the wealthiest men in Elburgon.

The problem was her father, Wairiri. He did not talk or interact with ordinary people, and was not liked by most of the people in the community. He was proud, conceited and arrogant.

Wairiri had made his fortune as a supervisor on a settler's farm. After he retired, he opened a restaurant in Nakuru. Being a thrifty man, he had saved considerable amounts and grew wealthy. He even managed to get an exemption certificate from the authorities which allowed him to borrow more than two hundred shillings from the bank, should he so desire. Very few of such certificates were given out. I recall that he told me he had Certificate 11, that is the eleventh one to be given to an African throughout the whole of East Africa.

Later he also purchased two plots in Elburgon where he built a shop and another restaurant. These were large profitable establishments and he was thus a very wealthy man by local standards. His daughter, Wariara, managed the shop, his wife managed the restaurant and the old man supervised. However, he still clung to the fierce colonial mentality he had absorbed as a farm supervisor and his personal relations with people were patronising and snobbish.

I had first met Wariara at her father's shop. She was a beautiful and hard-working girl and as we got to know each other we fell in love almost immediately. She had gone to school in Elburgon Scotland Mission School but had only gone up to Class Sub B, just enough to acquire some basic math and writing skills which she could use in the shop. Her father did not allow her to continue thereafter. Wariara's mother, Wanjiku, had never been to school at all but nevertheless, they were able to run their shop quite efficiently.

Her father, by the way, was taught how to write his name when he was already in business by a relative who helped him to open a bank account in 1942. He knew how to count, and relied on memory for the rest.

---

25   The name *Wa-riara* refers to *"one who came from Riara."* It is likely that whoever Wariara was named after must have come from Riara, not far from my ancestral home in Kiambu.

I knew Wariara's mother well since I used to have tea and bread at the restaurant when I was around. The mother, a polite woman, knew me as a young businessman. I was a regular customer and I remember that on two separate occasions, she gave me too much change and I only realised it after I left the shop. Both times I returned immediately and gave her the extra amount. I learned later that she considered me industrious, conscientious, polite and honest. But if her husband, Wairiri, knew anything about me, he never gave a sign. He never greeted or acknowledged me. Therefore, I did not know anyone who could approach Wairiri in order to broach the subject of marriage to Wariara. The elders in my clan who would normally have taken over this responsibility were far away in Kiambu.

Things did not improve when I informed my own father that I had found a girl to marry. When my father heard who the girl was, he roared with laughter and told me to stop daydreaming. No one could approach Wairiri's home, leave alone marry his daughter.

"And from which entrance do you propose to enter Wairiri's house, young man?" my father, Karume, asked me, in reference to the fact that there were very few people who were welcome at Wairiri's home. He told me to stop daydreaming. He had already chosen a girl for me to marry. The girl was Wanjiku Mungai, a young lady from a family whose status was more or less equal to our own.

But I was adamant and stuck to my choice. I left my father, went to think about my predicament and then had a bright idea. One of the few people that Wairiri talked to and tolerated, was a senior Forest Warden called Jackson Mwangi Macharia. Jackson was a wood merchant, selling firewood from the forest to East African Railways. Wairiri was well acquainted with Jackson because he also dealt with timber and charcoal.

So I talked to Jackson and told him of my difficulty in getting someone to approach Wairiri. Jackson was fond of me and said that, although it was nearly impossible, he would try to discuss the matter with Wairiri and put in a good word for me.

I came to learn about their conversation later. As expected, Wairiri hit the roof when Jackson informed him there was a young man interested in his daughter. Wairiri loved Wariara and doted on her. She managed the shop and was hard-working and helpful. Who was this cheeky young man who wanted to marry her?

"Just a local boy," answered Jackson. "He sells charcoal and timber."

Wairiri could not believe his ears.

"A charcoal burner wants to wed my daughter! What is the world coming to?" The old man ranted and raved, and Jackson left him fuming.

The fact is that Wairiri would have considered any young man beneath his notice and too poor to be acceptable, no matter what his status.

Wariara's mother had heard the commotion, and called Jackson into the back of the restaurant. Jackson explained everything, telling her that Njenga Karume wished to marry her daughter, Wariara. She hesitated a moment and then replied that she would have no objection. She told him that I was an honest and industrious young man, even though I was not as wealthy as her husband would have liked.

However, like any clever woman who knows her husband's nature well, she knew she could not give her opinion to Wairiri directly. At the time, our society was very conservative and subtle. She and Jackson devised a scheme. She would go to the shop and Jackson would bring me in so that the three of us could try to talk to the old man again.

I was taken to the shop and the old man looked at me with loathing and scorn. His wife, however, greeted me cordially. Jackson kindly extolled my virtues of hard work and he exaggerated my brilliant business sense while Wairiri's wife added compliments about my honesty and diligence. Wairiri was highly doubtful but said he would think over the matter and deliver his views the following day.

And, when he did give his views, he said that I could marry his daughter, but only if I could afford a bride price of three thousand shillings, an amount that had previously been the highest on record for Elburgon. This exceptional dowry had been paid sometime earlier by one John Njenga for a daughter of the village and it was considered to be an enormous amount, enough to buy a car!

After some haggling, Wairiri agreed to a bride price of two thousand six hundred shillings which I said I could afford to pay. Later, the traditional wedding took place and all ended well.

During the ceremony, I wore a second-hand suit I had bought at Kariokor in Nairobi. It was an almost new, light grey woollen suit that lasted me for many years. Contrary to everyone's expectations, Wairiri eventually took a liking to me and even gave me a lorry to use in order to go to Nakuru for the wedding photographs. On seeing the empty lorry and realising that Wairiri had totally changed his mind about me, the guests shook their heads in disbelief. As the Kikuyu say, *Ng'enda thĩ ndĩagaga mũtegi*, (nothing that walks the earth is impossible to trap.) And so Wariara and I started our married life. It was 1952 and I was twenty three years old.

During my younger days.

My mother Teresia Njeri, in 1973.

With Wariara before our wedding in 1952.

My children and my two wives Njeri and Wariara, around 1973.

My first shop in the Indian Bazaar, Kiambu 1958.

Myself, Muiruri Laban and James Gakuya, 1951.

My father, mother-in-law (Wariara's mother) and a relative, 1958.

Wariara, my first love, 1959.

With my father at Banana in 1958.

With my two wives, Njeri and Wariara with children and friends, early 1970s.

Margaret Njeri (extreme left), Njau, my long-time driver (third left), Maryanne Wariara (7th from left), my grandmother Nditi wa Kamonyo and other relatives while visiting Lynton Farm in 1976.

Kenyatta admiring my prize bull at Nakuru Agricultural Show, 1970s.

Greeting Kenyatta at State House, Nakuru in 1975, with other GEMA officials: Kihika Kimani (extreme left) and Duncan Ndegwa (centre) and Kiragu Stephen. Looking on from behind is Wilson Macharia.

Delegation from Yugoslavia – with Mbiyu Koinange (second left), President Kenyatta (centre), Dr. Kiano, myself, Matu Wamae and Kinyanjui Kabibi all in the front row.

GEMA officials with their Patron, President Jomo Kenyatta (centre). From left are Jacob M'Mwongo (GEMA National Treasurer), Njeru Ireri, Kihika Kimani, myself (GEMA Chairman), Jomo Kenyatta, Duncan Ndegwa (GEMA Vice-Chairman), Wilson Macharia (GEMA Ass. Treasurer), and Reuben Kigathi at Gatundu in October 1973.

With Fred Mbiyu Koinange (Jeff Koinange's father) at my cigarette shop in Kiambu in 1965. Fred Mbiyu was a step-brother to the renowned Mbiyu Koinange who was a cabinet minister in Kenyatta's government.

Duncan Ndegwa, Samson Muriithi Nduhiu, Mwai Kibaki and myself at a Harambee for Kimathi Institute of Technology – 4 June 1978.

Handing over a cheque to President Jomo Kenyatta as Mbiyu Koinange looks on.

New Year celebrations in Nakuru 1976, from the left Kim Gatende, Duncan Ndegwa, myself, Paul Kihara wa Wacu, Mayor Mburu Gichua, PC Isaiah Mathenge and Vice President Daniel arap Moi.

New Year's Eve with President Kenyatta and Mama Ngina and other invited guests, 1975.

With Muiruri Laban wearing identical clothes in 1952.

With grandmother Nditi Njoroge in 1960s.

This was the period when a number of passionate nationalists were traversing the whole country calling for independence and encouraging people to rebel against the colonialists. One day, around 1951, Jomo Kenyatta came to visit Elburgon.[26] He was accompanied by other political luminaries such as Eliud Mathu, Achieng' Oneko and Fred Kubai. The leaders called a public meeting and there were many Europeans in attendance as well as the Africans. Most of the whites were security people perched on Land Rovers. The crowd was tense and the atmosphere was stiff with apprehension because a violent showdown was looming between the Europeans and the nationalists.

Kenyatta talked about such issues as land and religion. It was the first time I saw Kenyatta in person, and I was deeply impressed. I have to admit that this initial admiration of Kenyatta would eventually lead to a lifelong friendship between the two of us.

Then the gathering was addressed by a Luo firebrand called Achieng' Oneko. Oneko was viewed as a radical and he had no time for euphemisms. He tore into the white man's colonial repression, telling the people that they needed to stand up and demand their rights since the white man had no right to cling to any part of Kenya. Pointing at the various Europeans in attendance, he finished his blistering speech with the Kiswahili words, *"Mnaona hawa Wazungu? Ni wapumbavu wote hawa! Msiwaogope!"* (See all these white people? They are all idiots. Do not fear them!) Even I did not think any African would have openly gone that far in front of his adversaries.

To say that those attending the meeting were shocked is an understatement. They had never in all their lives heard a white person insulted while he was present. They were quite used to mutter darkly among themselves and to talk in whispers about the colonialists, but none had been bold enough to confront a European face to face.

I remember that people in the crowd started whispering among themselves and wondering where Kenyatta had gotten this Luo. They asked themselves why the Luo did not know that whites should not be

---

26 Jomo Kenyatta had gone to Britain in 1929 and stayed until 1947. He was an official of the Kikuyu Central Association and it was they who sponsored his travel abroad. During that time he was the leading agitator for freedom, (especially for Kikuyu rights, land and freedoms) among the moderates and when he came back from Britain he held many public meetings all over Kenya. He had been educated in Kikuyu Scotland Mission and had worked briefly as a meter reader for the government in Nairobi and Nanyuki.

insulted. In fact, they were worried they could be imprisoned, or even killed just for listening to him, and they slowly started leaving.

The colonialists were clamping down harder on African rights. White soldiers and their African collaborators, especially the chiefs and their guards, could stop anyone and search them. They could detain a person for days if they were not satisfied with his or her behaviour. Ridiculous 'offences' such as failing to stop and take off one's hat when a white man's vehicle passed by, was punishable by three months in prison. Any African lorry driver who failed to give way to a white man's vehicle was guilty of a crime. Drivers who committed this offence would be taken to Molo police station by the 'offended' settler and would get a three-month jail term. In short, the colonialists were using terror tactics to intimidate and subjugate Africans in order to stamp out the rebellious spirit that pervaded the land.[27]

I personally got a taste of this treatment when I went to buy the *East African Standard* newspaper at a certain shop in Elburgon. The shop, owned by an Indian called D.H. Patel, was the biggest grocery shop in the area. Settlers made their purchases here, and there was a big sign at the entrance saying *'Europeans Only'*. However, there was a small kiosk at the back where Africans did their shopping. Somehow I did not notice, or did not read the sign at the front and went right in, picked up a newspaper and queued like all the other customers.

A strong hand suddenly gripped my collar and I was dragged out. A big white man then pointed at the sign and asked me whether I had read it. I answered in the negative and was warned never to step into the shop again and then shoved with such force that I fell to the ground.

That moment opened my eyes to the contempt that the white man held for the African. I could not understand why I had been hurled out. After all, I too could read the newspaper, which is why I was buying it in the first place, and I had the money to pay for it. So why could they not let me buy it? I then understood that the African was treated as though he was a dog and I felt bitter about the humiliation and injustice of it all. Dusting off my clothes, I left with the newspaper, which I had not even paid for. I could hear the whites roaring with laughter in the shop.

---

27 It was not only black Africans who were fighting for independence. Many Indians were actively involved in the liberation struggle. Markhan Singh, a trade unionist, had almost been deported to India for instigating workers to strike. During his trial, he told the white judge that it would be understandable if he was being threatened with deportation by black Africans but it was laughable that this was being done by a *Mzungu*. Those who helped the cause of liberation struggle included J.M. Desai and lawyer R. Kapila, among many others.

Some time later I went to Molo to see the District Officer, with Kanuti Ng'ang'a, a friend of mine. Both of us were riding bicycles. After we had finished our business we started making our way back. Although Elburgon is higher than Molo, there are quite a number of valleys and Kanuti and I sped down the slopes. As we enjoyed coasting down one of the hills, a police pick-up truck with two white policemen in it came up beside us and then swerved, trying to block our way. Kanuti came to a screeching halt and nearly fell. He was immediately arrested. I managed to narrowly slip by on the footpath and continued riding.

After a short time I noticed the police car behind me again. They came up beside me and then skewed directly onto my path. I was sure I was going to crash violently right into the side of the car. There was nothing I could do but clench my fists over the brakes and hope for the best. My bicycle slid over the dirt and I went into a skid but at least managed to keep my balance. My heart was racing and I came to shuddering stop. I did not understand why these policemen had made such a dangerous manoeuvre. I could have been seriously injured.

Well, the policemen threw me and my bicycle into the back of the police car. When I arrived at the station, I was locked up in the same cell with my friend Kanuti Ng'ang'a.

A sympathetic police inspector, an African man called William, said he would release me on bail once the *Wazungu* officers left. As soon as the whites went off duty, he released me on a one hundred-shilling bail.

It was already after dark. I waited till 11 pm and then got on the train headed for Elburgon. When I reached home I found my wife very worried, but I reassured her and told her what had happened. She was glad I had not been hurt but was anxious about the court hearing which was to be the next day.

The following morning I presented myself in court, and Kanuti and I were separately charged with riding our bicycles at eighty miles (about 129 kph) an hour!

We had never heard of anything more ridiculous. At that time, most cars could not do eighty miles an hour, even on a slope. How could we possibly do eighty on our old-fashioned sturdy steel bicycles with fat wheels and rigid frame?

The white officer who arrested us turned out to be the prosecutor as well. The judge, of course, was a white man, too.

"We could not even catch him in our vehicle!" exclaimed the arresting officer.

Knowing how such things worked, I knew it would be useless to try to contradict the policeman, or to explain that it was physically impossible for such types of bicycles to get up to such a speed.

I just said, "I had not realised I was riding that fast. I'm very sorry and will never repeat the mistake."

These are the words I spoke, but you can just imagine the words I would have wished to say, which were running through my mind.

We were each fined eighty shillings, for riding our bicycles at eighty miles an hour. Some justice!

The fever of impeding war was everywhere. Mau Mau oaths were being taken with unprecedented frequency. Inevitably, I was soon pulled into the maelstrom.

In early 1951, Nairobi was to be given a Royal Charter which would give it the status of a city. To many Africans, this was yet another move by the British to entrench themselves in Kenya. In fact, common opinion had it that the "Queen"[28] was annexing all the land in Nairobi for herself and that the whites were declaring the city as their permanent home. The propaganda mills churned out all sorts of rumours.

Many African politicians and freedom activists in Nairobi spoke against the move, but there were some few who supported the Charter. This faction was composed of loyalist councillors, among them a wealthy man, Muchohi Gikonyo of Pumwani. The Nairobi Mau Mau Council[29] decided that this group ought to be eliminated in order to prove a point to other Africans who might have similar ideas.

Three Mau Mau leaders, Fred Kubai, John Wamuti Muhongi and a man called Dominic, were assigned the task of eliminating Muchohi. The Mau Mau War Council had decided that the best place to execute Muchohi would be in his off-licence bar in Pumwani[30] since he used to drink there every evening in a back room. So Kubai, Wamuti and Dominic went there one evening under cover of darkness. Muchohi, as expected, was there entertaining his friends.

28 Although Queen Victoria was long dead at this time, and Queen Elizabeth II had not yet succeeded to the throne, many Africans still referred to the Empire as "belonging to the Queen".
29 The Mau Mau War Council is often confused with its military wing called the Mau Mau Central Committee. The Council met clandestinely in Nairobi, either in Kiburi House on Grogan Road or in private houses in Pumwani under the chairmanship of 'Chief Justice' Githua Muchohi from Kangema. Their role was resource mobilization and transporting arms to freedom fighters in the forest.
30 No Africans had fully licensed bars at the time.

The three entered the bar, boldly stepped up to Muchohi and without a word the one who had the gun, fired at him from close range and Muchohi fell to the floor bleeding. Unfortunately, or perhaps fortunately, the gun man was totally inexperienced in the use of firearms so when he opened fire, the bullet just grazed Muchohi's scalp. Not taking the time to check whether Muchohi was actually dead, the three Mau Mau ran off into the night, pleased that they had accomplished their assignment so speedily.

I am not sure who ordered this assassination but thank God that Muchohi did not die. He and his children later became my friends and, although Muchohi himself has passed away, I still meet with the family.

Muchohi had recognised his attackers and after he recovered from the shock, he immediately reported them to the police. By the following morning the manhunt was on. Soon, Kubai and Dominic were arrested, but Wamuti, who had apparently learned that Muchohi had survived, went undercover. In a panic, he took temporary refuge in a Mau Mau hideout within the African estates, but, with the police hot on his trail, he realised that he would soon have to shift elsewhere. The Mau Mau leaders also felt that the city was not a safe place to hide him. As I was told later, they made inquiries among members of the Mau Mau movement in Nairobi, and found out there was a young man from Elburgon who had taken the Mau Mau oath and could be relied upon to give Muchohi a safe house until things cooled down. That young man, of course, was me.

I had come to know several of the Mau Mau leaders in Nairobi during my travels to the city. With my partner, Muiruri Laban, we met them on quite a few occasions and they were aware that I came from faraway Elburgon, that I dealt in timber and fencing poles, and that I was therefore familiar with the forests around that area. They therefore decided I would be the ideal person to give Wamuti a temporary residence. I actually did not know about the murder attempt and Wamuti never told me why he had fled Nairobi and was in hiding. I only found out later when I was questioned by the police. Elburgon was far from Nairobi and I could hide Wamuti in my home and, if need be, in the forest.

A few days later, two Mau Mau leaders from Kiambaa, Mbiyu Koinange and Kuria Gathunguri came to visit me in Elburgon. Mbiyu was already acquainted with me because he and Jomo Kenyatta used to dine in my father-in-law's house when visiting the town. They explained the sketchy background of the events, just stating that Wamuti needed temporary lodgings and asked me if I would agree to hide him in my home.

I promptly agreed. Actually, it would have been impossible to refuse because, since I had taken the Mau Mau oath, I had vowed to be loyal to the movement and to do everything I could to further its progress. Being asked to do something for the Mau Mau was therefore not a request as such. Rather it was a duty expected of those who had taken the oath.

Anyway, arrangements were made to bring Wamuti to Elburgon by bus, and I welcomed him to stay with me. For the first few days, he stayed silently hidden in my house, but after some evenings discussing the matter in quiet whispers, we decided that it might not be very safe for him. The local police already suspected me of underhanded and shady activities since they knew I had considerable funds and furthermore, I never attempted to befriend or influence the administration.

Fortunately, during my logging forays into the forest, I had found an abandoned stone bungalow, deep in the bush. Its presence between the trees was inexplicable and strange but it seemed that the bungalow used to belong to a European settler who had deserted the area. It was dilapidated, virtually a wreck and the little yard was overgrown with tall grass, brambles, bushes and saplings. However, some of the crumbling rooms were still barely habitable. Wamuti and I decided that this ruin might be much safer for him than my own place, since few people ever wandered so far into the forest. In fact, as I found out later, this portion of the woods was sealed off by wardens, anyway.

Wamuti and I did our best to clean the inside of the house, chasing out the birds and little field mice, sweeping out their nests and the dust with makeshift brooms made from branches of nearby trees. However we left the outside exactly as it was, filthy with bird droppings, entwined with wild vines and sprouting plants in every crack in the walls, so that anyone passing nearby would never even imagine someone was living inside it.

That night we carefully made up bundles of bedding, basic kitchen utensils and any supplies that Wamuti might need. By the light of the moon we cautiously retraced the faint path between the trees and once we arrived at the little bungalow, we stored everything away in one of the inner rooms. This was to be Wamuti's new home.

Since my home was just on the outskirts of the woods, I could easily visit him almost every day, and sometimes, when he felt lonely and it seemed safe, he would come to sleep in my house for a change. He would stay out of sight, and we were constantly on guard, careful that he would not be seen in my house too often. He never stayed for more than a day or night during his visits, but while in the forest, he would help me cut down trees sometimes, just to alleviate his boredom. No doubt he was idle and claustrophobic, stuck in one place like that for several months, and felt stifled and frustrated. Occasionally, I would walk to Elburgon with Wamuti and introduce him as Edward, my friend from Kiambu. He was just Edward, and had no other name.

However, the situation was too good to last. One Sunday morning while we were walking down the slope towards Elburgon Township, Wamuti suddenly stopped dead in his tracks. Right in front of us, there was a man staring at Wamuti. He had an air of authority and was scrutinising Wamuti so closely and intently that I suspected he was a policeman.

Wamuti quickly murmured that he would see me later. He turned back the way we had come and strolled back up the hill. I walked straight on, not looking at the man in front of me, and I passed him by, trying to maintain a casual attitude. He glanced at me briefly and then, with quick steps, followed Wamuti up the slope. When I noticed him trailing Wamuti, I realised that my suspicions had been correct. I knew we were in trouble.

Later I learned that the man was from the Criminal Investigation Department and that he had come to visit his family in Elburgon. It was pure bad luck that put us on the same path.

I pretended to spend a little time in Elburgon and then I went back to my house, wondering what was going to happen. I did not dare head out to the bungalow in the woods, so I just sat there anxiously, worried about Wamuti. As it happened, after midnight, Wamuti was arrested in his forest hideout.

We never actually discovered if the investigator had followed Wamuti all the way, but it was very probable. The investigator and other policemen surrounded the old house and broke down the door. Wamuti had no chance of escaping, so he was handcuffed and taken to Nairobi in a police vehicle. The following day, just as I was getting ready to leave in order to see how Wamuti had survived the night in his forest hideout, three men came in and arrested me. They did not bother telling me the grounds for my arrest. They just informed me that they were there to escort me to Nairobi.

In Nairobi, I was locked up in the same cell as Wamuti. We talked a little but both of us were anxious about the future. Some few days later we were taken to court and Wamuti's charge was consolidated with that of Kubai and Dominic, who had earlier been charged with attempted murder. Like his co-accused, Wamuti was denied bail. On my part, I was charged with harbouring a fugitive and was luckily freed on bond which I paid in cash and found myself out of prison the same day.

When the trial came up, we were represented by R. Kapila, an Indian lawyer who was being paid by the Mau Mau Central Committee and who represented most Africans, especially those charged with Mau Mau activities.

The judge in the case was Thacker Holland while the prosecutor was Sommerhon.[31] My case, as less serious, was dealt with quite speedily.

When I appeared before the judge, he asked me whether I knew Wamuti. I admitted that I did and that I had known him for many years from my days in Kiambu. I told the judge that even our grandfathers had been friends, which was actually true. The judge then asked whether I had housed Wamuti in Elburgon and again I admitted it.

"Did you know that you were harbouring a fugitive?" he asked.

"No, Sir," I said. "Wamuti came to work for me. He needed money to buy spares for his taxi." Then I added, "I did not know that he was a wanted person."

The prosecutor informed the court that Wamuti's Christian name was John, however, I had been introducing him as Edward in Elburgon. He even brought a witness, a government officer from Elburgon, to corroborate this fact.

"You changed Wamuti's name to hide his identity because you knew he was being sought," the prosecutor charged.

"No, Sir! I have always known Wamuti as Edward since our early days," I insisted.

Fortunately, Wamuti's identity card read 'Wamuti Muhungi' without any baptismal name. The prosecutor therefore could not prove that Wamuti's Christian name actually was John. As a result, the judge sided with me and I was released.

The case against Kubai, Dominic and Wamuti continued for some weeks. When the time came for the ruling and the sentence, I made sure I was in the courtroom, and so did many Mau Mau leaders and the accused's relatives. Fred Kubai was found not guilty and released. Wamuti was sentenced to six months imprisonment or a fine of four thousand shillings. The surreal shock came when Dominic's sentence was read. He was found guilty of attempted murder and was jailed for seven years without the option of a fine.

As soon as I could, I organized a fund-raising meeting to offset Wamuti's fine. We held a *harambee* that same week in Kiambaa, and

---

31   Incidentally, the same judge and prosecutor would hear the case of Fred Kubai, along with Jomo Kenyatta and four others, during the infamous Kapenguria trial in which they were accused of being the leaders of an illegal movement, the Mau Mau.

managed to collect quite a sum from Wamuti's friends and other Mau Mau supporters. I can recall that two of the most prominent Mau Mau supporters who donated funds were John Mbiyu and Kuria Gathunguri. The funds were then sent on to Mau Mau leaders in Nairobi who topped it up and Wamuti was freed.

I am not sure what happened to Dominic but I believe he served his full term because I never heard of him again. However, Wamuti survived to become a very good friend and I often visit him in Karuri.

Oathing had started as early as 1947 and by 1950, the name Mau Mau was widespread—it became known as the "Mau Mau oath". Those who took the first Mau Mau *muuma wa kũiguithania* (oath of unity) in 1950 vowed allegiance to all causes of the movement. I took the first oath in 1951 in Elburgon and then later, when the State of Emergency and a full-scale war against the Mau Mau was declared in 1952, I took a second oath, also in Elburgon. It was a very secretive oath, which went by the name of *muuma wa mbatuni* (oath of the warrior's army—'*mbatuni*' was a corruption of the English word 'platoon'). There were various stages of oaths, depending on a person's reliability, initiative and commitment towards the cause. The latter oath was only administered to a trusted few because these individuals would be aware of the most secret plans such as who was to die, and when and where. What is more, such persons were the ones who were entrusted with executions.

Some people say there were up to seven oaths, all of increasing secrecy and severity. But as far as I know there was only the third oath, taken by those who fought in the forests.

Incidentally, my wife, Wariara, had taken the oath much earlier, even before we got married. During the visit of Jomo Kenyatta and his friends to Elburgon, Kenyatta had taken his dinner at the house of Wairiri wa Kigera, who was later to become my father-in-law. Kenyatta had said that he could only take his meals in the house of a trusted patriot. Wairiri was given the oath shortly thereafter, together with his three wives and adult children, who included my future wife Wariara.

When I married her, she did not disclose this secret. A person who had taken the oath could not divulge secrets of the movement to a person who had not yet taken it, irrespective of their relationship. I would occasionally see my wife in consultation with elders and other women but I never suspected that they were talking about the freedom struggle.

In fact, Wariara only revealed her status after she learned that I had taken the oath as well.

The oath was being administered all over Kikuyuland and by Kikuyus in Nairobi. Anyone who did not take the oath was viewed with suspicion and was considered a traitor and an outcast. This category included the collaborators, such as the home guards and religious leaders. They were considered non-patriotic and would never be told any secrets that involved the freedom struggle. In some cases, such people were killed if they betrayed the movement.

An example, which occurred in Elburgon, can illustrate how seriously the Mau Mau oath was taken. As I remember, it involved Willie Mwangi Michuki who had come into the area from Othaya. This was the same Willie who had tried to arrange a clerical job for me earlier. He was a good man, respected by the community and, after we had patched up our differences, was also my business partner.

However, Willie did not believe in taking the oath and skilfully dodged any effort to make him take it. The elders and others who had taken the oath were uncomfortable with this situation. They did not directly accuse Willie of being a collaborator, but felt they could not trust him either. They liked him, they knew he was an industrious and good person and did not want any harm coming his way. Nevertheless it did not matter how moral and upright a person was, it was the oath that was necessary in determining loyalty and support for the freedom struggle. We had heard reports that some people were given the oath by force, and if they refused they could even be executed. So the elders decided that Willie would be forced to take the oath one way or another.

However, all the tricks they used to get Willie to come to one of the secret locations where the *muuma* was taken, did not succeed. Somehow he always became suspicious and avoided any night appointments, when oathing would most likely take place. Finally we came up with an ingenious plan to lure Willie to a secret place where he would take the oath by force.

Now, one of the most beautiful women in Elburgon was a girl called Njeri. Many men admired her for her beauty, but she ignored them all. Her most ardent admirer, as everyone knew, was Willie Mwangi, himself. Willie had a strong desire to marry Njeri as his second wife, but he could not get her to agree.

Njeri had vowed she would never be a second wife to anybody, and she had gone as far as telling Willie to leave her alone. But Willie still harboured the dream that one day, she would be his.

Peter Kamau, another business partner of mine, and I devised a plan which we discussed with others who had taken the oath. The plan was to lure Njeri first and give her the oath and then use her as bait for Willie. And so, not much later, Njeri was given the oath.

After a month or so, our group informed Njeri of the plan. We assured her that we did not really care what sort of relationship she might or might not have with Willie. That was her personal business. What we wanted was for her to use her charm and lure Willie into a trap.

Having taken the oath, Njeri was obliged to do as we wished or the consequences would be serious for her. So Njeri spoke to Willie and, oozing charm, stated that she was thinking of changing her mind about their relationship. She asked Willie if he could meet her just after dark in a certain deserted hut in the outskirts of the village so that they could discuss their future. She told him that they would have the place to themselves because the owner of the hut was Njeri's cousin and he was away.

That afternoon I was in Willie's house, and I have to say, I have never seen him so happy. He changed shirts, suits and shoes, trying on different clothes to see what looked best and asking me for my opinion. I had to laugh when he practised winning smiles in front of the mirror.

But he was very secretive and refused to tell me why he was going through all these preparations.

"What's the big occasion, Willie?" I asked him as he posed, staring at his reflection.

He chuckled and said, "I'll tell you tomorrow."

I felt a little guilty. Poor Willie was in such a happy mood of anticipation. He was sure he was going to have a wonderful time with Njeri, yet we had something totally different planned for him that same evening.

Willie was exactly on time for the rendezvous near the hut. He expected to have a nice time with Njeri and perhaps some happy discussion about their future. When Njeri arrived, she held his hand and led him near the hut. His heart was beating quickly in anticipation. Njeri opened the door and into the darkness they went, closing the door behind them. All of a sudden, bright flashlights shone into his eyes. A stunned Willie saw a group of about ten men, all armed with *pangas* and directing the lights at him.

One of the men told him sternly to sit in the middle of the hut. Njeri was told to wait outside. When Willie's eyes grew accustomed to the light he saw his friends and business partners, Peter Kamau and me. His face registered betrayal rather than hatred. He knew he was caged with no escape route.

"*Wūūi, Njenga na Kamau, mūtikanjūragithie. Oyai ciothe no mūtikareke manjūrage!*" (Please, Njenga and Kamau, do not have me killed. You can take all my money and assets in the business, but don't let them kill me!) Willie pleaded. "Please, if you have hired them to kill me, tell them not to. I will sign any document giving you all the money, please."

But of course the only reason he had been tricked into the hut was in order to get him to take the oath. Once he was in the hands of the oath givers he had no other option.

Njeri, who was waiting outside, was called after the ceremony was over and told to escort Willie back. She was told that whether she and Willie spent the night together or not was totally up to the two of them. The oath givers had accomplished their mission and now they could trust good old Willie.

Willie did not spend the night with Njeri, and he never married her. However his friendship with Peter and me grew stronger. Until the time of his death recently, the three of us remained friends and would laugh heartily at our clever trick.

At this time I was living in a rental house owned by a man called Benjamin, who was the uncle of my partner, Muiruri. It was in this house that I brought my new bride, Wariara, and it was here also that we were blessed with our first born child, Wanjiku. Everything was going smoothly and business was good, and we were living quite comfortably. However, peace in the neighbourhood was disrupted when a government patrol led by a white officer came round, trying to smoke out those who had taken the oath. They knocked on the door and I opened it immediately. The white man had a look around and apparently my attire and the furniture in the house impressed him. He seemed particularly astonished by my gramophone. He asked me whether I was a clerk and I lied—I said I had been one but was now a businessman.

Benjamin, our landlord, was not so lucky. He was a shabby old man and he was accused of having taken the oath, a claim he denied vehemently.

"I own all these buildings, businesses and this house," he told the *Mzungu.*

"Shut up, old man!" the white man exclaimed. "We have already met the owner of the premises."

He had a hard time convincing the white officer that he was a man of God, but he succeeded all the same.

After this incident, Benjamin started seeing strange characters visiting my house at all hours. Benjamin was a staunch Christian, and, like nearly all those affiliated to churches, he was opposed to people taking oaths on the principle that it was a pagan ritual. He suspected that I had taken the oath and that those who were coming to visit me were my partners in the Mau Mau.

One evening Benjamin called Wariara and myself to his house. He asked his wife, who was just as religious as he was, to read a verse from the Bible and he then led us in prayer. After concluding the prayer, Benjamin informed us that, even though he loved us both, we would have to vacate his place within three months because he did not want trouble with the authorities. Naturally I understood. I knew Benjamin as an honest and upright fellow but unfortunately we were on different sides of the issue. I told Benjamin that we did not need three months—three weeks would be good enough.

As it turned out, I had another friend, an uncle-in-law called Patrick Mwaniki, who had a shop in the neighbourhood. Mwaniki had some vacant land behind his shop and he gave this to me so that I could build a house.

Wairiri heard about the expulsion of his daughter and me and became incensed. He offered us free iron sheets from his hardware shop and gave me permission to use his lorries to ferry building stones without charge. Within three weeks, our house was ready for occupation. It was the first stone dwelling house in Elburgon and everyone was impressed. Generally, the few who had stone buildings before this time used them as shops and residential premises combined.

Unfortunately, the home guards and fellow collaborators were most mistrustful. They had always suspected that I was a Mau Mau adherent, but the evidence of my new stone house was, in their warped view, a certain confirmation. It seemed to them that I had an endless supply of money. They concluded that I must be the Mau Mau treasurer in the area and that the new house would be the meeting place for the Mau Mau to plan their strategy.

After that, the home guards started monitoring my every move and I, together with other family members, knew I was in danger of being arrested and detained without trial, as had happened to a great many others.

In early 1953, I went to Molo on my bicycle to see the District Officer on a business matter, since there was no DO in Elburgon. After I returned from Molo, Wariara went to stay with a neighbour who had just had a baby and whose husband, James Mwanu, had earlier been arrested as a suspected Mau Mau, and detained without trial. One day while Wariara was away, a man called John Kimwe, who was a known *komerera*[32], came to visit at lunch time. I was just about to eat some *githeri* that my aunt had prepared and so I invited Kimwe to join me. As we ate, he informed me that my name was on the list of those who would soon be arrested as Mau Mau suspects. Kimwe said that some friends of his who were home guards had told him the raid would take place that night. He felt he had to tell me since he would not like me to suffer in detention.

I thanked him and thought quickly. I knew what happened to people detained on suspicion of being Mau Mau. The authorities would first freeze my bank account and impound my money on the assumption I was connected to Mau Mau. I rushed to see my wife at my neighbour's home. I told her what had happened and that I would have to flee Elburgon. Of course Wariara was distressed but she knew the consequences of detention.

I had enough money in my pockets to ensure my wife's survival, and neither of us was worried about maintaining our little family. My primary cause for concern was what was to become of all my savings. There was only one phone booth in the area and that was near D.H. Patel's shop. I inserted thirty cents into the slot and called my bank manager at Standard Bank, Nakuru, which was 37 kilometres away. When I identified myself and gave my request, the white manager told me that it was not possible to perform account transactions over the phone.

"I'm sorry, Mr. Karume. I just can't give you details of an account over the phone, nor can I do any transactions. How can I know if you are really who you say you are? How can I know who is speaking to me?"

I pleaded with him to no avail. The manager told me that it was impossible and instructed me to come to the bank personally at nine the following morning. I hung up. I could not tell the manager that the following morning would be too late. By then I might be in the back of a lorry, heading to a detention camp in Athi River or somewhere else. In desperation I went to consult my father-in-law, who was quite experienced in matters concerning money.

---

32 *Komerera* was the title that Kikuyus gave to those sitting on the fence (double agents), cowardly opportunists who were neither committed to the Mau Mau cause nor to the colonial administration. They rode with the wind, exploiting either side according to their convenience. Mau Mau adherents were referred to as *itungati* while collaborators and home guards were called *ngati*.

Wairiri advised me to make an estimate of the money I had in the bank and write the equivalent in a cheque to Raju Patel of Elburgon Trading Company. Patel would then receive the money from the account and hand it over to my family. Naturally, I could have written a cheque to Wairiri, but after discussing the matter we decided it might seem too suspicious.

Raju Patel owned the biggest shop in the area and Wairiri owned the shop right next to Patel's premises. As a result, the two were trusted friends. So I quickly estimated my bank balance and concluded it could be no less that six thousand three hundred shillings. I wrote a cheque for six thousand shillings to Patel and in further precaution, I backdated it for thirty days. This way, if I was caught and detained, Patel could claim he had been paid for some purchases made on credit long before I had been arrested. Raju was a good friend of my father-in-law and he gave the cash to Wairiri immediately. Once that financial matter was settled, I started on the most urgent part of my arrangements.

Night was approaching and there was little time. I quickly visited my friend and age-mate, Stephen Nduru, and informed him of the latest events. Nduru too, had taken the oath, and I said that he might be on the list, as well. Nduru agreed with this assessment and we decided to flee Elburgon and go to Limuru in Kiambu. We would, God willing, take the night train. I said a sorrowful farewell to Wariara and gave one last look at the brand new house where I had lived for just ten days, and then left Elburgon for good, never to live there again. This was early 1953 and I was twenty-four.

Chapter 4

Detention and my Fruitful Relationship with Beer

The plan was to sneak to Elburgon railway station and then proceed by train to Limuru and thereafter on to Kiambu where we would stay with my relatives until the hunt for us had cooled down. We knew we would be safer there because we were less known by the authorities and their collaborators in Kiambu.

Nduru and I made our way safely by avoiding roads where we might have encountered roadblocks and government officials. Then, we hid in the house of a friend and Mau Mau operative, Gichura, who worked for a saw mill known as Marioshoni Timber Company. Gichura happened to have a house near the Railway staff quarters. Other Mau Mau members had notified him that we were coming and he had no choice but to agree to hide us in his house until we left again. We stayed out of sight until nightfall because we knew the train would roll into the station around 11 pm.

Since we had sent word through the underground Mau Mau network, that we were fleeing the area by train, Nduru and I knew there would probably be quite a few members at the station to help us. The Mau Mau had a well-organized network and communication was quite efficient despite being clandestine.

But there was one particular problem that had not occurred to us earlier. A person could not book a train ticket if he did not have permission to travel. In order to travel, one had to have the relevant 'pass'. I had been issued with a permanent pass by the Nakuru District Commissioner owing to the nature of my business which involved a lot of travelling. I could go to Nairobi any time I wished, but my colleague, did not have such a pass. We struggled to think of a solution.

Then, as we tried to find a remedy for our dilemma, I was momentarily stunned. What astonishing luck! Incredibly, I actually had an extra pass, right in my pocket!

I had forgotten that my neighbour, James Mwanu, had given me his pass a few weeks earlier, so that I could renew it for him. Since I had a good relationship with the DC Nakuru, (naturally a white colonial officer), Mwanu thought I would be able to get the renewal done quickly, without too many questions being asked. But just two days after he had given me the pass, he was arrested and detained, so I had just kept it, not knowing exactly what to do with it.

Nduru was amazed when he saw that I actually had an extra pass, but when I suggested that we alter the pass by erasing Mwanu's name and inserting Nduru's instead, he hesitated. Nduru was very nervous about the idea. He said he might end up in prison if the forgery was discovered but I went ahead and prepared the altered pass anyway. I told Nduru not to be so fearful. Prison and detention was the same thing, and if Nduru remained in the neighbourhood, chances were that he would end up in detention anyway.

Gichura, our host, went to the station to book the tickets while his wife prepared a meal of chicken for us. We had to eat it in complete silence, in a darkened room, since word of our attempt to leave the area had leaked out somehow, and government undercover agents were swarming all over the station looking for me in particular. By good luck, on duty that night was an Asian Station Master who we called *babu* (a term of respect for a clerk, or grandfather), who happened to have become acquainted with me through my extensive business travels. The Station Master just read the names in the passes that Gichura gave him and issued the tickets. Gichura then returned home with the papers and Nduru and I were much relieved. Our risky forgery had not being detected. Now that we had passes and tickets, all we had to do was to wait for the train.

That night we surreptitiously crept out of the house, watching carefully for anyone lurking about, and stealthily made our way across the road to the station. As we approached the boarding platform we noticed a couple of home guards who were scrutinizing the faces of every passenger boarding the train. I suspected that the home guards were probably looking for us, but I did not care to hang about to confirm this hunch. Nduru and I stole away and concealed ourselves in the dark night shadows of a bush a little distance from the boarding platform and waited for the train to start moving. The Mau Mau operatives hidden around the railway station had also been keeping their eyes open for us and quickly located Nduru and I in the shadows. They approached the two of us, stuffed some money into our pockets and wished us well.

That was how the Mau Mau operated. They would not have let one of their own go into hiding without some means of survival, and had a contingency fund for just such a purpose.

The train hooted and started moving on its way towards Limuru and Nairobi. As it gained speed, Nduru and I jumped aboard and were soon rolling down into the Rift Valley and away from Elburgon where the search for us intensified. For the moment, we were safe. Whether our luck would last when we arrived in Kiambu was a different matter all together and we were both anxious about it.

We alighted at Limuru station the following morning and did not see any signs of home guards this time. Then we went onward from Limuru to Kiambaa, travelling on a bus christened *Kĩhooto*. Luckily I knew the driver, Gitu wa Mubiira, since my school days, and as we approached Kiambaa the three of us discussed the latest events in the country. Gitu informed me that the situation in Kiambu District was just as bad, if not worse than Elburgon.

Many people had taken the oath in Kiambu and, owing to its proximity to Nairobi, it was considered a hotspot of Mau Mau activities. It was ranked at the same level as Nairobi, Mt Kenya and the Aberdare regions where the Mau Mau rebellion was in full swing. The colonial governor requested Britain to send more soldiers to stem the uprising and subsequently, military operations to flush out the Mau Mau and their sympathizers intensified.

There were various camps in Kiambu where suspects were held awaiting detention. Many of my acquaintances in Kiambu were in these screening camps or already in detention. If Nduru and I were to escape the notice of the authorities, we had to keep an exceedingly low profile.

When Nduru and I finally made it home to Kiambaa, we were welcomed and given lodgings by my uncle, Gatenjwa Munge.

A short time after we arrived, a friend of mine, Gathigi Njoroge, who I have mentioned in an earlier chapter, joined us. He had also left Elburgon in a hurry and come to stay with his relatives in Kihara, just a few kilometres from Kiambu. However he found it quite crowded and when he found out that I was staying in Kiambu, he joined us. So Gathigi, Nduru and I all stayed together.

After some time in Kiambu, Gathigi told me he wanted to visit his relatives in Kihara. I was worried. Many people had recently been killed by the colonial authorities and others had been rounded up and detained after the murder of Chief Waruhiu by the Mau Mau in nearby Gachie. I warned Gathigi about the danger but he was not worried and insisted on travelling. He said he would just make a quick trip and be back by nightfall.

He asked me if he could borrow my jacket and shoes since his were quite worn out and he did not want to look disgraceful when visiting his relatives and naturally I agreed. So off he went.

I never saw him again. I later learnt that he had been shot dead by his own relatives who had since become home guards. Any land belonging to detainees or people in hiding was quickly snapped up by such collaborators, and since they imagined that he had come to reclaim his father's land, they eliminated him. I was very sad about his death and this incident just shows how dangerous it was to move around during that time.

I did not waste time getting back down to business again. For me, every chance was an opportunity to do business—*Irīaga na mbugi o na kūrī ūgwati,* (cows graze with their cowbells despite the presence of danger.)

Several of my timber clients in Nairobi owed me money and my father-in-law sent me the funds from the cheque I had written to Patel earlier, so I had no difficulty getting together enough capital to get started again in Kiambu. Peter Kamau, Peter Kamande and I decided to become partners in a general shop in Kiambu. Kamau had been my old business partner in Elburgon, and he and I had been in the timber business together. Just like Nduru and I, he had also escaped the crackdown on Mau Mau when he joined his relatives in Kiambu, the original home of his parents.

The three of us, Kamau, Kamande and I, decided to rent a shop in Kiambu from Bedan Njoroge, Kamau's father-in-law. Bedan had started building the shop but had failed to complete it. So we bought construction material and finished it on the understanding that the money we invested would be deducted from the rent.

When this first shop was up and running, we rented another one in Ndumberi township from Ngugi Karanja who was Peter Kamande's brother. In those suspicious days it was best to work with relatives, who could be a little more trusted than the general public.

As for Nduru, I employed him in the shop I set up in Ndumberi, as my assistant. Nduru was hardworking, but not very ambitious, and he was content to work for other people. After we all settled down, Nduru fell in love with the daughter of my uncle, my cousin Wanjiru. However, Nduru did not have goats or money for the bride price so I came to his rescue. I did not want Nduru to miss the important things in life just because he could not afford them. Furthermore, since I was the one who brought him from Elburgon and introduced him around, I felt a certain amount of responsibility for him. I did not want to harm either of our reputations. I therefore secretly gave him 200 shillings to use as bride price, with the caution that he should never mention the matter to any one.

When the time for the *rūracio*[33] (bride price negotiations) came, Nduru and his few friends went to the bride's home. I, as a cousin was naturally in the receiving committee at the bride's home, and, as usual in those days, with a lot of banter and pretence, a protracted argument started about the amount of the bride price. Each side argued its points and the debate went on for a while. Finally Nduru produced the 200 shillings I had secretly given him a few days before and said that that was all he had been able to raise, but that he would be able to bring more in the future. Wanjiru's father said that it was reasonable and accepted the money and blessed the young couple.

"Two hundred shillings is not very bad but it is not very much either," I insisted, tongue in cheek. "Won't you add even a little money, *Bwana*?"

Nduru could not help bursting into laughter despite the fact that this was a very serious and solemn ceremony. I was making a joke of the matter but was also indirectly stressing the importance of responsibility.

From then on Nduru was happily married and years later, the two of us would chuckle heartily at the memory of my cheek. Up to the time of his death, we would joke about the matter and I would tell him that he not only took off with my cousin, but he also used my money to do so.

The above episode reminded me of another incident that involved paying bride price that happened much later in the 1970s. This time, it was at David Wainaina Waruhiu's home in Githunguri. (David was the son of Chief Waruhiu who had been killed by the Mau Mau). Once again I was on the side of the bride since I was a friend to the father. The man coming to pay the bride price was Amos Kinuthia, a businessman from Ndeiya in Limuru who owned a number of schools and was a friend of mine. The spokesman for Kinuthia's side was another friend, Godfrey Muhuri Muchiri, who was a Member of Parliament.

---

33 The ceremony involved in Kikuyu *rūracio* or the verb *kūracia* (paying of the bride price) was very elaborate. Deliberately, representatives of the bride's clan would make things very complicated for the visitors, insisting that their daughter was worth much more than they were offering. They would recount the amount invested in her upbringing. On the other hand, the visitors would raise countering arguments, and after a while the two sides would reach an agreement. The arguing was a central part of the ceremony but unless the groom's side was offering a ridiculous bride price, the ceremony always concluded with an agreement. This elaborate course of argument still happens in many dowry ceremonies to date. According to Kikuyu customs, the groom never finishes paying the bride price.

The bride, Wanjiru Waruhiu, was a qualified medical doctor, one of the few university graduates at the time, and the bride's family emphasised this fact, implying that Kinuthia's delegation should pay substantially more than the regular bride price.

Now Muhuri was a shrewd man, and he quickly devised a way to counter this argument. When his turn came to speak, Muhuri rose and put on the airs of a very serious man.

"I am very happy today to speak on behalf of our son here, Professor Amos Kinuthia, who wants the hand of your daughter, Doctor Wanjiru, in marriage. He has just come from his studies in America and thus it will be a marriage between two intellectual souls," said Muhuri.

It was a struggle to keep myself from bursting into laughter. This was because Kinuthia was not a professor at all, nor had he just come back from the US. Muhuri was lying through his teeth, and Kinuthia and Wanjiru kept straight faces, nodding as if this was the gospel truth. I am not really sure but I think Kinuthia was in fact a Form Four graduate. As it happened, in the end the proceedings were successful and Kinuthia married Wanjiru, but up to now many of Kinuthia's friends, including myself, call him "Professor".

But that was the style of marriage negotiations of the past. Both sides had to use tactics to secure either a good dowry for the bride's family, or to limit the expenditure, in the case of the groom's family. These negotiations were often very interesting and entertaining, and it is refreshing to see many people still uphold these traditions today.

The three of us worked well together and the shops showed good profits. Because of our success, I decided to start a third shop at a place called Raini[34] in Kiambaa. I asked my wife to manage the shop. I knew she was very skilful in business and was highly experienced. Of course I could not sit back and do nothing while my wife was working and the money was flowing in. A short while later, in 1953, I opened a charcoal business in Kiambu. This was not a step backwards, but I realized there was a demand for the commodity and decided to once again take up this enterprise.

---

34 Raini is a Kikuyu version of 'line'. It was called Raini because the demarcation line between the white settler farms and the native reserve passed through the area. My bar in Raini still exists, but I have now leased it out.

Things were going well for us, and I decided it was time to move on to something more challenging. Peter Kamau and I decided it was time to make an attempt at a commercial enterprise in Nairobi where most big businesses were situated. We decided that we were not going to open the usual general shop. This time we wanted to try our hands at running a wholesale business. Opening a wholesale shop might not seem very impressive today but it is important to keep in mind that there were only two other wholesale shops operated by Africans in Nairobi at the time. Most African traders did not even know that they could operate wholesale shops. They thought such enterprises were the preserve of the Indians and in their ignorance, many of them stuck to their small retail outlets despite having sufficient capital to invest in wholesale businesses.

This time Kamau and I joined with two brothers, Waihumbu and Kang'ethe Murihia from Loitokitok. When we opened our shop on Grogan Road (today's Kirinyaga Road) there were, as mentioned earlier, only two similar shops owned by Africans. One of these belonged to George Njau Mwagiru and his two partners, while the other belonged to Gikang'a Kuria.

I named this shop 'Nararashi Produce Store', a somewhat Asian-sounding name for a very good reason. Whereas there was no law forbidding Africans from owning big businesses, the higher classes of Europeans and Indians nevertheless frowned upon the trend. I suspect there was an element of protection against African competition. All over Kenya, big businesses were the preserve of Indians and this held for Grogan Road as well. Therefore I decided it would be prudent to give my business a name that seemed to be Indian. In actual fact Nararashi is the name of a certain acacia tree that grows in Maasailand. I was quite fond of the name and retained it even after Independence.

The business grew quickly since many African customers preferred to purchase their supplies from fellow Africans rather than Europeans or Asians. We had all kinds of goods in stock, ranging from cereals to sugar to household goods. I was the shop manager, while my colleagues travelled the country purchasing maize, beans, *njahi* (black beans), sugar and other commodities, from farmers. We opened an account with the National Bank of India (later the Kenya Commercial Bank) shortly thereafter and its profile grew as the shop's profits grew.

Such accomplishments were not easy to achieve during the State of Emergency. Movement was restricted, and not only were our own travels limited, but so were those of many potential customers. One can assume that the shop would have made a great deal more money had we been able to operate under more favourable circumstances. My partners and I managed to avoid regular swoops by the colonial government for quite some time, but our luck was bound to run out sooner or later.

One day Peter Kamau went missing for the whole day. I was not especially worried, but when Kamau did not turn up or send any sort of message the following day, I sensed that something was wrong. I phoned Kamau's cousin, Kuria, and we combined forces to conduct a search but he was nowhere to be seen. Later, we heard that Peter had been arrested and sent to Lang'ata Mau Mau screening centre. The majority of people picked up in this manner ended up in detention, so Kuria and I had little hope of seeing Kamau in the near future. However, my remaining partners and I tried to continue our business as best we could despite the fact that the threat of arrest or detention was imminent.

Around that time, at the end of 1953, I bought my first car, a pickup manufactured by the British Motor Corporation. I used the pickup for general transport duties, and I hired a driver to run it. The driver, Kimani 'Kibiru' Kameero, was my childhood friend from Kiambaa who had taught me how to ride a bicycle when I was just a boy. Kibiru was a diehard Mau Mau member and when he was not working for me, the vehicle was used to ferry Mau Mau adherents to diverse places for various clandestine missions.

In some cases, our pickup was used to ferry guns and other arms. The guns would be hidden under an assortment of commodities which were supposedly being transported to other locations, but after the weapons were delivered the goods would find their way back into our shop.

I knew that the arms had been stolen from European homes or from police stations. It was a most risky business but it had to be done. The Mau Mau soldiers who operated around Nairobi seemed to have great respect for this contribution because, at the time, there were very few Africans with vehicles and hardly any of these were willing to cooperate with the Mau Mau. For this reason I was protected by the Mau Mau and was viewed as a vital and important supporter. African traders, especially the Kikuyu working in Nairobi and its environs, were expected to contribute to the struggle for liberation, and any trader who was foolhardy enough to collaborate with the Europeans could expect nothing but retribution from the Mau Mau, in the form of looting, arson and even death.

On the same day that we realised that Kamau had been detained, disaster struck and it was the Mau Mau who came to my rescue. After a long day working in the shop, I had retired to a back room behind the store. I had guests with me, namely Kuria, Kamau's cousin, and

Gakuya Muthongo, a business associate from Murang'a, and they all took advantage of sleeping there overnight. Our bedding was nothing fancy, merely used sacks piled on the floor for mattresses and some blankets to cover ourselves.

Just before I retired for the night, I counted the day's takings, which came to 12,500 shillings. I wrote up a deposit voucher so that I would take the money to the National Bank of India on Government Road (now Moi Avenue) branch which stood in the building which now houses the Kenya National Archives. I put the deposit slip and the money in a little bag and hid it under the sacks which served as my pillow.

The following morning at around 5 am, I woke up as usual to open the shop. I had a few chores to clear up and then I expected to head for the bank to deposit the money. But when I pulled the bag out from under my pillow, I found that it was much lighter than it had been the night before. Anxiously I counted the money and found out that 6,000 shillings was missing. And strangely enough Kuria, Kamau's cousin, was missing as well. Gakuya was still snoring away and I woke him in a panic. I explained that I had 12,500 shillings the night before and now half of it was missing. Gakuya, barely awake, said he had no idea what could have happened to it. He did not even know there was any money in the building.

Both of us suspected Kuria. Gakuya suggested we go to the police at once and report the matter. Perhaps Kuria would be found and the money recovered. But I objected because I was apprehensive. I explained that Kuria was a Mau Mau member and if the police captured him, they would most likely take him to detention. Even worse, the police might torture him and force him to reveal Mau Mau secrets, and that would be a disaster for the Nairobi Mau Mau cell. In any case, Mau Mau members had agreed to deal with reprobates within their ranks in their own way, without involving the colonial authorities. The solution, I explained to Gakuya, was to inform the Mau Mau operatives and they would surely be able to trace Kuria and deal with him.

I sent Gakuya to the Mau Mau cell in Kamukunji and four operatives promptly turned up at my shop to get the full details and then set off to apprehend Kuria. They did not even ask me for money to conduct the search because the Mau Mau had a contingency fund to deal with such matters.

One of them was aware that Kuria had been seen that same morning in Dagoretti, so the four took a taxi and headed there. Through various informants they finally found Kuria sleeping blissfully in a house in

Dagoretti, and when they woke him, they forced him into the taxi. They then all drove back to my shop. When they arrived they asked him to hand over the money he had stolen from me but he said he did not know what they were talking about. He had no knowledge of any missing funds, he declared. The four Mau Mau wasted no time. One of them walked out of the shop and returned a minute later with a rope.

"If you do not tell us where the money is, comrade, we are hanging you here, right now," he threatened Kuria. "We are trying to protect our country and we cannot entertain thieves among our ranks." He knotted the rope, made a noose and put it around Kuria's neck.

I was watching the proceedings, but when they put the rope around Kuria's neck I protested and said I would rather lose the money than have Kuria killed, but I was told to keep out of the matter. The Mau Mau tightened the noose around Kuria's neck, and he immediately confessed. He told them he would take them where he had hidden the money.

As I learned later, they got into the taxi once again and, under Kuria's directions, drove to Pumwani estate. Kuria pointed out a house and they all went up to knock on the door. It was opened by a woman who did not, by any standards of the day, look very decent. The Mau Mau asked the woman for the money she had been given that morning, and when she hesitated, she was slapped. In terror, she immediately gave them the cash. However some was missing and Kuria revealed that the balance was in Dagoretti where they had found him that morning.

They therefore drove back to Dagoretti. Kuria retrieved the last bit of the funds and they once more returned to my shop. I counted the money and found that sixty shillings was still missing but Kuria fearfully explained that he had used it to hire a taxi. The four Mau Mau declared that I should bear the loss myself, since, in their opinion, I had been careless with the cash in the first place. They said I should have known better than to put money under my pillow and that I would be better advised to put it in a safer place. Before they left they gave Kuria a severe warning and then disappeared as sniffly as they had arrived. Kuria, greatly embarrassed and ashamed, left as well. I heard later that he moved back to the rural areas.

This was the way the Mau Mau in Nairobi operated. They did not tolerate nonsensical distractions from any of their own members and discipline was meted out on the spot when it was required.

One day another of my friends was 'arrested' by the Mau Mau in Nairobi. This was Muiruri Laban, my former associate in the timber business in Elburgon. The industrious Muiruri had, on escaping Elburgon, started a charcoal business and a general store in his native Githunguri. The business was doing well, and he had even purchased a lorry which was used to transport charcoal to Nairobi. At that time it was difficult, almost impossible, for an African to obtain a pass from the colonial authorities.

The Mau Mau in Nairobi looked at Muiruri's situation critically and began to ask themselves how he had managed to obtain a pass and then commute every day. They concluded that Muiruri must be collaborating with the Europeans and after some deliberation decided that he should be killed. 'Death to all collaborators' was one of the primary mottos of the Mau Mau.

So it happened that one day they got hold of Muiruri. They took him to one of their hideouts at the back of a retail shop along Grogan Road. Once at the shop, which belonged to a Mau Mau, Duncan Maina, they intended to question him about his betrayal and subsequently execute him. One of the investigators who was the Mau Mau secretary in the Rift Valley, Jonathan Kamau, was aware that Muiruri was a friend of mine, so Kamau came straightaway to see me and informed me that Muiruri was being questioned and would soon be dead. In alarm, I sent my driver and Kamau back to the hideout in my vehicle to plead with the others to wait until I got there.

Before I even closed my shop, two of the interrogators and Kamau returned in my vehicle and tried to convince me that Muiruri was a collaborator. I insisted that Muiruri supported the Mau Mau effort but they did not want to listen.

"Njenga," one of them said, almost in tears, "Look at this pass! How can a good man manage to get a pass from a European DO? It's just not possible! A white DO would never give this to a good man! Maybe he has become a traitor!"

I continued trying to persuade them. I informed them that Muiruri and I had taken the Mau Mau oath together, in Elburgon, and that both of us were fully committed members of the *njamba cia ita* (warrior fraternity). I stated that I, myself, was the person who had helped Muiruri acquire a transport licence from the DO in Kiambu, a white man named Mathews, who was an acquaintance of mine. I further declared that Muiruri was one the staunchest supporters of the freedom struggle in Githunguri and that he had contributed considerable resources for the cause. I managed to convince the Mau Mau and thereafter the last words the Mau Mau told me was "*Kawīra gathiĩ na mbere*". (Continue with the good work.) Muiruri was set free and when we met shortly thereafter, both of us were in shock.

All this time, meanwhile, I had been told that the home guards at Kiambaa intended to implicate me in any way possible and have me jailed. They noted my prosperity with suspicion.

I was doing well at the time. I was a partner in two shops in Kiambu and in a larger store in Nairobi. The shop in Raini was doing very well, too. However, jealous collaborators were not at all pleased with my success. This envious faction was led by a turncoat called Mwathi Njucu who worked for the colonial authorities in Kiambaa. Mwathi was an inept bully who had been entrusted with the unenviable task of hounding his countrymen, and was a loathed individual. But that was no problem for him. Like most other home guards and headmen, he received considerable benefits from his disgraceful job.

I was perpetually worried and anxious about being arrested and detained. Nearly all of my business associates, partners and friends were already locked up in detention camps in far flung places like Hola, MacKinnon Road, Manyani, Mwea and other locations. I was aware that many of my contemporaries in Kiambaa had become collaborators and that they were covetous and resentful of my success, but I soldiered on. I was resigned to the fact that I would be arrested sooner or later, but this did not make me stop my business activities.

My partner Kamau and I owned a shop in Kiambaa. Kamau's wife was managing the shop while Kamau was in detention. My wife Wariara was managing our shop in Raini but she would come on market days on Tuesdays and Fridays to buy stock for the shops and would drop in to visit Kamau's wife. She would also come into the shop to assist. One day two strangers entered the shop in Kiambaa while Wariara was visiting. Neither of the women realised that the strangers were plain-clothes policemen. They made a show of comparing the cereals that were each sack, dipping their hands into the sacks and examining the contents the way choosy customers do. They left without buying anything, but Wariara observed that there was something disturbingly unique about them. They were too well dressed, and they did not behave like her usual customers. They had gone about examining the maize and beans in a very business-like manner. Anyway, the women soon forgot about them and went on with their usual business around the shop.

The following morning, a police vehicle drove up and Mwathi Njucu, the chief home guard, emerged together with an Inspector of Police and five African policemen. The police went directly to the sacks containing cereals and started an examination of their contents. One of the officers dug something out of the bag of maize and held it up for all of us in the shop to see. He was holding out three bullets, which he had just 'discovered' in the sack.

I was amazed and expected to be arrested immediately but surprisingly I was merely given a reprimand. The white Police Inspector informed me that they would be watching me carefully and warned me that I was facing a very long stretch in jail. As they left, we remained in the shop, shocked by the developments. Wariara and Peter's wife told me about the two strangers who had been in the shop the previous day and their strange behaviour. It was obvious that these men had planted the bullets. There was nothing to do but wait, so we eventually went about our business, although in an anxious and uneasy frame of mind.

About a week later, the police returned and took me to Kiambu Police Station. The inspector informed me that I was lucky because the bullets had been examined by a forensic expert and declared to have come from the police armoury. The inspector, whose name was Davis, was well aware that I could not have got into the armoury. So, he asked me, how had the bullets made their way into the cereals in my shop? I explained about the two mysterious men who had been in the shop the day before the 'discovery' of the bullets. It was obvious that the bullets had been planted by someone out to incriminate me, I explained, and I told him that my wife could identify the strangers if she saw them again. With no alternative, the officer released me and I returned to my shop, sighing with relief.

Not long thereafter however, I once more found myself the object of police scrutiny. A few weeks later, a little after two in the morning, a government lorry stopped on the street and I was summoned to come outside. I knew I was in trouble when I saw the lorry. I recognised it as the one used by soldiers to conduct their night swoops in search of Mau Mau and their sympathizers. In addition, I saw my old nemesis, Mwathi Njucu, between the policemen, with the smirk of triumph on his face. As I was bundled into the lorry, Mwathi sneered.

"I know about the store in Ndumberi, Njenga. I will make sure all your businesses are closed down and left in ruins!" he exclaimed.

This was in May 1954, during Operation Anvil, which was a swoop on all suspected Mau Mau adherents and sympathisers. On my part I just wondered how I had inspired so much malice in Mwathi.

The lorry drove away with me and many other captives in it, and Wariara was left behind sobbing and clutching our little daughter.

We drove towards my Ndumberi shop which was managed by Stephen Nduru. His assistant was a young boy called Kiarie Gichua. When we got there, the police jumped out, searched the shop and arrested Nduru who was ordered to join me in the lorry. As we were taken away again, I yelled back to Kiarie to look after things for us.

And as the lorry drove off I looked at Mwathi and shook my head bitterly. "Now you have all my properties, Mwathi. You have won!" I told him.

We were taken to Kiambu police station, which had holding cells for Mau Mau suspects from the area before they were subsequently ferried to screening camps. My old friend, Stephen Nduru and I discussed the irony of our escape from Elburgon, only to be arrested together in Kiambu. It seemed that our destiny on the Mau Mau issue was linked by providence.

Around three in the morning another friend of mine was brought in together with more suspects. Joseph Kiarie Mbugua, a businessman, had no fear. He was outspoken as usual. I heard him talking.

"You cannot arrest James and me!" he said. At that time he called me by my baptismal name. He faced the arresting officers and exclaimed, "Njenga is the one who feeds our families. Keep all of us here, but let him out to continue with his business!" he shouted.

I told him to shut up. When I spoke at his funeral recently, I very fondly remembered this incident and the way he bravely stood up for me.

We slept at the station, very poorly of course, and the following day our group was bundled into the lorry and taken to Lang'ata screening camp.

I was not necessarily worried about myself or my safety. What worried me excessively was the fate of my young family and the future of my businesses. All my partners had been arrested and were detained in various parts of the country. Although my wife Wariara and my daughter were financially secure, I was worried about their safety. I well knew what happened to the property of those who were judged to be Mau Mau. It was all confiscated by the colonial authorities on the basis that it had been acquired illegally, or would be used to further the Mau Mau cause.

Once in Lang'ata, we were body-searched before being locked up in a general pen for screening. After the screening we would then be secured in particular pens depending on the results of the 'investigation'. Aware that all my personal effects would be taken away, I cast about for some means of protecting the cash and the cheque book I had in my pocket. If these were confiscated, I realized it would be impossible for me to ensure my own safety, my relative comfort and even my survival.

Then I noticed that a white policeman, part of the search team, was admiring my neck scarf. It was a lovely green colour with white polka dots—I had paid sixteen shillings for it, which was a considerable sum in those days. I am not sure, but I believe it was made of silk. No other opportunity had presented itself, and I tried my luck.

"Do you like it?" I asked the white officer in English, indicating my scarf.

"Sure," said the policeman. "Where can I buy one?"

"This kind is very rare," I lied. "But then, why don't you take mine. You can have it. You look like a good man and anyway, even if I keep it, the other prisoners will probably steal it."

I gave the policeman the scarf and he in turn made sure the *askaris* let me keep my money and cheque book. The black officers glowered at me, but they would not dare harass a prisoner who was speaking to *Bwana* in English and exchanging gifts with him. And so I started a whole year of detention, without trial, naturally.

Lang'ata was the holding camp for detainees from Nairobi and its environs. Here the suspects would be questioned, screened and divided into various categories according to the level of their supposed guilt or lack of it. The European authorities would bring in colonial collaborators from various areas and they would identify and point out the hardcore Mau Mau members. These collaborators were the most despised individuals. They were referred to as *tūkūnia* (gunny bags or sacks) as they would hide their identities by covering their heads and bodies with hessian sacks that had eye slits to see through. The reason they concealed themselves, of course, was that if their identities were discovered by the Mau Mau, a sure and painful death would follow for their betrayal.

The suspected Mau Mau would line up and the *tūkūnia* would scrutinize them, pointing out the Mau Mau members who were then immediately isolated from the rest of the group. The prisoners' classification of status would additionally be based on the testimonies of the *tūkūnia*, who would explain the 'crimes' of each suspect and reveal their position in the Mau Mau hierarchy.

The most dangerous terrorists, as the colonial authorities classified them, were referred to as *makara* (charcoal) and isolated even further. Most of them were denounced as murderers and sometimes hanged, usually at Kamiti Maximum Prison. The *makara* who escaped hanging were condemned to such harsh detention camps as Manda Island in the Indian Ocean, Kapenguria and various others in the scorching Northern Frontier District. Those who were identified by the *tūkūnia* as hardcore were classified as *grey* and were detained in camps with very harsh conditions, such as Lamu Island and Mackinnon Road. The conditions were difficult and were similar to high security prisons.

Those who were deemed guilty, either by association or as Mau Mau sympathizers, but not necessarily active in the freedom struggle, were referred to as *white* in the screening camps. They were then sent to detention camps in which conditions were not quite as severe, such as Kangubiri in Nyeri and Mwea. These prisoners would usually be detained for short periods before being released. Those who were judged to be absolutely innocent were set free, though this was very rare. Each category was put into isolated pens (*ciugũ*) awaiting transportation to whichever camp they would be sent to.

Luckily I escaped being placed in the ill-fated *makara* group by what I attribute to the grace of God, sheer luck and some ingenious disguise on my part during the screening exercise. As was the procedure, a *gakũnia* came round with a sack over his head to point out those who were 'notorious' Mau Mau. He started with a neighbouring pen and I noticed the collaborator point out David Kibe Waweru, who had a second-hand goods shop which was next to my business along Grogan Road. Waweru was a friend of mine and I feared that if the informer, whoever he was, knew Waweru, then he might well know me and might point me out, too, which would have been equivalent to condemnation.

I prayed hard and came up with an idea. I quickly exchanged my clothes with an old man from Lari who was dressed in a ragged overcoat and then roughed up my beard, which had grown out since my arrest. I also grimaced and squinted. When the *gakũnia* came to the next pen, the prisoners were lined up and the informer began to pick out his victims. When he looked at me, he paused for such a long time that I could feel my heart beating violently and my blood rushing frantically in my veins. The *gakũnia* passed me, then, after a few steps, he turned and came back to me. This is it, I thought with dismay, fearing the worst. However, the *gakũnia* shook his head after looking at my face for some time and proceeded down the line.

I wish I had the foresight to try to see what happened to the old man who gave me his coat, but I never saw him again.

I was thus placed in the area of *grey* prisoners who were destined to be held for long periods in the toughest detention camps. If I did not think fast, I realised I would soon be in a lorry on my way to a distant detention camp for an indefinite incarceration. This would place me still further away from my family and businesses.

Of course, what I did not realise at the time, was that my prime business, the wholesale shop on Grogan Road, had already been raided by the authorities and all the merchandise confiscated as required by the law. All known property of Mau Mau suspects was declared property of the Crown.

I decided I would pretend to be sick.

When a prisoner became ill at Lang'ata camp, one other prisoner would carry him to the gate of the compound. They would then wait for the police lorry to come round in one of its many inspection trips. The sick person would be laid on the ground with a blanket while the prisoner who had brought him would squat beside him and put his hands on his head. (This was the gesture of submission which all prisoners had to make while roll-call was taken.)

When I got 'sick', I was taken to the gate by a colleague and I lay there, prostrate, until the prison lorry came. I can remember the prisoner who brought me to the gate was almost crying, saying, *"Aee! Anakufa! Anakufa"* (He's dying! He's dying!)

When the authorities came round, the colleague explained that I had collapsed with an unknown ailment. I was then thrown into the truck like a sack of potatoes and taken to the prison dispensary, where I was admitted.

I, in the guise of being a 'patient', was in a serious condition, but the doctors could not diagnose my illness. My temperature was taken and I was given antibiotics while they kept me in bed for observation.

Luckily for me, most of the nurses and paramedics were fellow detainees. I confided in them, admitting that I was not sick at all, and they colluded in my deception. They would take my temperature and inflate it on the records so that when the white doctors checked my records they would conclude that I was quite ill. Two particular medics who helped me carry out my fraud were Gachamba, a man from Murang'a, and James Njogu from Dagoretti, whom I remember Njogu very fondly. He was a tall lanky young man with a brown complexion. I would occasionally give these medics gifts, such as money for soda and the like, and they seemed to appreciate it a lot.

Njogu was among the first Africans to be trained as pharmacists. He now has a number of chemist shops in Nairobi and we still meet. He is a close friend and any time we get together I never forget to treat him to as many double whiskeys as he can take as he was the one who saved my life.

I was admitted, supposedly, for heart problems, and, according to the falsified records, the problems were proving quite difficult to control. When the white doctors came around I would shake, convulse and hallucinate like a dying man, and my act convinced even the most suspicious.

While I was in the dispensary 'dying', my fellow detainees were taken to Manyani detention camp. It seemed I had escaped that fate, but my relief did not last for long, for soon I contracted typhoid, a disease that almost killed me. On occasions I was on the brink of death and I would not have survived if it had not been for the tender care of Njogu, Gachamba and other fellow black medics.

I remember once, when I was half conscious, I overheard Gachamba whispering to another medic about me, "This one is gone."

I must have been extraordinarily weak.

I attribute the disease to divine intervention. God had finally given me what I had asked for, when I pretended to be ill in order to be admitted to the hospital. I prayed for a disease and that is exactly what He gave me. This is something I will never ever do again!

In life there are some things that defy logic and some mysteries that are beyond our power to explain or understand. My respect and fear of God has encouraged me to trust in His power, to always do good, and to avoid doing wrong. This way, I believe, blessings will always abound.

After my bout of typhoid cleared up, I was taken back to the holding pens. I was positively tired of hospital beds and by then it had been about six months since my arrest. At night I would lie in my tent and listen to or join in with other prisoners in singing Mau Mau songs in the dark, when the guards in their watchtowers could not identify the singers.

I remember the guards would take stones up into the watchtowers and if a prisoner ventured out of his tent at night, they would hurl the stones at him from above, sometimes with fatal results.

Although the living conditions in the camp were terribly bad and the fate awaiting us was even more horrifying, very few of the Mau Mau prisoners had their defiant spirit crushed. They did not betray their colleagues in order to be released, and those who became informers were to live forever with the invisible label of traitor. Most accepted whatever fate had in store for them and hardly any of them cooperated with the ruling authorities.

I remember one particular prisoner from Meru for his cheek. There was a white Catholic Priest from Machakos who would come occasionally to pray for the prisoners. The priest was very kind and we thanked him for coming all that way to pray for us. He was very courageous, and afterwards he would ask if there were any basic necessities we required. If so, he would organize the supply with the authorities. This Meru prisoner looked the clergyman in the eye and told him yes, there was one thing we were missing. Could the chaplain please organize to supply us prisoners with four *debes* (casks) of tobacco? The chaplain was outraged and stormed off.

October 20 in 1954, is one day of my detention experience that I remember vividly. On that day, in order to mark the arrest of Jomo Kenyatta and his colleagues two years earlier, all the prisoners decided to boycott any food that was served on plates. We were thus indicating that we were not reliant on the white man's cutlery or his ways, and so we ate our meal of beans from our hands. This defiance stymied the prison authorities to no end as there was no way they could enforce a particular manner of eating.

While in prison, I would write cheques when I required money. I had to hide my cheque book and move it from place to place, because we would be searched quite often. Then my friends among the guards would cash the cheques for me, and although I was not exactly comfortable, I was able to survive, and able to purchase small favours like meat and bread. I remember one unscrupulous guard who would cash my cheques. If I gave him a cheque of forty shillings, he would cash it and bring me twenty shillings only. He would claim that the other twenty had been deducted by the authorities, since I was a Mau Mau suspect. To cap it all, he also demanded five shillings for his 'labour' and thus out of forty I would be left with only fifteen shillings. I knew he was exploiting the situation, but I had no alternative.

Thus, basically, I missed only my freedom. At least I was still able to send letters to Wariara, who continued carrying on with our business in the Kiambaa shop. As they say, money is not everything, but it helps to have it, especially under such dire circumstances.

Every now and then, new prisoners would be brought into the camp while those who had stayed the longest were transferred to other detention camps. It was only later that I got to know that the more stubborn a prisoner was, the longer he was kept in prison, or even taken to distant detention camps. On the other hand, if a prisoner behaved in a mild and cooperative manner, things were not so bad and he could find his way out of the 'pipeline' faster. After about a year, around March or April of 1955, I was set free. I consider myself lucky. Some of my colleagues were to remain in detention for five years or more.

The State of Emergency was as its height when I came out of prison. Young people, especially men, were an endangered species in Kikuyu land and I knew I would have to be extraordinarily careful. Many ex-detainees were re-arrested and I had to avoid this fate. I realised the precarious position I was in a few days after my release when a home guard summoned me and took me to Karuri Market. Here, I was shown the bodies of three young men and a woman who had been shot dead. I was told to take care lest I ended up like them. Such grotesque display of corpses was a tactic the authorities used as an example of what would happen if people became Mau Mau. Why the home guard had chosen to show me this grisly example I do not know, but I clearly understood that they had a careful eye on me.

I understood that, as with everything else in life, jealousy and evil were constantly present in the relationships between the homeguards, prison warders, the police, the chiefs, the people and the detainees and ex-detainees.

Once out of prison, I found out that most of my businesses had been ruined. The shop on Grogan Road had been raided by the authorities long ago and closed. Those in Kiambu and Ndumberi had also closed down since all my partners had been detained as well. Only the shop in Kiambaa that was managed by Wariara had prospered. However, I was not overly worried about my financial state. My wife was an amazing and thrifty woman who had saved a considerable amount of money while I was in prison, so we had sufficient funds in the bank. It was time, I knew, to start all over again. In any case, my one year of detention was nothing compared to the seven years sentence that some of my friends had to serve.

At the time I was released, the colonial authorities were in the process of creating forced villages. This was the practice of coercing the Gikuyu, Aembu and Ameru to settle in cramped settlements in order to control them more easily. Such villages were surrounded by deep moat-like trenches with sharpened stakes at the bottom so that any person trying to enter or leave the village at night would be impaled. These barricaded settlements were under a dusk-to-dawn curfew and the circumstances were aimed at controlling the flow of food supplies and arms to the Mau Mau and their supporters.

Here I found another business opportunity. Contrary to the common trend, I asked the authorities to allocate me a market business plot, instead of one purely for a residence. Once I was granted a commercial plot I built a shop constructed of wood and *mabati* (corrugated iron sheets) with the aim of selling hardware. I converted the back of the shop into living quarters. Most other occupants of the village in Banana Hill were constructing houses, and luckily I was quite successful, selling them nails and other construction materials. After a short while, I leased a restaurant from Silas Mwaura in Banana Hill. There were many casual workers in the area and they ate at my restaurant. It became quite popular with them.

It was around this time that I discovered that Africans were now able to acquire licenses to sell liquor. Apparently the authorities were not keen on publicising this change in the liquor licensing laws. Previously, no African was allowed to sell or drink bottled liquor and those who did have outlets, ran them as off-licenses. In my uncle Gatenjwa's shop, for example, customers would come, buy beer, and take it away. Alternatively, they would drink in a back room somewhere behind the shop. This law had been repealed and Africans were now allowed to own real bars, but not many had taken advantage of the opportunity.

I should make it clear that there were severe consequences to drinking bottled beer and other liquors before this period.

One of my uncles, Paul Mwobi, was once caught with empty bottles in his bedroom. He believes that someone must have informed the police that he drank bottled beer.

One day, a white police officer came in and ordered his African *askaris* to search the house. After rummaging around they found four empty bottles under my uncle's bed and he was arrested.

When Mwobi was taken to court and charged with the offence, he admitted that the bottles were indeed found in his house but he denied that they had contained beer. The arresting officer asked the judge to take a sniff of the bottles, and when he did so, he confirmed that they indeed smelled of alcohol.

However, Mwobi said the bottles had been left by some women who were on their way to work on a farm. They had left the bottles in his keeping, as they usually did, so that they could put kerosene in them and carry them home in the evening.

The judge did not find this explanation satisfactory and in the end Mwobi was sentenced to serve three months imprisonment or pay a fine of one hundred shillings. The relatives quickly contributed money, my uncle paid the fine and was freed. However the fact is that my uncle Mwobi freely admits that he used to sell contraband beer and sugar.

As a matter of fact, as of that time, only two Africans had opened bars in Nairobi town. These were Muchohi Gikonyo who owned a bar called Africa Corner, and Waiganjo Mukangu, father to the future Nairobi Provincial Commissioner, Fred Waiganjo, who owned Kimwangu Bar. However, there were no bars run by Africans in the rural areas, and I decided I may as well be the first and applied for a license.

Chief Karuga Koinange, son of Senior Chief Koinange, had a building in Raini, and when I decided to start a bar in 1957, I asked him if he could let me lease the premises. I told him that if he was interested we could become partners in running the bar. One might argue that our friendship and business relationships had side benefits. As a Chief, Koinange had clout with the authorities and the *Wazungu* respected him. On my side, I had financial support and wide business experience, all important ingredients for prospective investors.

Even before I did so, the colonial authorities in Kiambu scoffed at the idea of Africans running bars due to 'security' concerns. Many whites believed that Africans could not handle alcohol and that their drinking should be monitored and controlled.

In those days the liquor licensing court for Central Province was located in Thika. Central Province, by the way, included today's Embu and Meru regions. At any rate, the court sat once a year, and had not yet dealt with bar applications from an African. Previously they had only given permission for 'off license' premises. I was aware of the European attitude towards Africans' supposed drinking habits and I was also aware of their bias against native entrepreneurs. Therefore I hired the services of a radical Nairobi lawyer, Marvin Morgan, to represent me before the Licensing Board. The usual arguments of insecurity in a rural area were brought up, but Morgan was ready. He knew these arguments were based on racial prejudice and stereotyping.

Morgan stated that the business was owned by Chief Karuga Koinange and myself. Koinange had hundreds of Africans under his supervision and had been sufficiently able to lead them and ensure their good discipline, Morgan explained. And if this were so, how could the respected Chief fail to control a small crowd in a single room in a bar? Morgan's argument won the day and I guess I made history by being the first African granted a license to run a bar in a rural area. This impetus of getting the license was the start of my long and fruitful relationship with beer.

I was happy that my bar in Raini was a hit. Its novelty was the talk of the region. Most people had never imagined that an African could walk into a bar, sit and be served beer in a glass just like a white man, without being harassed or arrested by the colonial authorities. It was almost unbelievable that, instead of being forced to hide in some back room, we could now sit, discuss and generally enjoy ourselves.

At the drinking dens we previously patronised—popularly referred to as *masanduku* (boxes) because we generally sat on planks and boxes—we drank silently, or quietly murmuring among ourselves. We did not want to attract the attention of the police and our patronage was at our own risk. In Kiambu District, only two permits for selling take-away liquor had been granted prior to 1948. One of these shops belonged to my uncle in Karuri and the other to Charles Kigwi in Gatundu.

However my bar now attracted customers from as far away as Kikuyu and Limuru. People would come just to sit, drink beer and marvel at the liberated atmosphere. The employees of Bata Shoe Factory in Limuru, about twenty kilometres away, were some of my most loyal customers. The staff would come in a company vehicle every Saturday to enjoy their drinks in the bar.

A few weeks after the bar opened, however, the settlers in the area wrote to the Kiambu District Commissioner demanding its closure. The reason they gave was that *shamba* boys (gardeners), cooks and other farm workers were now drinking too much and failing in their duties. In one particular case, a cook got drunk and staggered home to his wife in the servants quarters. When his European boss came home later that night with some guests, he called the cook to make them a meal. The drunken cook told him off, declaring that he was not a woman to engage in such domestic chores. Even when the cook's wife pleaded with him to attend to his employer, she was threatened with dire consequences if she did not leave him alone.

"That little *Mzungu* thinks I am drunk on traditional *mūratina*. Tell him I was drinking whisky and brandy, too, just like he does!" he roared.

As a result a special court was arranged in Kiambu with DO1, J.S. Simmance, presiding. As the owner of the licensed bar where the cook had got drunk, I was party to the proceedings. Once again, I enlisted the legal services of Marvin Morgan. The court was informed by the settlers that my bar had become a nuisance and a threat to development, and that it should be closed. The DO, unknown to the settlers, was my friend through Chief Karuga Koinange. The DO agreed that I should close down my bar, but Morgan argued that I should be given another plot in Banana Hill, far from white settlers. Till then, he stated, I should be allowed to operate the Raini bar for at least a year till I could construct a new one.

So I continued to operate the Raini bar and started constructing a building at Banana Hill. I had just built the foundation when I abandoned the whole structure as my plans were overtaken by other events. The settlers were no longer as powerful, and they could see that Independence was on the horizon. An African DO had been posted to Kiambu and it seemed that Kenyatta was going to be released.

Simmance advised the settlers that they should wait and present their case the following year at the Thika Liquor Licensing Court. The farmers did so, but their appeal was turned down and I continued enjoying the profits brought about by my license.

Since the bar was performing so well, I decided to buy two farms measuring about eighteen acres in total. They were the first of many such investments in farms and farming that I was to make in later years.

The 1953 pickup, which I found safe after being released from detention, came in handy for the beer business since I could use it to transport beer for my bar from Nairobi to Raini. While all this was going on, I was still seeking more business challenges. If one does not continually move ahead, one can fall behind. So I was contracted by W.C. French Limited, a company which had been awarded a contract to construct sewers by the City Council of Nairobi in 1958. I agreed to ferry workers from Banana to Nairobi, so I sold my pickup for three thousand shillings which after adding to my savings, I bought a three-ton Ford 6 ex-army lorry thereby almost tripling the number of workers I could ferry. The workers would spend the day digging trenches and laying pipes, and W.C. French would then pay me as per the agreed terms. I would, in turn, pay the workers every week. In this way, I became one of the largest African employers in Kiambu and Banana. The drains we constructed went through Westlands (where Jacaranda Hotel is now), St. Francis, MP Shah Hospital and down to Kariokor.

I would estimate the amount of labour that each worker was to complete in a day and I expected each worker to finish that portion before he was paid. However, I did more than just supervising. In order to get a good estimate of the amount of work that could be done in a day, I also climbed down into the trenches to work alongside the labourers on my own portion. I think this created good morale and also saved me some money. Saving even a little is something I have always admired and acted on from a very young age. Regularly putting aside some funds gives one extra capital to expand when new opportunities come up.

Later W.C. French was contracted by the government to construct barriers to block the flow of Nyamindi River in Mwea, near Embu. This was to create what became the Mwea Irrigation Scheme. When they were awarded this contract, the company contacted me again, to supply them with extra labour and to transport sand from Sagana for the project. I therefore bought another lorry and went to work on the project. All this while I would travel back and forth to Banana to keep an eye on the bar, and neither business suffered. My staff may have pilfered a bit here and a bit there but in general I trusted them. Unscrupulous petty theft was not a habit of the time.

Throughout this time, I had kept in touch with Bryan Hobson, the *Mzungu* who had once been impressed by my mathematical knowledge during a dispute between my uncle and the accountant at East African Breweries. After that first meeting, the two of us occasionally met and while I was in the charcoal and timber business, I would bring bags of potatoes from Elburgon to Nairobi, as gifts for Hobson. I strongly believe in retaining old friends, not only for the sake of golden memories, but also because one never knows when one might require some assistance. Our first meeting, of course, had been while I was a school boy. Now I was a businessman with various interests while Hobson was a director of East African Breweries Limited (EABL).

One day Hobson sent Raymond Kuria Gathunguri, the senior-most African manager at EABL, to inform me that he wanted us to get together. When I arrived at his office Hobson informed me that he had a business proposal. The only Kiambu beer distributor, Charles Kigwi Gatheca, was in a financial crisis of some kind and was willing to take on a partner. Since I had the necessary resources and experience to engage in the business, Hobson asked me if I would be willing to become that partner. It seemed that Kigwi had a loan of two hundred thousand shillings with the Breweries and was unable to keep up with the payments. Hobson, being the humane person he was, did not want Kigwi's property auctioned. This was the reason he was looking for a partner for Kigwi, and he thought that I would fit the ticket perfectly.

I was uncertain and dithered over making the decision. I knew little about beer distribution, and my experience was limited to the beer supply for my bar. I told Hobson I was more at home in the construction industry. Hobson argued that whereas construction was seasonal, beer distribution was a guaranteed profit-maker all year round and it would just keep growing. I was finally convinced by this argument, in addition to the fact that I was acquainted with Kigwi, and so I agreed to meet the Breweries Chairman, Michael Blundell, to discuss the deal further. Blundell was one of the leaders of the white settlers and was a senior politician in his own right.

If any one person ever influenced my life and the direction and success of my businesses, it was Brian Hobson. While the majority of Europeans spent a lot of energy ensuring the enforcement of racial segregation, Hobson fraternized with friends of all races and was married to an African woman.

Chapter 5

The Founding of a Nation

O ver the years, I had acquired a considerable amount of property, and my own presence, or that of my wife, always seemed to be required for strict supervision of the enterprises. Managers had been employed to run the business but they never seemed to work as efficiently or honestly as they should have.

As a result, I went to my father-in-law, Wairiri, and informed him of our dilemma. He suggested that the best alternative would be to marry a second wife. After all, he himself had three wives and my own father had three. For wealthy men this was the solution to such problems. They would marry additional wives to assist in business and management of property, and naturally for prestige, too.

Initially Wariara was not very supportive of this decision. However after I married Njeri, she eventually warmed up to the idea. It may sound ridiculous in modern times, but polygamy was the order of the day in Kikuyuland, especially for those endowed with property.

While Wariara and I were busy managing our large shop in the Indian Bazaar, my new wife, Njeri, continued running the older shop we had rented in the Kenya African Teachers Union (Kenyatu) building. By this time we had closed our shop at Raini. Our beer depot was also at Kenyatu for a while but when I got new premises in the Indian Bazaar, I transferred it there. It was a difficult period and political temperatures were at boiling levels. It was apparent to all of us that Independence would be coming soon and, although the Mau Mau rebellion had all but been quelled, other political activists consisting of both the educated and uneducated classes were openly campaigning for Independence. The whole country was buzzing with talk of impending freedom.

Dedan Kimathi, the Mau Mau commander, had been hanged in Kamiti Maximum Prison on 18 February 1957. Kenyatta and the rest of the Kapenguria Six were still languishing in jail, but rumours were rife that they would soon be released. More Africans, in addition to Eliud Mathu, had already been appointed to the country's Legislative Council (LEGCO) and it was obvious that Africans were being given a larger chance to chart the destiny of their country. Excitement and anticipation was rapidly spreading all over the country. In 1946, Mathu had been joined by B.A. Ohanga and by 1952 the number of African representatives had risen to six. In 1957 elections were held in the eight constituencies (Provinces) and Africans, for the first time, chose their own representatives to the LEGCO.[35] We were moving forward.

The opportunities, challenges and possibilities that would come with Independence were infinite and, though undefined, hope was in the air. The change of administration and new freedom would change the lives of the people, and many of us knew it could only be for the better. However, there was a great deal of confusion in African political circles. Despite the loose cohesion of nationalists from all tribes who were agitating for Independence, the glue to stick them together was missing. The body politic was composed of Africans, who, while united in the common goal of freedom, were actually working at cross-purposes.

The party that was predominant in the late 1950s was the Kenya African Union (KAU), which had been founded in 1944 with James Gichuru as president. Harry Thuku, a member, was persuaded by the colonial governor to change the name to Kenya African Study Union, something that would be regarded as less threatening. This annoyed some radical members of the party and Thuku was forced to resign. It reverted back to KAU in 1946. It was banned by the colonial authorities from June 1953 up to 1955, a period during which there were no political parties in Kenya. James Gichuru was President of the party, a post he held until he relinquished it to Kenyatta on 1 June 1947.

On 27 March 1960, James Gichuru and Oginga Odinga, Chairman and Vice Chairman of KAU respectively, called for the formation of a more formidable and nationalistic political party. I was present during a meeting at Kirigiti Stadium in Kiambu when the idea of the new party, the Kenya African National Union (KANU) was proposed, and the people accepted it. It was launched in May 1960.

Shortly after the formation of KANU was agreed upon, a party constitution was drawn up. The educated elite in African Corner Bar

---

35 The eight who were elected were as follows: Ronald Ngala (Coast), James Muimi (Ukambani), Bernard Mate (Central), Tom Mboya (Nairobi), Daniel arap Moi (Rift Valley), Oginga Odinga (North Nyanza), Lawrence Oguda (South Nyanza), Masinde Muliro (Western).

huddled around a table for many evenings, drafting the constitution. There was Joseph Gatuguta, a lawyer who had just come from India, Mwai Kibaki, a former Makerere lecturer, Tom Mboya and a host of others. I was often there with them and I recall that someone, it may have been Mwai Kibaki, brought a copy of the draft of Uganda's Congress Party Constitution to examine.

I recall that when KANU was formed, Gichuru was the President, Tom Mboya was made Secretary General, Ngala was made the Treasurer, and Moi was the Deputy Treasurer. Whites were not comfortable with KANU so they encouraged Ngala and Moi to create the Kenya African Democratic Union, KADU,[36] their own party. As a result Moi, Ngala, Muliro and a few others resigned.

There was the usual suspicions among the politicians, especially between the two political parties that had emerged. The Kikuyu and other large communities dominated KANU's leadership, while KADU was led by personalities from the smaller Rift Valley communities, the Kipsigis, Tugen, Nandi, Marakwet, Elgeyo and others going under the collective name of Kalenjin,[37] and the Miji Kenda at the Coast. Political activism was at an all time high all over the country, but there was considerable uncertainty about where Independence, when it came, would leave the various tribes and their leaders. In particular, there was always the question of which tribes would benefit most.

Naturally all political parties tend to seek the support of the wealthy because they realise that they need resources for mobilization and administration of their campaigns. This is why, the world over, many governments are swayed, not so much by their individual leaders, but by lobbies and special interest groups. So, since I had considerable resources at the time, I was bound to catch the eye of African politicians.

I was generally known to be an independent-minded person and due to my business contacts, I had the opportunity to come to know, befriend and form acquaintances with some of the most prominent personalities of the day. These were the persons with the highest positions in the colonial government and also in the political arena. Most of them were well educated and knew that they would be pivotal in the African government which lay ahead. They were the ones who had taken the mantle during

36 KADU was formed by leaders of minority groups such as the Kalenjin, the people of North Eastern and Coast regions. KADU hoped to avoid Kikuyu and Luo dominance in independent Kenya by pressing for a more federal constitution. Its leaders were Ronald Ngala, Daniel arap Moi, Masinde Muliro and Justus ole Tipis. In 1964 KADU dissolved itself and its leaders joined KANU.

37 The word Kalenjin was coined by Rift Valley leaders to identify the related peoples who lived in the region. It is not certain but Taita Towett is often credited for coining the term.

the agitation for self-rule and they would be the ones at the helm when Independence finally came.

Because there were very few places we could meet and a limited number of upmarket cafés and restaurants for Africans in those days, we all had a chance to become acquainted and got to know each other. I have to admit that I enjoyed fraternising with the high and mighty in politics.

In 1958, Jaramogi Oginga Odinga had coaxed Mwai Kibaki to leave Makerere University, where he had been a lecturer in economics, and return to Kenya to be the KANU Executive Officer in order to run the party secretariat. Kibaki was one of the personalities with whom I became acquainted. We met after an encounter in the African Corner Bar in Nairobi, off Race Course Road, and the two of us have remained friends ever since. We met often for drinks and held sessions to plan strategy, even though I held no official position in KANU. I also met Jaramogi Oginga Odinga there. Odinga, since he was much older, used to call me his "young businessman".

Another of my friends who was among the politically prominent individuals of the day was Tom Mboya, a charismatic Luo politician who held the position of Secretary General in KANU and whom I also met at the African Corner Bar. I had major objections to the manner in which Europeans treated their African labourers and shared these sentiments with Mboya, who was a trade unionist. We became very close, and one of the saddest days of my life was when Tom Mboya was later assassinated in 1969.

There was a time when Mboya and I wanted to become business partners in a petrol station. We wanted to buy the Damji Petrol Station which was operating under the umbrella of Standard Oil Company. It was situated at the intersection of Ronald Ngala Street and Racecourse Road, where a petrol station now stands. The manager more or less agreed, but for one reason or another, the deal did not go through.

It was Mboya who introduced me to such political heavyweights as Dr. Njoroge Mungai, Dr. Munyua Waiyaki, Kariuki Njiiri, Dr. Julius Gikonyo Kiano and many others. Tom Mboya had come back to Kenya from America, where he had gone for some Trade Union meetings, around the same time as Dr. Mungai and the others now formed the political elite.

My home, which was situated behind my shop in Kiambu town, became the un-official meeting place for many members of this African political elite. These politicians would meet for discussions and planning in my home and although the house is not big by today's standards, at the time it was considered quite a large, comfortable residence. I would slaughter goats and provide whatever drinks my guests desired. Not one of my get-togethers was complete without freshly roasted goat ribs.

One such session was arranged by Tom Mboya, who phoned me and suggested that we have a get-together for some returning graduates who had just returned from America in early 1960. Mboya wanted to introduce them to me. Naturally I would not throw away a chance to cultivate contacts and I saw this as an excellent opportunity. I knew people like Mboya would be Kenya's leaders in the very near future and it would be foolish not to befriend his associates. I do not believe I have ever passed up an opportunity to make and maintain contacts, and I think this is a factor that has helped me enormously in my business and political ventures. After all, having friends, no matter what their financial status, is a form of wealth in itself.

Some of my more affluent acquaintances have occasionally asked me why I mix with the poor. All I can say is that these people, and others like them, form the heart of humanity. I respect their hard work and struggle; I admire their down-to-earth wisdom and, more often than not, they help me to understand myself and the world around me. I value their friendship.

Needless to say, the party was arranged, and I had a ram slaughtered for the occasion. Among those who turned up with Mboya were Kariuki Njiiri, from Murang'a, Dr. Njoroge Mungai, Munyua Waiyaki and others. I had also invited my own friends, Mwai Kibaki, Margaret Wambui Kenyatta, a daughter of Jomo Kenyatta, and a few others. Wambui and I had met earlier around this time, when her father was in prison. Like Jomo, she was also in a political career. And so, after the introductions were completed and the feast consumed with relish, our topic of conversation spontaneously turned to the state of the politics in the country.

The party went on till late in the night and by the end of it I had fortunately formed bonds of friendship with all of these future leaders, bonds that would last for a lifetime. I felt quite humbled by the fact that these African leaders were proud of me as a model businessman and that they wanted to use me as a model of what an African could achieve if he or she was given the opportunity. Apparently they saw me as a beacon of hope for the Africans who had been impoverished by colonialism and they were openly proud that I had done so well for myself and my family. I think perhaps they wished to associate with me because, while most of them were well educated and they knew my own education was limited, I had nevertheless managed to become wealthier than they were.

❖ ❖ ❖

I remember that one day Dr. Gikonyo Kiano called and asked me for a favour. He wanted me to host a luncheon for a visiting American. He was a high-ranking government official and I believe his name was Mackenzie. He was in the country ostensibly to gauge the attitude of Kenyans towards Independence and to assess how well prepared they were for it. He was being taken around the country by Kiano, who was the Minister for Commerce and Industry.[38]

Kiano's plan was to take the visitor around the country so that he could see for himself how colonialism had affected the Africans. Kiano intended to take him to poverty stricken areas like Ndeiya near the capital, where all the suffering and economic squalor could be blamed on colonialism. He would afterwards, as a contrast, take him for lunch in my 'palatial' house. I was a bit embarrassed by this honour, but knew that it would be an interesting contrast for the visitor to see and I agreed to the plan.

So Kiano took the visitor to places like Ndeiya in Kiambu, where they witnessed jigger-infested citizenry living in run-down mud-walled and grass-thatched dwellings. He also took him around the villages in Kiambu where they saw the vast European settler farms and the small squatter farms allotted to the Africans, which were hardly large enough for their subsistence. Then they came to my house for lunch.

The American could not hide his surprise, much to the joy of Kiano and myself. Whereas he had seen nothing but raw poverty a few minutes before, here was an obviously prosperous home owned by an African. Wariara and I had decorated the house with the finest furniture and linen and tried to present the perfect evidence of prosperity. Kiano and I also showed the man around our well-stocked store, and he expressed surprise when I said, hesitantly in English, that my wife and I managed it ourselves.

Kiano's black American wife had dropped in earlier to help Wariara prepare lunch for the guest. Being a westerner herself, Mrs. Kiano had wide knowledge of European cuisine and as a consequence the meal was of several courses and was as good, if not better, than any that the official could have taken in a settler's house. We also had a very wide range of

---

38 Kiano had been given the Trade and Industry Ministry by the colonial government. Other leaders had vowed to decline any political appointments until Kenyatta was released from detention, but Kiano went against the grain and accepted the prestigious position. Those who were close to him say that he accepted due to pressure from his American wife, who was apparently quite a dominating woman.

wines and spirits for the visitor to choose from. Of course Kiano and I had orchestrated the whole show in order to impress the visitor, but we made our point. By the time he left, the visitor was thoroughly impressed and he commented that what Africans lacked was not initiative but opportunity. He was convinced that he should support our cause.

I was always happy to hold meetings for politicians although I did not consider myself one of them. History was being made all around me every day and I was proud to have a small role in the process by playing host to future leaders. Many decisions and topics were discussed and plans concluded in those informal meetings at the back of my shop that were to have a great effect on the politics in both the pre-Independence and post-Independence periods. And when it came to the formation of KANU, these meetings were held in my home as well. And they were also to have a profound effect on my future.

It was a momentous occasion when Kenyatta was released in 1961. Many viewed him as the messiah who would lead Kenyans to the promised land of freedom, although some of the Europeans, especially the settlers, did not agree. In fact they could not even contemplate the fact and called Kenyatta a 'leader unto darkness and death'. They stubbornly closed their eyes to the fact that the dream of a British Empire "where the sun never sets" had turned out to be just that, a dream. Independence was on the horizon, the British authorities accepted the fact and were forced to release Kenyatta after all other African leaders refused to negotiate until he was freed.

Even before Jomo was released, it was widely accepted that he was the *de facto* leader of KANU and that he would lead the country towards self-rule.

Earlier on, before Kenyatta was jailed, Gichuru had given up the presidency of KAU (which later evolved into KANU) in favour of Kenyatta. James Gichuru, who was the KANU President, was just holding brief for Kenyatta, and he stepped aside as KANU President, the moment Jomo was set free.

When he was released, Kenyatta quickly asserted his authority in KANU (not that he needed to) by holding a series of private and public meetings all over the country. There was euphoria everywhere he travelled, for Africans knew it was now just a matter of time before self-rule became a reality. Kenyatta spoke on his vision of a new Kenya wherever he went, and he inspired the confidence of everyone, even those who had never met him before. I recall a casual statement Kenyatta made in one of his speeches before he went to prison. It was something like, "This tree of freedom has to be watered with blood. That blood is not from a chicken or from a goat but from you." He spoke in proverbs, and there was another one I recall.

"I will hold the animal by the jaws and you people will have to bear its kicks until we subdue it."

Jomo held planning sessions with his lieutenants, both in the KANU office in Nairobi and at his home in Gatundu. This home, by the way, had been built for Kenyatta by KADU, perhaps to influence him. His original house at Gatundu had been demolished by the colonial authorities. When it became apparent that he was to be released, KADU and KANU both vied for Kenyatta's support because whichever party he joined would surely become the ruling party of independent Kenya. KADU was very well funded because of considerable support from the European community. KANU, on the other hand, relied on membership fees and could not afford to make any grand gestures.

So when Kenyatta was released, Ronald Ngala and Daniel arap Moi of KADU handed over the fully furnished house.

One of them said, "Since your old house was demolished, we in KADU have now built you this new one. We could not let you come out of prison, just to sit outside."

I remember that KADU also bought Kenyatta a car, a Vanguard, with the registration number KHA, and we used to say the letters stood for "Kenyatta Home Again." I cannot recall the other details, though, but this is the car Kenyatta used after his release. Unfortunately for KADU, Kenyatta chose to join KANU instead.

Those of us in KANU felt we had to do something for Kenyatta as well. Dr. Njoroge Mungai, Mwai Kibaki and Tom Mboya bought a Mercedes 110 on hire purchase so that Kenyatta could travel in true presidential style. A few months later, the Mercedes was almost towed away for non-payment of the instalments! But he kept and used both cars after that.

The house KADU built is where Kenyatta hosted international press conferences and met his many guests. I believe he was still under some sort of restriction, because he did not come out of the compound.

Thousands and thousands of people from all over the country, including myself, went to Gatundu and stood outside the fence to have a glimpse of Kenyatta, and to hear him speak.

Upon his release there were often large press conferences and Kenyatta was once asked whether he preferred the new house, or the old one which the colonials had demolished.

"This one is also good," he replied. "But you know, when you build a house yourself, you might set a certain stone in the ground. Then, when you see how it lies, you might decide to turn it to face the other direction."

So the crowds would come and Kenyatta would walk around the interior of the fence, waving his flywhisk and greeting anyone he might recognise. One day, as he spoke on his vision for Kenya, he noticed a familiar face in the crowd. The person he saw was Rawson Macharia, the person who had given false testimony against him during the Kapenguria trial.[39] Kenyatta asked the officers manning the compound to let Macharia in.

"Oh, look! That is my friend there! I want him to come in!" He quipped.

The guards allowed Macharia to enter the compound and he was visibly embarrassed, but Kenyatta gave him a hug.

"We haven't met for a long time. How are you? What have you been doing?" Kenyatta asked.

Macharia said something inaudible and I do not think anyone who witnessed the spectacle knew whether Kenyatta was being forgiving or sarcastic.

A short while after Kenyatta and the rest of the Kapenguria Six were released, they held a very big meeting in Pumwani ground, to tell the people that they were back.

When Paul Ngei was given a chance to speak, he said, addressing his remarks to the British officials in the audience, "Although we have been released, I want to remind you that the land in Kenya still belongs to us, not to the *Wazungu* . . . We will continue to fight for our land and freedom."

The colonialists were of course very disappointed and upset. After a week, the Provincial Commissioner asked Kenyatta to comment but Kenyatta merely said, "Ngei is a politician like me, and he has own opinions."

---

39   Rawson Macharia went down in Kenyan history as a traitor because his lies caused Kenyatta's imprisonment. When it dawned on him that Kenyatta would be released, or perhaps out of remorse for what he had done, he confessed and revealed that he had been bribed by the prosecutors to lie about Kenyatta and Mau Mau. He was jailed for two years for perjury and he faded into oblivion after independence. He was knocked down by a motorbike and killed in 2008.

Then a little later the group held a meeting in Nyeri for released detainees and former freedom fighters. The meetings were organised by Joe Mathenge, a brilliant politician who was Kibaki's nephew. The speakers were people like Kenyatta, Odinga, Mboya, Gichuru and many prominent leaders but, quite interestingly, Ngei's name had been removed from the official government permit that was required for such meetings.

The Provincial Police Commissioner was present because this was expected to be a highly charged meeting. I was there in the crowd and I remember that the grounds were overflowing with people waiting to hear the leaders' speeches. When the scheduled time came, Mathenge stood and opened the meeting. He introduced the speakers and said that each one of them would have a chance to address the crowd, except Ngei. Now this statement was met with a great deal of surprise and everyone in the audience began to talk to his neighbour, speculating on this strange exclusion.

When Ngei was introduced, he just waved to the multitude and then, suddenly, he went nearer to the microphone and said, "Although I am not allowed to speak to you today, I can say the prayers to open the meeting." Everyone removed their hats, including the European administrators and the police. They bowed their heads and he then started praying solemnly in Kiswahili, "Our God in Kenya, please tell me that the *Wazungu* will go. This is our land. Tell the *Wazungu* God in England that they are not wanted here. They must go back to England."

The crowd erupted in cheers, all the women shouted ululation and over the whole grounds people were shaking with mirth and approval.

Ngei intoned a deep solemn "Amen!" and the gathering heartily replied, "Amen!"

The whites did not understand. The white PC was bewildered. He had never seen so much cheering for such a short prayer. He asked Joe Mathenge for a translation of Ngei's prayer and when he learned what had been said, he was most upset. In fact, he was furious, but there was little any of the colonialists could do. The meeting went on and the leaders all got their chance to speak.

But afterwards the British looked for a chance to prosecute Ngei. Since he was praying, the matter was legally difficult. Eventually, after three months, Special Branch's Ian Henderson, the same person who had arrested Mau Mau leader Dedan Kimathi some years earlier, arrested Ngei and advised the government to prosecute him on the technicality that he had introduced politics into church matters. Apparently there was some such bylaw in force and, furthermore, his name had not been on the permit as one of the speakers.

When the case finally came up in court about three months later, people from all over the country came to observe the proceedings. After all the discussion and argument, Ngei was found guilty and fined five hundred shillings. Just as soon as the sentence was pronounced, someone went to the clerk and paid the fine as quickly as possible. When Ngei came out of the court house, some sympathisers pressed money into his hand. He must have collected quite a bit of money that day, and he just put all of it in his pocket.

Just to conclude that little story, one day before going to Lancaster House Conference in London where the details of Kenya's Independence were being worked out, Ngei and Kenyatta had a big meeting in Machakos. I would have liked to attend, but I was caught up elsewhere. Nevertheless, I heard the details from my friend Godfrey Muhuri Muchiri who managed to attend. As I understand it, Ngei stood up and said, "I want you people to pass one resolution here. I was fined. I was fined because I prayed to God in Nyeri yet I did not have a license. I want to tell all of you to go to your priest and make sure the priest goes to the DC to get a permit every Saturday for whatever sermon he will give on Sunday."

Ngei was a brave warrior and a hero of the freedom struggle.

I was one of the people who wished to be introduced to Kenyatta. After all I had heard a great deal about Kenyatta and I wanted to meet this political force who was certain to become the next head of the country. For one reason or another, I like to situate myself in the middle of things, especially when there might be some benefit to come in the future. In addition I had extraordinary admiration for Kenyatta's courage and charisma.

Although I did not know Kenyatta personally at the time, I did not have difficulties in arranging an appointment with the man. It so happened that my partner in the beer business, Charles Kigwi, was a stepbrother to Chief Muhoho wa Gatheca, who in turn was Kenyatta's father-in-law, (being the father of Mama Ngina). Muhoho was also a friend of mine and was a constant visitor to my house in Kiambu.

Before I went to visit Kenyatta, in 1961, I happened to mention the facts of my visit to my friend, Brian Hobson, of the East African

Breweries. Hobson was a man of keen ambitions and he knew it would be beneficial for the company if he had the opportunity to meet and get to know Kenyatta. They had apparently met once before, very briefly, before Kenyatta had been imprisoned, and now Hobson saw the chance to renew the acquaintance and hopefully start a friendship. He asked me to try to set up an appointment for him and other managers of the brewery.

So I went to meet Kenyatta in the company of Kigwi and Muhoho. Muhoho introduced me and then Kenyatta said that he had already heard about me and my business activities during the time I was in the timber business in Elburgon. When I told Kenyatta that I had often seen him at my father-in-law's home in Elburgon, he conceded that he frequently visited Wairiri, my wife's father, every time he visited the area and said that he had enjoyed many good meals there. In addition, Kenyatta said he had heard about my business activities in Kiambu while in prison, and he stated that he was happy to meet me at last. He said he was proud of me, a young man, setting an example of African industriousness right in his own district. He was also aware that politicians often met in my house and he thanked me for my hospitality. My modesty was quite overcome by this kind praise.

Looking back on this meeting, I think I am right to say it changed my destiny. The two of us started a friendship that was to last till Kenyatta's death and which significantly affected my fortunes, especially politically. From then onwards our lives were intertwined in quite a number of ways, and that night I entered Kenyatta's inner circle in a manner which I had never imagined. We talked politics while we took tea, and Kenyatta kindly listened to my modest ideas and aspirations of a new independent Kenya. Kenyatta also told all of us in the gathering of his vision for Kenya and his anticipation for Independence. It was a turning point in my life although I did not recognise it as such at the time.

Later in the same meeting, I nervously asked for an appointment for Hobson, the Managing Director of the East African Breweries. I do not think I was tactful enough, particularly in dealing with such an elder and I did not know how Kenyatta would react to my request that he meet with this *Mzungu*. He had undergone quite an ordeal in European hands during detention, and I did not want to antagonise him, especially in our first meeting. But I need not have worried. Kenyatta did not take the request badly at all.

Kenyatta told me that he knew Hobson well. It seems that Hobson had once tried to compromise him in a certain way and although he did not elaborate the point, Kenyatta told me that he would reveal everything when Hobson came to the meeting. This was a characteristic evasion that Kenyatta often made use of. Kenyatta then called out to Achieng' Oneko, his trusted private secretary who had been staying with him at Gatundu ever since they were released from prison, and he told Oneko to check his diary and pencil in Hobson for an appointment. Kenyatta's schedule was packed with meetings and appointments, but Oneko booked the appointment for seven o'clock on a certain evening the following week. Thus I had the opportunity to meet Oneko as well, and this also became the beginning of another lifetime friendship. After that we left.

Hobson was very pleased to secure the appointment. The two of us went for the meeting in Gatundu accompanied by Charles Kigwi, my partner and neighbour, and Joseph Thuo, the first African director in the board of East African Breweries. Also in the delegation was Raymond Kuria Gathunguri, a senior manager with the Breweries. Hobson wanted to impress Kenyatta with the fact that his company was not racial and had Africans at the highest levels of management. Also accompanying the delegation was John Njenga who was my cousin. At the time he was a manager in the Breweries, although he later left the company to join Nararashi Distributors where he rose to the position of Managing Director. Kenyatta observed that Hobson had done well by employing many ex-detainees and Hobson replied that he had employed them because they were skilled, educated and honest. I found the conversation fascinating.

In the meeting, Hobson was full of praise for Jomo Kenyatta, telling him that what he was doing was best for the country's future. Kenyatta on the other hand praised Hobson for selecting former detainees to senior levels in his company, and Hobson explained that he had appointed them on merit. Hobson requested Kenyatta to tour the Breweries and see for himself what the company was doing to empower the Africans working for it. Kenyatta said he would create some time to visit, but Oneko broke into the conversation and informed Jomo that he would have to go alone. Oneko would never agree to step near any brewery.

At this Kenyatta just laughed. He told us about a previous tour he had taken at Allsopps Breweries factory sometime before he was imprisoned.[40] This was before his relationship with the colonials had broken down irretrievably. He had been escorted by Achieng' Oneko, and after being

---

40   There were two breweries in Kenya at the time. One was Kenya Breweries, (later called East African Breweries) founded in 1922 by Charles and George Hurst. Allsopps East Africa Limited was founded some time afterwards and was later acquired by East African Breweries.

shown around the plant by some of the managers, the two were given a crate of beer each to take home. Oneko carried the crate on his shoulder up to the car and they had then both gone home. Some press photographer must have been lurking nearby and noticed the two leaders, for on the following day, the newspapers had a big picture of Oneko hauling a crate of beer on his shoulder. The picture had a nasty caption below it, and this incensed Oneko to no end. So, he repeated, he was not going anywhere near a brewery ever again.

There was one major reason Hobson wanted Kenyatta to tour the breweries, though. Shortly before he had been detained, Kenyatta appealed to his fellow Africans in various public rallies to boycott East African Breweries products and European cigarettes as an act of economic defiance against the colonial administration. Many people agreed with Kenyatta and avoided the company's products, seriously affecting its profit margin. Kenyatta's call was taken so seriously, especially around the Mt. Kenya region, that, at the time, one could face serious consequences, including caning and death, if the Mau Mau found them taking the products. Therefore a reversal of this boycott would significantly open up the market potential among Africans and it would be a public relations coup if Kenyatta would visit the company and give it accreditation.

Kenyatta then told us all that Hobson, together with his boss Michael Blundell, had once tried to compromise him by offering, on behalf of the colonial authorities, a quarter of the breweries shares in exchange for toning down his fiery speeches. Kenyatta had flatly declined and informed Hobson that he would never compromise his policies while his people remained under the yoke of colonialism, even if the whole plant was offered to him. Hobson was greatly embarrassed by this revelation, but Kenyatta narrated it in a jocular manner, as a thing of the past. They were laughing about it and I learned something new.

In general, the meeting was a success for Hobson. Kenyatta promised full cooperation with him in future. After all, Hobson's company was one of the biggest taxpayers to the government, and Hobson promised that this relationship would no doubt continue to expand and improve after independence. Unlike many other whites, Hobson actually loved Kenya and he saw himself as a Kenyan. He intended to stay in the country even after Independence and after his European wife died, he married an African woman.

At this time I was a nominated councillor. I had been nominated to the Karuri Local Council by my friend and business partner, Charles Karuga

Koinange who was the council chairman.[41] By this time I had not even dreamt of elective office and so when the council nominated me, I agreed to serve. Although I was only in the office for one year, I learned a thing or two about how councils operated.

Most of those who were elected to these councils were ex-detainees because the KANU youth were very hostile to any former home guards or collaborators trying to vie for a post. Any collaborator making the attempt was knocked about and his nomination papers torn up when he went to present them to the Kiambu DC's office.

In those days the position of Councillor did not attract a salary. We would meet to debate various issues and be paid an allowance of two shillings per session. That sounds like a small amount, but I remember I would be able to buy *nyama choma* for myself and a colleague for only fifty cents.

The Councils gradually became hotbeds of corruption and lethargy and eventually the allowance system was scrapped by Jomo Kenyatta in 1963. One example was the Kiambu District Council. The ex-detainees in the Kiambu Council complained to the Chairman, Philip Ngugi Muimbo, over their allowances. They told him, sarcastically, that they had not been paid salaries while in Manyani detention camp. Now, without a salary, they would be forced to come to the Council meetings in rags. They demanded to be loaned a sum of forty thousand shillings, or about Sh. 1,500 per councillor, in order to buy smart clothes, and generally spruce up as befitted their status as councillors.

Ngugi argued with them for a long time and after the stormy session, the council agreed to write a cheque of one thousand five hundred shillings to each member so they could better their wardrobes. But it was not free money—this was a loan that each councillor had to pay back. In those days, that amount was quite a princely sum. Whether this money was ever repaid is a matter of conjecture!

Anyway, as a result of these daily allowances, members of the council would debate a simple subject for days on end so that they could be paid more.

After discussing a topic for hours they would say, "Mr Chairman, let us postpone this meeting until tomorrow. It is not as if the problem will rot or be eaten by rats if we leave it until tomorrow." In this way they would drag out deliberations for weeks.

---

41   Local and District councils preceded the current County and Municipal councils. They were comprised of councillors who had been elected by the public and others who were nominated.

Local Government Minister Lawrence Sagini noticed this habit in many Councils and decided to do something about it. He informed Finance Minister, James Gichuru, about his concerns and Gichuru in turn reported it to Kenyatta. Gichuru told Kenyatta that the District Council in Kiambu was one of the most notorious council exploiting the system.

Kenyatta therefore scrapped the sitting allowance system and decreed that members would be paid a fixed salary. From that time onwards, there was a great change and issues in the Kiambu District Council would be debated and resolved in minutes.

In 1962, Father Sheridan, who was in charge of Riara Diocese, approached the Kiambaa Local Council with a proposal. He wanted the Council to allocate land for the construction of Kanunga Secondary School. This school was intended to complement Kanunga Primary School which was already in operation. Father Sheridan had received sufficient money from Rome for the construction of the school.

Thirty five acres of land had been set aside for public amenities after land demarcation in Riara in the late 1950s. Kanunga Primary School stood on a portion of this land and it was expected that Kanunga secondary school would also be located nearby.

Among all the Councillors in the Kiambaa Local Council, my former teacher, Peter Muhoho and I were the only Catholics. Some were from the Anglican Church while others were ex-detainees who belonged to various denominations. When the Council met, and the time came to discuss the allocation of land for the secondary school, all the Councillors, other than Muhoho and I, were vehemently opposed.

This majority, led by Gideon Gathunguri, did not want to allocate any land for the school.

"That land is part of our land. We are the ones whose land was reduced in size in order to set aside land for public amenities," said Gathunguri. "If the *Mūbea* (Catholic priest)—this actually is a Gikuyu corruption of "Mon Père", French for "My Father"—wants to build schools, let him go back to Italy and do it there."

Muhoho was incensed at this selfish logic. He had been a teacher since 1938 and he knew the value of education.

"Look here you people," he fumed, "you only see as far as a fly". He shook his head in disgust. "Don't you realize that the *Mūbea* doesn't have a single child? The schools are not for him! This school is ours, for our own children."

The other councillors were still not convinced. They were very rude about it, and they said that they were not giving away their land to any white man.

Muhoho tried again.

"The Father wants to finish construction and open the school before January," he explained. "If he cannot start, the money from Rome might be sent elsewhere."

But the councillors did not listen. They still equated the church to colonialism and they were very touchy on the issue of land.

So we went to Father Sheridan and informed him of what had happened during the meeting. But he was not discouraged. He told us that no matter what happened Kanunga Secondary School would be in existence by January 1963.

Father Sheridan, who truly believed in the advancement of Christianity and education among Africans, was determined to start a secondary school. I recall that we held a small *harambee* in Riara and I donated one thousand shillings for the school.

Before the end of the year, he set aside two classrooms at Kanunga Primary School and replaced the grass-thatched roofs with corrugated iron sheets. That was the beginning of Kanunga Secondary School and my brother Munge was among the first students to enrol in the school the following January.

Before long, the son of one of the councillors who had opposed the allocation of land for the school, came to ask if he could join Kanunga Secondary School. He had been rejected by all the other schools in the area due to his poor grades. Kanunga did not accept him either and after that his father went around saying that my brother had only been accepted because I had donated some money during the *harambee*.

Father Sheridan became a very close friend of mine and he often approached me when he had development issues concerning the church and Catholic schools. Shortly after Kanunga Secondary School was started, Father Sheridan was faced with yet another challenge.

The Diocesan Bishop, J.J. McCarthy, had received a donation of two hundred and forty thousand shillings for the construction of churches in the diocese. Now, as it happened, the Kiambu Catholic Church in Kiambu Town was not actually a church. People worshipped in a social hall, which was neither big enough nor suitable for church activities. However, Bishop McCarthy was not willing to release all the money for the construction of a church in Kiambu Town. He had other ideas about how the money should be used.

Father Sheridan approached Peter Muhoho, Phillip Kamau, a church leader called Kingati, myself and some other businessmen who were members of the church. He asked us to accompany him when he went to see McCarthy and try to convince him to release the funds for the construction of the church. I recall that Father Sheridan carried some of the delegation in his car and I carried the others.

When we arrived at the Bishop's residence, Sheridan introduced us as the representatives of Catholics in Kiambu. Each of us made a plea for the construction of a proper church in our town. But Sheridan could see that Bishop McCarthy was not much impressed. Since Sheridan knew how to speak Kikuyu very well, he whispered to me and told me to tell the Bishop that I was willing to donate twenty thousand shillings for the construction work to begin.

When I told the Bishop about this intention, he seemed to reconsider. Finally he said that he would come to Kiambu the following Sunday, see the congregation and the premises and make a decision.

When we got back, Father Sheridan called Peter Muhoho to plan out a strategy. And so it happened that Father Sheridan informed the Riara Catholic Church faithful that there would be a special mass in Kiambu Social Hall the following Sunday and that they should all attend. That Sunday when Bishop McCarthy arrived, he was surprised at the size of the congregation, which spilled out of the hall and on to the road.

He conducted the mass, and afterwards declared that he had seen the willingness of the people to worship and that he would release the donor funds immediately for the construction of the church. We were overjoyed.

The following morning, Father Sheridan came to my shop in Kiambu Town and asked for a soda. He told me that the funds the Bishop had promised them would be enough to build the church. He said I should keep my twenty thousand and improve my business, instead. But I would have been willing to give it out if need be.

Later we identified a plot near the Kiambu Club and that is where the church stands today.

Whatever people say about the growth of the church, I believe that without Father Sheridan, Muhoho and a few others, the Catholic Church in Kiambu would still be far behind.

All the while, the train of Independence was gradually approaching its destination. The colonial authorities had decided to grant Kenyans self rule in June 1963, with a Prime Minister in charge of government. The Prime Minister would work alongside the Governor of the Colony, Malcolm MacDonald. However Foreign Affairs and National Defence were still dictated from London and the Head of State was still the Queen. Nearly everyone felt that Jomo Kenyatta, KANU's leader, should become Prime Minister, but there was strong opposition from KADU, which was led by Ronald Ngala and Daniel arap Moi.

In addition there was a minor glitch in the programme. The Constitution, as it stood, required that the PM first had to be a Member of Parliament. Kenyatta was not an MP, unfortunately. Gatundu constituency, where he lived and later stood for election, did not exist as a separate entity at the time and Kenyatta therefore needed a platform from which to vie for Parliament. It was extraordinarily strange to see that the many Members of Parliament who claimed to respect and honour Kenyatta, nevertheless refused to step down for him, claiming that their seats in Parliament belonged to their constituents and were not their own.

However, Kenyatta's close confidants and I were not overly worried or dismayed by this predicament, and we quickly contacted a true patriot of Independence to consider stepping down for Kenyatta. The man we approached was Kariuki Njiiri, the MP for Kigumo, and he promptly agreed to stand aside for Kenyatta.[42]

I remember that our approach to Kariuki was accompanied by a rather funny incident. Since I did not want to attract any special attention during our discussions, I asked a patriot called Robert Njenga to slaughter a goat for *wazee* at his home in Karura, rather than holding a party in my own house. My friends and KANU operatives Kariuki Njiiri, Mwai Kibaki, Bernard Njenga, Bernard Hinga, Dr. Munyua Waiyaki and Henry Wariithi attended. We were inside having drinks and the meat was roasting nicely outside in the garden. At one point, we were informed that half of the goat was ready and had been brought to the kitchen. Since I was considered to be the better carver, my friends told me to slice some selected joints for them. I should explain that my friends often teased me,

---

42 Not many people are aware that Kenyatta first got to Parliament as the MP for Kigumo. Njiiri was later re-elected during the first post-Independence elections for the same seat, and Kenyatta rewarded him with an Assistant Minister's post.

claiming I had a great deal of experience with goats, having lived in the Rift Valley.

I went into the kitchen and began to cut up the deliciously crisp and juicy meat. As I was slicing, one of my friends, a mischievous young man called Mwai Kibaki, said he was going to the kitchen as well, to help me. When he joined me he asked me to cut up the ribs first, so that we could nibble on them as I worked. I thought this was a great idea and as we chatted and I continued cutting, we ended up eating all the ribs. In the other room, Dr. Munyua Waiyaki was getting hungry and decided that we were taking far too much time so he decided to come and see what was causing the delay.

When he came to the door, he was shocked to see that the meat was gradually disappearing. In conspiratorial whispers, Kibaki told him to sit down and shut up. He invited Waiyaki to start eating one of the front legs and told him to ignore the others and let them talk *siasa* (politics) in the sitting room. Dr. Waiyaki thought this was a good idea and so we sat round the kitchen table and ate the leg as well.

Shortly after, Bernard Hinga decided to find out what was going on. When he came to the room, Kibaki asked him to sit and be quiet and we could all start on the hind leg of the goat. But Hinga was not as mischievous as we were.

"These rogues have eaten everything," he roared out for the whole homestead to hear.

Everyone came rushing into the kitchen to see for themselves and you can imagine how they shouted at us when they saw the bare bones on the table. With a great deal of teasing and laughter, we were banned from carving any more meat and soon another goat met its end.

By the end of the party, we managed to convince Kariuki Njiiri to relinquish his Parliamentary seat for Kenyatta. Later that night there was another celebration held for KANU officials and supporters at the United Kenya Club in Nairobi and Kariuki's decision was met with much joy and festivity. This put us one step closer to Kenyatta's ascension to the leadership of Kenya.

About four years ago, during the funeral of a friend from Kigumo, Francis Thuo, I read the condolence message from President Kibaki. During the occasion, I also thanked the people of Kigumo for allowing their MP to step down for Jomo Kenyatta and told them that their patriotism speeded up Kenya's independence.

But back then, there were many people vying for nomination for positions as Members of Parliament, and KANU and KADU both offered candidates in nearly all constituencies. Kenyatta and KANU tried to work out a strategy which would have the strongest candidates standing in areas where they would have a chance to defeat KADU members. For example, James Gichuru was asked to vie for a seat in Limuru where there was no other strong candidate, and leave the Kikuyu seat for Joseph Gatuguta, a lawyer who had high potential.

During the nomination day, Gichuru and Kenyatta met at the Kiambu DC's office, the venue which was to be used as the returning station. All candidates were supposed to hand in their papers between 9 am and 12 pm. If there were many candidates vying for one post, the list would be released after 12 and they would have to fight it out during the subsequent elections. If there was only a single candidate who had handed in his papers by noon, he would be declared the unopposed winner and would be an MP-in-waiting. By 10 am, Kenyatta and Gichuru had handed in their papers.

However, it was not seemly for the KANU President, who was resplendent in a costume festooned with KANU colours, to idly hang around the DC's office until noon. Therefore, as I was informed later, Kenyatta asked Gichuru if he knew a place where they could relax and wait for the results. Gichuru knew just the place. He said he had a friend who had a house nearby, where they could rest and receive first class hospitality. The friend happened to be me, and Gichuru explained to Kenyatta that I had played a significant role during the struggle for independence.

They got into Kenyatta's big Mercedes Benz, the one KANU had purchased for him, and drove to my house. In all respects, he was the President-in-waiting and had already started enjoying the trappings of power, such as the limousine and numerous bodyguards. Following behind them was a small entourage of key supporters. The convoy attracted shouts of approval from the people as it made its short journey from the DC's office to my home. Most Africans in the vicinity closed their businesses, stopped their farming activities and gathered nearby to welcome, cheer and applaud this legend who they revered.

Once the convoy arrived at my house and shop, they discovered that I was away and my wife, Wariara, informed them that I had gone to Nairobi on business. All the same, she warmly welcomed them to my office at the back of the shop.

Gichuru, who enjoyed taking liquor, asked Wariara whether they could get some drinks. Wariara called up our neighbour, Poppatlal, an Indian shopkeeper who at one time had opposed the allocation of the area's plots to Africans. She knew he carried a stock of spirits so she informed him that she had guests and let him know who her guests were. She asked him to send someone with drinks and said she would pay for them later.

At this time, despite the fact that quite a few prominent Indians had supported the movement for independence, they were living in conditions of uncertainty because they were unsure of their future under an African government. Poppatlal of course knew who Kenyatta was, and knew he was likely to be the President soon. So the drinks, one bottle of whisky for Gichuru and one bottle of brandy for Kenyatta as specified by Wariara, were delivered almost immediately.

Meanwhile, my wife was dividing her attention between entertaining the guests and making frantic phone calls to all my contacts in Nairobi in order to let me know that I had important guests in the house. She could not get me at the breweries depot or at any other business premises where she would have expected to contact me. She tried various restaurants and bars, but I was nowhere to be found. She told her guests that she could not reach me but Kenyatta told her not to be concerned. After all, he said, a man had to work and they had not even given notice that they would be coming. Kenyatta told her not to lock up the shop because of their presence and asked her to tend the counter as usual. Naturally Wariara would have preferred to lock up the shop and attend to the guests, but Kenyatta was never easily contradicted.

For whatever reason, some nagging sixth sense told me that I should be at home in Kiambu. However my car was being fixed in a garage and the mechanics were not through with the repairs. I was bored at the garage and did not want to remain idle, so I asked my friend, Mikuga Kibe, to give me a ride home and told the mechanics I would return for the car later.

When I arrived I was shocked to see an enormous crowd gathered around my shop, talking animatedly. I almost jumped out of the vehicle before it came to a stop. My mind was racing as I bolted from the car. What had happened? Had there been a fire? Had thieves struck? Was Wariara safe?

I made my way through the crowd and was puzzled to find my wife at the counter, selling goods as she always did. Bewildered, I asked her what was happening and she told me that we had two guests in the back who were having a drink and relaxing. The guests, Wariara informed me, were the ones who had attracted the crowd. This left me perplexed.

I then made my way to the back rooms and I was incredibly surprised by the identities of my guests. I found two highly important visitors, the leaders of the struggle for independence, sipping their drinks quite comfortably and looking very much at home. After greeting them, I started gushing apologies but Kenyatta cut me short. He told me that they were quite at ease and that my wife had welcomed them very graciously.

"Karume's father," Kenyatta said cheekily, "where else in this town would you have expected *wazee* to relax as they waited for the nomination results?"

By that time it was fifteen minutes to noon and the results of the nomination were about to be announced. Kenyatta asked me to keep their things (meaning their bottles) for them while they drove to the DC's office to hear the results and said that they would be back after the announcement. After they left, I hurriedly purchased the fattest rams available and had them slaughtered. I then asked Wariara to close the shop for the day. We then moved to the rooms behind the office. We had always regarded the rooms we occupied behind the shop as a temporary residence till I got round to building a proper house, but, if there ever was a time to decorate, this was it. A Persian carpet that I had obtained while in Mombasa on business was laid out in the sitting room and our house quickly smartened up. After all, our visitor was the future President of Kenya.

The results were announced, and both Gichuru and Kenyatta were declared winners since they had been unopposed. A local politician called Gatabaki Mundati and Karuga Koinange, who had by this time been promoted to DO, Kiambu,[43] joined them and they all came back to my house. All the crowds which had gathered in the town cheered wildly as the future President drove by. Once they arrived, celebration was in the air, and celebrate we did. I do not believe those rooms behind our shop have ever held such a spectacle. I even gave drinks to the supporters and bodyguards, who were on duty outside.

At that time I had a new gadget in my house, a television set, and Kenyatta asked me to switch it on so we could see how nominations were proceeding in the rest of the country, but I explained that it only broadcast at night. We could, of course, have listened to the news on the radio but unfortunately I did not own one.

"Then ask those *Wahindi* (Indians) to give you one," Kenyatta suggested, referring to my neighbours. "We need to know what is happening." He was already talking like a President.

---

43   Karuga Koinange was a brother to Kenyatta's third wife, Grace Mitundu, who was the daughter of Senior Chief Koinange. He was eventually promoted to Provincial Commissioner.

So I approached my next-door neighbour, a fellow shopkeeper, and asked him to lend me his radio since *Mzee* wanted to hear the news. The man, an Indian who owned Karani Kiambu Service Store, knew that it was the President who was being referred to and selected the largest and most expensive radio in his shop. He handed it to me and asked if his children could come and greet Kenyatta. I checked with Kenyatta and of course he agreed, and for many minutes thereafter, Indian children, accompanied by their mothers, came into my house to greet and welcome Kenyatta and his friends.

Kenyatta was very gracious but occasionally had mischievous moments. He introduced his companions properly but when introducing DO Karuga, who was in official uniform, he became a bit sly.

"And this person here," he said, "is your next DC."

This made us all look at each other with amusement and a certain amount of speculation. No one could predict what was on Kenyatta's mind. As it happened, Karuga did indeed become the DC for Kiambu and was later promoted Provincial Commissioner for Central Province.

The celebrations continued and the party went on both inside and outside the house. Kenyatta was a natural leader who expected authority to be respected, and he would not have protocol breached even as the festivities continued. Through the windows he noticed his bodyguards drinking outside the house and he instructed me to ensure that his subordinates outside did not drink while on duty.

"Njenga," he said, "I can't drink together with my bodyguards. Can you do something about it?" Then he continued, "If you want to throw a party for them in the future, that's fine, but not while I'm here."

So I sent them all to my 'Maendeleo Bar' that was a little further off, opposite my shop, and invited them to drink on my account but warned them to stay alert in case Mzee wanted to leave and they were needed.

Meanwhile the radio continued to broadcast news that we wanted to hear, and some that we did not. Most of the seats which had been unopposed had gone to KANU, with personalities like Oginga Odinga sailing through. In KADU, Moi won unopposed in Baringo, as did a few others like Ronald Ngala. As the announcements continued it became clear that KANU was going to win. The drinks flowed on. Everyone removed their jackets and relaxed. We had more drinks and we were all very happy. Kenyatta was extremely pleased and, right there in my house, the political leadership began to plan the line-up of the new government which KANU intended to form. I felt very proud of being a part of it all, and, since I knew most of the people in Kenyatta's camp, I found myself slowly beginning to participate in the discussion although I knew this was not my strong point.

I never planned to be involved in the events that occurred during that turbulent period of Kenya's history. I believe it was providence, or coincidence, that arranged matters so that I just happened to be on the scene when history was unfolding and thereafter I was inextricably caught up in the events and became part of them. If anyone had asked me at the time, I would never have got involved in the murky pools of politics, at least not at that period of my life. My view was that my business was doing business. I had no interest in elective politics, which I considered time-consuming and which would have disastrously interfered with my various commercial enterprises, which I still regard as my true calling. All the same, through no ambitions of my own, I was slowly being drawn into the political arena and I have no regrets.

My view on the whole matter is that what God wills, will be, no matter what a mere mortal tries to do to change the circumstances.

But I would still like to explain the incident about the radio and the television. You see, I never bothered purchasing a radio because I felt a television was even better. The TV set that I owned was very special to me because it had been given to me by my closest friend, Muiruri Laban.

When I left Elburgon, Muiruri went on to Githunguri where he purchased a transport lorry. We lost touch for a while and, although I never found out exactly what happened, all his wealth gradually disappeared. I was worried that I never saw him any more, and wondered why he was avoiding me. One day Muiruri's sister-in-law came to buy something at our shop in Kiambu. My wife talked to her and learned about Muiruri's misfortunes. My wife was very sympathetic and she tactfully pleaded with the sister-in-law to tell Muiruri's wife, her sister, to visit.

That following Tuesday, a market day, Muiruri's wife did indeed show up, and we talked for quite a while. I asked her what had happened to Muiruri and she said that he had no money anymore. He apparently did nothing but stay at home, or, if he did go out, he would just play draughts with idlers at Githuru-ini market centre, and sometimes even walked barefoot. I asked her why he did not ever just drop in to see me, and she replied that he was ashamed. This made me feel terrible. I told her to tell him that I was ordering him to come the following Friday.

Muiruri finally came in to see me and I slaughtered a goat for him. We roasted the goat, ate, drank, told stories and talked. It was great being together again. I asked him why he had not visited and he confessed that he felt too embarrassed to come and see me. We continued drinking till very late, slept a little and then, sometime in the early morning, I asked him to come outside with me. I showed him one of the lorries which was standing in front of my shop and told him it was his. It was an old five ton lorry I had bought at an auction for about two thousand five hundred shillings and I gave it to him.

"*Mwanake*, you are in luck! I just bought this lorry last week and since I have enough vehicles for my business, you can have it."

We used to call each other *Mwanake* which literally means "young man" but would be better translated as "buddy".

I expected him to be happy, but instead he became even more embarrassed. He stammered his thanks but, after I asked him what was wrong, he told me that he had nothing, not even money for fuel. What could I do? I gave him enough money to buy diesel for a week and told him that I wanted him to start a new life. He was a very dear friend.

Interestingly enough, this was just around the time Africans were starting to plant coffee because the colonial authorities had finally changed the law and allowed Africans to plant coffee. Coffee needs a lot of manure to ensure fertile soil for the young plants. Many people were in this business of supplying manure, but most of them had two- or three-ton lorries. Suddenly Muiruri's five ton lorry was in big demand because he would sell at the same price as the other merchants. He would go to Kajiado, buy and bring the manure and sell it by the lorry load. He made so much money that he was quickly able to buy another lorry and soon became financially stable again.

Naturally, with two lorries in his business, Muiruri was buying lots of diesel. Now it so happened that in Eastleigh there was a petrol station having a promotion for anyone purchasing more than ten gallons of fuel. The Asian owner of the station had put out a large jar of beans and challenged his customers to guess how many there were, and if anyone could guess correctly, they would get a brand new television set, something recently arrived in Kenya. Muiruri made a guess whenever he bought fuel, and on the day when the correct amount of beans was announced, he found himself winning the new television set.

When Muiruri picked up the television set with the intention to take it to his house, an Indian came up and asked him to sell the TV to him for 1,300 shillings. Muiruri was very tempted to sell. The offer was a considerable amount of money at that time. But then Muiruri's wife, Wambui, interrupted them.

"How can you sell this TV?" she asked. "Surely we can find something better to do with it."

"Well, with 1,300 shillings I could just add a little extra and buy another lorry. But, alright, if you so wish, we can take it home."

"What do you mean? This gadget does not use paraffin. It needs electricity and you know we don't have electricity at home. What would we do with it?"

Muiruri realised that Wambui was trying to tell him something indirectly and paid more attention to what she was saying.

"What do you think would be the best thing to do, then?" he asked.

Wambui thought for a moment.

"Well, you know Njenga Karume has electricity at his house," she said.

Muiruri really wanted to sell the TV and buy a new lorry but his wife's words made him reconsider.

"Without Njenga's help, we would still be without a lorry," Wambui continued. "Wouldn't it be nice to give him this? Without the lorry which he gave you, you would not have won the TV in the first place. Or would you have drunk the diesel through your mouth?" she joked. "He was very generous and we should show some appreciation."

Wambui was very persuasive and Muiruri finally agreed. Sometimes it takes the wisdom of women to help men see their obstinacy. So Muiruri called me and said they would be coming to visit us the following Friday and sleep over.

That Friday Muiruri and Wambui came and we had quite a party. They had carried along a big wrapped parcel and Wariara and I were curious about it. When they gave it to us and we opened it and saw the TV, we were extremely happy. When it got late, our wives went to bed and Muiruri and I caught up on all the past news. Muiruri was very honest and when he got tipsy, he confessed that if it had not been for his wife, he would have sold the TV.

I laughed at his frankness. He was a very humorous man, and after this incident, Mwai Kibaki and I would often visit his hotel at Juja for *nyama choma* and drinks. I wish I could recall all the stories he used to tell! At any rate, I was very happy and pleased to have done something for my friend so I did not really need his thanks, but the TV was now a wonderful extra bonus.

In 1962 I bought my first real farm, Lynton Farm, near Cianda in Ndumberi, Kiambu. The farm was sold to me by a settler named Ivorine who was a Queen's Counsel and a judge who had presided at the infamous Githunguri trials over the Lari massacre in 1953. Like many Europeans at the time, he was leaving the country. The farm had a large colonial style house where my family and I lived for the next 17 years until I moved to Cianda in 1979, where I now stay.

I still own the 142-acre Lynton Farm. It was originally planted with wattle trees but when I bought it, I cut and sold the wattle trees and planted tea instead.

One year later, on 1 June 1963, when Kenya was finally granted self-governing status, Jomo Kenyatta became the country's first Prime Minister, and the future of the foundation and structure of the new government began to be constructed.

I was ecstatic about Independence and was thrilled to have so many friends among the most prominent and powerful in the administration, but I personally did not feel the need to get involved in either politics or government, for three basic reasons.

First of all, I had no background in elective politics and all that goes with it. I had no idea of the procedures, the campaigns, or the compromises which are vital to such a role. And of course, without understanding or going through such measures, one cannot have a place in the higher echelons of government. I admired many of the new leaders and felt that people such as James Gichuru, Mwai Kibaki and others were more qualified to handle roles which would surely bring so many benefits to *wananchi*. I left such things to the professionals and felt privileged to be in constant social contact with Kenyatta and his lieutenants. These friendships expanded after Independence but I preferred to remain backstage, behind the scenes, and never felt the calling to be on the stage myself. I am sure if I had ever expressed the desire for a public role, Kenyatta would have found a position for me.

The second reason I felt no ambition to be involved in politics, was that I had other priorities. At that time, I did not want to dedicate my life to politics at the expense of other efforts which were much closer to my heart. Most particularly, I was intensely dedicated to being successful in business matters and I felt I had no limits in regard to expansion. Some people may have felt I was already thriving and could thus relax, but I have never held that attitude. I feel it is always possible to do more, and to do better. With Independence, I knew there would be great opportunities.

Africans could now work freely, expand and exploit business possibilities to whatever extent their destiny and enterprise permitted. To my mind, merely owning a large shop, with the addition of some bars in Kiambu, did not strike me as an ultimate achievement.

The final reason that a political role held no attraction for me was that I still had a young family who occupied me considerably. I felt that the public focus and the forces involved in politics would not create an atmosphere suitable for raising my family. It should be remembered that by Independence in 1963 I was only 34 years old and I had a young family and children who needed a father. I thought that I would be a better influence and be closer to them if I avoided direct involvement in politics.

On 12 December 1963, Kenya gained her full Independence. My family, some friends and I went, like thousands of others, to Uhuru Gardens to watch the British flag come down and to celebrate as the new Kenyan flag was raised at midnight. It was a wonderful occasion and we were so overwhelmingly happy that it is hard even to describe. There was an incredible euphoria that surged through all of us in the massive crowds. People were thrilled that their century-long period of suppression and battle was finally over, and that they were now free.

As earlier mentioned, during the early 1960s I married a second wife, Margaret Njeri. After our marriage, she assisted in our businesses in Kiambu but later we established another home in our newly purchased farm in Molo.

We bought Kambara farm in Molo from a government settlement scheme. The land, originally belonging to a European lady, had been advertised for sale by open tender.

I later learned that the then Minister for Agriculture, Bruce Mackenzie, already had plans for it himself. He wanted his Ministry to acquire it and use it for research since it was very fertile.

As it turned out, my bid of Sh. 150,000 was the highest. The next closest bid was Sh. 120,000 by Eliud Mahihu, a friend of mine and a Provincial Commissioner then. I knew there were many interested parties who wished to purchase the farm, and was rather worried that Mackenzie would break the deal, so I knew I had to pay in the twenty percent deposit, Sh. 30,000, as quickly as possible. As soon as I got the letter stating that I had won the tender, I paid the whole amount in cash.

The next day Bruce Mackenzie phoned Cyrus Gakuu Karuga, the estate manager who had advertised the sale of the farm. Mackenzie wanted to discuss the deal and buy the land for the Ministry of Agriculture for use as an Agricultural Development Corporation (ADC) research site. But since I had already paid the deposit, there was no way he could break the sale agreement. I was, naturally, very happy that I had closed the loopholes. I understand Kenyatta only came to know of the details a year afterwards.

Later we purchased additional parcels until we had a sizeable farm. Njeri managed the farm and the cattle and supervised the workers. She was highly competent and we consistently had good profits. In addition the cattle always won prizes at Agricultural shows. We had hundreds of grade cattle which were purchased from the Agricultural Development Corporation and from Delamere's farm where my father had once been a herder. These are the small ironies of life.

In 1977, we bought the Highlands Hotel in Molo but some years later we sold it. After the death of my second wife Njeri in January 1990, I started making losses on the Molo farm as well. I therefore decided to sell it, too, and buy another tea farm closer to home, bordering Lynton Farm, so that I could personally manage it. The Molo farm, by the way, was bought by the Government in 2006 for the resettlement of squatters.

In 1965, the British American Tobacco Company, the main tobacco manufacturers in the region, advertised for distributors. Since I had established a series of wines and spirits shops in Kiambu, I believed these would also be good outlets for cigarettes. My applications were successful and I was given the distributorship rights for Kiambu District under the trade name of Kiambu Tobacco Wholesalers. I am still in the business under the same name today, and it has been very profitable. Despite all the controls over cigarettes, I still make handsome profits today. However I have never been a smoker, and I detest the habit which I believe is not good for ones health. If today there was a total ban on cigarettes, I would welcome the move.

There was another business in which I got involved in that almost turned out to be more complicated than it was worth. At this time, there were no African wines and spirits importers or manufacturers in Kenya. All imports were in the hands of whites in companies such as Saccone and Speed, Jadin, L.N. Lakani, Mackenzie, Benco and others. It was felt that there were too many of such businesses in the hands of whites, and the Kenya Government, according to the Africanisation policy of the time, wanted Africans to take over. Many industrial and business concerns underwent a similar transformation.

The Government, through Joe Kibe, the PS in the Ministry of Commerce and Industry, decided to create a separate agency, Kenya Wines Agencies Limited, (KWAL) under Kenya National Trading Corporation (KNTC) which itself was under the Industrial and Commercial Development Corporation (ICDC). ICDC was an investment company which had been created by the government to help Africans own and run large businesses. It was intended that KWAL would manufacture wines and spirits locally, to add to those products from abroad.

Companies like Wanja Enterprises, Joles Ltd., Waiganjo Wines and Spirits, W.G. Murathe and Sons, and my own Nararashi Distributors, were heavily involved in distribution and when we heard that KWAL was being created in order to produce spirits within the country, we formed an informal association to enable us exchange information on the market. Then, when we heard that shares in KWAL were coming up for sale, we met and decided that since we could well afford it, we might as well purchase the majority shares.

My fellow distributors knew that I was friendly with James Osogo, the Minister for Commerce and Industry, and asked me to convince him to let us buy the majority shares in KWAL. When I went to see him, however, I was told that he was away on official business in Singapore, so I decided to speak directly to Kenyatta about the matter. It seemed to be the most promising option.

Soon thereafter, my fellow distributors and I met Kenyatta at State House Mombasa. I explained the advantages of allowing distributors to purchase the majority shareholding in KWAL, and the benefits that would be gained by Africans owning the business. Kenyatta agreed and told me it would definitely be rewarding, however we would have to wait for Osogo to handle the matter. I believe that if Osogo had been in Kenya at the time, we would have been assigned KWAL straightaway.

When ICDC leaders got word that we planned to acquire a majority shareholding in KWAL, Matu Wamae, the ICDC Chairman, and others, acted quickly to halt our attempt. They told Charles Njonjo, the then Attorney General, that our companies were not purely African-owned, either. They further told the AG that most wine distributors had whites and Indians as partners, and that we were just a front for non-African businessmen. Matu and others in the ICDC leadership found out about this anomaly and told the Attorney General that if we bought majority shareholding in KWAL, it would not be truly Africanized and the industry would remain in the hands of foreigners. I admit that this was true to some extent because some wine distributors had foreign partners who chose to remain in the shadows.

Unknown to us, Kenyatta was briefed by Njonjo and thus was not in the same mood he had been earlier, when we met him again on the matter. Osogo had returned from Singapore and I made a new appointment with him and the President, to be held the following week in one of the State House board rooms.

On the day of the appointment we were quite jovial as we went in to see the President, confident we would be allowed to purchase majority shares in KWAL. When we were admitted into the board room, however, we were somewhat perplexed to find Matu Wamae, Charles Njonjo and Daniel arap Moi already there. We had expected James Osogo, as the Minister for Commerce and Industry, since he held the portfolio concerning matters such as KWAL, but why were the other three present?

When the meeting began, I was given the first opportunity to speak, since I was the nominal spokesman, and had arranged the meeting. I pointed out the advantages we had gained now that Africans were governing themselves and running their own industries. I explained to the President how grateful we were for getting the opportunity to buy shares in KWAL, and I promised that we would run it professionally for the benefit of the government and for Kenyans. My colleagues nodded in agreement as I raised each point, but I did not like the frosty looks on the faces of Moi and Njonjo.

Then Kenyatta spoke. "I have heard what Njenga has said, but he is too quick and clever for me to catch him. I want someone else among you to speak," Kenyatta stated, leaving us wondering what he meant. He told me to sit down and asked my fellow distributors to speak.

A number of my colleagues raised their hands to be allowed to expound on our suitability to buy shares in KWAL, and W.G. Murathe of W.G. Murathe and Sons was given the chance to speak. Murathe had originally worked as a driver at Saccone and Speed and had risen through the ranks before starting his own small distributorship. I knew Murathe well because he lived in Mucatha near Banana in Kiambu, where I had run businesses in the past. He spoke along the same lines I had, saying what a great thing it was to see the wine trade being Africanized.

Then Kenyatta confounded us all. He took a document out of his desk drawer, unfolded it and started studying the contents. "Do you have a partner?" he asked Murathe as he raised his eyes from the paper.

"Yes," Murathe replied. "My wife, Njeri. No one else."

Kenyatta's face hardened and his eyes glared as they always did when he was angry.

At that moment I realised we were not in for a smooth ride.

Kenyatta again read from the dossier he was holding.

"What about Mehta?" he thundered. "And what about so-and-so Patel? And what about this other *Mhindi* called so-and-so? Are they your brothers?"

"I have employed them, Sir! They are my employees," answered Murathe, meekly shaken.

"Kwenda huko! Kaa chini!" (Go away! Sit down!) Kenyatta roared.

As Murathe slunk back to his chair, Kenyatta glowered and asked us if anyone else would like to speak. Those who had previously raised their hands looked away nervously, avoiding the President's eyes. They now understood that he had all the details of their partnerships and most of them had non-African partners. It seems that Njonjo had dug out all our business records and given them to him. In short, those of us with foreign partners, whether active or dormant, had compromised our standing.

"You see, Njenga?" Kenyatta exclaimed. "It's too bad that some of your people still want to do the bidding of foreigners."

"But Mzee," I argued, "what about those of us who are genuine? What about those of us who do not have foreign partners and interests?"

Kenyatta stared at me and then whispered with Osogo for a few minutes, consulting him on the issue. I remained hopeful because I knew Osogo had a good heart, but as for the President, one never knew what he might come up with.

"Alright," said Kenyatta after some time. "You distributors without foreign partners will get five percent of KWAL. ICDC maintains the rest."

So we got our little five percent of the shares, and ICDC retained ninety five percent. The meeting ended at that point and I think I saw a look of triumph in Njonjo's eyes.

Before the State House meeting, we had organised a large barbeque at PanAfric Hotel. We had been looking forward to feasting on a number of roasted goats in celebration of our victory in acquiring shares in the biggest liquor manufacturing industry in the country. We had been so confident! We thought it would be a simple matter to convince the president of our suitability and that the appointment was just a formality. But we had forgotten the Kikuyu saying, *Mwīro wa ngoro ndūkinyaga* (Wishes of the heart rarely become reality).

After emerging from such a defeat at State House, rewarded with merely a crumb instead of the whole loaf, I wondered why we should go to celebrate.

"Why should we go to PanAfric now?" I asked aloud. I was very disappointed at the developments.

"We might as well go and console ourselves," said one of my colleagues. "Drown our sorrows, you know?"

We drank the expensive champagne we had ordered in advance, and feasted on our *nyama choma*, but it was a little depressing, despite the five percent consolation.

Life is like that. You win some, you lose some. Nevertheless, I still have my portion of the KWAL shares we acquired at the time.

Chapter 6

Gema and the Reluctant Leader

GEMA. The word, or acronym as it is, still raises controversy to this day. It is an organization that continues to elevate temperatures and debate in political circles, and is associated with ethnic bigotry, elitist tribalism and the abuse of power in its extreme. Yet many do not know the facts behind GEMA, the Gikuyu Embu Meru Association.

For one reason or another it seems that my name somehow became synonymous with the organization, and on numerous occasions I have sought to set the record straight. Contrary to many myths about GEMA, I was not even part of the group that conceived and founded the organisation. I was, at the time GEMA was founded, just an ordinary businessman who happened to be a friend of President Jomo Kenyatta. I was not even an MP and had no aspirations of joining politics. I only wanted to mind, literally, my own business. How I came to be GEMA chairman in later years and became the most recognised face of the assembly was not through my own doing. It was, in fact, actually against all my wishes.

GEMA was formed in 1971. Many people, including the tribes that were supposed to be members, were not aware of what it was or of its agenda. It was seen by many as a tribal alliance that gave the Mount Kenya communities leverage to dominate other tribes and, by extension, the whole of Kenya. While member tribes cautiously welcomed the founding of the body with a combination of reluctance and enthusiasm, the rest of Kenya's tribes were definitely not pleased. The reason for this critical reception was that the Kikuyu already dominated all areas of governance and commerce, and every place one went was either headed by a Kikuyu or was manned by a majority from that tribe.

From the Civil Service to private business to the diplomatic corps and other institutions, the Kikuyu were, in most cases, the top administrators. The Kikuyu elite and academia of the time tried to justify this preponderance by arguing that the tribe dominated all fields by virtue of being the majority and by having taken early advantage of European education which was required for the high ranking jobs that arose for Africans after Independence. After all, the apologists said, there were also more Kikuyu in prison, in hospitals and in mortuaries. So why would one expect there to be a minority of Kikuyu in government? It was not their fault, they declared, that they had a bigger population or that they were more educated and better qualified.[44]

Before the dawn of Independence the small tribes had already formed KADU in order to counter KANU, in fear that the larger tribes would push them to the periphery. They were led by Ronald Ngala and Daniel arap Moi, who constantly reiterated that the small tribes would be reduced to insignificance if KANU took power after Independence. The beliefs of Ngala and Moi and of other KADU leaders were influenced by the settlers who wanted to remain behind after Independence. The settlers intended to create spheres of influence in the new nation and they thus wanted to establish a system of federalism, or *majimbo*, as it was called. They believed that this system, by generating autonomous regional governments, would enable them to have greater influence in areas where they had interests such as the Coast and Rift Valley Provinces. This system of government was actually put in place when Kenya gained self rule in 1963 but was abandoned after Independence when a central government took its place.

Kenyatta and other nationalists had never favoured *majimbo* and had conceded to its adoption as a matter of political expediency, thus hastening Kenya's independence. Later KADU was dissolved and all its members joined KANU in 1964, with Kenyatta as the party leader and President of the republic.

But the suspicion that the Kikuyu wanted to dominate other communities still remained. Kenyatta's kitchen cabinet was full of members of his own tribe. There was James Gichuru, the man who had given up the Presidency of KANU after Kenyatta was released from detention in Kapenguria. Then there was Charles Njonjo, the favourite son of a former colonial chief; Mwai Kibaki, the tough economist with a degree from Makerere and a First Class degree from the London School of Economics; Kenneth Matiba, Gikonyo Kiano, Mbiyu Koinange and a horde of other Kikuyu Embu and Meru who were constantly in Kenyatta's presence wherever one looked. There were several 'outsiders', too, such

44 Because the Kikuyu have purchased farms in areas outside their traditional homeland they are accused of grabbing land, government positions, and stealing from other tribes. This has led to murder, displacement and other atrocities following tribal clashes, which usually occur around each General election since 1992.

as Tom Mboya, Ronald Ngala, Jaramogi Oginga Odinga, Daniel arap Moi, Kitili Mwendwa, James Nyamweya, Taita Towett and a few others. Kenyatta had tried as much as possible to strike a regional balance in his government and the Civil Service, but it was obvious that it was the Kikuyu who were dorminant.

To a large extent, the country was virtually being run by the Kikuyu community. One may blame Kenyatta for this state of things and accuse him of tribal bias, but it would be short sighted to do so without considering all the other facts.

There are a number of factors that stand out in Kenyatta's over-reliance on his own tribe. First of all, Kenyatta, at Independence, personally knew many Kikuyu who were available and who could fill up the various positions in government that required education and knowledge. Next, many GEMA politicians felt that their own community had led the main struggle for freedom and it was now time to reap the benefits. For example, out of the 200,000 people arrested and detained in Nairobi Province when the State of Emergency was declared in 20 October 1952, eighty percent of them were Kikuyu.[45]

And so this Kikuyu majority took over the government and running the country when Independence was declared on 12 December 1963. Many of the small tribes were not happy with the state of things, and it was only a matter of time before discontent increased. Jaramogi Oginga Odinga resigned in 1966 and started the Kenya Peoples Union (KPU) in protest. But Kenyatta silenced all voices of dissent by ensuring that none of Odinga's supporters made it back to Parliament in the mini General Election in 1966. KPU was proscribed in 1969 and the dominance of Kenyatta, the Kikuyu and KANU allies continued.

It was against this precarious and unstable background that the Gikuyu (Kikuyu), Embu, Meru Association (GEMA) was formed. A group of Kikuyu, Embu and Meru MPs felt that they were under threat from the other tribes who, when combined, far outnumbered them. They were also concerned about the issues which began to divide them after the realisation of independence. They therefore decided to form an association to strengthen and protect the communities they represented and which they could fall back upon in any eventuality.

GEMA was ostensibly set up as a welfare association. As I see it, the sentiments of Kikuyu superiority or need to dominate were actually absent

---

45   Many more were held, tortured and killed in various Kikuyu reserves, while the other tribes recorded very few casualties in the war for Independence. It may sound bigoted, but it is a fact that whereas there were many patriotic freedom fighters from all over the colony, the majority were Kikuyu.

when GEMA was formed. I believe that there was no aim, ambition or even notion that the Kikuyu were superior.

When GEMA was formed there were other tribal organisations already in place such as the Luo East African Union which had been in existence for over 40 years and was led by Paul Mboya, the New Akamba Union, which was over 25 years old and led by Mulu Mutisya, the Abaluhya Union and also the Kalenjin Enterprises Union. There were also others, such as the purely commercial Luo business, "Luo Thrift", headed by Jaramogi Oginga Odinga, which had been active before that time.

As such, the GEMA leaders felt no guilt when they formed the organization since it seemed that all the various tribal groupings existing in the country were established for their members' welfare.

At the time it also seemed that tribal animosities were few and far between, and atrocities such as tribal clashes were non-existent. Tribal associations therefore gave people a greater sense of belonging and identity and were never intended to divide the country. I earnestly believe this to be true but I know that not everyone agrees with this assessment. I feel that ethnic identity is something to be proud of, but the whole issue of one's tribal origin was twisted by politicians to create suspicion and hatred.

Before the formation of GEMA, James Gichuru, a close confidant of Kenyatta, sensed that MPs from central Kenya did not seem united nor did they speak with one voice. Gichuru suggested that all MPs from the region take their tea together in the Parliament cafeteria, in order to bond more fully with each other. These informal forums led to the proposal to form a more regular union.

The MPs took their idea to Kenyatta and convinced him that there was need for such an umbrella organization to cater for the needs of *Mbarĩ ya Mũmbi* (the House of Mumbi), meaning the Gikuyu, Embu and Meru who are related by language and lineage and are considered by historians to be close cousins. Consequently the groups felt they should be united and they wanted a legitimate organization to push their agenda. Kenyatta accepted to the formation of the union and consented to become the association's patron.

When Kenyatta agreed to the formation of GEMA, I doubt that he knew what a force GEMA would become. I say this because I personally witnessed a time when Kenyatta became quite uncomfortable with the influence of the organisation and even rebuked its leaders, telling them to stop imagining that they were the government. He thought of GEMA as a cultural movement and allowed its formation in order to retain the support of his lieutenants. Whatever the case, he permitted its creation and subsequent events were virtually beyond his control.

GEMA was registered under the Societies Act in a single day by the then Attorney General, Charles Mugane Njonjo, who was acting under the instructions of Kenyatta. However Njonjo later came to intensely detest the movement. He never attended GEMA meetings nor did he want to see his name associated with it in any way. In general, we have had a somewhat cold relationship over the years.

At this point I should tell you about how I became acquainted with Charles Njonjo. We actually first met when he was a clerk at the Attorney General's Office in 1958. Charles Kigwi and I had gone to the Office to register our company, Kiambu General Transport Agencies Ltd., the partnership we had created in order to distribute beer. When we entered, we started looking around for anyone who might possibly give us advice on how to proceed.

Kigwi saw Njonjo sitting inside and told me, "Oh, look! That's the son of Chief Njonjo. I'm sure he can help us." Kigwi knew Chief Njonjo because he had been a chief himself before he retired to concentrate on business.

And so he did. Njonjo assisted us and gave us plenty of good advice.

I met Njonjo again later in the year at Dr. Samson Mwathi's farm in Ngemwa, near Githunguri. Dr. Mwathi was a great friend of mine and also a director of the East Africa Building Society. He had just bought some land and he invited us for a goat barbeque. Njonjo was one of the guests who came along with others like Paul Mirii and Mareka Gechaga. All of us ate and drank. We talked a lot and I recall it was a happy social get-together. At around this time, Njonjo and I were not very close, but neither did we have any differences.

I am not sure exactly when it happened, but Njonjo changed after he became the Attorney General. There was one case I recall in particular, when I definitely noticed a difference in his personality.

At one time, Stanley Munga Githunguri, who was the Chairman of the National Bank of Kenya, was accused of stealing the institution's money and arrested. Githunguri was a good friend of mine and by this time I was already the Chairman of GEMA. When I heard the news I called another friend, Mbugua Murihia and we went to Githunguri's house to see if we could learn the details, or if there was anything we could do to help. We were told by his wife, Karungari, that all she knew was that he had been locked out of his office at the bank and then arrested.

So in the morning I phoned Njonjo, made an appointment and went to his office.

James Karugu, Njonjo's deputy, announced us. "Mr. Njenga Karume is here, Sir."

"Come in," Njonjo said.

Karugu was also asked to come in with me. Being Njonjo's deputy, Njonjo would never speak to anyone on official matters unless Karugu was present.

Karugu took up a seat next to me.

After the usual greetings, I asked Njonjo my question, "Why can't you release Githunguri on bond?"

"You know why. He has stolen money from the Bank's customers. I cannot release him."

"I find that very difficult to believe. Why would he stoop so low to steal customers' money? It's impossible. You must give him a bond."

"No. I've told you I will not. There is no reason why I should."

I tried to think of another approach. "Look, I know that no one is 100% honest, maybe we all slip now and then, but he has helped many people. Can't you balance it out somehow? He has done so well in every other respect. Weigh his good deeds against the alleged bad ones, Mr. Njonjo."

Njonjo continued turning me down. I pleaded with him for about an hour and finally, at the end of it, Njonjo reluctantly agreed to grant Githunguri release on bond.

"Alright!" Njonjo finally said. "I will let him out. But you warn him not to continue stealing!"

I thanked Njonjo profusely and we left. I was so relieved!

Later, I learned that, following this meeting, Karugu phoned Githunguri and told him the whole story.

After relating what had happened, Karugu exclaimed, "Githunguri, you are so lucky to have a friend like Njenga! He was desperate to get you released! He continued begging for over an hour, and he was almost in tears when he was pleading with Njonjo! He is the best friend you will ever have!"

But what Karugu did not know was that it was his own actions that had prompted me to continue for so long. Remember that while we were sitting at the table in Njonjo's office, Karugu was seated next to me. Every time it seemed like I was just about to give up, Karugu would stamp his foot down on mine, under the table. I do not know why, but this encouraged me to keep going, keep beseeching Njonjo to have mercy on Githunguri. And so I continued pleading.

Later on I met Karugu and we had a good laugh. Over a drink, I reminded him that I suffered from gout.

"I almost screamed out in pain every time you stomped on my foot!" I exclaimed. "Did you want me to scream and burst into tears in front of the Attorney General?"

"I did it for a good reason," Karugu explained. "I also wanted Githunguri released and I was so happy when you proved willing to take on my boss."

Anyway, to get back to GEMA, the leadership ranks of the association consisted of the many prominent personalities in Kenyatta's inner circle. The interim officials were as follows:

Chairman: Julius Gikonyo Kiano (MP for Mbiri, Minister for Commerce and Industry)

Secretary General: Lucas Ngureti Kamau (MP for Kirinyaga)

Treasurer: Mwai Kibaki (MP for Bahati and Minister for Finance)

Vice Chairman: Jeremiah Mwaniki Nyagah (MP for Embu and Minister for Agriculture)

Assistant Sec. Gen.: Jackson Harvester Angaine (MP for Meru, Minister for Lands and Settlement)

Organising Secretary: Waruru Kanja (MP for Nyeri)

A number of Kikuyu leaders and leading Civil Servants were not amused by the actions of the group. They believed that they should have been included and involved in an agenda that so intimately secured their tribal destiny, and they felt short-changed by the MPs.

This dissatisfied group wondered how the MPs had managed to convince Kenyatta that they alone were best suited to lead the organization, while there were highly capable people outside Parliament who could make significant contributions to GEMA communities. They held high offices in other circles and considered themselves leaders, despite the fact that they held no elective offices. Why had the MPs usurped the role of leadership for themselves yet there were many others who had made massive sacrifices for the nation and were heavily involved both in the battle for Independence and in entrenching Kenyatta as the leader of the republic?

The spirit of rebellion rose and those Kikuyu leaders who had been left out of the GEMA leadership decided to take actions to alter the current arrangement. They were led by Karuga Koinange who had been gradually promoted from the position of DO which he held in Kiambu during the 1962 elections. He was now the Central Provincial Commissioner and was a friend and in-law of Jomo Kenyatta.[46]

Karuga was, as already mentioned, a friend of mine, and together we decided to formally invite the Kikuyu leaders who shared this dissatisfaction to a meeting at Wambugu Farm in Nyeri in 1971. We chose Nyeri because this was Karuga's base as Provincial Commissioner, and it was quite far from both Nairobi and Kiambu where our activities would have been severely scrutinised. Our intention was to discuss and deliberate on our standing in the wake of this new association that purported to represent the welfare of the tribes 'that fought for the country's Independence'. Karuga and I, after wide consultations in all regions in the province, selected a group of Central Province leaders and professionals for the Wambugu Farm meeting. Kiambu elders led by Gatabaki Mundati also kindly and unanimously selected me to act as their representative.

When the meeting took place, the participants did not take long to agree that it was mischievous for the MPs to elect GEMA leaders from among their own ranks only. Not everyone could fit into Parliament, they argued, and there were many other leaders outside the House. There were numerous individuals who had been involved in creating the emerging nation and they should not be ignored or neglected. They decided to select three delegates from among themselves to present a petition to Kenyatta at his home in Gatundu. Those selected were Matu Wamae, Duncan Ndegwa and myself. Wamae was the Chairman of the Industrial Commercial Development Corporation while Ndegwa was the influential Governor of the Central Bank of Kenya. Although I did not hold any public office myself, due to my friendship with Kenyatta, I was sent to inform him of the intended visit and fix a date for the discussion and presentation of the petition.

As happens in many political intrigues, word leaked out and GEMA MPs soon knew of the intended meeting. It is not clear who informed the MPs, but I believe it might have been Kenyatta himself. We all knew that Kenyatta liked to play the middle ground. He would invite warring

---

46 Kenyatta had married Karuga's sister, Grace Mitundu, and was, in turn, a close friend of Karuga's father, Senior Chief Koinange, and his eldest son, Mbiyu Koinange, who became Kenyatta's closest friend and confidant.

parties, who would be shocked to find themselves in the same meeting with their adversaries, and then let them confront each other. Instead of the usual backbiting and rumour mongering that took place in such political altercations, the facts would eventually become clear. Kenyatta would listen to the dispute, ask insightful questions and consider all sides of the argument before reaching a decision. He had little time or patience for petty squabbles and personal arguments.

Whatever the case, when the Wambugu Farm group went to Gatundu, we found the group of GEMA MPs whom we had grievances against. What we had thought would be a closed door meeting with just the three of us and Kenyatta, turned out to be a meeting of more than fifty people. Ninety percent of the GEMA MPs were present. Kenyatta pretended that it was a mere coincidence, but he felt that, since both groups were represented, the issues could now be clarified. Of course we did not like it, but we knew that Kenyatta had arranged it and so we had to play along.

The GEMA MPs were well-prepared. They knew they had to counter the accusation that they were an elitist group of parliamentarians with ulterior motives. They had therefore invited various KANU leaders, who were not MPs, to join them. These included the likes of Kihika Kimani, the Nakuru KANU chairman, among others. The MPs wanted to demonstrate that they had consulted widely and that GEMA was representative of people from all walks of life and all areas of the GEMA tribes. In the face of this development, our Wambugu Farm group was confounded, but we were determined to pursue our case all the same.

And so the meeting got off to an acrimonious start. Both sides traded accusations as Kenyatta listened. The MPs accused the Wambugu group of meddling in affairs they did not understand, while our Wambugu group accused the MPs of seeking self-aggrandisement, leaders who were using the GEMA tribes as a vehicle for their own selfish motives. Mwai Kibaki, one of the MPs, belittled "the so-called Wambugu farmers" by stating that we lacked the intellectual capacity to understand GEMA's rationale and objectives. In reply, I told Kenyatta that the *"tu-MPs present"* (the little MPs present) did not represent the views of the people and that they operated from the ivory towers of Parliament. If they wanted to scorn us as the "so-called Wambugu farmers", I thought I might as well play their game, too.

One MP, George Mwicigi complained that Mzee was giving me too much time to air my views while the MPs themselves had to jostle for the microphone. Both sides dug into each other, and finally, after lunch, Kenyatta suggested a solution.

He suggested that both groups begin working together to form a stronger GEMA, rather than operating as two warring factions. An interim committee of six MPs and non-MPs was to be formed in order to tour Central and Eastern Provinces and collate the views of the people at the grassroots. The people could then explain what they expected of GEMA and give suggestions to make the organization more powerful and meaningful to them.

Three of us, Matu Wamae, Duncan Ndegwa and I were chosen, while the MPs representatives were GEMA officials, that is Mwai Kibaki, Waruru Kanja, Gikonyo Kiano, Jackson Angaine, Lucas Ngureti and Jeremiah Nyagah, so we were nine altogether. Grudgingly, the MPs accepted this arrangement, which was not, of course, a suggestion but rather a ruling by Kenyatta. As I have mentioned, it was very difficult to say 'no' to Kenyatta. In any case, at this initial stage, the real objectives of GEMA as an organization were ill-defined and not all those present were reading from the same script.

Not much later, the selected team toured Central Province as they had been instructed and collected the views of the people. At the end of the exercise they presented a report to Kenyatta. It included various suggestions and complaints from all of the GEMA tribes, including the shortage of land, insufficient infrastructure and the lack of other resources. The report was then presented to Kenyatta and he called the same selected teams to Gatundu. Meru and Embu people complained that the Kikuyu had gotten the lion's share of Ministerial appointments while the Nyeri Kikuyu complained that the same Ministerial appointments had all gone to Murang'a and Kiambu. At that time there was no full Minister from Nyeri.

Kibaki was then the MP for Bahati in Nairobi, but he was originally from Nyeri. When Kenyatta read this latest point, he asked jokingly, "*Kaĩ woriire Nairobi Kĩbakĩ?*" (Kibaki, did you get lost in the pleasures of Nairobi?)

Kenyatta was trying to diffuse a tense situation by his remark. It was true that Nyeri had no Ministers. The President was trying to demonstrate that although Kibaki was a Nairobi MP, he was a Nyeri man who also held a very powerful portfolio as Minister for Finance.

At the end of the day, it was agreed that the leaders who were not MPs should also be granted life memberships in GEMA and should be involved in all decision-making bodies of the organization. The life membership, which MPs had already taken, cost the newcomers 500 shillings.

However, despite all this, during that early period GEMA was more of a theoretical concept rather than a practising association. It took some time to set up a working network within the province it purported to serve, and a number of public meetings with provincial leaders had to be organised in order to enlighten the people on the objectives, goals and meaning of the alliance.

Since the GEMA constitution stated that the election of officials should be held every two years, the tenure of the interim officials expired in 1973. At the time, however, the spirit of rebellion had infected GEMA's ranks. Many members viewed the officials, under the chairmanship of Julius Gikonyo Kiano, as highhanded and proud intellectuals who did not represent the ideologies of the majority. They were seen as highly inaccessible and furthermore members believed the leadership acted as a barrier between themselves and Kenyatta. Most members no longer wanted such officials to represent them.

Many people believed that the person who would be most suited to chair the association should be simple, accessible and available, and simultaneously well-connected and influential. And thus they proposed me.

I was definitely not interested. When people came to ask me to agree to the proposal I refused. I recall that Dr. Munyua Waiyaki was very persistent but I just did not have the ambition to get involved in politics. In fact, although I was enthusiastic about the organisation, I can confirm that when my name was proposed for GEMA chairmanship, I was appalled. I did not want anything to do with leadership. My profession and skills were centred on business, an activity to which I was fully devoted.

This is why, even while I sat with Kenyatta and Gichuru listening to the election results over the radio in my house in Kiambu, I never once gave a thought to elective politics. I simply had no ambitions in that field. I considered politics and leadership to be the preserves of those who had specific talents, and I felt I was certainly not one of them. Therefore, when I was approached with the proposal to lead GEMA by many delegates, (some from Kiambu, but most from other areas) I flatly turned it down.

GEMA had by this time become a major force in the political landscape, and any leader from the community who ignored the association would be doing so at his own peril. Kenyatta, as the patron, was highly interested in the daily affairs of GEMA and its leaders briefed him on everything of significance. So when Kenyatta learned that I had refused to consider the chairmanship of GEMA, he summoned me to Gatundu. I am not certain who informed Kenyatta of my position, but I think it was someone like Dr. Munyua Waiyaki, James Gichuru or Mbiyu Koinange. The three had been attempting to persuade me to take up the chair, but I had politely refused.

Naturally when Kenyatta called me, I had a fairly good idea why he wanted to see me but from the outset I pretended it was just another social visit like the many others I had had with him. I took Jackson Kamau and Charles Kibe Karanja along with me. The two were my neighbours in Kiambu and Kamau was the Chairman of Kenya Tea Development Authority while Kibe was the organization's General Manager.

As usual, Kenyatta started the meeting with casual small talk with us before getting down to the real business. He asked me how things were going "out there in the country" and I said it was all just fine, everything was okay. However, Jackson Kamau and Karanja did not think so.

"Why not tell Mzee the truth?" Kamau asked. "The people want you to lead GEMA but you have refused!"

Kenyatta asked me why, as a matter of fact, I had refused to lead the society. I was not happy about the way the conversation was going, but I replied that I was completely committed to my businesses and it would be impossible for me to perform satisfactorily on either activity if I were to take on the responsibilities of both.

"If the GEMA leadership was meeting in Nakuru and one of my beer distributing lorries crashed in Thika, I would go to Thika," I protested. Seeing that I had made no impression I continued, "My businesses will always come first."

Kenyatta could not be persuaded to change his view, however. He proposed that I chair the association for two years until someone suitable could be found. Again this was not actually a suggestion, but rather a directive. Reluctantly, I accepted the post of chairman which had, in reality, been imposed on me even before the elections had been held. I was not exactly certain how the consequences would affect my businesses, but I was displeased with the whole prospect. Elective politics and leadership had never held any appeal for me, but due to my relationship with the President, I was unwilling to disappoint him.

I guessed that the matter must had been discussed and settled long before this particular meeting and my suspicions were confirmed when the President's wife, Mama Ngina, came to the room to serve us some tea afterwards. As we conversed she mentioned that she had heard that I had refused to "serve the people", and asked me whether this was true. I assured her that I was willing to serve in whatever way that was necessary, and that the matter had been settled. She thanked me for "offering" myself.

That was that. I was forty four years old at the time, and the new GEMA chairman would doubtless be me, Njenga Karume. Kenyatta may have "talked" Kiano out of seeking re-election, and it was settled.

The GEMA elections of April 1973 were hotly contested. In fact, they were a great deal more acrimonious than the previous parliamentary elections. It seemed that most of the candidates had realized that GEMA's position in the Mt. Kenya region, in Nairobi and in the Rift Valley was even more strategic than Parliament and that it would be more prudent and tactical to be in GEMA, if not in both bodies. GEMA had the support of the President and the electorate, and furthermore, endorsement by GEMA was as good as a ticket to Parliament. Wambugu Farm in Nyeri was selected to be the venue for the elections because it had been the site where the original group of non-MPs had first met to air their complaints about GEMA. Holding the elections in the same locale seemed to be a symbolic victory of sorts for the non-MPs.

Nearly all delegates supported me for the position of Chairman, but the battle for the post of Organizing Secretary saw the fiercest competition. Kihika Kimani attempted to oust Nyeri MP, Waruru Kanja, and they both went full out in their campaigns. The two rivals traversed the GEMA region drumming up support in the days prior to the elections and they spent considerable sums of money in the attempt to achieve their ambitions.

On the eve of the elections, Kihika Kimani camped in a hall in Nanyuki town with his supporters. Waruru, on the other hand, was with his supporting delegates in an Embu hotel. Each camp was afraid their supporters might defect to the other and so they were entertained lavishly. Both contending camps held magnificent feasts, and many goats faced the knife. Copious amounts of drinks were consumed and money changed hands.

It is said that the feasting at Kihika's camp was most ostentatious and extravagant. The guests ate and drank till they could hold no more. Kihika even bought mattresses which were placed on the floor in the hall so that his delegates could sleep overnight ahead of the following day's elections.

However, Kihika was so suspicious of his supporters that he would allow none of them to step outside the hall for fear they would be compromised by Waruru's supporters. Kihika, it later emerged, held the keys to the hall and positioned himself on his mattress in the doorway. Anyone wanting to pass through the door, for whatever reason, was escorted by Kihika himself to guarantee that they would not desert his cause. He even accompanied the delegates when they went to the toilet!

There was a lot of tension in the elections in which Jeremiah Nyagah was the Returning Officer. Kiano, the previous Chair, was not present at the venue, nor was he expected to attend, and, since I was unopposed, I was voted in as Chairman. The member who proposed me was Njagi Mbarire, (father to Cecily Mbarire who would later be nominated to Parliament by President Mwai Kibaki in 2003). After a great deal of heckling and shouting, Kihika Kimani trounced Waruru Kanja for the Organizing Secretary's post.

Other positions were not as bitterly contested, but they had been carefully scrutinized in advance and were virtually pre-determined. This was because GEMA, in order to cement its unity, found it essential to delicately balance the leadership to reflect all regions and communities of the association. Duncan Ndegwa, from Nyeri, got the Vice Chairmanship while Ireri Njiru from Embu was elected Secretary General. Jacob M'mwongo from Meru was elected National Treasurer since Mwai Kibaki did not defend the position. The Assistant Secretary General's post went to Wilson Macharia from Murang'a while Stephen Kiragu from Kirinyaga became the Assistant Treasurer. The previous MPs had more or less decided that they would not contest.

All in all, the original founding MPs were the heavy losers in the 1973 elections but the fallout did not seem significant, and all regions and communities were more or less satisfied with the results. Of all the founding MPs, only Waruru Kanja contested. Lucas Ngureti wanted to contest, but we talked him out of it because the seats of Chairmanship and Vice-chairmanship had already gone to the Kikuyu.

My wife, Wariara, and my mother, Teresia Njeri, accompanied me to the election venue and sat in the car waiting for me to finish. After the GEMA meeting, we all intended to leave for Molo.

At this point, I think it is would suffice if I mentioned what was going on in the life of my parents. My father and mother had been repatriated from Elburgon to Kiambu during the State of Emergency and from there they stayed on my farm for a while, but they were not very happy. They had been away from Central Province for more than fifty years because it had been 1923 when my grandfather first moved to the Rift Valley, so I believe it was a problem for them to adjust. For some reason, they also found the people in Kiambu somewhat unfriendly and felt they did not belong. So in 1975, I bought them a farm in Nyahururu. They were quite pleased to move to Nyahururu and I was happy to see them settled there.

After the GEMA elections, I was resigned to taking up the challenge of leading the organization, but all the same I vowed not to abandon my businesses and farming activities.

This was just the beginning of GEMA's influence, and its impact on national politics was later seen in the General Elections of 1974. Now that we felt secure on the standing of central Kenya, we decided to expand our horizons by trying to influence the elections in Nairobi. Our ambition specifically extended to promoting members of our associated communities to the positions of elected MPs in the city. Consequently most of the candidates running for seats were handpicked by GEMA leaders. Those we saw as unlikely to succeed were asked to step down in favour of others.

It was at this time that Mwai Kibaki's political history took an interesting turn. We in GEMA were making plans to take all the seats in Nairobi. Since Kibaki was from Othaya in Nyeri, we were convinced that he could stand there while we put someone else to vie in Bahati.

Gerishon Gichuki, other friends and I convinced Kibaki to stand in Othaya, his home constituency, where he had better chances of winning. Gerishon and Kibaki were in-laws as they had married two sisters. We felt Kibaki would have a safer political future in Othaya compared to metropolitan Nairobi—and he has never lost an election there since 1974!

Kibaki phoned me one morning and when we met over a cup of tea at the Norfolk Hotel, he told me that he had decided to concede to our wishes and relocate to Othaya constituency. I assured him that he had done the right thing and promised to support him in any way I could. Somewhat later in the campaign, I was invited to be the chief guest at a *harambee* intended to raise funds for laying water pipes in Othaya constituency.

With Kibaki's withdrawal from Bahati, however, GEMA was faced with a problem. The Election Day was approaching rapidly and they still did not have anyone with sufficient popularity to oppose Jael Mbogo and others. However, GEMA knew that, provided they made the right choice of candidate, they had the voters and the finances to ensure that such a person went to Parliament. Money was one thing that the GEMA leaders did not lack. Therefore when I asked Kibaki to recommend someone to succeed him in Bahati, he suggested Dr. James Muriuki,[47] who was in his car at the time, and who was a friend of his, also from Othaya. Kibaki brought Dr. James Muriuki in, introduced him and we had a cup of tea together. Afterwards I advised Kibaki to take Muriuki to the GEMA officials in Nairobi and Bahati so that they could coordinate his campaign.

Unfortunately, I believe that the choice of Dr. Muriuki in 1974 was a disaster from the beginning and we almost lost the seat. Muriuki was a stubborn individual with no knowledge or experience in politics and had no notion of how to go about a campaign. By the time the GEMA leaders realized this, it was too late to put someone else in his place. Dr. Muriuki, in his naïveté, selected young men from Nyeri district as his youth wingers and chief campaigners, and foolishly left out those from other districts in the larger GEMA region.

The GEMA leaders decided that this would absolutely not do. The Bahati GEMA Chairman, Kirimania, and the Nairobi Branch Chairman, Mwangi Mathai, informed me that the candidate for Bahati was a total failure. They suggested that Mwaura Gatete or Muthoni Likimani would stand a better chance of taking the seat if they had good support from GEMA. The two were renowned political activists. However, I told them it was now too late to make a change, and I gave GEMA leaders the mandate to campaign in Bahati, independently of Dr. Muriuki. They would be campaigning for GEMA rather than the candidate. Likewise, I asked Dr. Muriuki to continue his own campaign and let the GEMA leaders do theirs. After all they shared the same goal.

As it happened, Dr. Muriuki won the election, but I feel that the seat was actually won for him through the use of GEMA funds and influence. All the seats in Nairobi were taken by members of GEMA. Dr. Munyua Waiyaki won in Mathare Constituency, Mwangi Karungaru in Embakasi, Maina Wanjigi in Kamukunji, Dr. Njoroge Mungai in Dagoretti and Charles Rubia in Starehe. A relatively unknown candidate, Wachira Waweru, trounced Samuel Kivuitu to become Parklands MP while Mwangi Mathai won in Lang'ata.

---

47 Dr. Muriuki later went on to challenge Kibaki himself but that was much later, in 1988, when Kibaki was the Vice President. Moi was the only MP who was unopposed in the 1988 *mlolongo* (queue voting system) for the General Elections. Perhaps Moi wanted to show his superiority and did not want Kibaki to go unopposed, so in that year, he sponsored Dr. Muriuki, a tactic which would also stop Kibaki going to campaign for others who Moi was opposed to.

For me, this accomplishment was a major triumph because it conclusively proved the strength of GEMA. To take all eight seats in metropolitan Nairobi was no easy feat, and it had only been made possible through the massive influence of GEMA. When I was invited to Gatundu shortly thereafter, I was sure Kenyatta was going to congratulate me for a job well done. GEMA had bared its teeth and shown what it could do.

When I arrived at Gatundu, I found Kenyatta in the company of Eliud Mathu, Mbiyu Koinange, Mama Ngina and Kenyatta's brother, James Muigai. There were no congratulations for me, however. Although he did not directly censure me, Kenyatta expressed concern that Nairobi, as the metropolitan capital of Kenya, should have a diversity of MPs in terms of ethnic origin.

"Couldn't you have left even one seat?" he asked. "You should have at least spared *kamwe ka igongona* (one ceremonial seat)[48] for the other communities!"

I had thought *Mzee* would be very pleased with all our hard work and suddenly I understood what he was talking about. It was a revelation.

"Sorry, Mzee. You know I really don't know anything about politics," I said meekly.

I think Kenyatta had discovered, after it had already happened, that it did not look quite proper to have all the MPs from one community. This GEMA domination would not look good to the other tribes, nor would it do anything for the unity of the country. Added to that fact, GEMA communities had taken over ninety percent of the seats in the City Council, as well, and so Kenyatta had reason to be concerned. Even his daughter, Margaret Wambui, was elected the Mayor of Nairobi.

The more I thought about it the more I realised my mistake. I had not thought about the elections from this perspective, but I immediately understood Kenyatta's logic. I confessed my ignorance of political manipulation, however, and reminded Kenyatta that the murky world of politics had been unknown to me even when he chose me to head GEMA. After all, I was not an elected MP myself and would never consider vying for such a post. I promised, however, that I would never make such a mistake again. It is probably because of this ignorance that Kenyatta nominated me a Member of Parliament, probably so that I could learn a thing or two about politics.

---

48 In Kikuyu traditions, every homestead should have at least one animal (goat or sheep) which can be used for ceremonial purposes should the need arise. Even if a person's entire flock was confiscated, for example to pay a debt or a fine, the complainant could not take all the animals – they had to leave kamwe ka igongona.

GEMA thus became very powerful.

I remember years earlier, I used to meet Pius Gumo at the Mt. Elgon Bar where most KADU bigwigs used to meet. Gumo became my friend, and after independence he bought many farms around Kitale.

So, when members of GEMA hosted a party for me in Kitale, I found Pius there. During the party, Pius told me about his son, Fred, who aspired to be the mayor of Kitale. Pius asked if I could help his son to realise his dream.

It so happened that among the councillors who would vote for the mayor, three were members of GEMA. If I could convince them to give Fred Gumo their votes, he would sail through. I called one of them, a man called Julius Wang'ang'a, who was the local GEMA chairman and a nominated councillor.

"Pius is a great friend of mine," I said as I introduced the two, "and he has a son who needs help to become the mayor."

Wang'ang'a and Pius exchanged small talk and got to know one another.

Then Wang'ang'a said, "We councillors had decided to give our votes to a Mt. Elgon Maasai councillor, but now, since you, Njenga, have made the request, we are willing to oblige. You're our Chair and we respect your advice."

Pius was overjoyed and thanked Wang'ang'a. However Wang'ang'a interrupted and said, "Just make sure your son works hard and brings progress in the council."

And so when the election were held, Fred Gumo won the seat, from which point he started to build a political career. He is currently the MP for Westlands in Nairobi and a Cabinet Minister in the Coalition Government. I count him as one of my friends and continue to refer to him as 'Bwana Mayor'.

In 1975, it was again time to elect new GEMA officials. For me, the time could not have come too soon. I was exhausted by the day to day running of the organization which took so much time and energy, and I was only happy to hand over the mantle to new blood. I wanted nothing more than to concentrate on my businesses and my family and leave elective politics to politicians. I still felt that I did not belong.

The meeting which was set to elect the new officials was held at the Desai Memorial Hall in Nairobi. But I was in for a surprise. While various leaders wrangled about the positions they wished to vie for, one member, Njagi Mbarire, stood on a point of order and declared he had a proposal. While all the seats would be contested, he said, everyone was in agreement that the Chairman should retain his seat unopposed. I think my face was the only one in the hall that held an expression of dismay and worry, while other members cheered wildly at the proposition.

I stood up to protest and reminded the delegates that two years previously, I had agreed, with extreme reluctance, to lead the organization. My two-year term was over, and I did not want to seek re-election. I reminded them of the GEMA motto, *Kuuga na Gwĩka* (Words with Actions) and declared that endorsing me in such a manner was contrary to the whole spirit of the motto and to the society's constitution, which clearly stated that democratic elections were mandatory.

That Sunday afternoon at around 4 pm, I went to Gatundu and found Mzee Kenyatta with Eliud Mathu, James Muigai and Mbiyu Koinange.

"You know, *Mzee,* I've been elected again," I said in despair. "I think they elected me by force. Now, what should I do?"

Kenyatta shook his head. "You should have seen me yesterday, Njenga. What can I do now? If you had come to me earlier, I could have issued a statement that you are a thief or something," he joked.

"Please, *Mzee,* surely there is something you can do."

"It is too late," the old man said. "Now you will have to wait another two years."

In 1977, there was another GEMA election in Nakuru. This time I had made up my mind that, no matter what happened, I would never be Chairman again. I had come armed with the GEMA Constitution which clearly stated that a person could only hold the office of Chair for two years. We had already breached this clause and surely the members would not do it again.

As I explained my stand to the members there in the gathering, I heavily emphasised my reluctance and argued that it was my time to go.

"Please give the chance to someone else," I pleaded. "I simply cannot be Chairman any longer. The Constitution does not allow it."

One delegate from Murang'a, a man with a powerful authoritative voice stood up to speak. This was Kenneth Stanley Njindo Matiba, a close friend of mine and who was the Chairman of Kenya Breweries Limited (KBL).

"Mr. Karume, you are always giving us problems. We can amend the constitution to make it a four year term. Constitutions are made by men," he declared, "and they are also changed by men."

He immediately proposed a motion to change the GEMA constitution so that the Chairman would serve a four-year term. Other officials would still serve for two years as the constitution stipulated. The delegates endorsed this unanimously.

I tried to plead my case, but they would hear none of it. After all, there were other more educated and qualified people who could lead the union, I argued. Nevertheless, it seemed that my words fell on deaf ears, and I was elected Chairman for another term.

After that, albeit with a lack of enthusiasm, I immersed myself fully in my duties in GEMA. The organization acquired various farms and properties, and every paid-up member received shares in these concerns. In this commercial part of the organisation, at least my business acumen came in handy and, through various loans and business arrangements, the group was able to gain substantial property all over the country.

Some time previously, in October 1973, shortly after I first became Chairman of GEMA, a team of officials and I visited Kenyatta in Gatundu. I explained that GEMA was having cash flow problems, which was a major hindrance to its activities. Very few people were contributing their yearly membership fees and the organization's coffers were in the red. I presented Kenyatta with a proposal. GEMA was a union, and if the President would allow the formation of GEMA Holdings Limited, my team and I would use our expertise to turn the subsidiary organization into a profitable outfit. This would make it more viable and give it relevance and credence among the members.

GEMA Holdings, as I envisioned it, would be a company that would invest heavily in various fields. In my view, the membership would be composed only of members of GEMA communities. GEMA would sell a share for one hundred shillings, and the maximum value of the shares a member could purchase would be ten thousand shillings. Kenyatta gave the go ahead, and I contacted Waruhiu and Muite Advocates, a leading city law firm, to form and register the company. Githongo and Associates were contracted as the company's auditors.

And so GEMA Holdings started doing business. Our first acquisition in 1975 was the Clayworks brick factory along Thika Road. The owners, some Italians who went under the name of Gonella and Company, contacted me and informed me that they were selling a majority shareholding in that company, in order to concentrate on other businesses. The price for seventy five percent of the shares was six million shillings.

I could have bought the company for myself, since I had been approached in an individual capacity, but I chose to let GEMA have it. I wanted to demonstrate to Kenyatta that the association was capable of much more than mere community politics and welfare. So I met with the board of Standard Chartered Bank. My own most significant accounts had always been held in this bank, and Standard Bank handled my major transactions, therefore, with this in mind, the board naturally trusted me. GEMA Holdings subsequently opened an account and negotiated a loan of six million shillings and payment terms.

Shortly afterwards, GEMA Holdings purchased seventy five percent of Clayworks, and later on purchased the remaining twenty-five percent, which it still owns to this day. As a matter of fact, GEMA Holdings offices and secretariat are located in the factory near Githurai. The factory produces bricks and other clay products and it still declares dividends to its shareholders. I have been re-elected chairman ever since the purchase and I still chair the board.

The second acquisition GEMA Holdings made was the purchase of two parcels of land, one measuring forty-four thousand acres in Gilgil, and the other measuring thirty-one thousand acres in Rumuruti in Laikipia. At this time, many European settlers were still selling their land in the country, and one, Arthur Cole, had heard about me and my keenness on acquiring land. So he invited me to buy his two ranches for twenty million shillings. Cole, who was returning to the UK, wanted the money paid directly to his account in England.

GEMA Holdings and I had a problem. The group did not have that kind of money and even if we had it, only the Central Bank Governor could authorize such a massive bank transaction involving accounts in different countries. I briefed Kenyatta and thereafter, Cole and I were invited to State House.

Kenyatta began with a bit of flattery. He informed Cole that he himself was a great friend of his uncle, Barclay Cole. Kenyatta had been employed as a meter reader by the colonial government in the 1920's and had worked with the older Cole in a water project in Nanyuki. Kenyatta said that Barclay had been the first European in the area to invite a black man, that is Kenyatta himself, as a guest to the whites-only Muthaiga Country Club. So, Kenyatta told Cole, he had no objection to getting down to business.

I used my negotiating skills as a businessman and managed to convince Cole that I could organize a one-off payment if Cole could reduce his asking price to twelve million shillings. Kenyatta said that Cole would be the first *Mzungu* to receive such a favour. So Cole did not take long to accept the offer. Although it was considerably lower than his asking price, he still had the two advantages of receiving the money in London, and receiving all the money at once, rather than in instalments. Kenyatta called the Central Bank Governor, Duncan Ndegwa, and told him to facilitate the transfer. I had been fairly sure my offer would be accepted, and had, previous to the meeting, negotiated the twelve million shilling loan with Kenya Commercial Bank, which was headed by John Njoroge Michuki, a talented financial manager, so everything was completed quite smoothly.

But I would like to explain that when Jomo Kenyatta phoned Ndegwa, right in front of Cole and me, it was obvious that he was himself a very shrewd businessman and clever judge of human nature. He knew that Ndegwa would not be very pleased to receive Presidential instructions to facilitate such a large transaction. Kenyatta knew it would hurt Ndegwa's ego to be commanded to do this and that for Njenga Karume, so the President decided to play games in talking about the whole affair.

"Yes Ndegwa, how are you?" Kenyatta asked in Kikuyu, over the phone.

He listened a while to Ndegwa's reply and then asked, "How many Central Bank Governors are there in Kenya?"

I assume that Ndegwa told him there was only one.

"Are you still the GEMA Vice-Chairman?" Kenyatta asked. "And does Njenga Karume let you sometimes take over GEMA's chairmanship in interim capacity when he goes for his businesses abroad? . . . You mean he does not? Selfish fellow!" said Kenyatta.

As we were only able to hear one side of the conversation, we speculated on what Ndegwa might have said.

"I will send him to your office with a *Mzungu* and when he comes," Kenyatta told Ndegwa, while winking at me, "keep him waiting at the reception for about thirty minutes. We don't want him to think he is so important that he grows horns now, do we? And then facilitate the transfer of twelve million shillings to the *Mzungu's* account in England, okay?"

Ndegwa must have complained that twelve million was far too much to transfer abroad, but then Kenyatta assured him that with the acquisition of the farms, the money would easily be repaid. The farms had cattle that would be productive and the land was collateral as well. After all, with Africans controlling agriculture the value would remain here forever.

No doubt, in this short conversation, Kenyatta demonstrated that Ndegwa, as Central Bank Governor, had authority over financial transactions in the country. Ndegwa, of course, was quite pleased with this recognition, especially since he did not know that I was with the president at the time. Kenyatta often did things like this, always trying to keep his friends happy and rarely taking sides.

When I went to see Ndegwa, he did not keep me waiting at the reception as Kenyatta had suggested. After all, he was GEMA's Vice-Chairman and this transaction would be of great benefit to the association. I went to John Michuki of Standard Bank to facilitate the transaction and thus the funds were quickly on their way to England.

However, GEMA Holdings now had to find a way to repay the loan. I consulted Duncan Ndegwa, my fellow director in the organisation, and the two of us came up with an idea. We decided to keep the land and manage it as a set of ranches, since there were already seven thousand head of cattle that came with the acquisition, which would enable us to repay the loan.

GEMA's Annual General Meeting (AGM) at Kikopey in Gilgil, was opened by the Rift Valley Provincial Commissioner, Isaiah Mathenge, that year, and was attended by over six thousand members.

I informed the members of the purchase of the land and informed them that we would utilise the land as a ranch and repay the loan from the proceeds. However the majority of the members, who had purchased one share for one hundred shillings, were opposed to this. Many of them were landless and felt they would be better off if the land was subdivided.

I tried to convince them that the land was not viable for cultivation but they would not budge. I further told them some of it was even on the rock. But they were the majority, and after four hours of argument they won the day. So we subdivided the land into parcels, which were sold to members at one thousand shillings per acre. After all, I felt that the company had been formed to empower the members economically and if it was sub-division they wanted, sub-division they would get.

But a difficulty arose. We explained that chaos would ensue if the members were allocated land according to the shares they held. Whereas there were many people with only one share worth one hundred shillings, there were others with shares worth ten thousand shillings. How was the sub-division to be carried out? Those with a majority shareholding would be entitled to most of the land while the small shareholders would get insignificant pieces or even end up with nothing. It was quite a dilemma, and a great deal of time was spent on the debate.

I thought about it for quite a while and finally came up with an original concept whereby neither those with many shares nor those with few would feel cheated. Each acre would go for one thousand shillings. In the face of that, I proposed that those with shares worth ten thousand shillings would be allocated two acres of land, worth two thousand shillings. Two acres would also be allocated to those with shares worth one hundred shillings. However, those with a single share had to pay the balance of one thousand nine hundred shillings, to raise their shareholding, in order to get a two-acre plot. All members agreed to this proposal and the money that was realised from the sale was used to pay off the bank loan.

In addition, we told those members whose shares had been undervalued, meaning those who received two acres for shares worth ten thousand, that they would be compensated with money from the sale of the unused land in the Clayworks factory. The Clayworks land measured two hundred and eighty-three acres, but the factory occupied only eighty-three acres. The other two hundred acres did not have clay soil and so was not beneficial to the factory. We proposed that the rest of the land be sub-divided into eighth-acre plots and that these be sold to individuals, hopefully, persons from GEMA communities. The plots, being in a semi-urban area, were bound to fetch better prices than the semi-arid land in Gilgil. The proceeds would then be shared out in proportion to the value of a member's shareholding.

In the end of these proceedings, for example, those who had shares worth ten thousand shillings were paid out a whooping two hundred thousand shillings, those with five thousand shillings worth of shares were given one hundred thousand shillings and so forth. I did this to help the poor people and I was pleased with the result. The poor were very happy to have a piece of land to call their own. If we had sold the land to those most able to buy it, the rich would have got nearly everything, and the poor would have got virtually nothing.

There was a large colonial house on the Gilgil ranch land which a certain European lady wished to purchase. She was already leasing it from GEMA and managed a wool shearing and sales business on the premises. However, GEMA members, those who had bought the smaller parcels, were opposed to selling her the house. They did not want a European in their midst. After all, it was the whites who had stolen their land in the first place, they argued. Kenyatta had said that Europeans were going back home, so the members felt it was preposterous for me to consider having one of them buy the house.

One member, Wanjohi Kirogo, came up with a proposal. He said that since I was the Chairman I should buy the house and the adjacent land myself, so that I could 'look over my people'. He wondered why I was abandoning them there. He said I should lead by example. The other members agreed unanimously, and I was forced into agreeing on the purchase. An independent valuer assessed the house and set it at seven thousand two hundred shillings and thereafter I bought the house, including the compound. I called in three business partners and together we refurbished the building and converted it into a hotel. We also built thirty three cottages on the plot. The outcome today is Jacaranda Elementaita Lodge.

Meanwhile, a dark cloud was gathering on GEMA's horizon. The organization had managed to take control of Central Province and Nairobi politics and all the MPs who had won in the 1974 General Elections in those areas were backed by GEMA. Furthermore, other GEMA officials and I were very close to the President.

Little by little, GEMA was becoming an overwhelmingly strong and influential body and this caused alarm and concern in certain circles. I, as the Chairman, had just become a nominated MP, but to some people it seemed that I had more power than many high-level government officials. The tribal exclusivity was also making many outsiders uncomfortable. They viewed GEMA as a meddlesome, sinister and formidable creature whose elusive tentacles were continually growing and influencing the society by underhand means. Kenyatta was also growing older, and many people outside GEMA's inner circle felt that the organization was an impediment to the eventual Kenyatta succession. Complaints and grumbling grew and opposition to GEMA's insidious power was becoming more and more obvious.

At the height of GEMA's power in 1978, members went to visit Kenyatta one day in Gatundu. These members would be flying out to attend an agricultural show in England and as the overall Chairman, I introduced the GEMA branch chairmen to Kenyatta and told him that the union had representatives all over the country from Mombasa, to Kisumu, Garissa and Moyale.

Kenyatta warned GEMA not to go overboard, to imagine that it was the government or more powerful than KANU and the government. I do not believe that Kenyatta was actually worried about GEMA's success; he merely issued this warning for the benefit of GEMA's critics, such as Vice President Daniel arap Moi and Attorney General Charles Njonjo, who were present at the meeting. Kenyatta never believed that GEMA would become a threat to the country. After all, he nominated me to Parliament in 1974 as a sign of his confidence in me.

One of the factors that made GEMA hated among other communities was that it took its slogan of *Kuuga na Gwĩka* to the extreme.

Other tribes and tribal organizations had watched GEMA buy thousands of acres of land, a large clay industry, and saw its membership soar to hundreds of thousands of registered and active members. It had gobbled up all the parliamentary seats in the capital city and acquired properties left, right and centre. No other tribally affiliated group had ever operated on such a massive scale before, and all this had occurred within four short years. Those who were not GEMA members or those with an eye on the Kenyatta succession felt that GEMA was unstoppable and would sooner or later take over the leadership of the country.

Among all the other critics, there were two people to whom the whole concept and existence of GEMA was an abomination. These anti-GEMA individuals were Daniel arap Moi, the Vice President, and Charles Njonjo, the Attorney General. To my mind, Charles Njonjo was an arrogant and self-conceited fellow who felt that he was intellectually superior to all those who were close to Kenyatta.

Charles Njonjo was the son of Josiah Njonjo, a colonial chief, and as such he had been born into a privileged childhood. He had attended the best schools and attained a law degree from Fort Hare University in South Africa. He then proceeded to England for his pupilage before coming back to Kenya. Kenyatta appointed him to the post of Attorney General shortly after Independence and since his appointment, he carried on in a supercilious and haughty manner, ignoring or sneering at those who did not agree with his ideas. All those who knew him describe him as an ambitious man who had the aspiration of becoming the President upon the death of Jomo Kenyatta. He was close to the President, who was somewhat of a father figure to him, and Njonjo would never contradict Kenyatta openly. But once out of the President's vicinity, he made no secret of his opinion that Kenyatta was surrounded by idiotic advisors.

Then there was Moi, a loyal Vice President to Kenyatta and who was, according to the Constitution, supposed to be the successor, should Kenyatta die. Moi served loyally, never disagreeing with his boss, and he was a patient man who knew his time would eventually come. After all, he had willingly made a sacrifice and dissolved his party, KADU, in order to join KANU and support Kenyatta. Moi and many other leaders outside GEMA felt that it would only be justice for him to ascend to the presidency. Moi embodied the united ambitions of the small tribes, who had originally formed KADU in order to protect themselves from the dominance of the large tribes. Consequently they expected Moi to take over the highest post in the land. A great many members of these tribes felt that the Kenyatta regime had ignored and sidelined them, and that Moi would correct this situation.

Despite being a Kikuyu, there was no love lost between Njonjo and GEMA. GEMA simply was not significant enough to gain his attention.

Moreover he did not get the respect he thought he deserved from the association. He viewed the group as a horde of ignorant villagers who neither had the intellect to understand power, nor the facility to do anything but accede to Kenyatta's whims out of sheer ignorance. He especially loathed Mwai Kibaki, a graduate of the London School of Economics who was now the Minister for Finance. Kibaki was the favoured intellectual among GEMA leaders and he carried out his job as expected and did not engage in petty politics. Nevertheless, Njonjo viewed him as a rival for the top seat.

In my opinion, Njonjo did not have much respect for Moi's intellect either because, after all, Moi just had some basic primary school education. But Njonjo feared Kenyatta. He knew that those who had shown the slightest bit of insolence or contempt to Kenyatta had done it at their own peril. Njonjo therefore befriended Moi, probably believing that he would be able to manipulate him and the law, when the right time came. And given Kenyatta's age by the mid 1970s, the time was not far off.

Njonjo and Moi viewed GEMA as an obstacle standing in the way of their succession plans. The association's leaders included most of those in Kenyatta's kitchen cabinet and Njonjo knew that it would take careful manoeuvring by Moi and himself to succeed in attaining power after Kenyatta's death. He was also uncomfortable with the powerful coterie of Kiambu leaders who formed Kenyatta's inner circle. This group did not take Njonjo seriously and they were irritated by his pretentious aristocratic mannerisms.

However, Njonjo underrated the power of GEMA, as he discovered when the "Change the Constitution Movement" began. This movement began with a conversation that took place on a plane one day in 1976. Kihika Kimani and I were flying to a meeting in Geneva. We were discussing a topic that had become the subject of many discrete conversations in and outside the corridors of power. We were talking about Jomo Kenyatta's declining health and what would happen if and when he died.

Kihika, who was the MP for Nakuru North, was a somewhat arrogant politician with questionable ideas of his own grandiosity. He was reasonably wealthy and had helped settle many people, especially the Kikuyu, in Rift Valley Province. He had accomplished this through setting up land-buying companies such as *Ngwataniro Mutukanio* Company and thus many Kikuyu in the Rift Valley had a great deal of respect for him. He was also Kenyatta's eyes and ears in Nakuru and the Rift Valley and had clashed with Moi over many issues including power politics and supremacy in the province.

On his side, Moi did not like Kihika because Kihika had taken Kikuyus to settle in the Rift Valley and this reduced Moi's influence as he was not assured of Kikuyu support. Kihika attacked Moi in every forum available and apparently hated him. I often told Kihika to be careful about how he talked about Moi in public since Moi could become the President someday and then he, Kihika would be in a tight spot indeed.

Kihika was however least bothered. He could simply not envision the possibility of a Moi presidency and was of the opinion that it would be business as usual following Kenyatta's death since it was certain that another member of the House of Mumbi (in other words, a Kikuyu) would automatically take over. He was not alone in this view. Many of the individuals in the Kiambu group of leaders were of the same school of thought. Kenyatta had created such an aura of invincibility around himself that even the idea of his death and succession never created uneasiness in the minds of those around him. Kihika and many other Kikuyu leaders just assumed, quite naïvely, that one of them would take over in case of any eventuality. The Kikuyu formed an overwhelming majority in the government and some of the leaders assumed that this was just the nature of things, a *fait accompli* and that it would always be so.

Now, as we flew over the continent below us, I shattered that assumption.

"How would Moi become President?" Kihika asked, astonished by this possibility. "Where would our Kikuyu leaders be, if and when this happened?"

I reminded Kihika that there was the small issue of the law.

"The Constitution," I informed him, "states categorically that the Vice President takes over as acting President if the President dies in office."

This shocked Kihika. He had no idea that the law had anything to say on the matter. Moreover, Moi was his political enemy and then, perhaps even worse, he was not a Kikuyu. Kihika was the worst kind of Kikuyu chauvinist, and the very idea of Moi becoming President appalled him. Something had to be done quickly to prevent this eventuality. As he thought over the matter, Kihika hatched an idea which he shared with me.

"The best option," he said, "is to campaign to have that ridiculous clause in the document changed, to ensure that Moi never becomes acting President."

We both knew that Moi would have a distinct advantage in any presidential election if he had already occupied the position in an acting capacity for 90 days.

We devised a plan. We would campaign, both in Parliament and outside, to have three different individuals stand in as acting President for those 90 days. The three proposed stand-ins would all be senior civil servants appointed constitutionally. But Vice President Moi would not be among them. He was completely omitted from our scheme.

The three people thus selected to stand-in should preferably stay in the capacity of acting President for three months prior to the election. This would give the leaders from GEMA tribes and those from other tribes who did not favour Moi, ample time to organize their supporters and elect a person who they would be comfortable with for the Presidency. The three individuals we had in mind to stand-in were the Head of the Civil Service, the Parliamentary Speaker, and the Chief Justice. I have to state that up to today, I am still very uneasy with the section of the Constitution which allows the Vice President to automatically take over for 90 days. In the wrong hands, this could be a recipe for disaster.

Among the forerunners for the Presidency, Kihika and I supported Mwai Kibaki. We decided to enlist support from our colleagues who shared anti-Moi sentiments and then start a campaign to have the Constitution altered.

When we returned to Kenya, this is just what we did. We secretly began to canvass for supporters among our parliamentary colleagues. Leaders from GEMA tribes needed no inducement whatsoever, but the support from other community leaders for the "Change the Constitution Movement" was somewhat surprising. We, as the leaders of the movement planned to go round the country addressing *wananchi* (the citizens) and gather support for the idea before going to Parliament to change the law. This way, the idea would appear to have more authenticity as it would demonstrate the full cooperation of the people.

The first meeting of the "Change the Constitution Movement" was held in Nakuru in 1976. It was, to use a phrase that Kenyan journalists have rendered a tired cliché, 'a mammoth rally'. Thousands of Kenyans attended and leaders from various tribes, other than the Kalenjin, addressed the crowd. They spoke unflatteringly of Moi's style of leadership and told the people that the person who would take over from Kenyatta should be a strong character who could steer the country forward. They depicted Moi as the antithesis of this person and urged *wananchi* to support their goal of changing the constitution. They convinced the crowds that giving the acting capacity of President to just one person would ensure that that person would 'cement' himself into the seat and refuse to budge even if he were defeated in an election.

"Let me tell you people," Paul Ngei, the Minister for Cooperatives and Housing, told the crowds in Afraha Stadium, "If my wife, Emma, and I were to go to State House and I was in the acting capacity of President for three months, I would never get out for any other person to occupy the seat. Not even the strongest animal in the world would pull me out of there."

This summarized the gist of the leaders' speeches in that particular, highly-charged rally. Speaker after speaker expressed misgivings about Moi in leadership, and there were many speakers. There was Kihika himself, Paul Ngei, William ole Ntimama, John Konchellah, Dr. Njoroge Mungai, Taita Towett, James Gichuru, Jackson Harvester Angaine, myself and many others. This Nakuru meeting caused a stir all over the country and spread alarm among Moi's supporters. We organizers felt it had been a success because the people's apparent support had given it legitimacy. It no longer appeared to be just a GEMA plot, and we rode home that day on a wave of jubilant success.

Njonjo, Moi and his camp were not surprised by the tactics and strategy of the "Change the Constitution Movement" but they were appalled and shocked by the enormous popular support from the leaders of other tribes. It could have been dismissed as a GEMA delusion and belittled as mere trivial tribal ambition, but with such colossal espousal, it could not be swept under the carpet. The massive turnout in the Nakuru meeting was not a good indication for either Moi or Njonjo. They felt that something had to be done, and done quickly. If the "Change the Constitution" group continued to go around the whole country creating negative propaganda and gathering support from *wananchi*, Moi's future looked bleak.

After considerable deliberation, Njonjo came up with a fairly simple, yet totally devastating solution which surprised the rest of us. As the Attorney General, he called a press conference and announced that all those who addressed the Nakuru rally would be arrested and charged with treason. The Penal Code had an interesting little section which stated that it was an offence for anyone to imagine the death of the sitting President. The offence amounted to treason, whose sentence, according to the same document, was death. Therefore, Njonjo said, those who had addressed the Nakuru rally had not only imagined the death of the President, they had stated it outright, through the use of loudspeakers. They were on record for having uttered words that insinuated the President's death, and Njonjo told the press that he had a watertight case against them. No doubt Njonjo was congratulating himself as he spoke. His counter-attack was ingenious.

The Nakuru meeting had made headlines in all the papers and Njonjo's declaration, a few days later, made headlines again. No one in the history of Kenya, had ever been charged and convicted of treason and this in itself was big news. Furthermore, the people whom Njonjo intended to arrest were prominent leaders from across the whole political divide, and charging them all with a capital offence was almost unimaginable. The consequences of charging them and finding them guilty would be sure to shake the whole country and would alter the Kenyan political landscape forever. What the world would think of such an action, if it were to ever take place, was another thing altogether.

Being an early riser, I was up before 5 am and started my day by reading the newspaper. I was absolutely stunned to see my name and those of the other leaders who had spoken in Nakuru, on the front page. I immediately understood, with great dismay, that Njonjo actually had a water-tight case against all of us. According to the Penal Code we were all guilty of treason, without a doubt.

I immediately phoned Paul Ngei and informed him about the development. Next I called James Gichuru and we discussed it with a sense of urgency. We realised that our only sure source of protection was Jomo Kenyatta himself.

Kenyatta was in Nakuru that weekend, and we decided to go see him at State House. We also called Angaine and asked him to meet us in Nakuru.

So the four of us, Ngei, Gichuru, Angaine and myself, together with Kihika Kimani, who joined us later, sat at a table at Midlands Hotel in Nakuru and reviewed our predicament before we went on to see the President. If Njonjo actually carried out his threats the lot of us would be in prison in a short time. We all agreed that Kenyatta would probably be willing to intervene, but informing him about the whole matter was somehow a very different, uncomfortable and distasteful thing.

I dialled the Nakuru State House number, which we all knew by heart, and asked for the President. As I waited to be connected, my courage just trickled away, I lost my nerve and, in a fluster, I gave the phone to Gichuru. Gichuru was the most fearless and daring among us. Gichuru informed Kenyatta that the five of us were in Nakuru and would like to talk to him about a certain issue. Kenyatta told us to join him at State House and so we all drove there.

As usual, the inscrutable Kenyatta appeared to know nothing of the reason for our visit. He pretended to be pleasantly surprised and welcomed us to Nakuru. Although he did not reveal any knowledge of

Njonjo's threats, he obviously was well aware of what had been going on. However, he allowed Gichuru to struggle with the explanation of the whole embarrassing story. It was not easy to mention that so many people were virtually anticipating Kenyatta's death but somehow Gichuru laboured through. Finally Gichuru revealed that the Attorney General, Charles Njonjo, was threatening to charge us with treason. Then, Gichuru hesitantly asked Kenyatta to give his views on the matter.

The rest of us sat silently, quite worried and anxious about the President's reaction.

Kenyatta did not react immediately, then he suddenly laughed so uproariously that he had tears in his eyes. He was shaking with mirth when he pointed at us, sitting there in such a subdued manner. In between his laughter he said, "I did not know I have so many cowards in my government!"

Gichuru and the rest of us smiled uncertainly, not knowing whether to join in Kenyatta's laughter or not. But how could we when he was laughing at us? But a wave of relief passed through us all nevertheless.

When Kenyatta wiped his eyes and recovered from his amusement, he promised that he would talk to Njonjo and tell him to drop the whole issue. However, serious once again, he advised us to lobby in Parliament if we truly wanted to have the Constitution changed.

After that, we toned down our anti-Moi vitriol but the public rallies continued. There was another big rally in Meru which had been convened by Angaine, which I did not attend since I had gone for business in Mombasa, but the speakers were less critical this time.

Njonjo was not pleased with the campaign. Perhaps he had really imagined himself putting us all in prison, but now there was nothing he could do about it. We were Kenyatta's men, and although the President did not support us openly, he obviously knew what we were doing and did not intervene.

Stanley Oloitiptip, a burly Kajiado MP who was a Moi supporter organised a petition, and about 100 MPs signed against the motion to change the Constitution. After that no one had the courage to take the motion to Parliament. Gradually the movement fizzled out and died with a whimper.

As I see it, the "Change the Constitution Movement" leaders genuinely believed that what they were doing was right for the country. We were not just thinking of the situation at the time. We were thinking of the future.

Njonjo's relationship with me continued to sour thereafter. At one time, Njonjo vindictively decided to delay approval of GEMA's documents for the transfer of the seventy-five thousand acres of land in Gilgil and Rumuruti, discussed earlier.

All documents involving land transactions of public companies had to pass through the AG's office and it was quite inconvenient to have the approval delayed for long periods of time. On a visit to Kenyatta in State House, I happened to express my displeasure at Njonjo's delays in handling my papers. Kenyatta immediately phoned Njonjo, and the Attorney General appeared to be amazed, saying he had the document ready for collection on his desk. Kenyatta then asked him to deliver it immediately to State House and to do so personally. I remember the conversation, or rather one side of it.

"Njonjo, how are you?" asked Kenyatta over the phone. "Now, there are these papers for your friend Njenga Karume for these GEMA *shambas* they are buying. He tells me you have refused to sign them. Is that so?"

Although I did not hear what Njonjo said at the time, Kenyatta later told me that he had exclaimed, "You mean he is there making accusations against me again! I signed those papers long ago and they are just here on my desk waiting for him to collect them."

"Oh," said Kenyatta. "You mean you signed them a long time ago but you haven't been able to hand them over because you haven't met him for some time? Good, very good. As a matter of fact he is here at State House. You bring them over."

When Njonjo arrived, he was invited to join Kenyatta, who was having tea in the shade under a tree[49] with Mbiyu Koinange[50] and myself. The four of us conversed on trivial matters for a while, and then Kenyatta got to the point. He informed Njonjo and I that he did not like infighting among his ranks and that the two of us had better make peace and learn to cooperate.

What was it, after all, that the two of us were fighting about, Kenyatta asked. Njonjo replied that I always opposed his initiatives for unknown reasons.

---

49 Kenyatta had an eccentric habit of holding important meetings under trees. Sometimes, the whole Cabinet would deliberate on matters of national importance under one of the many trees on his farm in Gatundu. This is the traditional Gikuyu way. Elders deliberated under certain ceremonial trees, away from disturbances and especially from women and children.

50 This can be very confusing because it happens that Senior Chief Koinange wa Mbiyu had six wives and six sons named Mbiyu, (one from each wife). Peter Mbiyu Koinange was the one who was closest to Kenyatta and was a Minister in the Office of the President.

In turn, I accused Njonjo of being petty. He was always accusing me of siding with his rivals such as Dr. Njoroge Mungai, with whom he had differences. Yet I was not a politician and never took sides. I did not understand.

Njonjo told Kenyatta that at one point, he had even sent a team of arbitrators to talk to me and end the feud, but I had continued with my attacks against him. These arbitrators had been Central Bank Governor, Duncan Ndegwa and Assistant Minister for Lands, G.G. Kariuki.

I explained that I had no time to criticize Njonjo. I informed Kenyatta that on one occasion I was enjoying drinks at my Jacaranda Hotel with Police Commissioner Ben Gethi, head of Special Branch James Kanyotu, Ignatius Nderi, Director of CID and Jeremiah Kiereini, the Permanent Secretary in the Office of the President and deputy Head of Civil Service. Some people might wonder why such a group of important people in the government would all drink with me, a nominated MP, but we were just friends. I am not sure, but it may be closer to the truth to say that, at this particular time, by virtue of having Kenyatta's ear, civil servants befriended me 'just in case'.

Anyway, this group of friends and I talked about various matters of national importance and I mentioned Njonjo, very deliberately, in the course of the conversation. I complained about Njonjo and his attitude towards me. I did this intentionally because I wanted word to reach Njonjo. I was fairly sure one of the people I was sitting with would pass word along. And sure enough, later that night, Njonjo phoned me and accused me of backbiting him.

When Kenyatta saw that his arbitration was failing to make headway and that there was more to this feud than met the eye, he asked us to discuss the matter on our own like *wazee* and solve whatever problems we had between us.

I recall that as we were on our way out, Geoffrey Kariithi, the Head of the Civil Service, came in to see Kenyatta and Koinange.

Njonjo invited me to his car, an Audi, on our journey back to Nairobi while my driver followed us in my Mercedes. The two of us had a serious conversation. Njonjo pleaded with me to stop supporting the "Change the Constitution Movement" since it was in bad taste. Kenyatta was not dying and there was no hurry. He asked me to support Moi for the presidency, since this would ensure a smooth transition and continued stability. In turn, he promised me that he would make sure that my friend, Mwai Kibaki, would become Vice President to Moi.

"You know that Kibaki is a very intelligent person," Njonjo told me. "With him as the Number Two, we are going to be very safe. He will contain Moi."

In turn I told Njonjo that I could never trust him since recently he had threatened to charge me with an offence punishable by death.

I informed Kibaki about Njonjo's statement and we both concluded that he was probably just trying to manipulate us. All the same, upon Kenyatta's death and Moi's accession to power, Mwai Kibaki was actually named Vice President and Njonjo phoned me after the announcement, making sure that I noted that he had kept his promise.

GEMA engaged in quite a number of activities for the benefit of its members. One such an event was a trip to Coventry in England in 1978. GEMA farmers were to tour an International Agricultural Show at that venue, in order to learn about better farming techniques and the latest farm inputs available.

One evening, Kibaki invited me to a harambee at Kimathi Institute as the Guest of Honour, and since there were many GEMA members at the venue, we met at Duncan Ndegwa's home near Nyeri town after the function. We were entertained by a famous Kikuyu singer and accordionist, Wagatonye, who enthralled us with his popular folk songs which always carried one message or another. In one of his songs he passed along a message, which sounded very witty in its original Gikuyu.

"Mr. Chairman,
Let me also put my foot on the eagle
Taking people to Europe.
The highest I have ever gone
Is the top of a tree."

In other words, he wanted to come along on the plane and visit England with us.

We all found this quite amusing, and I called John Mubia Wairagu, one of the first African Land Valuers, and told him that he should now raise money from his friends to pay for Wagatonye's airfare. I thought it would be very entertaining to have Wagatonye with us. So John went round the groups at the party asking people to make donations. The fare was ten thousand shillings. Samson Muriithi Nduhiu, a businessman, gave a thousand, Kibaki gave a thousand, Mayor Nahashon Kanyi Waithaka, the Nyeri KANU Chairman, gave a thousand and money was starting to pile up. I told John to go outside because there were plenty of people in the garden and he could try his luck there. After an hour he came back and told me that the job was done. He had raised eleven thousand shillings.

When he heard that he would be able to accompany the farmers, Wagatonye sang another song for us, a song which poked fun at his own appearance. Again, an English translation cannot do justice to the poetry and wit of the original.

"Two things I am good at
Are ugliness and music.
Since we are here for music
And not competing in ugliness
I will now sing for you with all my heart.
And if I get lost,
If you cannot find me,
Don't look for me in the river valleys.
Look for me in England."

In the end he travelled with the farmers to the UK and kept them entertained. Altogether there were about one hundred people who stayed for two weeks. It was a mixed group, mainly GEMA members, but also others from organisations such as the Kenya Farmers Association (KFA) and the Agricultural Society of Kenya (ASK). I arrived a little later than the rest, coming in a week after the tour started. All through, people were constantly complaining that they had to drink draft beer, but what they really wanted was Tusker.

At the end of the tour, we hired a hall there and had a big party. As a special treat, I phoned Kenneth Matiba, another GEMA official and Chairman of Kenya Breweries, and asked him to send thirty crates of Tusker Premium Beer by air, which we served at the party. Everybody was incredibly happy and the beer was drank to the last drop. Even the whites at the counter enjoyed it and complimented the flavour. I am not sure how it happened, but at the end of the party, six crates were missing!

Although I do not want to mention his name, I remember there was a certain person, a church elder who was also a councillor. He had always claimed he was 'saved' and never drank. But he felt that no one knew him at that distant venue, so when he saw the liquor being served, he started shaking and sweating and, finally overcoming his scruples, he asked for brandy. By the end of the evening he was completely drunk. When he encountered a woman, one of his fellow church-goers in Nyeri, he got a real shock.

"Don't report this in Nyeri," he pleaded with her. "This is London. It doesn't count!"

Kenyatta passed away on 22 August 1978, and the many events surrounding and following his death are described later. Moi took over power as the "Change the Constitution Movement" had feared, and he stayed there just as Ngei had predicted. Indeed, he stayed on the Presidential seat for 24 years. All those who had been opposed to his ascendancy were forced to pledge their loyalty to him, and they backtracked and swallowed their words, as many politicians do, in order to survive.

Those who did not toe his line were kicked out of government. Many Permanent Secretaries, parastatal chiefs and other senior Civil Servants whom Moi did not like or who were from the 'wrong' tribes were retired. What the GEMA leaders had feared would happen, had happened.

The time was now ripe for Moi and Njonjo to give me my reprimand. Shortly after Kenyatta's death, Njonjo told Parliament that GEMA was an illegal institution and a criminal one at that. This caused bitter arguments in the House, and I responded by saying that I would never lead a criminal organization and then accused Njonjo of jealousy. Why, I asked the Attorney General, had he agreed to register an illegal movement and let it operate from 1971 to 1979?

Nevertheless, the die was cast. A few days later, Moi banned GEMA, and the news was broadcast on radio and TV. It was now an illegal movement.

My associates and I had expected that this would eventually happen and we knew there was little we could do about it. However, there was another matter, and I booked an appointment with Moi at State House to discuss it. Unlike President Kenyatta, who hated State House and who never once slept in it, Moi enjoyed staying in the official residence. Once I got to State House, I told Moi that I had accepted his decision to ban the GEMA Union, but there was a registered limited liability company called GEMA Holdings that operated various businesses and had shareholders who had invested in it. The company had been registered in September 1973. One cannot just ban a company from operation, I told Moi, trying to reason with him. What would happen to its assets and the investments the shareholders had made?

Moi thought for a moment and then stated that he was opposed to tribal organisations. He made it clear that the company could continue to operate, but it had to change its name. GEMA was tribal, and it had to go. I was told to decide on a new name for the company and it could continue its business. So I spent some time thinking over the issue and finally wrote down a number of possible names. Among them were Kirinyaga Holdings, Mumbi Holdings and Kirimara Holdings.

When I returned to State House I took the names to Moi, who was in the company of Njonjo. Njonjo looked at my list and smirked. Kirinyaga and Kirimara, he told Moi, both meant Mt. Kenya, where the Gikuyu God, *Mūrungu*, was supposed to have his abode. Mumbi of course meant the House of Mumbi, the mythical mother of the Gikuyu tribe. They were, in short, all tribal names.

At a loss, I finally suggested Agricultural and Industrial Holdings Limited and the name was accepted.

But Njonjo was not done with me yet. I remained the Chairman of Agricultural Holdings, and thus he still felt dissatisfied. Shortly after GEMA was banned, Njonjo called the company directors Kihika Kimani, Kiragu Stephen, Jacob M'mwongo and Kigathi Rueben, and gave them one directive. He wanted them to ensure I was removed as Chairman.

This group met at Ambassedeur Hotel to plan out their strategy and decided they could easily just throw me out. Kihika was offered the chance to be Chairman but he declined. Then Kiragu Stephen was offered the post, and the others tried to convince him by saying that the chairmanship would come to his home in Kirinyaga. In the end, Kiragu agreed.

The rest then assigned themselves various directorships and called a press conference at which they announced that I had been removed from my position and Kiragu elected in my place. (The Chairman of a Board is usually elected by the directors, so they were within the law.)

The following morning the newspapers had large bold headlines announcing the change. They ran something like, "Njenga Karume kicked out of GEMA Holdings". Shortly thereafter newspaper reporters phoned or came to ask whether I had anything to say about the new developments.

In response I merely said that after twenty one days, I would call a Special General Meeting of all members, in order to officially hand over the office of Chairman to Kiragu Stephen.

Interestingly enough, when the Special General Meeting took place in Gilgil, about 8,000 members came for the meeting, but none of Kiragu's and Kihika's supporters showed up. I informed the crowd that I was no longer the Chair, stated that I had tried my best to serve them all through my time in office and concluded by thanking them for their cooperation in all our endeavours together.

But the members were in uproar. They were outraged by the actions of the new Chairman and his fellow directors.

All through my little speech of farewell, they shouted and interrupted.

"Where are they?" the members yelled wildly. I do not know what they would have done to any of the directors if they had showed up at the meeting.

The members dismissed the company Directors and the new Chair and elected new office bearers including Matu Wamae and Ngengi Muigai, among others.

"Bwana Chairman," one of them said, "we have now given you a new team to work with and we want you to continue as Chairman. We have also given you power to kick out any Director who undermines the company."

Another shareholder said, "If any of these new Directors go and have lunch or tea at Ambassedeur behind your back, sack them. Pick others and we will support you and endorse them in the next AGM."

Perhaps that shareholder, a farmer from some rural place, thought that the biggest and most impressive place for directors to plot their schemes was Ambassedeur Hotel. But his words were taken very seriously.

To date, the resolutions of those shareholders still stand and I continue to be the Chairman of Agricultural Holdings. The company continues to operate under that title. It still owns the Clayworks factory and several plots in Nairobi, and it continues to declare dividends. It has several employees and continues to sell hundreds of plots to Kenyans. Annual AGMs are still held, and I have remained in my position, having been re-elected unanimously since the 1970s.

As a result of the attempt to oust me, Kihika and I fell out badly for a while, but thereafter we re-united as friends. However when we formed the Democratic Party in 1991, we once again had a dispute which basically ended our relationship.

In 1992, Kihika was contesting a parliamentary seat on a KANU ticket, and he talked disparagingly about Mwai Kibaki and myself. He had changed allegiance and was now supporting Moi, who he had previously regarded as an enemy.

Although a lot of his criticism against me was mostly a campaign ploy, it nevertheless broke up our friendship. Kihika later joined our party and won the Laikipia seat but we never became close friends again after that and I was somewhat surprised when, after his death in November 2004, three of his wives called me to say that his dying wish was that I should be the master of ceremonies and that I should be in charge of the whole event.

I had initially refused to go for the funeral, and sent a cash donation instead. However, three of his elder wives (for he had more than ten) came to me and pleaded with me to attend.

One of the wives said, "The family will be haunted by a curse if you refuse to come."

"Kihika insulted me many times during Moi's rule," I replied, "and I'm just not willing to be present."

"If it is about insults, we should be the ones complaining," another said. "Kihika insulted us all, all our married lives, and even physically assaulted us!"

What could I say? In the end I went for the funeral.

"You see all these people?" one of the elder wives asked me during the funeral service. "Most of them have been insulted by Kihika at one time or another."

I found it sad that people sometimes utter words without thinking, never realising how deeply they can hurt, and then death catches them unawares, with no chance to apologise.

But to get back to GEMA, it seems that many people misunderstood the nature and intentions of the organisation. It was created to benefit its members economically, and it was successful in achieving this goal since thousands of people are now settled on their own land in the Rift Valley, courtesy of belonging to the union. GEMA was never meant to be a source of income for its officials, and none of them benefited from GEMA's existence in any way different from ordinary members.

As for the political side of things, I have to explain that the union was formed to unite the people of the GEMA tribes, just as other tribes had formed various unions. I have no regrets and can declare that the GEMA years were among my most fruitful, in terms of my efforts to serve the people of Kenya.

Recently GEMA was revived and interim elections have been completed. Its title is now GEMA Cultural Association and its Chairman is Reverend Bishop Lawi Imathiu. The revival took place after the community's intellectuals, church and political leaders realised that there was need for unity in order for the community to progress, and talk as one. A good number of groups have been meeting in various forums with the sole aim of uniting and creating peace between GEMA and other communities, and many of these have been amalgamated in the GEMA Cultural Council. Among the Kikuyu themselves, a need has been identified to unite the Nyeri, Murang'a and Kiambu peoples.

In addition, concerned leaders were highly distressed after the GEMA community bore the brunt of the post election violence in December 2007. The leaders, who have held a number of brainstorming meetings, raised concerns that the government has not been doing enough to protect members of certain tribes and that there is need for a welfare organization to help those affected by post election chaos. The proposed new GEMA also intends to spearhead a cultural renaissance among the GEMA tribes since many of its proponents feel that the people are slowly losing their cultural identity. The government has kept its hands off the new proposed movement, and it remains to be seen what will come of it.

Chapter 7

Reminiscences – Times with Jomo Kenyatta

In 1961, Jomo Kenyatta, the new leader of Kenya who was to pilot the nation into a new realm of Independence and infinite possibilities, was released from prison. He had been jailed with five other leaders on 22 October 1952, after being arrested and convicted of leading Mau Mau activities. Incidentally, I recall that before the trial, people everywhere donated one cent each in an effort to raise enough money to pay for his lawyer, Denis Pritt, from London, whose fees were to be twenty-eight thousand shillings. Somehow they managed to collect the required amount.

The Kapenguria Six, as they were called, had denied the charges, but after a trial marred by bribery and deceit, they were imprisoned by the colonial government, all the same.[51]

Now that Kenya was independent, Africans had every opportunity to realise their dreams. Earlier, as mentioned in Chapter 5, I had met Kenyatta in Gatundu, not long after his release, and the two of us had struck up an unusual bond of friendship that remained for life. Kenyatta immediately felt an affinity towards me, perhaps because I was hardworking and ambitious. I believe he might have seen me as a symbol of what young Kenyans could accomplish once we were freed from the chains of colonialism. Possibly Kenyatta felt that if I could manage to make so much headway, despite considerable opposition from the colonialists, the potential for all Kenyans was unlimited, now that restrictions had been lifted. In turn, I had great admiration for Kenyatta,

---

51 On 20 October 1952, Jomo Kenyatta and other suspected leaders of the Mau Mau were arrested. The top most leaders who faced trial in Kapenguria were referred to as the Kapenguria Six. These were Jomo Kenyatta, Kung'u Karumba, Fred Kubai, Bildad Kaggia, Paul Ngei and Achieng' Oneko.

as well. He was the father of the nation and a figure of inspiration and hope for all Kenyans.

With this strong friendship between us, things could not have been more favourable for me. I was not directly interested in politics, but I saw *Mzee*, who was over seventy at this time, as admirable and wise. Although I was young enough to be his son, this did not seem to stand in the way of our blossoming relationship.

Reflecting on our first meeting, I would have to say that I was thrilled to meet the famous old man, but Kenyatta's deep, searching eyes did not frighten me the way they did most people on first acquaintance. On the contrary, I think there was immediate acceptance between us.

Kenyatta, of course, had friends and colleagues who were more intimate with him by virtue of their political leanings and their closeness in age. Compared to these others who congregated in Kenyatta's Gatundu home and at State House, I suppose I was a mere boy. But they seemed to enjoy my company and very graciously treated me with almost the same amount of respect as they did each other, and thus, within a few years, I was lucky enough to become a part of Kenyatta's inner circle.

The majority of the men who were closest to Kenyatta were from the President's home district of Kiambu. Kenyatta relied on these individuals to assist him in deliberations and in the analysis of momentous decisions affecting the country, much to the chagrin of the leaders of other communities.

This circle of men was led by Kenyatta's closest friend and associate, Mbiyu Koinange. Kenyatta and Mbiyu were constantly together. Where Kenyatta was to be found, Mbiyu was somewhere close by. Mbiyu held the prestigious portfolio of Minister of State in the Office of the President. The old men had been friends for a long time, and the two had recently met again in London when Mbiyu was on his way back to Kenya after finishing his M.A. at Columbia University and Kenyatta was in the UK agitating for Kenya's freedom and the return of stolen lands. They had also been teachers together at Githunguri Teachers College, which Mbiyu had founded and headed as principal. As far as I was aware, if everything went as expected, rarely a day passed without Kenyatta and Mbiyu meeting for a tête à tête. Kenyatta infuriated many politicians and government officials by including Mbiyu in all his meetings, when they apparently deemed the appointments secret or private.

I had known of Mbiyu since my early twenties while I was engaged in burning charcoal in Elburgon. At that time, Mbiyu and Jomo Kenyatta were holding public meetings all over the country agitating for independence, and creating awareness of the issues involved in the struggle. In short, they encouraged people to demand Independence. These two politicians had deeply impressed me with their rhetoric and apparent boldness. After one such meeting, they had taken lunch at my future father-in-law's home in Elburgon.

After Nduru and I fled Elburgon for Kiambu, Mbiyu's younger brother Charles Karuga, and I had started a business together. As such, I was readily accepted by the influential Koinange family including the old man, Senior Chief Koinange, who was Mbiyu's father, as well as Kenyatta's father-in-law. This new relationship with the Koinange family also opened doors for me in Kenyatta's political inner circle.

I remember one incident in the early 1960s when I went to visit Muhoho Gathecha. I met him and his family outside in the garden, all dressed and ready to go to Gatundu, where they had been invited by Kenyatta. His wife, Mama Ngina Kenyatta, had just had a son whom she named Muhoho, after the Chief, and the whole family was going to see the newborn. However, when I arrived, Muhoho decided that he would not join the family in travelling to Gatundu but would stay at home and play host to me.

The others tried to persuade him, saying that such a snub would not look good to the President. We all put forward arguments to convince him. I pleaded with him to no avail. He ignored us and told his eighth wife, Nyokabi, who was Ngina's mother, to bring a *gĩtumbĩ*, (a massive gourd) of traditional *mũratina* beer, for me to enjoy. Then he asked his son Peter Gathecha to slaughter a certain special goat for us.

Despite all our objections, Muhoho refused to consider accompanying his family on the visit and retorted that Kenyatta was a son-in-law, someone he could see any time. I, on the other hand, was a close friend who he would not wish to offend.

Later Kenyatta was told that Muhoho would not be visiting with the rest of the family because I had popped in and he had decided to chat with me instead.

Kenyatta laughed. "Even if Muhoho was going to see God and Njenga turned up at his house, he would keep God waiting," he joked.

When the family returned at around seven in the evening, I was still worried about Muhoho's cancelled trip. I asked my partner Charles Kigwe what had happened when Kenyatta heard that Muhoho had refused to come but I need not have been so anxious. Apparently, Kenyatta had taken it in his stride, since he knew my close relationship with Muhoho.

This friendship with Muhoho started in Kiambu while Kigwe was my business partner. On one occasion Kigwe brought Muhoho along to visit me and we had a talk about Muhoho's land case. Apparently during the Land Demarcation in the late 1950s, there were about twenty-one acres of land in his ancestral home of Murang'a which had been grabbed by some relatives who were former home guards. Muhoho had tried to appeal to the Murang'a Land Tribunal but his appeal had been rejected.

At that time, Peter Gacathi, a great friend of mine from Kiambaa, was the Murang'a District Officer and was in charge of land demarcation, so I told Muhoho I would discuss the matter with him. Quite a while earlier, when Gacathi was in Makerere, I used to help him with fees and such matters so I was sure he would be willing to help.

I phoned Gacathi from Kiambaa and told him I would slaughter a goat for him the next time he would be in Kiambaa and he agreed to stop by the following Saturday, at about 10 am. I invited Muhoho and Kigwe as well, and got beers and roasted the goat. When Peter Gacathi arrived I introduced Muhoho as the father of Mama Ngina Kenyatta, explained his case and asked Gacathi to please see if he could be of assistance, especially now that Kenyatta was in prison.

Once Peter had heard the details, he said he knew about the case but unfortunately the file was closed, and no more appeals would be allowed.

I pleaded with him to open it once more and finally Gacathi said he would see what he could do. He looked at his diary and said they should come to Murang'a after two weeks.

So the case was reopened and Gacathi himself heard the particulars from the disputing parties. Subsequently it was ruled that a mistake had occurred and the land was returned to Muhoho. From that time onward Muhoho told all his friends that "Njenga is my lawyer and I don't need any other lawyer."

Another member of this inner circle who probably facilitated my easy acceptance was James Gichuru. Gichuru, despite being older than me, and of course more educated by far, (he had been a student at Alliance and Makerere and later a teacher at Alliance) was a jovial old man and became my bosom buddy. The bright but hard drinking and devil-may-care Gichuru, who was Minster for Finance in Kenyatta's government, had been the President of KANU and its predecessor, KAU, but had relinquished both positions in favour of Kenyatta. He had taken a liking to me many years before, when we became acquainted in business circles. Before Kenyatta's release from prison, Gichuru was a frequent visitor to my Kiambu home where we discussed politics as Gichuru knocked down shot after shot of whisky. We eventually became partners in beer distribution.

The rest of Kenyatta's kitchen cabinet also quickly became my friends. There was Dr. Njoroge Mungai, Kenyatta's brother, James Muigai and Rev. Musa Gitau, Kenyatta's *mūtiiri*.[52] There was also Eliud Mathu who was the comptroller of Kenyatta's State House.[53] Mathu was very close to Kenyatta, but he had always had political ambitions. So much so, in fact, that in 1974 he resigned his portfolio to contest the Parliamentary elections in Lang'ata constituency. Kenyatta tried to persuade him to stay, but he was adamant, saying that the people had called him to serve. Kenyatta reminded him that whatever happened, he would have to bear the consequences, since the policy in this regard was that any civil servant who resigned to contest would not be re-employed in government.

Unfortunately, Mathu was trounced in the Lang'ata election. Kenyatta then called up Alexander Gitau, a son of Reverend Musa Gitau, to take over the job of comptroller but Gitau only stayed in the position for one year.

Apparently Kenyatta missed Mathu considerably, and called him back to 'forgive' him. Mathu then returned to State House and resumed his position up till the time of Kenyatta's death. Kenyatta seemed to love Mathu because he would directly reveal what many others would not. He would tell Kenyatta the straightforward truth even if it was not very palatable. In this, he was very much like Gichuru.

I had known Mathu for many years. He was one of those who had been invited by my father-in-law in Elburgon when I was paying bride price for my wife Wariara in 1951. Mathu and Wairiri had been friends for some time, and he travelled all the way from Kiambu to Elburgon to witness the ceremony.

Naturally there were a few individuals who were not comfortable with my presence, but they were polite enough not to mention it to Kenyatta. One of these was the newly appointed Attorney General, Charles Njonjo, as pointed out in the previous chapter.

As I saw it, Kenyatta was faced with many problems and crises in the early years, but these were the normal events that happen in any high office. Usually Kenyatta handled them by issuing decrees, but he was not

---

52   *Mūtiiri* is the man who escorts a boy to his circumcision and in effect becomes his guardian into adulthood and for life, much like a godfather in western countries.

53   Eliud Mathu was the first black African to be nominated to serve in the colonial Legislative Council (Legco) in 1944.

averse to using political trickery, as was the case when his lieutenants decided to create posts for eight Vice Presidents in order to reduce the influence of Jaramogi Oginga Odinga who had communist leanings and working links with the Soviet Union. I think it was Mboya who proposed the move. This was proposed and passed at a KANU Conference in Limuru in March 1966.

Later that month, Odinga resigned and formed his own party, the Kenya Peoples' Union (KPU). A little later in April 1966, Tom Mboya brought a motion to Parliament which stated that if one was voted in by one party and then joined another, he would have to go back for fresh elections. This motion was passed and in the subsequent elections Odinga was re-elected to Parliament, but many of his lieutenants were not. Odinga became the leader of the opposition but in 1969 KPU was banned following disturbances in Kisumu when Kenyatta went to open the Nyanza General Hospital. Odinga was placed under house arrest and detained without trial a few weeks later. That was the end of Odinga's life in Kenya's corridors of political power until 1992 when the multi-party system was re-introduced and Odinga became the leader of the Forum for Restoration of Democracy (FORD) Party.

With the exception of Luo Nyanza, (Odinga's home area) Kenyatta enjoyed wide popularity. But he was often more of a feared powerful ruler than a benevolent President and he would destroy the political career of anyone who was particularly obnoxious or who refused to cooperate. In his own words he told me that he wanted to mould this country that was still in its infancy and he had no time for '*vinyangarika*' (spoilers). He believed he had to be firm in order to prevent Kenya from going the way of African countries such as the Congo, Angola and others which had plunged into civil war immediately after independence due to differences in ideology.

In fact Bildad Kaggia, who also had some socialist leanings and who had demanded free land for all ex-Mau Mau freedom fighters, was, apart from Odinga, one of the major casualties. Kenyatta and Kaggia had been in jail together; they were two of the Kapenguria Six, but the camaraderie died after Kaggia opposed Kenyatta's policy of buying land from the departing colonialists on a willing buyer, willing seller basis. The acrimony between the two reached such a crescendo that Kaggia was coldly and efficiently removed from the political limelight and ended up in near oblivion. In a public meeting in Kaggia's native Murang'a, Kenyatta once accused Kaggia of living up to the meaning of his name.

Mitgliedsbeitrag
ALA Abteilungen
betragen
Komitttee
Fahrkarte

Fiction - History -
criticism

1 - Virtue d...
Prehmatey,
2 - Ethiopie
Script

8662273327

$ - 4560

May 22 / 448.42

Marc

04464 WB535

96.6204
K1496

323
H88

96.9.6014

Kagia in Gikuyu means 'one who disturbs or irritates'. Out of all the Kapenguria Six, Kaggia ended up the most frustrated. He died in mediocre circumstances at Kenyatta National Hospital in March 2005.

After dealing with Odinga's KPU, the next crisis for Kenyatta came in 1969 when Tom Mboya was shot dead outside Chaani Pharmacy on Government Road (the present-day Moi Avenue) in Nairobi. The murder occurred on a Saturday and Kenyatta received the news from Bernard Njinu, Head of the Presidential Escort in Gatundu.

Seated in his garden in Gatundu, Kenyatta was watching traditional dancers, a practice which was part of his normal relaxation during weekends, when Njinu hurried up to him and gave him a slip of paper with a message about the assassination. According to a witness who was seated just behind Kenyatta, he read the paper, gazed ahead and asked, "What have my people done?"

Riots started a few hours later, when University of Nairobi students and some members of the Luo community began to blame Kenyatta's government for the death of Mboya, and demanded answers.

At that time, I was attending a *harambee* in Githunguri, Kiambu, where I had been invited by James Gichuru, who was the chief guest. As Gichuru and I watched the dancers entertaining us, Gichuru's son, Gitau, came up and gave his father a note. On it were the words, "TOM MBOYA SHOT DEAD IN NAIROBI". Gichuru read it, rubbed his eyes, read it again and gave it to me. I was shocked beyond belief. I had just talked to Mboya the previous night on the phone and everything had sounded fine. And now this!

"Is this possible?" I recall asking Gichuru.

"It must be. My son would not play such a sick joke on me," Gichuru answered.

The two of us quickly made our donations and hurried out of the venue, leaving the other people behind to conclude the event. When we arrived in Nairobi there was chaos on the streets. There were running battles between the police and rioters, and there was teargas everywhere. Nevertheless we managed to confirm that Mboya had been rushed to Nairobi Hospital and declared dead on arrival.

There was a great deal of tension in the country after that sorrowful event, I remember. Very many people believed that Kenyatta's government was behind the murder, but no one had definite proof. The suspect who was arrested and subsequently charged and convicted was a Kikuyu[54] and this fact convinced people of the government's involvement even further.

It was an extraordinarily tense situation during Mboya's memorial service at the Holy Family Basilica. Kenyatta was in attendance with other senior government officials. I was there as well, as a great friend of Mboya. I had not been sure exactly what would happen. I did not even know if Kenyatta would show up, so I was very watchful. Suddenly rioters started pelting the Basilica with stones and charging towards it. They were repulsed by police using teargas, but the fumes also wafted into the church through the windows and the mourners ended up with burning eyes, running noses and terrible coughs. The rioting was directed at Kenyatta's government, so he did not speak at the service. He did not want to add a single word that could cause the volatile situation to explode.

Although no one has disclosed who gave the orders for Mboya's execution, I am most certain it was not Kenyatta. Mboya was very close to Kenyatta, and as KANU's Secretary General, Mboya was extremely useful both in and outside Parliament. The two had always been friendly and in addition, Mboya was Kenyatta's pointman in Nyanza and among the Luo. Kenyatta would lose a great deal, and gain nothing by the death, therefore it is impossible to imagine that he would have been behind it.

At this particular time, Kenyatta badly needed Mboya's support. After all, he had groomed Mboya as the Luo who could counter Odinga's influence. However, whether Kenyatta ever speculated that Mboya might succeed him is another question altogether. I feel that some people might have felt that Mboya was growing too close to the President and thus arranged the assassination.

On my part I was very bitter about this death, and I hope one day the real killers of Tom Mboya, J.M. Kariuki, Pio Gama Pinto and Dr. Robert Ouko will be known.

There was enormous discontent during that difficult period. The Luo were grumbling and suppressed, and the Kikuyu were more divided than ever before. Other tribes felt they were sidelined and neglected when it came to the benefits of *uhuru*.

---

54 The suspect, Nahashon Njenga, was convicted on flimsy grounds and he was largely seen as a scapegoat. When he was questioned in court, he is reported to have asked, "Why don't you get the big man?" It is thought that there was pressure to convict him to quell the disquiet in the Luo community.

Kenyatta's close confidants were worried about the situation. During this time, shortly after Mboya's death, it was said that Mbiyu Koinange, Arthur Wanyoike Thungu (Kenyatta's trusted bodyguard) and a few others, suggested that the Kikuyu community take a loyalty oath and commit themselves to the President, personally. This way, those who took the oath would forever be religiously bound to support Kenyatta, no matter what else might happen.

I have to say that I am extraordinarily bitter about that oath. It was administered all over Kikuyu land and was referred to as *"chai"* (which in normal circumstances merely means tea). It had already started at Kenyatta's own home in Gatundu, and then, one day, while I was in my office, I was phoned by Kariuki Kimani wa Mbagi, who was the manager of Kenyatta's farm in Njiru area. Kariuki informed me that the president wished to see me urgently in Gatundu. Kariuki and I arranged to meet in Ruiru and then drove to Gatundu together. When we arrived, I was surprised that I was not taken to Kenyatta's house as usual. Instead, Wanyoike Thungu told me, without elaboration, that the President was in another house. Then he escorted me towards the area where houses of the security men were located. I knew there was something funny going on and I was suspicious and somewhat fearful. I realised that, for whatever reason, I might be in trouble and my suspicions were confirmed when I stepped into one of the buildings.

Once inside, I realized something was terribly wrong. First, Kenyatta was nowhere to be seen. Second, there, in the dark interior, I noticed my old friend, Kaniu Kinyanjui and others, who were holding *pangas* (machetes). Many dreadful thoughts raced through my mind. Why had my friend Kariuki Kimani tricked me into this?

"Mũthoniwa ruta nguo," (Remove your clothes, my in-law) Kaniu told me. That was the nickname we used to refer to each other, not because we were really in-laws, but because of mutual respect.

I immediately realised that this was an oathing session. I was furious that I had been tricked into the situation in such a manner, right in Kenyatta's home. I had taken oaths before, notably Mau Mau oaths, and I recognised the setup straightaway. Holding back my resentment, I stripped. Basically, the oath involved chewing some mucky stuff and pledging my loyalty to Mzee Jomo Kenyatta, the government and his Kikuyu leadership, and to stand united with my tribe at all times. I pledged to do so and after a few minutes the whole thing was over. I was also asked to 'contribute' some money for the cause and, feeling resentful, I did so.

Wanyoike Thungu told me that Kenyatta had not intended to see me at all, and that I could now go back to my business. The others even had the audacity to wish me a good day.

As I walked back to my car I felt very disappointed, furious and enraged. My friend Kariuki, who had duped me into the situation, was seated in my car wearing a knowing grin. Apparently Kariuki thought that the oath was a small matter but I believed otherwise. I had not known that any such thing was going on, and I never asked Kenyatta about it later, either.

In silence I drove over to my Amani Bar in Kiambu and when we both ordered our drinks, I expressed my displeasure.

"How stupid are you people to hold this thing in *Mzee's* home? What will happen when the public gets to know about this?" I asked Kimani, who just shrugged as he had no answers to these questions.[55] I did not mind taking the oath so much, but I could not understand how it could be done at the president's home. I wondered if maybe Kenyatta was getting too old and losing control of what his lieutenants were doing.

In my opinion the supposed purpose of the oath was never well examined and the people behind it were suspect. The idiots behind this oath were so sloppy that they even administered it to children, which was totally against the whole cultural concept. The oath actually achieved the opposite of what it was meant to accomplish.

Religious people were very disappointed and antagonised and the oath polarized the Kikuyu community. The 1969 *"chai"* therefore worsened the existing situation by a considerable degree.[56]

I will never forgive those who organized that *chai (muuma)*. *Muuma*, according to Gikuyu tradition, is a serious affair and is only taken in times of national crisis or to resolve extremely serious disputes. But this *"chai"* was a haphazard and expedient affair whose goals and intentions were muddled by ignorance and ulterior motives.

---

55 Actually many senior Kikuyu, including Cabinet Ministers, were tricked into going for the oath in Gatundu in a similar manner. Some members of Kenyatta's kitchen Cabinet believed that if senior figures pledged their loyalty it would make them more steadfast against the onslaught of other tribes. Why the oath givers believed that the oath could have the desired effect on the takers, even Christians, will never be known. The politically beleaguered President is said to have accepted the idea rather reluctantly.

56 The oath may have caused other problems. Historically, even before this time, some groups had never fully accepted each other, despite being members of the same community. It is a pity that there are some from Kiambu who still scornfully refer to their Nyeri cousins as '*tūmūndū twa Nyīrī*' (those little people from Nyeri) and believe that the Kikuyu from Nyeri are inferior. Some Nyeri Kikuyu, on the other hand, with a similar attitude, refer to the Kiambu Kikuyu as '*Tūmūkabete*' (those uncultured people from Kabete) and accuse them of being wily, conniving and materialistic.

The oathing was done in Nairobi, all over Central Province, and also brought to the Kikuyu who lived outside these locations, coordinated by the associates of Thungu and others. The huge amount of money that was collected in the oathing ceremony was never accounted for, nor was anyone told of its purpose. I believe that it probably went into the pockets of Wanyoike Thungu and his fellow goons.

Although it was supposed to be secret, word naturally got round the country that the Kikuyu were taking an oath. What secrecy did the organizers expect when they were giving the oath to children? The oath created even more suspicion against the Kikuyu and I feel that it caused immense deterioration in inter-tribal relationships and heightened tribal animosities. The oath was a big political blunder. The matter actually came to Parliament and Vice President Moi, as Leader of Government Business, defended Kenyatta over the matter.

Although I still attended to my expanding businesses, I had a hectic schedule and an exciting life during the Kenyatta years. After I had worked backstage in the political theatre for many years, Kenyatta finally nominated me as MP in 1974. Mbiyu Koinange was the Kiambaa MP at the time.

I was already the Chairman of the powerful GEMA Union and being a nominated MP did not hurt my position. Kenyatta invited me to many informal sessions, both at State House and in Gatundu and perhaps many people relied on my ties with him and his inner circle.

For example, before I was nominated MP after the 1974 General Elections, there had been considerable jostling for Parliamentary and Civic seats. My GEMA colleagues and I planned to win as many seats as possible, especially in Nairobi. The GEMA strategy in the city was quite simple, merely to win all the seats. I had no serious problems with this strategy, but there were a few difficulties. For example, I had close friends with political ambitions. They were from other tribes, yet they wanted to vie in the city. One such friend was Mulu Mutisya, the Chairman of the New Akamba Union, who was also the Councillor for Bahati Ward.

Mutisya was an influential figure among the Kamba, especially those who lived in the city. Owing to his charisma, eloquence and his connections in high places, he was revered by the members of his community. However, he had absolutely no education and he could never hope to pass the Parliamentary Proficiency Test.[57] Therefore, instead of vying for Parliament, he had gone for the post of Councillor which he won easily, and he seemed happy enough to stay in that position and not aspire further. His only rival to the 'kingship' of Ukambani was Paul Ngei, then a powerful Cabinet Minister who was the Kangundo MP and was close to Kenyatta due to the fact he was also one of the six that had been imprisoned at Kapenguria.

Mutisya was a good friend of mine. He was Chairman of the New Akamba Union and I was Chairman of GEMA and thus we had worked closely in many areas. GEMA often worked closely with similar tribal organisations and the stereotype which pictures GEMA as an organ of Kikuyu chauvinism is not accurate. At one time in early 1974, for example, Mutisya invited me to be the chief guest at a *harambee* in Machakos. I believe I was quite good at mobilising resources from all GEMA branches and animating such events, so I was often asked to attend this type of function. The *harambee* was held in order to raise funds to buy water storage tanks for public schools in semi-arid Machakos. The *harambee* realised Sh. 520,000, a colossal amount at the time, and most schools in the region were able to acquire a tank. As a gesture of thanks, the New Akamba Union kindly held a party for me in Nairobi where I was made a full Kamba elder.

However, to get back to the elections of 1974, Mutisya, as stated above, intended to retain his Bahati civic seat. Meanwhile the area former MP, Mwai Kibaki, with whom Mutisya had cordial relations, had shifted his political base back to his native Othaya Constituency. At any rate, the largest obstacle that Mutisya saw looming over him was the power of the GEMA machine, which seemed to be sweeping the political scene in Nairobi. John Murugu, the Assistant Secretary of the Transport and Allied Workers Union wanted to vie for Mutisya's civic seat and, becoming quite worried, Mutisya called on me for help. I then approached Murugu and tried to convince him not to compete against Mutisya, but my request fell on deaf ears. Murugu was ambitious to capture the Bahati civic seat because his friend Muhuri Muchiri was vying for the Embakasi Parliamentary seat.

The elections were duly held and due to GEMA's influence, Murugu beat Mutisya hands down. Mutisya was crushed by the loss. Without a position of status, not even a civic seat, Mutisya saw his influence significantly reduced among the Kamba.

---

57 Anyone intending to vie for a parliamentary seat in Kenya has to sit and pass a proficiency test to show he is literate enough to understand the working of the House.

Seeing my friend so unhappy, I assured Mutisya that I would do everything possible for him. I went to Gatundu, spoke to Kenyatta and tried to convince him that if Mutisya was nominated to Parliament, the Kamba community would be jubilant and extremely thankful to Kenyatta since Mutisya was a most influential man and Chairman of New Akamba Union. Mbiyu confirmed my assessment, stating that Mutisya was the 'king' of the Akamba. Kenyatta, as always, was non-committal and said he would think about the matter. Kenyatta rarely gave an immediate yes or no answer—he carefully thought over most issues before he reached a decision and did not normally act arbitrarily.

When I left, I prayed that the President's decision would benefit Mutisya. Kenyatta, on his part, made a few inquires about Mutisya and some days before the list of nominated MPs was released, the Eastern Provincial Commissioner, Charles Karuga Koinange, contacted me and informed me that Kenyatta had been asking questions about the character of my friend, Mulu Mutisya. The President made these inquiries from Koinange as Mutisya was from Eastern Province and Karuga would naturally have a dossier on him. I pretended to be ignorant of Kenyatta's intentions, but became more optimistic about Mutisya's chances after that. A few days later, at 1 pm, the Voice of Kenya (VOK), which was the government-owned radio station, announced that Mulu Mutisya, and I, among others, had been nominated to Parliament. I was thrilled that Mutisya had been nominated, but I have to say that I was appalled that I had been nominated, too.

However what happened when Mutisya heard the news is quite amusing. Mutisya was a gifted speaker and he liked holding court at his house in Eastlands. Many Kambas in Nairobi looked upon him as a community elder. That afternoon he had been talking to a number of Kamba friends when they suddenly heard the announcement of nominations on the radio. It was a shock that caught all of them, especially Mutisya, totally by surprise.

Mutisya later told me that he was so excited when the announcement was made, he turned the volume so high that the knob broke, incapacitating the radio. A few minutes later, even before Mutisya could fully understand the impact of the announcement, people from all over the estate poured in to congratulate him, referring to him as *Mheshimiwa* (honourable). It was overwhelming, but all too much for him to absorb, and he still did not actually believe it could be true. So he quickly sent one of his friends to buy a new radio and at 4 pm the announcement was repeated. Slowly the truth started to sink in, but Mutisya still had doubts.

The following morning when I arrived at my Kiambu office at 7 am, Mutisya was already there patiently waiting for me. He had a lot of suspicion that I was involved in his nomination, since we had discussed it earlier, but was so overwhelmed that he was not exactly sure what had happened. I invited him in and once we were inside and seated, Mutisya thanked me profusely for arranging the nomination. However, Mutisya had one question which had been disturbing him ever since the announcement was made.

"Have you heard the announcement on the radio?" he asked me.

I told him I had and congratulated him on his nomination.

"Is the Parliament we are nominated to the same one which Paul Ngei is sitting in?" Mutisya asked. Ngei was Mutisya's arch-rival when it came to Kamba leadership.

I laughed and assured him it was the very same one.

Pumping a triumphant fist into the air, Mutisya shouted, *"Ni usu!"* (That's it then!). Soon thereafter he departed, leaving me bemused and chuckling.

Mutisya was overjoyed that he would now be facing his adversary on an equal footing. As fate would have it, Mutisya was later elected MP, and even became a Director of Kenya Power and Lighting Company, among other senior appointments. Mutisya perhaps holds the dubious honour of being Kenya's first illiterate Member of Parliament. But no matter what favours Kenyatta extended, he always kept a card up his sleeve, and granting a favour, was often not without some strings attached.

At one time I had gone to Eldoret to give evidence in a case where a man had been accused of obtaining money by false pretences. It was a rather ridiculous case.

A man had gone to the shop of my friend Ngugi Gitonga, who was the Uasin Gishu GEMA Branch Organising Secretary in Eldoret. This man told Ngugi that he was a clerk at GEMA headquarters in Nairobi and that he was on his way to Kitale. However, his car had broken down and he had no money.

"Njenga Karume said that if I get into any difficulties along the way, I should come to see you," he told Ngugi. "Now my car has developed a problem and I really need to get it fixed so I can get to Kitale."

Ngugi did not hesitate and gave him the money. However, the man was back the following morning.

"Look, I'm sorry to bother you again," he told Ngugi, "but fixing the car has turned out to be more expensive than I thought. I need a bit more money to get it running again."

Ngugi was sympathetic and went to get some more cash, but his wife became suspicious. She called her husband to another room.

Softly, so as not to be overheard, she whispered to him, "There's something not right with that man. I don't know what it is, but I'm suspicious."

Ngugi brushed off her doubts and started back to hand over the money but his wife stopped him again.

"This is not how Njenga does things. He would have phoned by now," she murmured softly.

Ngugi stopped and thought it over. After a few moments he nodded and then quietly called the police. He then went back to the shop.

"Just wait a little. I've sent for some money from the bank," Ngugi told the man. "It won't take long."

The man waited patiently, not suspecting a thing. When the police came into the shop, he was shocked when he was arrested and protested his innocence.

I was summoned as a witness in the case when it came up for trial, so I travelled upcountry. I planned to make quite a few stops along the way, finishing up with a visit to my friend Makanga, who was the DC Kitale. I therefore spent a few days in Nakuru and went to many of the bars in town, taking a beer in each of them and meeting GEMA officials. On Wednesday night I slept in my house at Molo and on Thursday, the day of the court case, I travelled to the court in Eldoret.

In court, I was called forward and the accused was told that if he had any questions for me, now was the time to ask them.

"No, Sir. This is the first time I have met Honourable Karume, so I don't have any questions for him," he told the magistrate. "But thank you very much for calling him." He paused and then smiled at me. "This is a big day for me! I am so pleased to finally meet you, Honourable Karume. I have heard so much about you and it is wonderful to actually see you here!"

Everyone in the courtroom was laughing quietly. The accused was so audacious!

When it was my turn to speak, I testified that I had never seen the man before and that he was definitely not a clerk at the GEMA office. Therefore, I stated, I could never have sent him to Ngugi or anywhere else.

I left before the sentencing and proceeded to Kitale to my friend the DC, and I do not know what sentence the man was handed. But I will never forget his cheek!

That same weekend there was a by-election in Nakuru following a successful petition by Kabiru Kimemia against Mark Mwithaga who had won in the general elections. The group around the Attorney General, Charles Njonjo, did not like Mark Mwithaga. This group, who were Kenyatta's confidants, did not like his views or the fact that he was a good friend to Nyandarua MP, Josiah Mwangi Kariuki, or JM, as he was popularly known.

"JM was a thorn in the flesh of Kenyatta's kitchen cabinet. He had criticized the leadership many times for ignoring the poor of the country. In addition to having a close relationship with JM, Mark Mwithaga was also a friend of mine and this incensed Njonjo a lot. One way or the other, the group felt that Mwithaga had to be stopped and it is likely that, in this respect, the President shared Njonjo's views.

About twenty months before this, Mwithaga had been involved in a minor domestic scuffle with his wife. The wife had complained to the police at the time and the case had been shelved, but the complaint was now dug up and the incident proved to be a godsend for the Attorney General. One of the AG's men in the Rift Valley was the Provincial Police Officer, James Ephantus Mungai, who put in a lot of effort on the case.

The matter was exaggerated and what should have been a storm in a tea cup became a virtual gale. All the newspapers, television and radio stations belaboured the story and it seemed that the exposure given to the case was just a little too exaggerated. We were suspicious that someone, somewhere, was deliberately arranging as much publicity as possible.

Charges of assault were then drawn up against Mwithaga just a few days before the elections and he was arrested and taken to court. He was released on bond but on the Friday before the elections were held the following day, Saturday, Mwithaga was sentenced to jail for over a year.

People were angry that their MP of choice, Mark Mwithaga, was being jailed for a minor offence which had lain dormant for nearly two years. As I explained earlier, on my way to Eldoret for the court case, I had spent time in Nakuru, visiting bars and talking to GEMA officials. Everywhere I went, the spirit was the same. Despite the government's obvious wish that the people should elect Kabiru, they all expressed support for Mwithaga. By the time I left Nakuru, I was quite convinced that if the government wanted the people to vote for Kabiru Kimemia and kick out Mark Mwithaga, they would be in for a rude shock.

After visiting the DC Kitale, he decided to come back to Eldoret with me for a party which we had both been invited. The party was at the house of a friend, Muchiri Kibui, and many people were present, including the Eldoret Mayor and the area DC. There was the usual *nyama choma* and lots of beer, and we all had a good time.

But at around 7 pm a new guest arrived.

"The little man has been jailed!" he exclaimed joyfully, referring to the diminutive Mwithaga.

I listened to his story, but as soon as I could get away, I approached the Uasin Gishu GEMA Secretary, John Macharia, who was also at the party with us. I asked him to go to the next room and make a call to State House Mombasa. I knew the President was at the coast and felt I should speak to him.

When Macharia got through to State House, he first asked whether the president was around, or if he had already gone to be entertained by traditional dancers as he was wont to. When he was assured the President was still available, he called me and I took the receiver. I asked to speak to the President and when he was on the line, I told him that I was in Eldoret and started out with small talk. I told him that people were very happy since he had arranged for them to settle in the area, and such things. Kenyatta enjoyed hearing about the state of the country and all his conversations were started with these informalities.

"So what can I do for you, Njenga?" Kenyatta asked after we finished with the warm ups.

"Now *Mzee* . . . I don't quite know how to begin," I stated, somewhat hesitantly. "I want to inform you about something and I am almost sure you will think it is unimportant. However, I will tell you all the same and the decision is yours."

"What is all this about, Njenga?" He quipped.

"It's about Mwithaga. He has been jailed," I said timidly.

"I see," Kenyatta said, as usual pretending to be ignorant of current affairs. "You mean the little man has been jailed?"

I was concerned to hear the phrase "little man" again, but said nothing.

"Now Njenga, what do you want? What interest do you have in the matter?" Kenyatta asked.

"You see, *Mzee*, I was in Nakuru two days ago. I talked to the people, even our GEMA leaders, and everyone said they had decided to vote for Mwithaga, not Kabiru."

"So what do you want me to do?" the President asked.

"*Mzee* . . . I don't want us to be like Ghana. I don't want Kenya to be on the list of countries where a popular leader was elected while in jail," I said, referring to Kwame Nkrumah, the Ghanaian leader who was elected while in prison.

"We should not allow someone like Mwithaga to be elected while in prison," I continued. "It will look bad . . . like the government imprisons popular people for some reason."

"Listen Njenga," said the President, "even if Mwithaga was in church at his wedding and broke the law, he would still be arrested and imprisoned."

Kenyatta paused for a moment and then went on, "Most of the time, I would listen to your advice, but this time I don't think you have the right information."

"But I know he will definitely be elected, *Mzee!* The government will be embarrassed!" I said emphatically.

"It won't happen. My people have assured me that Mwithaga will be defeated," Kenyatta said confidently.

"Alright, *Mzee,*" I answered. "I just thought I should let you know. The decision about what to do is always yours. So . . . I will see you when you get back to Nairobi . . . but don't say you were not warned," I finished, and hung up the phone.

John Macharia, who was all along present during the conversation, was open mouthed with surprise. When we rejoined the party in the other room, he told the other guests that he had never met any other person as bold as I was, and that he did not know anyone else who could tell Kenyatta something to his face the way I had done.

The party went on but at midnight I went to the Highlands Hotel to sleep. Just before I nodded off, I wondered what the situation would be at the next day's election.

The following day I got up early and visited nearly all the polling centres. At each centre I was told the same thing; they were going to vote for Mwithaga. After I finished my survey, I headed back home.

At seven that evening, my wife Wariara and I listened to the news. When the results of the Nakuru by-election were announced, we heard that Kabiru Kimemia had managed only two thousand votes against Mark Mwithaga's over five thousand votes. I was overjoyed with this landslide victory and also with the fact that my predictions had proved true.

"Now, my dear Wariara," I exclaimed, "bring me the biggest bottle of whiskey in the house! If ever there was an occasion to drink, this is it!"

I would have liked to tell Kenyatta "I told you so" but did not make the call because I knew I had already made my point. However, Kenyatta was infuriated when the results were announced. He summoned the Attorney General, Charles Njonjo, the Director of the Special

Branch, James Kanyotu, the Rift Valley Provincial Police Officer, the Police Commissioner, and other officials who had been involved in the embarrassing mess and sternly rebuked them, without mincing his words. He declared that despite the fact that they had all the state machinery to work with, they were still unable to do anything properly. The government and the Judiciary had been severely embarrassed. I later learned that Kenyatta had told them that I was brighter than all of them combined because I had known precisely what was going to happen.

The following day Special Branch Director James Kanyotu and I met for lunch and, in a light-hearted manner, he asked me, "Chairman, why do you want to have us sacked by *Mzee?*"

I assured him that I had no such intentions. This gave me an inkling of the reception they had received at Kenyatta's hands. At any rate, although Mwithaga won, he fell ill while in prison and never took up the seat.

Over a period of time I found out that in addition to Njonjo, many other people were uncomfortable with the close friendship between Kenyatta and myself. Out of the blue, Kenyatta would occasionally consult me on various issues that were better dealt by Cabinet Ministers, or officials in various departments. This naturally caused some resentment, but I had no say in the circumstances. At other times Kenyatta would let me sit through in his meetings with senior officials who would remain tense and ill at ease because of my presence. Unfortunately for them, there was nothing I could do about it!

Many of such meetings were the informal sessions that were held in the gardens of Kenyatta's home in Gatundu. The grounds had a sort of arena with a dais and if there were many visitors, we would meet there. However, if there were just a few of us, we would go to the small house which had been built for him by KADU on his release. If it was quite confidential and Kenyatta wished to speak to only one or two of us, we would go out and sit under a tree.

I remember one particular occasion when Kenyatta spoke to me privately in the garden. This happened shortly after independence, when Europeans started selling their coffee farms in Kiambu. The DC Kiambu, Eliud Njenga, (who grew up with me in the Rift Valley) had learnt about a farm on sale in Gatundu, near President Kenyatta's home, and invited Makanga, who was his DO 1 at the time, and I, to be his partners. The farm was about two hundred and ninety acres, with one hundred and forty acres under coffee. The farm was going for 1.2 million shillings and so we went to have a look at it.

Kenyatta's chief bodyguard, Wanyoike Thungu, got wind of the information and was not very pleased. Thungu was a distrustful person with a nasty character and had a tendency of trying to drive wedges between Kenyatta and anyone who got too close to him. Since he used to ride in the Presidential limousine, he had plenty of opportunities to repeat malicious gossip to the President. One day as Kenyatta was driving up-country from Mombasa, Thungu told him that I had acquired a farm in Gatundu. He went on to say that the DC and I had organised things so that any available land in Gatundu would be sold to people from Kiambaa. In short, he implied that I was trying to undermine the President in his own backyard.

Kenyatta, of course, was not amused. When he arrived in Gatundu, he summoned the DC, who was at the venue in his official capacity, and told him, "I hear that you and Njenga have said that my people will never own farms in Gatundu. You go home and come here with him on Monday. I want to discuss this matter with the two of you."

The DC and I were rather concerned about the misunderstanding and talked about how to handle it. When we arrived at Gatundu on Monday, we found about one thousand people, of whom the majority were mothers with children and the very old, inside Kenyatta's compound. Later we learned that Wanyoike had already instructed their representatives on what they should to say to *Mzee* about me and the DC. He told them to complain about landlessness and the fact that available land was being taken by 'foreigners', that is, Njenga and I from Kiambaa.

When we arrived Kenyatta called me inside the house. He asked me about the story he had heard; that I was bringing in people from Kiambaa to buy farms in Gatundu.

I told him I had no such intention. I explained that we only intended to purchase a single farm and that I had organised for a loan of 1.2 million shillings from the National Bank of Kenya in order to do so.

Since I noticed that Kenyatta was still not very happy with this, I continued and told him that since I had many farms, I did not mind leaving this one for the poor people of Gatundu. Furthermore, I said, I would transfer the loan to any account the people would set up, so that once they started collecting money among themselves, they could service the loan after acquiring the land.

Kenyatta was very pleased about this offer and told me that he actually had never believed the story. Then we moved out under the trees. There were only two chairs for us. Then he told one of his aides to call Wanyoike, who then came and stood next to Kenyatta.

"Wanyoike, repeat what you told me about Njenga and the DC," Kenyatta told him.

"You see, Mzee, it is . . . it is . . ." he stammered.

"It is what?" thundered Kenyatta.

"It is people . . . the people say, they say . . ."

"Which people?" Kenyatta was now very angry.

"Eh . . . eh . . ." he fumbled for words, but none came to his mouth.

"Do you want Njenga to think I am an idiot? Say what you said from your mouth, not what the people said!" Kenyatta lifted his wooden walking stick as if to strike him. "Get out of here before I hit you! And if you ever come to me again, giving me such nonsense! . . . "

Wanyoike literally ran away, back to the crowd.

Kenyatta then sent for the Thika DO, Kibathi Thuo, and told him to help me purchase a big, fertile farm in Gatundu since the one I had intended to buy was too small for me. He also told the DO to make a list of all the farms on sale and bring it to him.

Meanwhile, when Wanyoike discovered that his little plot had not worked, he quickly changed his instructions to the leaders in the waiting crowd. He told them things were now different so they were not to mention anything they had previously rehearsed.

Kenyatta and I then came and sat on the dais, talking and laughing heartily, while Wanyoike cowered nearby. The DC opened the meeting, and then the leaders of the crowd were invited to speak. They complained about landlessness and about outsiders who came in to the area to buy the available farms. They mentioned Geoffrey Kariithi, the Head of Civil Service, and James Gitau of the Kenya Trading Corporation as some of the outsiders who had bought land in Gatundu. Not one of the speakers mentioned my name.

When Kenyatta rose to speak, he told the people that he had heard their complaints and something would be done. He called the DO over and instructed him to help people identify land that was up for sale. Then he told the people that I had also intended to buy a piece of land in the area but I had given it up for the poor. Kenyatta told them that I had 1.2 million shillings in the bank and I was willing to transfer the money to their account so that they could access the loan. The crowd went wild with joy and there were many ululations from the women.

Kenyatta then told his aides to give the people refreshments and then he, Mama Ngina and I went into the house for lunch.

❖ ❖ ❖

One night, the Rift Valley PC, Isaiah Mathenge, called me while I was at my Lynton farm in Kiambu to let me know that the President was visiting Keringet the following day. Keringet is in what is now Kuresoi Constituency in the southern Rift Valley. A departing settler had sold twenty thousand acres there, which had been purchased by members of the Kipsigis community and the President was going to give out the title deeds.

Mathenge said that on his way back, the President intended to pass by and see my Molo farm, mainly because I had often told him how proud I was about the productivity of the land and cattle. Kenyatta himself loved livestock and had many cattle on his big farm in Njiru, near Nairobi. He and I were always joking about whose animals were bigger and healthier and this visit would now give him a chance to compare.

So after I finished talking to Mathenge, I tried to phone my other wife Margaret Njeri in Molo, in order to inform her that the President would be coming to visit, and that Wariara and I would be coming in early to make preparations. Unfortunately the lines were down so I was unable to get through to her. I decided we would just have to hope for the best.

Mathenge, like any PC who expected a visit from the President to his Province, ordered the administration, the police and the security forces to make their usual preparations, and they got into action.

The following morning at dawn, Njeri was woken up by the roar of road graders working the nearby road, and she wondered what was going on. She was even more surprised when the graders started working on the road leading up to the house. Behind the graders were tankers sprinkling water to keep the dust away. Soon afterwards, the compound was teeming with vehicles and mean-looking men in suits who came out of them. They spoke little, but she panicked when they demanded to search her house.

Without waiting for her consent, they thoroughly searched every nook and cranny in the whole compound, including the toilets which they flushed and even checked inside the cisterns. Afterwards they locked the toilets and kept the keys.

They then set themselves up in different positions all over the compound and outside it. Njeri could not shout for help because the farm was vast, over one thousand acres, and the nearest neighbour was kilometres away. As the men rummaged around examining everything, she was near her wits' end!

She told me later that she felt I had betrayed her by not telling her that I was in debt; that she was sure that the farm had either been auctioned, or was to be. As more cars kept driving into the compound, she watched in horror and wondered what sort of auctioneers these people were.

When Wariara and I arrived we found that the roads had been cleared and the security people and their bosses were in place. Godfrey Muhuri Muchiri, the MP for Embakasi, had accompanied us.

My intention had been to drop off Wariara so that she and Njeri could help each other in preparing the lunch. But as soon as we entered the house, Njeri burst into tears and refused to greet me.

"Why," she asked me bitterly, "was I not told the farm was going to be auctioned?"

I calmed her down and explained that there was no auction and that all the preparations had been made because the President would be coming along shortly. I told her about the problems with the phone lines and comforted her as best I could. Wariara gave Njeri a hug and she gradually regained her composure. She and Wariara soon went into the house to prepare for the guests.

On my part, I made sure some goats were slaughtered and that everything was going according to schedule. As soon as I was satisfied with the arrangements, Muhuri and I left to join the President in Keringet.

Meanwhile Kenyatta was planning to play a trick on his entourage as he did every now and again. As the meeting neared its conclusion, Kenyatta called Mathenge and the Rift Valley Provincial Police Officer, Harrison Musau, aside and said that his visit to my farm was to be private. He wanted only a few people to accompany him and these would be Jackson Angaine, Eliud Mathu, Mbiyu Koinange, GG Kariuki, Daniel arap Moi, Mama Ngina and Mathenge. Apart from the Presidential security detail, everyone else should be stopped and turned back at a roadblock near Molo town at the junction to my farm.

As soon as we could get away, Muhuri Muchiri and I left the Keringet function to make the final preparations for Kenyatta's arrival on my farm. Nakuru Mayor, Geoffrey Kamau, was already there waiting for us, as well as a troupe of traditional dancers who would provide the entertainment. These were organised by the PC Isaiah Mathenge. Many goats were slaughtered and the meat was cut, cooked and roasted, and all was ready when Kenyatta and his entourage arrived.

As for the others, many chose to sweat in their cars for hours at the roadblock while Kenyatta and his friends enjoyed their lunch. Such tricks by the President certainly did not endear me to my detractors. After all, who was I to deserve a visit from the Head of State himself?

❖ ❖ ❖

Long before my entry to Parliament I had been harassed by a great many people who wanted to see Kenyatta and thought I could arrange an appointment for them. I remember an occasion in which a delegation of bus owners came to me and begged me to book an appointment for them with His Excellency. They wanted to complain about the new cheap mini-buses, called *matatus*, which did not require licenses from the Transport Licensing Board (TLB) and were thus driving the big buses out of business. *Matatus* had no timetable and did not have to pick passengers from any predetermined bus stage.

Some time earlier, Kenyatta had declared that *matatus* would not be required to pay TLB fees, perhaps because he wanted to assist the small investor. The Ministry concerned had also said that *matatus* were doing a good job by filling the gap left by buses. However, bus owners wanted the President to reverse this decision and ensure that the matatus also paid TLB fees and follow a set timetable, in order to operate on level commercial terms.

I agreed to book an appointment for them. After all, Peter Kamau (who had been my partner in the wholesale shop) and I were partners in Kenya Road Services Ltd., and we had twelve buses ourselves. Our buses plied the Kisumu and Mombasa routes. Meanwhile the bus owners organised a fundraiser and collected fifteen thousand shillings. The amount was to be given to Kenyatta during their meeting, as their contribution towards the completion of Gatundu General Hospital.

I thought about this issue. I knew Kenyatta had himself declared that matatus would not pay TLB fees. And I knew that once Kenyatta issued an order, it was most highly unlikely that he would ever reverse his decision.

So, on the day of the meeting, I told the bus owners I had a previous appointment and that they were to go to Gatundu on their own. I made myself scarce because I sensed that Kenyatta was unlikely to change his mind, and I did not want to be blamed in case an embarrassing situation arose.

And that is exactly what happened. A man named Njoroge Nduati, a public transport magnate who had more than eighty buses under the trade name "*Jogoo Kĩmakia*", was the spokesman for the group. He made his address, flattered Kenyatta and then produced the money for the *harambee* and gave it to the President, saying that the amount was the group's humble contribution towards the hospital. Ululation and applause met this generosity.

Kenyatta accepted the cheque, the largest so far in the *harambee*, and thanked them for their charitable contribution. Then he asked them what he could do for them and the bus owners explained their problem. They were under siege by the emergence of small mini-buses and wanted to have them banned or given a timetable. Otherwise, if that was not possible, perhaps the bus owners could also be exempt from paying fees to the TLB, in order to level the playing ground.

Kenyatta thought for a minute. Naturally he had contemplated the matter beforehand, and most likely he had already reached his decision. Kenyatta was 'old school' and had to give the impression of deep contemplation and ponderous effort as expected.

"What is the price of a bus?" he asked them.

"A hundred thousand shillings," they answered.

"And the cost of a *matatu*?"

"Twenty five thousand shillings," they said.

"Good, then," he answered. "It seems that you people don't know business. Let me help you." He looked out at the delegation and then continued. "Go sell your bus and buy four *matatus*. One *matatu* can go to Mombasa, one can go to Eldoret, one can go to Thika and the other elsewhere. This way your problems will be solved."

The leaders left, defeated and embarrassed.

I think I know why Kenyatta refused the request. He had been more sympathetic to the plight of the small investor who could not afford to invest a hundred thousand shillings. He often said that Kenya did not belong to a few, and in this case he would have been ignoring the plight of hundreds in order to serve the whims of a dozen.

In the end, Kamau and I later sold our buses, and Njoroge Nduati's company wound up. But I can proudly say that we were among the pioneers of the big bus fleets in Kenya.

Kenyatta never gave any indication of a chosen successor, and he continued to retain Daniel arap Moi as his Vice President. I believe he did not want to leave a legacy of conflict in the young independent country he had helped to create.

In Kenyatta's own words, the only other person who was suited for the post was his former Finance Minister, James Gichuru. Kenyatta believed that Gichuru was a true patriot and a principled man.

While Kenyatta was in prison, the British Governor, Malcolm MacDonald, came to Gichuru and informed him that the Colonial Office wished to deliver a message. They felt that since Gichuru was already the KANU President, the British Government had him in sight for the post of Prime Minister as soon as Kenya became independent. Gichuru rejected the offer outright and said that the only person who would sit on that chair would be Jomo Kenyatta.

Gichuru was a brave man and a true patriot. He believed in the power of Kenyans and had been vehement in his denunciation of colonial rule. I remember that once, shortly after I had commenced trading in my shop in Kiambu, Gichuru paid me a visit.

Quite some time before Gichuru's visit, during the shop's official opening, I had invited some guests for the ceremony. The chief guest on this occasion was Terence Gavaghan, the white Kiambu District Commissioner, and I had a small plaque to commemorate the occasion.

So when Gichuru later came to visit, he saw the plaque I had placed on the wall, memorializing the official opening. Gichuru hated Gavaghan. He hated all white colonial administrators, but he hated Gavaghan in particular because of his reputation of having tortured Mau Mau detainees when he was the officer in charge of Mwea detention camp.

"Njenga, if you do not remove that sign with Gavaghan's name, I will have to leave," he insisted angrily. So I quickly removed the inscription and he came into the house. Thereafter we chatted happily, and the matter was forgotten.

Gichuru had been a good Finance Minister in the early years of Independence. When he was transferred to the Ministry of Defence, he performed just as well. Power and wealth were not particularly attractive to him and he acted as an intelligent ally for Kenyatta, but he had a personal weakness which undermined his health. He tended to be hard on the bottle, sometimes with embarrassing results. Kenyatta however overlooked this shortcoming, and the two were more like brothers than mere friends or fellow politicians.

However Kenyatta realised it would not be easy to have a Kikuyu as Vice President. I feel that Kenyatta was realistic, with visions of a united Kenya, and was not actually a Kikuyu tribalist. He believed himself to be a Kenyan President, not a Kikuyu chieftain, and he wanted the best for the Kenya nation.

As would be expected, given my history and relationship with Kenyatta, I believe that Kenyatta's style of governance was, for the most part, a success. Kenyatta strived to achieve a vision of a prosperous Kenya, but the vision was thwarted by numerous odds, some insurmountable. Kenyatta did not tolerate the embezzlement of public property. Although embezzlement and corruption did occur during his time, it was without his approval or knowledge. For example, when Kenyatta's long-time friend Paul Ngei was accused of stealing relief maize when he was the Minister for Trade and Industry, Kenyatta suspended him and formed a Commission of Inquiry into the matter.

At Independence, Kenyatta took over the helm of a ship travelling through previously uncharted waters and there were bound to be many storms in the sea. I admit that some things could have been handled better, but despite Kenyatta's overwhelming personality, he still had to rely on advisors, many of whom had ulterior and selfish motives and who did not have the good of the country at heart. However, compared to other newly independent African states such as Tanzania, I feel that Kenya was a fairly successful country under Kenyatta's rule. Given the circumstances, Kenyatta tried his best to make Kenya a stable independent republic. Some things failed, and, indeed, Kenyatta should be blamed for them. Nevertheless, he should not bear the sole blame, because he had many lieutenants under him who made some quite bad decisions. Naturally, Kenyatta was not perfect, none of us is, and I certainly am not perfect myself, either.

I believe that one of the truly bad decisions that Kenyatta's government made was the mistreatment and injustice meted out to the real freedom fighters, the ones who went to the forest. When they came out of the forest, many found that their land had been confiscated and they had no option but to start living as squatters. Although Kenyatta advised Africans to obtain loans or use their savings to buy land from the departing Europeans, obviously the Mau Mau did not have any money. I feel that the government should have donated land to the freedom fighters for deserving cases.

Many of the fighters were thus very disillusioned with Kenyatta's government. They had previously put their faith in the new government which had been their beacon of hope while they fought and saw their companions die, or were detained in horrible conditions, but they felt the subsequent governments forgot them. It is a pity this problem was never addressed. Many things could have been done to help them right after independence.

The problem is, of course, that a great many people hide behind this label "Freedom Fighter", even when it is known that they were loyalists or sitting on the fence. Without an organised system of discovering their exact status, the resulting chaos would have led to more difficulties.

I am sure there would have been ways to honour the Mau Mau fighters but so far, Kenya's three governments have chosen to treat the Mau Mau as an embarrassing reality. The Kibaki regime erected a statue in Nairobi City Centre to honour Dedan Kimathi. This is a good start, and I hope that this is only the beginning. Perhaps one day we shall see a Mau Mau Museum, too.

There is also the perennial question of Kenyatta's decree of "willing seller, willing buyer" when it came to the disposal of the land previously occupied by the colonial government and European settlers.[58] Many people, especially those linked to the independence struggle, were furious when Kenyatta made the *"hakuna cha bure"* (there's nothing for free) statement concerning the disposal of that land. At the time, I believed that the land should have been given out freely to Africans after the *Wazungu* left. After all, the Europeans had never justly nor legally owned it. With hindsight, however, although theoretically the notion of free land for Africans would have sounded wonderful, I now believe it would have led to chaos, anarchy and even war if it had been implemented. Furthermore it would have set a wrong precedence on free assets.

I now feel that the only people who should have benefited from some sort of arrangements, should have been those who fought in the forests. For one, if land was to be given to everyone, who exactly would have been given what portion of land and where would the land come from? Take the Maasai, for example. They covered vast lands as they herded their livestock, but they were pastoralists, never settling in one place and never claiming ownership to particular areas. If they were to demand the return of all land that was stolen from their forefathers by the Europeans, how would the ownership have been determined, and who would have been the custodian? Before the Europeans came, no one had anything like title deeds to any land in the country. So who would deserve to be given land?

Bildad Kaggia advocated free land for everybody and approached the sensitive issue from a socialist point of view, which is why he fell out

---

58   When it became clear that Independence in Kenya was inevitable, most European settlers opted to leave. The British government gave Kenya money so that the government could buy land from the settlers in a sort of compensation system. The irony was that they were being compensated for land that had never been theirs in the first place. The government acquired some of the land and individuals bought privately from the Europeans on the "willing buyer, willing seller" basis advocated by Kenyatta. It was this land that the government sold to the people through land settlement schemes.

with Kenyatta. Kaggia and Jaramogi genuinely fought for the poor man and for freedom fighters, but they were somewhat misled. Their ideology was unpractical. The precedence of giving free land would have caused innumerable problems, as is evident these days in the Mau Forest issue where land was arbitrarily and illegally allocated, with dire consequences for the whole nation.

Unfortunately that concern and the other problems now facing Kenya such as corruption are due to the bad seeds which were planted during the previous regimes and they are now ruining our country. A leader has to have judgement and foresight. He has to understand that his every action will have consequences far into the future. The impact of each decision he makes has to be carefully weighed. In this short period of our nation's existence, some leaders have already left behind a disgraceful record in the history books, which will embarrass their descendants.

All the same, it is my belief that Kenyatta did the best he could in the circumstances that existed in the new republic. He was not perfect, but he got the country on its feet and running towards a bright future.

There was one other activity that I was engaged in during this period and which I am quite proud of. Paul Mirii, Peter Gacathi and I are the founders of the Kiambu Institute of Science and Technology (KIST), which is the biggest of its kind in Kiambu. The institute was established in 1976 by development-minded people from the area who decided that young people who did not manage to join university, should have the opportunity to learn other skills. A similar institution, Kimathi Institute of Technology, had been started in Nyeri in 1972.

Paul Mirii was the Chairman of the group that founded the institute. He was the Director of Agriculture in Kenya at the time. Peter Gacathi, a long time friend who was the Permanent Secretary in the Ministry of Education, was the Secretary, while I was the Treasurer.

Although the two hundred acres of land where the institute was to be sited had been identified, there was no money to make the purchase. As Treasurer, it was my job to raise funds to buy the land and start construction of the institution. So I lobbied among my friends and associates, here in Kenya and abroad, and we managed to collect eight hundred thousand shillings which was sufficient to give us a good start.

KIST now trains thousands of young people in various skills. Many of its graduates are well settled in life and earn their livelihoods with the skills they learnt at the institute. I am grateful that KIST still thanks me for my assistance in acquiring the land, during every graduation.

Every time I pass KIST I realize the value of education anew and although I did not manage to receive much schooling myself, I believe our young people should get every chance possible. This is the only way our country will prosper.

One morning, I phoned Kenyatta who was relaxing at his traditional retreat at State House Mombasa. Kenyatta sounded very jovial, and we talked about various issues. I informed Kenyatta that I would be leaving for London and the USA that night to escort my daughters, Lucy Wanjiru and Jane Mukuhi. Jane was going to study in Cardiff, while Lucy was going to a college in Kansas. I told him I would be back within a week and he wished me a good journey. I requested for an appointment with him when I came back

Kenyatta said he was going to see his people on the South Coast where he was due to hold a fundraising meeting at Msambweni Primary School, and that I should come down to Mombasa on the Tuesday I planned to return. Little did I know that that was the last conversation we would ever have, and his function in Msambweni was the last he undertook.

I left the country that night. When we arrived in transit in London the following day in order to board a connecting flight, I was surprised to find a man holding a placard with my name on it. I went over to identify myself and was shown into an office at the airport. I was told that my wife had called and left a message that I be intercepted, and that I should call her the moment I landed in London. With a feeling of panic, I looked for coins and a booth and phoned my Lynton Farm home. Wariara answered and when she spoke, I realised that something was terribly wrong.

"*Mzee* is dead," she told me in a miserable voice.

"Which *Mzee?*" I asked, puzzled.

"*Mzee,*" she answered, breaking into tears.

"I heard you the first time," I said. "What I am asking is which *Mzee* died, and where?" I was thinking of my father in Nyahururu, or perhaps my father-in-law in Elburgon. All respected old men were referred to as "*Mzee*".

"But he has just come from hospital and they said he was cured," I protested, referring to my father, who had been hospitalized a few days before for a minor ailment.

"Not that one, I am talking about the big one," said Wariara.

"What are you talking about? Who is the big one?" I was worried and all this circumlocution made me impatient. Perhaps I had a premonition who she was referring to because I was almost shouting at this juncture.

"Mzee Jomo Kenyatta is dead. He died last night in Mombasa," my wife finally let out the shocking words.

"But . . . but I talked with him only yesterday and he sounded okay," I stuttered in disbelief, not wanting to believe the news.

"Njonjo announced the news at 1 pm," Wariara told me.

"I will get the first possible flight back home," I stated and hung up the phone.

I was in shock. How could Kenyatta die? I had never really contemplated Kenyatta's death, not even during the days of the "Change the Constitution Movement" when we had argued about his successor.

That is how death is, I suppose. One never imagines the death of a loved one or a close friend, and when it happens it hits like a ton of bricks, overwhelming every other thing and reducing the rest of the world to insignificance.

What would happen to Kenya now? Who would take over the helm? Would the transition be peaceful? A hundred questions ran though my mind.

I told my daughters what had happened and told them that they should proceed onward to their schools but I would have to go back to Nairobi.

I did not manage to get a flight that day but I was able to acquire a ticket for the following day. I booked a room at the Churchill Hotel, which was my usual accommodation when I was in London. While leaving the airport I met Arthur Magugu and told him what had happened. I also ran into a friend of mine, George Muhoho, who was returning to Kenya with his wife after their honeymoon in America. When I broke the sad news to Muhoho, he reacted with disbelief and distress.

The following day I returned to Kenya and found the nation in a state of shock.

I went to State House every day to console Mama Ngina. I was quite worried and did not know what might happen next. I thought there might be a bit of trouble because it was very tense at State House and in the whole country. I was very sad and many leaders did not know what was going to happen. We were all in doubt about the future. We were not allowed to speak at the funeral and this may have been because the government, our detractors in particular, did not want GEMA making a statement.

We thought of Kenyatta as a hero and it was difficult to accept that he was dead. He was always a "larger than life" figure to all of us.

I remember that there was a story about one woman in Githunguri who heard the sad news at one o'clock and then rushed over to another woman who was working on the farm.

"What are you doing on the farm? Haven't you heard?" the first one cried out. "Kenyatta has died!"

"What?" exclaimed the second in disbelief, "You mean even *he* could die?"

Chapter 8

The Moi Years

There was considerable tension among Kenyan politicians when Kenyatta died, especially among those of us who were closest to him. Apart from all the shock and grief, politicians were aware that there would be a number of changes in government after the three months set out by the Constitution, during which a new election should be held.

As Moi took control as acting President, below the surface and the quiet lull of the mourning period, speculation and political manoeuvring was at a boiling point. Those of us who had campaigned against Moi in the 'Change the Constitution' movement knew well that if Moi was elected President, which was already virtually a *fait accompli*, we would definitely find ourselves at a distinct disadvantage. The group[59] who had been closest to Kenyatta and most influential, were in a panic and they were weak, squeezed into a tight corner since Kenyatta's death had caught them unprepared. They held a great many meetings, just as others did, all over the country.

The succession had not gone our way. I suppose we had been short-sighted and had conceitedly believed that a Kikuyu would automatically take over from Kenyatta and thus we were all divided amongst ourselves. Kenneth Matiba and I were for a Kibaki presidency, while the Kiambu group had not selected any candidate from their supporters. Despite believing in their supremacy, there were fierce internal jealousies because each thought he would be capable of leading the country. Dr. Njoroge Mungai was fighting with Charles Njonjo, while Mbiyu Koinange had his own ambitions. In short, none of them had resolved to cooperate with any of the others to counter a Moi Presidency.

---

59 The group of powerful Kiambu politicians who had coalesced around Kenyatta was derogatorily referred to as the Kiambu Mafia. However, it was not a close-knit group exercising power as one body but rather a set of dissenting entities. Their only common factor was that they were close to Kenyatta.

To Kenyatta's mind, apparently, Moi was a good choice because he had proved himself a loyal servant as Jomo's deputy, and more importantly, his origin was rooted in a very small tribe, a significant issue with all the rest of Kenya's population.

Naturally, Kenyatta was not clairvoyant and never imagined that the reign of his humble, loyal and God-fearing deputy would be transformed into a regime of ruthless dictatorship under whose rule Kenya's political, economic and social structures would shatter to pieces like a clay pot thrown out of the window.

During a 'Change the Constitution' meeting in Nakuru, Paul Ngei had observed that few people would be willing to leave State House after occupying it in acting capacity for three months. Sure as night follows day, over the 90 day period stipulated by the Constitution, Moi quickly solidified his power base and within a month of taking over it became obvious that he was on his way to becoming President.

An atmosphere of chaos, panic and fear pervaded certain corridors of power. Many strategic meetings were held in private clubs and the homes of Kenyatta's former lieutenants. Due to their past, mostly antagonistic relationships with Moi, they were certain that they would not feature in his long term plans and they began to re-evaluate their positions.

Although I was not privy to matters of certain Kiambu politicians, I had reason to be concerned. I had supported the 'Change the Constitution' movement which had vigorously campaigned in order to prevent Moi succeeding Kenyatta, and I was the chairman of GEMA, an organisation which Moi hated. Moi believed GEMA was behind the efforts to sabotage his political position during Kenyatta's reign.

But I was a nominated MP and, according to the constitution, I was safe till the end of the term, so I knew there was no way Moi could remove me. There was also my old nemesis, Charles Njonjo, who was Moi's confidante and who now looked at me disparagingly, whenever we met. Njonjo was sitting squarely in Moi's inner circle and his power and influence as Attorney General could only increase under a Moi Presidency. Njonjo had never seen eye to eye with me, and the situation had been worsened by the steady growth of GEMA and my contribution to the 'Change the Constitution' movement. I was also aware of the fact that Njonjo held grudges, and I was uncertain of what actions the Attorney General would consequently take.

There was nothing to do but wait. Moi had shown that he could be his own man and would not be held back by an inherited system. In 1978, shortly after he was sworn in, he demoted Mbiyu Koinange, undoubtedly

Kenyatta's chief lieutenant, from the powerful post of Minister of State in the Office of the President to the lacklustre portfolio of Environment and Natural Resources. We knew this was only the beginning.

Within the two weeks after Moi was named acting President, the Cabinet met and issued a strong statement which Mwai Kibaki read out to the public. The declaration announced that the Cabinet had resolved, as a body, that Daniel arap Moi was the right person to take over from Kenyatta and that he now had the endorsement of the Cabinet.

After such a proclamation of support, many of those who had any misgivings about a Moi Presidency retreated and kept their reservations to themselves. It was obvious that no one had the resources to marshal a sufficiently strong enough opposition.

A few weeks later I received a call from acting President Moi requesting me to stop in for a visit to his Kabarnet Gardens home in Woodley. My friend and Moi's close ally, Stanley Oloitiptip, and Justus Ole Tipis, accompanied me to the meeting. As we sat having tea, Moi asked various questions on a variety of topics. After discussing the trivialities, Moi then asked me who GEMA Union was going to support for the position of Vice President.

"Your Excellency, it is your prerogative, but I think Mwai Kibaki is best," I said.

Oloitiptip also echoed my feelings and supported Kibaki.

Sometime later I talked to the press and it was not until the subsequent article was published, that I realised I had inadvertently destroyed Kibaki's chances of being made Moi's deputy.

The reporter had asked me who I, as GEMA Chairman, would support for the presidency. This was despite the fact that no one had openly declared they would challenge Moi for the position. Perhaps the reporter tricked me into giving a specific answer. I told him that GEMA was not mine. It belonged to its members. I added that I intended to call a meeting of GEMA leaders and then we would debate the issue and declare our position on whether to support Moi or not.

I found out later that when Moi read the article, he was furious.

A certain lady, a friend of our family, worked in State House. She just happened to be present when Moi was talking to others about the article in the paper.

"Just who does this Njenga think he is? What is this little GEMA to me!" Moi had fumed. "Let him try! Whatever he says or does, I will rule this country!"

This lady friend said Moi had been outraged by the whole interview with me.

Well, I did not even realise that my personal outlook would hasten the death of GEMA and create further distrust between myself and Njonjo and Moi. At that time, I simply did not believe Moi was the right candidate and perhaps I was hoping that something would turn up to change the inevitable.

Nevertheless, I changed my mind to a certain extent a little time thereafter. Many KANU sub-branches had come out and openly endorsed Moi as the next President, and it became obvious that he held the advantage since no one else was running against him. Time was running out but no one came forward to challenge him. It is fairly certain that no one would have had much of a chance against Moi anyway. The three months time-frame was too limited for anyone else to mount a significant presidential campaign.

All KANU branches in other Provinces declared their support for Moi. Central Province, the home of the Kikuyu, definitely did not want to appear to oppose the man who was the President-in-waiting. All of a sudden, every politician who had previously been opposed to Moi was endorsing him for leadership. It looked like we had no alternative, so we also went to State House to show the support of the Kikuyu.

The delegation was led by Central PC Simeon Nyachae. On behalf of Kiambu District, Mbiyu Koinange declared that the sub-branch fully endorsed Moi for President. Dr. Gikonyo Kiano spoke for Murang'a and Deputy House Speaker, James Muregi Kabingu, vouched for Nyandarua's support. Kibaki spoke on behalf of Nyeri while James Njiru spoke on behalf of Kirinyaga.

During all this outpouring of endorsements, we were on the lawn outside State House, and I remember I covered my head with a newspaper because the sun was blazing down on us. When all the five District representatives had spoken, Nyachae, who was the Master of Ceremonies, took the microphone. He congratulated the five who had spoken and then he asked permission from Moi to call one *Mzee* to speak on behalf of all the leaders and for Central Province in general. Nyachae then called me up to speak as GEMA Chairman.

I was taken aback for an instant. This was a real surprise. I had not met Nyachae before the meeting nor was I one of the official speakers. I never panic in such situations since I have always been confident in addressing the public. But, since I knew the purpose of the gathering only too well, I knew I had been trapped.

With no alternative open to me, I was forced to state that I agreed with the other leaders, reiterated that Moi was the best choice, and confirmed that he was GEMA's choice, as well. The crowd cheered and Nyachae smiled happily.

I was bitter because I realised that I had been cornered. I could never have expressed any doubts in Moi's leadership at such a public venue. It would have been like one man fighting an army. And Nyachae knew, perfectly well, that I had my reservations about Moi.

The fact was that, as the Central PC, Nyachae would have been deeply embarrassed if all KANU leaders from the Province endorsed Moi and then I stood to contradicted them. PCs were very powerful at that time and Nyachae's image would have been deeply tarnished if his Province did not support Moi a hundred percent.

The news was then broadcast on VOK as was normal practice at the time and I felt my position had been completely compromised.

There was a Presidential election in 1978 and, since Moi was unopposed, at least one thousand voters from each province had to append their signature to approve a proposal to make Moi the President. A ballot, where there is only one candidate, would have been needless and expensive and therefore this was sort of an endorsement or confirmation that Moi was President.

The following year, Parliament was disbanded to pave way for a general election and many of the previous MPs had no choice but to campaign for votes. After all, only MPs were eligible for the Cabinet and there was always the question of whether or not Moi would retain the Cabinet members of his predecessor. Earlier on, when Kenyatta died, I started thinking about getting into Parliament as an elected MP. I mulled it over and decided that this was an opportunity to serve the people. The only challenge was that Mbiyu Koinange, who was my personal and family friend (and who had also been Kenyatta's right-hand man) was the current MP for Kiambaa. Competing with Mbiyu might look unseemly and discourteous, I thought. After all, Mbiyu had been the area MP since independence and had played a major role in the liberation struggle. I reflected on my options and contemplated trying for a seat in Molo, in Nakuru West, where my second wife, Njeri, resided. I had significant connections there, through my land and businesses, and a delegation had visited me in order to convince me to stand in the area. I was certain I could easily sail through.

However, the people of Kiambaa prevailed upon me to vie in their constituency, instead. There were a number of delegations from Kiambaa that came to visit me, to encourage me to stand. I recall one of the delegates was led by Ng'ang'a Muchiri from Ruaka, and another by Kuria Gathunguri. Others from church groups and women's organisations gave me their support. Apparently they were disappointed with Mbiyu's leadership and wanted change. They complained that, despite his powerful position as Kenyatta's close associate, Mbiyu had done little for Kiambaa. It seemed that the people felt that Kiambaa was least developed of all the other constituencies in Kiambu and they blamed Mbiyu for this situation.

As the Chairman of GEMA, my relationship with Moi and Njonjo continued to be frosty. Njonjo considered me a threat and I saw him in the same light. I decided I would be better off in Parliament. At least there I would have a forum to defend myself, to represent my people in GEMA and also to protect my businesses.

Thereafter I presented my nomination papers, as did eight other candidates including Mbiyu Koinange, Nginyo Kariuki and Peter Gacathi, the former administrator who had helped me in Chief Muhoho's land case. Mbiyu campaigned on the platform of experience, telling the people that Gacathi and I were greenhorns, although I was fifty years old at the time and had vast experience in GEMA leadership. My own campaign was based on bringing change and development. Gacathi's campaign was vaguely stated since he had been a Civil Servant and did not know the intrigues of politics well.

When the results were announced I had won by a landslide. I had garnered 19,000 votes, Mbiyu about 10,000, Kariuki 900 and the others ranged from about 700 to as few as 30 votes. Perhaps the people saw Mbiyu as an old man past his prime and, with Kenyatta's death, his relevance had diminished in the eyes of Kiambaa people.

Moi won the 1979 election unopposed and officially became the country's second President. By this time he had solidified his power base and the voices of opposition had all but gone silent. Naturally I was aware that my political career might be difficult under a Moi Presidency, but I left my fate in the hands of God to whom I always turned to in good times and bad. As was widely expected, many people in the previous government did not make it back into the Cabinet.

During and after 1979, Moi started dropping Kenyatta's people from the government line up. Bernard Hinga was removed from the post of Police Commissioner. My friend Eliud Njenga, the Kiambu DC, was shown the door as well.

However, in the case of Eliud Njenga, I believe he may have inadvertently hastened his own removal. After reading the President's Jamhuri Day speech on 12 December 1979, he put it aside and remarked in Kiswahili, "So there, people, you have listened to your President's speech." Just an innocent remark, but it was widely reported in the press, and the impression created by the sentence was that Njenga did not view Moi as *his* President. What a difference one little word can make!

In due course, many Kikuyu Permanent Secretaries who had served under Jomo were not re-appointed in the new line up. Just a few years after Kenyatta's death, there were virtually no Kikuyu Permanent Secretaries left.

Perhaps to placate the Kikuyu elite, many of whom were terrified of a non-Kikuyu President, Moi chose Kibaki as his Vice President, just as Njonjo had stated.

Kibaki's selection was commonly expected, mainly because he was popular and admired in the business and corporate circles. In addition he was the most outstanding Kikuyu in government in terms of education and experience. His performance in the Ministry of Finance had been exemplary. He was not aggressive, had never voiced anti-Moi sentiments and he was the ideal choice to strike a balance between the uneasy Kikuyu and the rest of the nation.

Of course, I was not in the new Cabinet. With Njonjo as Moi's chief advisor, no other scenario would have been expected. However, Moi retained quite a few prominent Kikuyu personalities from the previous regime. These included Central Bank Governor Duncan Ndegwa, Head of Civil Service and Secretary to the Cabinet, Jeremiah Kiereini (who incidentally, was Moi's close neighbour), the Head of Special Branch, James Kanyotu and a few others.

GEMA had always presented a knotty problem for both Moi and Njonjo. Shortly after the elections it seemed that the time had come to put GEMA and me in our place. Moi believed GEMA had always opposed him while Njonjo looked down on it as a tribal organization led by ignorant semi-illiterates. It was Njonjo who, while in a Parliamentary session, stated that GEMA was an illegal movement. Consequently there were heated arguments over the issue. I challenged Njonjo, wondering why he had registered GEMA if it was indeed an illegal movement. However, it was merely a matter of time before things came to a head— and the day came sooner rather than later. GEMA was proscribed.

I was happy though, that we were at least allowed to retain our commercial interests with the proviso that the company changed its name from GEMA Holdings to Agricultural and Industrial Holdings.

I knew that if I was to survive Moi's reign, I had to change my political tactics and style. Together with my wives Wariara and Njeri, I became a KANU Life Member in 1979. During Kenyatta's time I had been an ordinary member with no particular need to prove my loyalty, but now with Moi as President, in the context of our past relationship, I had to change tack. Ironically, it had become a condition that those who wished to stand for elections must be KANU Life Members.

At that time, that piece of paper, the certificate of KANU life membership, was the ultimate proof of loyalty. Under Moi's new administration, I knew it was the way to go.

But my relationship with Moi remained cold. My relationship with Njonjo was even colder. Since I had no Cabinet responsibilities, I continued to concentrate on my businesses and on my duties in regard to representing the people of Kiambaa. It was obvious to me and to others who had been close to Kenyatta that things were different now and it was time to adapt as best we could.

However, Moi was observant and apparently continued gauging my character.

I generally went down to the Coast every August, and took my whole family down to enjoy the school holidays and to attend the Mombasa Agricultural Show. I often sent some of my best cattle to the Nakuru Agricultural Show, so I enjoyed having a look at what other farmers were producing.

One day in August of 1979, the Deputy of the Special Branch, Stephen Mureithi, came to visit me at my house in Nyali. Moi, who was also at the coast to officially open the show, had given Mureithi a message to deliver to me. The message was merely that, once we both got back to Nairobi, he wanted to speak to me on various issues. This was after Moi had been President for about one year. Given the fact that we had not spoken, even once, during that period, my curiosity was greatly aroused.

I agreed to the meeting and Mureithi set it up. A little later, when I was back in the city, I found myself at State House, Nairobi. Moi was an early riser, like me, and when I arrived at around 7 am, I found Moi in conference with Njonjo and Laikipia MP, Godfrey Gitahi Kariuki. Kariuki, who was better known as GG, was the Minister of State in the Office of the President and was very close to Moi. Over tea, we had some discussion and then Moi asked me the same question that Kenyatta had often asked. Moi wanted to know why Njonjo and I were constantly in conflict. And what problem did I have with GG? Why were we always fighting and unable to cooperate?

I remember the conversation well. I informed Moi that it was Njonjo and GG who were actually prejudiced against me and not the other way round. I told the President that, if this scenario had been played out in Idi Amin's Uganda, I knew I would have been executed by this time. Moi agreed with my assessment but then told me that there was no cause to fear since this was Kenya and he himself was a staunch Christian who would never execute anyone. Moi said that Njonjo and I should show the people that we were together.

Njonjo then appealed to me to agree to bury the hatchet. He asked me to support Moi and put a stop to *fitina* (malice) against the President. I replied that I had no problem whatsoever in working with Moi, Njonjo or GG.

As a matter of fact, Njonjo and I immediately agreed to organize a public function in Kiambu so that people could see there was no animosity between us and that we were friends working together in the same government. It was decided that Njonjo be the guest of honour at a fundraiser for Gathanga Catholic Church which was in my constituency and also very near Njonjo's farm. I should explain that Njonjo's roots were in the area as well.

There is an interesting story about Njonjo that came out of this *harambee*.

I wanted to ensure the success of the fundraiser and I wanted to use the opportunity to show Njonjo that there was no enmity between us, so I made special arrangements.

I knew that Njonjo did not drink local beer, so I tried to get some imported Löwenbräu beer from Germany. It was difficult to find but I managed to locate an Asian shopkeeper who had it in stock and I bought about two dozen cans and put them in the boot of my car. I was trying to be a perfect host and cater for Njonjo's taste.

The *harambee* went on well. We raised a considerable amount of money and Njonjo and I acted like the best of friends, although I am not sure how convincing we were, even to ourselves.

Later, after the *harambee,* Njonjo, Oloitiptip, Arthur Magugu and some other VIPs and I were sitting in the VIP tent chatting and having some food. This tent was a little further off from the others, so we had a bit of privacy.

The rest of us were drinking Kenya beer but after Njonjo was seated, I sent for the German beer in my car boot and Njonjo was very happy to get his Löwenbräu to drink. He thanked me for being such a thoughtful host and began to tell Oloitiptip about the special qualities of this beer and why he enjoyed drinking it. However, he did not want to use the beer glasses we had out on the table. He called his driver, a man called Kabuco Wakori, and told him to bring his branded silver beer mug from his car. I was a little surprised that he carried his own mug around with him, but passed it off. After all, we each have our little idiosyncrasies. When he got the mug from the driver, he poured in the Lowenbrau and seemed very satisfied and content.

The drinking continued for some hours and then everyone slowly started to leave the venue. As for me, I went home early because I knew the next day was the day I scheduled to talk to my constituents.

So that morning, while I was in my office in Kiambu with a visitor, the DO, a friend of mine called Waweru, came in and since I could see he had something urgent to discuss, I quickly dealt with the visitor's problem and then asked the DO to come in. Although we used to meet frequently on various matters, I wondered what was so pressing, that he would interrupt my session with my constituents.

The DO seemed uncertain of what to say, at first, but finally he asked me, "Do you know what happened to Njonjo's beer mug?"

"Beer mug?" I asked in surprise. Naturally I remembered Njonjo's mug but I was surprised that a DO would come to my office so early in the morning to ask me about such a thing. I told him that I did not have any idea.

"It's a serious matter," Waweru said. "Mr. Njonjo phoned the PC, Mr. David Musila, at the Provincial Headquarters in Nyeri this morning. The PC was told to find out what happened to his beer mug after yesterday's *harambee*. Then the PC phoned the DC, and the DC has phoned me. No one knows what happened to Njonjo's beer mug. He can't find it. What shall I do?"

I laughed. It was pretty hilarious for this neighbourhood matter to go all the way to the Provincial Headquarters in Nyeri, which was almost two hundred kilometres away. But of course the DO, as a junior government officer, did not see it that way. He had his superiors on his back and was anxious to deal with the matter expeditiously.

I told him the name of the woman who had been responsible for the catering arrangements and the fact that she came from Gathanga. So the DO called together the Chiefs and the Sub-Chiefs from that area and told them to find the mug, even if it meant a door to door search. Luckily, one of the sub-chiefs knew the name of the lady and went straight to her house to see if she would know what had happened to the mug.

The woman was very surprised to see so many uniformed government officials at her door, asking about a beer mug.

"It's here," she said. "I didn't know whose it was. I brought it for washing along with the other dishes and cutlery."

So the Sub-Chief reported the matter to the Chief, who in turn reported to the DO and then the DO reported to the DC. The DO said that the mug had been found, but now they did not know what they were supposed to do with it. The DC then reported to the PC and asked him what they should do next. The PC was quite happy and said that he would phone Njonjo and find out how it could be delivered.

And when he rung Njonjo, the AG said, "Tell the DO he can bring it to my house in Muthaiga."

So the PC phoned back the DC to pass along the instructions. The DC in turn passed the directions to the DO and the DO came to see me around 4 pm, to find out where Njonjo lived. Apparently even the PC had been afraid to ask Njonjo where his house was. Civil Servants exercised considerable caution around Njonjo.

I gave them directions and a map to Njonjo's house in Muthaiga and I told them they would recognise the place because they would find a policeman at the gate. I also advised them to be in their uniforms and to wrap the mug in something presentable. I figured that if so much protocol was going to be involved, they may as well do it properly.

And so, when they got there, they saluted and handed over the mug. Njonjo told them to sit at the veranda and be served some tea and toast, and after that they left.

The most notable thing about this search was that the yard where the *harambee* had been held adjoined Njonjo's property. He or his workers could have easily followed up the matter themselves. Just imagine the time and government resources spent in pursuit of a beer mug!

Despite the Harambee, we never really buried the hatchet. But with old age catching up, I have decided that it would be much more gentlemanly to mend fences and nowadays we have an occasional chat. It is really regrettable that politics and money so often break up or prevent friendships.

The government and the political scene were running fairly smoothly during the first years of Moi's rule. Apart from a few minor hiccups here and there, which is to be expected in any government, the country was moving ahead at a relatively good pace. The economy was functioning and growing and there were little if any hostilities among the various communities. Moi was trying his best to run the country following the methods used by his predecessor and for the most part, he was successful. He was carrying out the promise he made to the nation in his inaugural address, which was that he would *fuata Nyayo* (follow in Kenyatta's footsteps). However, unlike Kenyatta who mostly administered the government from his Gatundu home, and who never once slept in State House,[60] Moi generally worked from State House itself. Apart from the reshuffles that Moi implemented here and there, it was virtually business as usual.

After three years of Moi's presidency, however, everything changed. On the morning of August 1, 1982, Nairobi woke up to the sound of heavy gunfire. Shortly thereafter, some rebels from the Kenya Air Force stormed into VOK Broadcasting studio and forced a terrified Leonard Mambo Mbotela (a radio announcer) to broadcast the overthrow of the government and state that all authority was now in the hands of the military.

The police were told to remain out of uniform and keep to their stations, and the rebels stated that they would explain the details later. After that, the radio continuously broadcast various patriotic and military tunes without interruption. Everyone was tense. People all over the country worried about the circumstances and their prospects for the future. There was no word from Moi. There had been coups in many African countries, but Kenya had only experienced rumours of plots and conspiracies. Now the worst had happened, and the whole country was stunned.

It soon emerged that the coup plotters were a naive group of disorganized Junior Air Force mutineers whose childish plans of overthrowing the government were quickly falling to pieces. Within hours, the rebels were crushed by the General Service Unit and the Kenya Army. Many of the rebels were killed while the remainder were arrested. Moi came out of hiding and the radio announced that the government was once more in control. However, a dusk to dawn curfew was imposed and it took quite

---

60   Kenyatta only slept in State House once. It is claimed that at night he heard the croaking of frogs and he declared that they were indeed the ghosts of colonialism. After that, he travelled from Gatundu to State House whenever he had business to execute at the official residence.

a number of days for life to return to normal, especially for Nairobi residents.

I was at home when the coup took place and I remember that my daughter Lucy phoned me early in the morning from her room and told me that she had heard on the radio that there was an attempted coup. I found out later that my wines and spirits shop in Westlands was totally destroyed, either by looters or by the military rebels. They apparently came in with vehicles and stole everything on the shelves. I was so disappointed that I closed that shop for good.

Mostly I was worried about my son, Wairiri. He had gone out the previous night and was clubbing with his friends in Nairobi. Apparently he and his friends had heard the gunshots and taken off. Not much later we found out he was staying with Leonard Kibinge, the Permanent Secretary in the Ministry of Finance. Kibinge's son and Wairiri had both made it safely from town to the house in Lavington and Kibinge brought him home that afternoon. We were incredibly relieved and happy he was safe.

I had a *harambee* scheduled at Kiambaa, in a village called Muthurwa, for the day and I remember I had to cancel it.

It is this single incident, in my opinion, that marked the drastic change in Moi's personality and style. All the soldiers who were suspected of supporting or collaborating with the rebels were given lengthy sentences. Those who were convicted of masterminding the coup were hanged. The leader of the mutineers, Hezekiah Ochuka, was actually the very last person to be hanged in Kenya in 1987. Politicians who were suspected of colluding with the plotters, such as Raila Odinga, were detained without trial.

From the time of the coup onwards, Moi was determined to prove he was in charge and he did so with a heavy hand.

Just a few months earlier Parliament had passed the infamous Section 2A which made Kenya a one party state, thereby making KANU the only legal political party, with Moi, of course, as its President. This now gave Moi a free hand to deal with any opposition.

I was not happy at all. A single party is just another name for a dictatorship. No one could question any action taken by those in power and I believe Section 2A divided the country.

In addition, detention without trial was used as a solution for anyone in disagreement with KANU and Moi. For dissident politicians such as

Raila and his father, Jaramogi, Koigi Wamwere and others, the next nineteen years were hell on earth for them. Scholars and journalists who were considered disloyal and anti-Moi also faced the same treatment. Free speech was no longer tolerated and freedom of the press was just an unthinkable ideal. Anyone who dared to criticize KANU or Moi was expelled from the party and faced political exile.

With the establishment of Moi's dictatorship, Kenya decay's began. Looting and corrupion became the order of the day. Many government institutions such as the Kenya Meat Commission (KMC), Kenya Cooperative Creameries (KCC), Kisumu Cotton Mills (KICOMI), Rivatex, just to name a few, collapsed. Even financial institutions such as Kenya Commercial Bank (KCB) and National Bank of Kenya (NBK) where the government had controlling shares started declaring huge losses. Huge sums of money were paid for non-existent services and kickbacks and bribes were as normal as the sunrise every morning. For the next nineteen years, Kenya's economy was to tumble down the precipice, from a fast growing financial success to that of a banana republic.

One of the most unusual regulations instituted under the regime was the toll paid for use of the Mombasa to Uganda highway and Thika Road. Every motorist had to pay a toll to use these roads. But the toll collected certainly never went to the upkeep of any roads as had been intended. The whole road network nearly collapsed during Moi's regime and motorists had to incur huge maintenance costs on their vehicles due to bad roads.

I should explain that, since the media was strictly controlled, we all relied on the gossip and rumours that circulated very efficiently. We knew nearly everything that was going on, from Moi's personal life, to those of his sons and those of his cohorts. There were a few secrets, but many things were leaked and everyone was aware. Many times we had a bitter laugh about their foolish personal antics that were costing the country so dearly and often caused serious harm to the others in their lives.

Moi's phobia for opposition blinded him to the fact that his henchmen did absolutely anything they desired, all in the name of serving the republic. The disastrous effects of Moi's rule on the economy and his disregard for the rule of law will be felt for generations to come.

All this time, the system was watching me and other powerful people in the country. One such person in Kiambu was Ngengi Muigai, whose actions were closely monitored by the government.

The day before the coup, in August 1982, Njonjo held a party in his house at Muthaiga and, as I learned later, informed his friends that he would use all means possible to ensure that I did not return to Parliament in the 1984 general elections. One lady from Kiambaa was present at the party. Like the other lady at State House who I mentioned earlier, she was a friend of our family, so as soon as she was free, she hurried out to see us and advised me not to vie in the next general elections. She told Wariara and me that Njonjo might be planning something sinister, and she was worried about my safety. My wife agreed with her and felt that I should not run for parliament. She decided it was too dangerous. But I was nonchalant. I was not cowed by Njonjo's bragging or his threats. I told the lady that God, not man, was in control of humanity's destiny and therefore Njonjo's raves and rants meant little to me.

Causing great surprise for many Kenyans, Njonjo had resigned his powerful position as Attorney General in 1981, in order to vie for the Kikuyu parliamentary seat. This was most astonishing because Njonjo was leaving an extremely powerful post and leaving the Cabinet to become a mere Member of Parliament.

I and others who knew his true character wondered how he could take the enormous downward step from the prestigious position of AG, in order to interact with *wananchi wa kawaida* (the common man) whom he looked down on. How could the aristocratic Njonjo endure performing *Nyakīnyua*[61] dances with poor barefoot women in Kikuyu Constituency, as the other candidates did, in order to garner support?

It did not seem possible that Njonjo had suddenly seen the light and decided that he would better serve his Kikuyu constituents as their Member of Parliament. Furthermore, in another suspicious incident, the immediate former MP for Kikuyu, Amos Ng'ang'a, conveniently announced that he would not be contesting and soon after, he was expediently appointed chairman of Tana and Athi River Development Authority. Njonjo easily won the seat as Member of Parliament and was appointed Minister for Constitutional Affairs.

Then, not too long thereafter, a thunderbolt out of the blue destroyed Njonjo's ambitions. While Moi was attending a public rally in Kisii, a Cabinet Minister, Elijah Mwangale, declared that there was a *msaliti* (traitor) in the country, and that this *msaliti* was planning to overthrow

---

61 *Nyakinyua* is a term that refers to communal dances by Kikuyu women. At that time, politicians would be entertained with these dances, and they would become a campaign medium in which the participants would praise the sponsoring candidate and deride and insult his or her rivals. The politicians always joined in the dances, sometimes with comical results.

Moi's government. Many politicians were puzzled by this *msaliti* matter, because Moi himself did not elaborate and no one else seemed to have a clue on the subject. Through innuendo and the clever manipulation of selected politicians, fingers soon began to point at Njonjo. Rumours and gossip gave out the supposition that Njonjo was the traitor and it was he who was planning to overthrow Moi.

Nevertheless, there was a confusing paradox in this conjecture. Njonjo and Moi had always been extremely close friends. Njonjo had consistently defended Moi and had contributed immensely in Moi's campaign to succeed Kenyatta, to the extent that Njonjo had earned the wrath of fellow Kiambu luminaries who had their own ideas about the succession. Moi had worked very closely with Njonjo, more so than with anyone else, both before and after he attained the Presidency. How could he now turn against his friend with such evil intentions? It did not sound quite right.

Consequently, Moi asked all KANU sub-branches in Central province to determine whether Njonjo actually was a traitor. Moi sent Arthur Magugu, who was then the Minister for Finance, to tell us that all Kiambu officials should meet and decide our stand on the issue. At the time, I was a member of the sub-branch, (and became the Chair almost immediately thereafter), Ngengi Muigai was the branch secretary and, together with the other officials, we invited Njonjo to the KANU office.

I am certain that Moi was deeply convinced that we would pass a guilty verdict on Njonjo. After all, Njonjo had continually criticised and pestered Ngengi and myself, calling us *Ngoroko*[62]. On many occasions he also sent Soki Singh of the Special Branch to harass and annoy us by forcing us to record statements with the CID. If we therefore united forces against Njonjo as branch officials, we would be able to destroy him. Perhaps it was time to pay him back for all the nasty things he had done to us.

We called the meeting. Magugu did not attend since he was away on official duties. Joe Gatuguta, who was the Kikuyu Sub-Branch Chairman, and I summoned Njonjo, who was, at the time, the Minister for Constitutional Affairs. A woman called Mumbi Gichuru, who was the Ndumberi branch representative went straight to the point and asked Njonjo if he knew anything about the traitor issue. Njonjo denied this vehemently, declaring that he had absolutely nothing to do with treason. After hearing his testimony, we then asked him to leave so we could discuss the matter.

[62] *Ngoroko* were supposedly "cattle rustlers" but in many cases this was just a term to cover up the covert and private military armies of some politicians.

We talked the matter over and at one point I told the branch officials that, in my lifetime, I had witnessed a lot of mudslinging. I said that during the state of emergency in the 1950s, I had witnessed many people being detained or even killed because of false evidence given by enemies and home guards. This matter regarding Njonjo, I explained, looked like witch-hunting. After debating for some time, the sub-branch officials concluded that the accusations were baseless and implausible.

In consequence, as Chairman, I asked all the sub-branches—Gatundu, Githunguri, Lari, Kikuyu, Limuru and Kiambaa—which comprised the Kiambu branch, not to support Njonjo's persecution.

"We Kiambu KANU Branch officials do not know what this animal called *Msaliti* looks like," I told the meeting. "We are very curious to know. Should anyone of you in the sub-branches see it, please immediately inform us so that we can take it to Moi."

"We should not waste more time on this issue," added Ngengi. "Remember it has been dry for a long while, but it rained last night. Go to your homes and start planting crops," he joked.

"And you people in the sub-branches go back and try to find this animal. We at the District level have not been able to discover it," I added.

The *Standard* newspaper which had sent reporters to cover the meeting, quoted us verbatim the following day and shortly after the newspaper hit the stands, I received a phone call from someone—I cannot now recall who it was—and was told that Moi was foaming at the mouth over my remarks.

After reading the newspaper and noting the stand we had taken in Kiambu, the Nyeri sub-branch headed by Kanyi Waithaka also dismissed the allegations that Njonjo was a traitor. In Murang'a the branch, headed by Gikonyo Kiano, first decided Njonjo was the traitor and then, after they were reprimanded by *wazee* and senior politicians in Murang'a, later backtracked and defended him in the matter.

These elders had told the Murang'a members, "Kiambu, which is Njonjo's home, has not found him guilty. Now who are you to decide that he is?"

I probably could have influenced the officials in Kiambu to judge Njonjo guilty, but my conscience would not allow me to do so. In retrospect, the issue was, of course, a total fabrication, errant nonsense and I believe it was one of those harebrained schemes, such as Mwakenya[63] which Moi and his henchmen used to punish their perceived enemies.

---

63   Mwakenya was an imaginary rebel movement which Moi's men created in order to be able to arrest and detain dissidents without trial at the infamous Nyayo House underground cells. The victims were tortured and some were maimed for life while others were killed.

Eventually, a Commission of Inquiry found Njonjo guilty but Moi 'forgave' him. This made the whole event look ridiculous. However, despite the fact that many people believed he was innocent that was the end of Njonjo's life in the public domain.

According to rumours from the people, and based on the theories of my friends who were close to both Moi and Njonjo, the two had an agreement, a sort of Memorandum of Understanding. This verbal contract was arrived at even before Kenyatta's death and encompassed the concept that Njonjo would do everything in his power to ensure that Moi became President after Kenyatta's death. In turn, Moi would govern the country for five years and then hand over the presidency to Njonjo, or at least to sack Kibaki and appoint Njonjo as Vice President. However, it appears that when the period of five years was nearing its end, Moi reneged on the agreement and betrayed him by creating the *msaliti* issue.

It cannot be proven, but this speculation sounds quite possible. The inquiry clearly demonstrated that Njonjo did not have the machinery to overthrow the government. He had neither the resources nor the men. It was completely implausible that he was a traitor. Yet the commission found him guilty. This point has never been well explained and still bothers many people today.

Again, one must ask oneself why Njonjo resigned from his prestigious position of Attorney General to become a mere Member of Parliament, representing the poor and illiterate whom he considered beneath his notice. Naturally Njonjo had to get into Parliament in order to become the President, if that was his intention, and Moi, who had tasted the sweetness of power, may have decided to betray Njonjo and thwart his ambitions despite any agreements they had made earlier.

In the general elections of 1983, I had no serious challengers and easily went back to the House. However in 1988, I was eventually fired from my position as Kiambu KANU Branch Chairman when I again refused to be used by Moi in the persecution of another politician, Jonathan Njenga, who was the MP for Limuru.

It happened that there was a time we had a motion in Parliament, and when we went to vote, it was only Jonathan Njenga and Charles Rubia who voted against it. Therefore KANU wanted to remove Jonathan from Parliament, and there was only one way to do it. If the KANU Limuru Sub-branch was to remove him from his party post, then the KANU

Disciplinary Committee could strike him off the list of Party members. He would then be party-less and thus barred from the position of Member of Parliament. The Limuru Sub-branch was therefore instructed to figure out a way to get rid of him.

So the Limuru Sub-branch made a recommendation to the District Branch to remove Jonathan. When it was brought forward, I began to wonder why this recommendation was made and asked around trying to discover the motive behind it. I knew very well that once an MP was kicked out of KANU he would lose his parliamentary seat.

As the Kiambu Party Chairman, I called a meeting of Party officials and, after hours spent considering the case, we were unable to come to any agreement. I therefore made plans to take it up again as soon as possible.

When all this was going on, Moi was planning a trip to the United States, and just a day before he left, he phoned and said he wanted me to accompany him. At the time, I did not realise why he wanted my company, but I made arrangements with various people to manage my affairs while I was away. I made sure that the meeting to conclude the Jonathan issue would be dealt with while I was in America.

Among other preparations, I wrote a letter to my deputy, the Vice-Chairman, Josephat Karanja, (who not much later became the Vice President of Kenya), instructing him to convene and chair a Branch meeting once again and that the main agenda should be the matter of Jonathan's censure. I informed Karanja that, since the matter seemed to be taking up a lot of time, they should not postpone the case just because I was going to be away. I told them to make a decision as quickly as possible.

So in the morning, Moi and I flew off to the US. I was fairly confident that, left on their own, the Kiambu KANU Branch would never kick Jonathan out.

When the meeting took place, Karanja read out my letter to the other officials. One of the members in Kiambu wondered why their Chairman had been "taken away".

Mr. Gathenge Njaci, a party official from Githunguri Sub-branch, thanked the Vice-Chair and also, sarcastically, thanked the President for inviting me, the Kiambu KANU Chairman on his trip. He said that all the members should be quite pleased. By honouring the Chairman with this trip, he told the members, President Moi was also honouring and showing respect for Kiambu District people. He told the Branch Secretary, Ngengi Muigai to make note of his words in the minutes of the meeting. Njaci was not a big-bodied person, but few could match his courage.

He said there was no need to continue with the meeting as there was no hurry. He proposed that the members should wait until I returned, to discuss the matter. He felt that, since I started it, I should finish it. Macharia Mandaba from Lari seconded the proposal and Mata Gitagia from Kikuyu did the same. Kimata Mukui from Gatundu, and Nduta Kore[64] from Kiambaa Sub-branch supported the suggestion as well. Then others stood to express their opinions and all wanted the matter to be delayed until my return.

Later these officials told me that they had realised that Moi had tried to get me out of the way so that I would not influence their decision. In fact, Karanja was the only one in a hurry to finish the matter.

While we were in the US, Moi sent Stanley Metto, an Assistant Minister who was also in the entourage, to invite me to breakfast in Moi's suite the following morning, where Moi asked me what was happening in the Jonathan case.

"This man is giving a lot of trouble," said Moi. "Is he just going to be left like that? Something must be done!"

I told him that I had written a letter to Karanja and instructed him to wrap up the case quickly.

"I have left the case with the members," I told Moi. "I am not sure what has happened but I'll definitely make sure that action is taken."

I had a feeling that Karanja, or perhaps someone else, had phoned Moi to tell him about the events at the Kiambu Branch, and that was why I had been invited to breakfast.

When we came back, I found the case still pending. I discovered that the members had refused to denounce Jonathan Njenga or remove him from KANU. I therefore called another meeting over the case.

Coincidentally, there was a meeting of the KANU Disciplinary Committee set for the following week, just one day after our scheduled Kiambu meeting. Okiki Amayo was the Chairman and Kariuki Chotara, Mulu Mutisya, Moody Awori, and I, among others, were the members. This Committee was responsible for throwing MPs out of Parliament and if an MP was expelled or suspended for six months, he would automatically lose his seat.

---

64 Nduta Kore's husband had died during the fight for independence and she herself had shared the same cell with Mama Ngina Kenyatta at Kamiti during the State of Emergency.

The Kiambu meeting started at 10 am I told the officials that we must wrap up the matter that day even if we had to sleep at the venue. So we started the hearing and the accusations came up one by one. I refuted each one and then informed the members that we, as Branch officials, had nothing to do with Parliament. Parliament had its own Standing Orders and could deal with Jonathan if there was truly a case against him. As a Branch, *we* had no case against him.

I instructed Peter Kihumba, the chairman of the Limuru Sub-branch, to tell Jonathan that we had no case against him.

The following day I went to Kenyatta International Conference Centre to attend the Disciplinary Committee meeting. One of the members, Moody Awori, informed the Chairman that he was having problems with a certain woman named Julia Ojiambo who was giving him a difficult time in his Funyula Constituency. Amayo sympathised. He himself had been thrown out of parliament by a woman, Phoebe Asiyo.

"When you talk about a woman giving you problems I understand better than anyone else," Amayo said. He told Moody to present a case against Julia Ojiambo who would then be summoned before the Committee.

"You bring this Julia and do not be like Karume, this King of Kiambu," he said, pointing at me, "who never brings any cases before this Committee."

"Mr Chairman," I said in protest, "I am only the Kiambu Branch Chairman, and I have to follow the decisions made by my members. If they have no cases, I cannot bring you one. They are very intelligent, they are leaders and I stand by their decisions."

I thought that was the end of the matter. But I later came to know that the Disciplinary meeting had been conveniently arranged the day after our meeting in Kiambu, so that the Jonathan issue would be settled once and for all. I suppose I was a considerable source of frustration to those involved in this case, and in other similar matters, but then, and now, I refuse to let my name be used as some sort of rubberstamp when it comes to accusations against someone I believe to be innocent.

After this case against Jonathan Njenga, I was a marked man and I encountered frustrations from all sides.

In 1988, both party and parliamentary elections were conducted through *mlolongo* (queue system), where voters queued behind the symbol of their candidate and then counted.

The first elections were for the various posts in KANU and it came shortly before the general elections. But I soon learnt that, despite having more supporters and longer queues, all the delegates who were in my faction were being rigged out. There was no one to complain to.

That evening, I went to Cianda where the names of the winners at that level were to be announced. I had been unopposed at this grassroot level, so I expected it to be a mere formality. However, I had a hint that something unexpected might happen, so I was very curious about the results. I took my mother, my two wives and my children with me.

The returning officer who had officiated at the voting that morning did not turn up and, instead, some other person read the names of the winners in Kiambaa. He was protected by a score of policemen and did not look at ease.

As he read through the list of winners, strangely enough, despite the fact I had run unopposed, my name was not read out. My supporters, ignoring the presence of the police, started picking up stones, ready to throw them at the administrator, but I intervened and restrained them.

This was a ridiculous situation but I knew that if I did not win at the Cianda level, there was no way I could contest for the District Chairmanship. I tried to remain calm and, after thinking it over, I became resigned. Nevertheless, I was determined to find out the facts. One of the reasons I was able to be fairly objective over the matter was because I had already had a tip-off.

A few days before the elections, my cousin Catherine Wanjiku came to tell me that she had learned something interesting. It seemed that Gichura, a certain KANU official who was rooting for Nginyo Kariuki's election as Chairman, had attended a dinner at Nginyo's house at Red Hill. The DC, Victor Musoga, was also present. During the dinner, the DC had reassured Nginyo over his ambitions of dethroning me.

"Don't worry! You will become Chair, Mr. Nginyo. I've told you that we've received instructions that Njenga Karume is not to win the elections anywhere!"

Although Gichura supported Nginyo, he had a certain amount of respect for me. Therefore, when he heard about this little plot, he decided to pass the message along via my cousin, Catherine.

I was concerned and decided that the best way to resolve the issue would be to face Moi directly and ask him if he knew about these plans to rig the elections. That morning I did not even take the time to shave. I called on Vice President Josephat Karanja at his house in new Muthaiga to ask him the whereabouts of President Moi. I told him I would like to see the President but Karanja told me that Moi had gone to Baringo.

I was resolved on the matter and decided I would drive to Baringo to see the President there. As I was driving through Gachie village, I saw my friend Godfrey Muhuri and waved down his car. I asked him to accompany me to Limuru, so that we could talk along the way—I told him I had an important matter to discuss with him.

Muhuri told his nephew, who was driving, to continue on to Nairobi and then Muhuri got into my car.

When he was seated, I drove off and said nothing. I guess Muhuri might have wondered what was disturbing me. When I drove right past Limuru and even past Naivasha, Muhuri expressed his surprise. He pointed out that I had said we were going to Limuru, yet we had passed Limuru a long time before.

I did not know what to say to him so I kept quiet, but when we drove past Nakuru and drove down Baringo road, I finally felt I had to explain.

I explained to him that I was going to see Moi. I told him that although I knew he was a brave man, I had been afraid to tell him earlier, in case he chickened out. Muhuri just sat there and stared at me. I do not know what he was thinking.

Some time back Moi had built a hotel in Baringo which was managed by the Kenya Tourist Development Corporation. Moi retained a suite at the hotel and I was certain I would find him there. However when we got there, the President was out. We were told that he had gone to church.

We went to have a snack in the hotel and then returned to the reception area to wait. Moi finally came in around 1 pm and although he had seen us, he did not even greet us. He just passed and went straight up to his rooms. Then, after about an hour Moi sent a bodyguard to come get us and when we went upstairs, we found him with some visitors.

I recall there was a friend of mine, Joel Burtut, who was the Chairman of Baringo County Council, a politician, Chelagat Muta, the Mayor of Kabarnet and quite a few others who were older men from the area.

As we entered, they were just having lunch. Moi asked us to join in but I told him we had already eaten at the hotel's restaurant.

Burtut had that day's newspaper, and showed us an article quoting many Kiambu MPs saying they would support Peter Muhoho for the Branch Chairmanship. Some of the quotes were from Samuel Ngigi Mwaura of Limuru, Kuria Kinyanjui of Lari and Zacharia Kimemia

Gakunju of Gatundu. Burtut showed the article to Moi and pointed out that I had always supported KANU, much more than any of the others. He told Moi that I should be given a chance to compete on a level ground.

But Moi did not answer. Because of his silence, I was almost certain he was the one behind the campaign against me, but that was what I had come to confirm.

After a while Moi asked me if I would like to see him in private. He said I should come to his bedroom for a chat. He sat on the bed while Muhuri and I sat on the two chairs in his bedroom suite.

First, I apologised for coming on a Sunday when I knew he was very busy, but I said it had been unavoidable. Then I told him about the dinner at Nginyo Kariuki's house and about the DC's assurances to Nginyo.

"I just wanted to know if the instructions had come from you," I informed the President.

"I don't even know the DC! I do not even talk to DCs! He is a fool!" Moi exclaimed.

Then, as I sat waiting, he phoned the Permanent Secretary in charge of Administration in the Office of the President, Hezekiah Oyugi, and talked to him.

"Listen. Do not to touch Kiambaa. Let Karume continue," he instructed.

After the phone conversation, I was very happy and said, "Your Excellency, I pray to God to keep you well."

Moi told me to take his house phone number and if I was bothered again, I should just call.

"No, I can't bother you about such a thing," I said and then asked Moi give me Oyugi's number instead.

I drove back home in a much more settled state of mind.

The next day, just to make sure that Oyugi had actually received the message, I decided to phone his house. I called the number Moi had given me and asked to speak to Oyugi, but the woman on the line merely asked me who I was. After identifying myself, she said that Oyugi had left the previous Friday.

I was astonished. I told her that this was not possible because the President had phoned him on that same number, the previous day. But the lady insisted that Oyugi was not in and then hung up. That is when I realised that I had to be prepared for any eventuality.

Another interesting event had also taken place prior to the elections.

Apparently the Kiambu DC, Victor Musoga, had already sent out a message to all the Divisions that "Mr. Karume must go!" I had learned that he had been promised a promotion to PC if he arranged things so that I lost. On the other hand, if I won, he would be sacked. This was a typical tactic of the time.

On the day of the election which was meant to select District Branch officials, there was a huge crowd at Madaraka Gardens in Kiambu. There were people from all over, including people from the surrounding farms, but I never attended. Since I had already 'lost' at Cianda grassroots level, I was not even eligible to compete at the District level.

However, sometime later, I was told what happened.

Apparently there was a gentleman in the crowd named Muthiora. He was a coffee picker at Gatatha Farm which borders my Cianda Estate. Press photographers were all over the place and Muthiora had his picture taken quite a few times and he felt quite flattered.

On the day following the elections, the General Manager of Gatatha Farm, a Mr. Johnston, read *The Standard* newspaper and was amazed to see Muthiora's picture. He recognised him as one of the regular coffee pickers, so he asked one of his supervisors to call Muthiora to his office. When the coffee picker came in, the manager showed him the photo. Muthiora stared at his picture on the newspaper.

"Oh! See, that is me! This is the very jacket that I wore yesterday," Muthiora exclaimed in excitement.

"And can you tell me what it means?" the manager asked.

Muthiora was puzzled. He was not quite sure if he was in trouble or not.

"I was just there in the crowd," he said. "We were told that the DC might have some jobs for us, so I went."

Mr. Johnston frowned. "Wait, I will read it out to you."

So the manager read the caption under the photo, and it clearly stated that Muthiora had defeated Mr. Karume in the Cianda sub-branch KANU elections.

Muthiora was amazed and rather afraid.

"How can I stand against Njenga?" he asked. "I am just a worker. Mr. Karume is the one who built this place. He built the school here, and my two children are in it and he has developed this area."

Muthiora had a hard time deciding what to do. Finally he told the manager to help him with two things. First he asked the manager to hide the newspaper with the picture so that I would not see it. Second, he wanted to go to the newspaper offices to find out what had happened, and make them retract the article.

Mr Johnston then called my farm manager, Bernard Kuria, and told him about the story in the paper. Kuria could not resist following up such an amazing event and went to Gatatha Farm to see for himself.

When Kuria asked Muthiora what had happened, he said he did not know. Muthiora explained that he had been in my queue, supporting me and had witnesses to prove it. Kuria then drove Muthiora down to the *Standard* offices and once there, Muthiora explained to the editor that he had never stood against Karume. He said that if the government wanted Karume's seat, they had better just take it, and not involve him.

They thought that would be the end of the matter, after all, the truth had been explained. But all of a sudden the CID started looking for Muthiora. He was quite scared and disappeared from his usual haunts, but after being in hiding for three days, he was found, arrested and taken to the DC's office. The DC, warned Muthiora that if he did not agree to the newspaper article and state that he had defeated Karume in the elections, he would go to prison. Muthiora was forced to sign a statement and thereafter had no choice but to cooperate.

"Oh, yes!" he said, "I now remember. I defeated Karume."

Poor fellow!

I also learnt about other actions that had been taken to make sure I would not go through. Moi must have been very worried to have taken so many separate steps against me.

Apparently, during the campaign period, some money had been dished out to the Kiambu MPs to ensure that they campaign against me.

It happened that Moi had a function at the Kikuyu PCEA Church. All of us Kiambu MPs were present, and later we went for lunch at the nearby Sigona Golf Club.

It was after I went home shortly thereafter, that a number of MPs, among them George Muhoho, Arthur Magugu of Githunguri, Peter Kinyanjui Kabibi of Kikuyu, Samuel Ngigi Mwaura of Limuru and Kuria Kinyanjui of Lari went to Josephat Karanja's house to discuss strategy.

Karanja had a briefcase full of money, two hundred thousand shillings for them to share out, in order to campaign against me. This was a common practice at the time whereby huge sums of money would be used to buy voters to ensure that an unwanted individual did not sail through.

As would be expected, an argument ensued as to how the money should be shared out. Some felt they should receive a bigger share than the others depending on the 'complexity' of their assigned task to remove me. Others felt that the money should be shared equally. At the end of it all they each got forty thousand shillings.

Kabibi was a friend of mine and we were open with each other. He phoned me a few hours after midnight and told me what had happened.

"When you left we went on to Karanja's place," explained Kabibi, laughing. "Imagine, we were given two hundred thousand shillings from Karanja and I got my share of forty thousand!"

He explained that they had been very happy when I left early, since they had been wondering how to get rid of me so they could go for Karanja's meeting.

So I told him jokingly, "From now on, until the elections are over, if we meet in a bar, I'll buy the drinks." With a smile I continued, "I don't want to drink beer or tea from the money you were given for selling me."

But when I phoned Karanja in the morning, I was no longer in a joking mood. In fact, I was furious.

"How could you share out money to campaign against me in your very own house?" I asked him. "I thought you were my friend!"

Karanja was quite shocked. "How did you find out?" he asked incredulously.

"I have my sources," I told him.

But since the meeting in his house had ended at 1 am, he knew it must have been a very close friend to call me at that hour. He suspected it was Kinyanjui Kabibi.

As I learned later, Karanja then went on to phone Kabibi.

"Why did you tell the Chairman[65] about the meeting and the money?" Karanja asked.

Kabibi did not deny telling me.

"Was I lying? It is the truth, and since it is the truth, there is no harm done," he said.

So, because of me, Kabibi also got into problems during the elections.

During the grassroots elections in Kirangari location, Karanja and his faction decided to teach Kabibi a lesson. They arranged to have someone stand against him in the sub-branch elections and had a little talk with the DO beforehand.

---

65   Since I was the Chairman of GEMA, KANU and many other organizations and companies, many people still refer to me as "Chairman".

The Returning Officer, the Kiambu DO, had a hard time trying to rig out Kabibi as he had been instructed. While more than two thousand voters in the station queued behind Kabibi, his rival's line had ten people only.

The DO knew that if he announced that Kabibi had won, he would lose his job. He knew he had to be subtle, but wondered what to do in the face of such blatantly obvious victory.

Kabibi was at the front of the queue and his wife was immediately behind him. With a frown on his face, the DO started examining the candidate's papers, searching for any way to disqualify Kabibi. After inspecting Kabibi's papers and finding them in order, without any tiny discrepancy to make use of, he asked for his wife's documents.

This is where he found a way out of his dilemma. Mrs. Kabibi's Identity Card stated that she was born in Murang'a. When the DO saw this, he made an issue out of it and told both her and Kabibi to get out.

"What are you doing here? Go to Murang'a!" he shouted. "You cannot vie here!"

Mrs. Kabibi explained that although she had been born in Murang'a, she had been married for decades in Kiambu and that she had always voted in Kiambu, as well. The DO refused to listen. Although he had no legal basis to do so, he told them both to get out and go to vie in Murang'a and even threatened to call the police if they did not immediately leave the venue.

It was ironic. Kabibi had been born in Kiambu, and he could easily see his father's home from the polling station, yet he had just been declared an alien. He and his wife left under protest.

As soon as the stunned couple was forced out of the area, the DO declared the person with ten supporters as the winner.

In December of that year, a friend of mine brought that very same District Officer to my house. He felt quite bad about the actions he had been forced into and wanted to apologize. We had a few drinks and since he felt rather bad, I think he might have taken one too many. Needless to say, once his tongue was loosened, he told me that the intelligence services had instructed all administrators, including chiefs and sub-chiefs, on the precise candidates who were to win the elections.

I slaughtered a goat for the two of them, and gave each a bottle of whisky. The DO explained that he had only done as he did because the DC, Victor Musoga, had said he would lose his job if Kabibi won. The DO implored me to go to Kabibi and ask him for forgiveness.

"If I hadn't done what they wanted," he explained, "I would have been sacked and someone else would have replaced me. My replacement would have made sure Kabibi got kicked out anyway."

Since it was in late December, I suggested that he look for a goat which we would give to Kabibi for Christmas. When the DO finally got a chance to explain the matter to Kabibi, he was forgiven. Kabibi understood the machinations of politics only too well. And is it not amazing how the truth will always come out, no matter how many attempts we make to hide it?

As expected, I lost the Kiambu KANU chairmanship to George Muhoho. Without a grassroots seat, I could not vie for the District Chairmanship. I did not even appeal. It would have been futile. As for Victor Musoga, he was rewarded for his efforts and promoted to Provincial Commissioner for Central Province.

That year the KANU elections were carried out in a ridiculous manner all over the country. It was a pure farce and kept those of us who were in the right frame of mind, wholly amused.

In Othaya, where Kibaki was vying, the results were indeed comical. When the District Commissioner read the names of those who had won the elections, everyone was amazed. It was astonishing! The 'winners' queues were all those which had the least numbers of supporters! In one sub-branch, Kibaki stopped the DC from proceeding with the announcements after he announced one winner.

"The candidate you have just named as a winner," Kibaki told him, "was a teacher. Unfortunately he died in November last year."

The DC was stunned and embarrassed.

"Perhaps it would be better," Kibaki suggested helpfully, "if you name someone who is alive. It would certainly make our KANU working sessions in Othaya so much easier!"

After the hoots and laughter of the crowd had died down, Kibaki said, quietly but succinctly, "Even rigging requires some intelligence!"

That line was much quoted in the media and was taken to aptly summarise the ludicrous 1988 *mlolongo* elections.

After the elections fiasco, my friend Kenneth Matiba resigned his portfolio as Minister for Transport and Communications. He said he just could not serve such an illegitimate government. Matiba has always been a somewhat dramatic fellow, so after he resigned, he went to the Kiharu KANU office, hired a lorry and carted away all the furniture. After all, he had furnished the office himself, at his own expense.

The following day he came to my home. He talked for a while with Wariara and me, and then made a suggestion.

"Get one of your lorries, James." He was one of the few people who called me James. "Let's go to Banana," he continued, "and take away all the furniture from the Kiambu KANU office, as well. Then after all the furniture is out, we can demolish it," he said. As a second thought he added, "I am sure *Mama* Karume here could use the stones and wood to construct something like a pig pen."

True, I had built the Kiambu KANU office and furnished it with my own money when I was the Chairman, but I protested against Matiba's suggestion.

"Yet how can you leave that office standing?" he asked in outrage. "Those hooligans have rigged you out!"

All I could say was that I did not, and still do not believe in such revenge. I am afraid Matiba was very disappointed with me.

My most difficult and demanding years in business came during Moi's years in power. This was the case, not only for me, but for many other business people as well. Those who had the right connections received many lucrative contracts, but those who were either seen as disloyal or were nonentities had a gruelling time, just keeping their businesses afloat. Inflation was rising by the day, especially after donors withheld aid to the country due to the regime's poor record of governance, mismanagement of the economy and abuse of human rights. The economy went into a recession from the 1980s right through to the 90s and most businesses suffered. The government began to print valueless money and the shilling suffered incredible damage. The government made erratic, naïve decisions based on whims and this applied to the economy as well as everything else.

I owned coffee and tea farms at this time, but the price both commodities were earning was minimal compared to the input these crops required. My Cianda, Lynton and Molo estates suffered heavy losses during Moi's era. I had also made considerable investments in the hotel industry but the existing conditions in Kenya ensured that business was slow and bed occupancy was always below economically viable expectations. Tourists were not coming in the large numbers they had in previous years. My hotels were suffering too. Each one of my enterprises was registering low income and occasional losses. Loans piled up and creditors were becoming impatient. Whereas well-connected individuals were getting unsecured loans from banks after 'orders from above', I could not access any of them. I was not one of the regime's favourites and I was out in the cold.

I had to devise a strategy to stay afloat. I had to sell off some properties in order to save the others from the auctioneer's hammer. But that was just a taste of things to come. Politically, I remained on the sidelines during Moi's time. I was, thankfully, still a force to be reckoned with, both in Kiambu and in Central Kenya politics, but Moi ignored my presence and this did not change until much later in his Presidency.

My friend Stanley Oloitiptip wanted me to join him in the Cabinet, and he talked to Moi. I do not know what Oloitiptip said to the President to make him change his mind, but subsequently I was made an Assistant Minister. I was moved from one Ministry to another quite rapidly. I started out in Local Government in 1980 and then moved to Urban Development, then to Energy, next Lands and Settlement and finally Cooperatives.

One thing I should point out is that if one is appointed an Assistant Minister, one is powerless, because it is always necessary to support the Government line. One can never speak one's own mind. Perhaps this appointment was a tactic to keep me close and monitor my movements and moods. In 1988, I was sacked and a few years later, in 1991, some friends and I decided to form our own political party.

I juggled the roles of representing Kiambaa people with my attempts to keep my businesses afloat. Somehow I kept everything in balance and managed to survive—many of my business colleagues were not as lucky. Fortunately my property was never placed under receivership nor was it sold off like that of many other prominent businessmen and personal friends, but it was an incredibly tough battle.

Chapter 9

Out of Moi's Shadow

Like the ludicrous KANU elections, the 1988 Parliamentary elections were a farce, as well. They are remembered for their gross irregularities and blatant rigging. Acting on his unique brand of 'wisdom', Moi decided that the elections would not be held by secret ballot but through the queuing system (like the ones for the KANU elections) whereby voters would line up for the candidates of their choice and then be counted manually. Such retrogression was an incredible example of the new style of government.

Protests were widespread when many candidates were rigged out because they did not meet dubious standards of slavish loyalty. Such actions were intended to kick out popular 'dissidents' who had the support of their constituencies. The rigging was so blatant that even when it was totally obvious which queue had the most voters, others would be announced winners. This went on to such an extent that in some polling stations, the supposed number of votes garnered by favoured candidates was far greater than the number of voters in the voting register. People were outraged and incredulous but Moi, as usual, was unmoved.

Luckily I survived the ridiculous queuing voting system with ease as I seemed to be quite popular with the voters. However, most significantly, my friend Mwai Kibaki, who had also been re-elected in Othaya, was nevertheless dropped from the Vice Presidency and appointed Minister for Health. At this time the Ministry of Health was bedeviled by mismanagement and corruption, and an appointment there was considered an insult. Dr Josephat Karanja was selected to replace him and this did not go down well with Kibaki's allies, or with the Kikuyu community in general. Kibaki was given a token Ministry to run and many of his friends and supporters viewed this as an insult. Surprisingly, Kibaki accepted the demotion without complaint and seemed oblivious to his humiliation. It was perhaps this embarrassing loss of Kibaki's status that agitated the people of Central Province more than any other factor, and it was one of the major dynamics that led to the return of multiparty elections four years later.

Towards the end of the 1980s, Moi's rule faced the strongest opposition it had ever had. People were tired of his authoritarian and irrational style of leadership and fed up with the extensive looting carried out by his lieutenants. The economy was at the lowest it had ever been since independence and whispers of opposition became more audible until they were heard throughout the land. Bold politicians such as Kenneth Matiba, George Anyona, Charles Rubia, James Orengo, Raila Odinga and his father Jaramogi among many others, were openly agitating for the repeal of Section 2A of the consitution. Moi's terror tactics could no longer stop his adversaries or the clamour for change, because the more he persecuted his opponents, the louder the shouts of protest became.

It was at this point that, Kenneth Matiba resigned from Parliament, and he and Charles Rubia started a serious and very vocal campaign to make Kenya a multiparty democracy. Chants of "Moi must go!" filled the land, and people started being openly critical of the President. Desperate to slow the tide, Moi threw both into detention. Moi's feeble excuse was that Kenya was not ready for multiparty rule and that chaos and anarchy would ensue if multipartysm was permitted. Not many people agreed with his point of view, however. The opposition was concentrated mostly in Nairobi, Central Province and Nyanza where people had never been fully comfortable under Moi.

In order to establish a basis for his refusal to permit multiparty politics, Moi gambled by sending out a team, headed by Vice President George Saitoti, to gather the people's views on the multiparty system. Perhaps it was not so much of a gamble as the team returned with the pre-arranged verdict Moi wanted. Kenyans supposedly did not want multipartyism.

KANU stalwarts such as Ezekiel Barngetuny and Joseph Kamotho still thought that KANU would rule forever. Barngetuny told the youth to chop off the fingers of any opposition supporters who flashed the "two finger salute". Kamotho said that KANU would rule for one hundred years.

Meanwhile, the protagonists of multipartyism led by Jaramogi Oginga Odinga, Kenneth Matiba, Charles Rubia, Ahmed Bahmariz, Paul Muite, James Orengo, Masinde Muliro, Martin Shikuku, George Anyona and others, formed an umbrella movement called the Forum for the Restoration of Democracy (FORD). This movement comprehensively included nearly all stakeholders in the fight for the so-called 'second liberation'. It was at this time that Mwai Kibaki flippantly made the infamous remark, stating that "trying to remove KANU from power was like trying to cut down a *mūgumo* (fig) tree with a razor blade."

It is said that guns can stop an army, but not an idea whose time has come. The agitation for multiparty politics went ahead full throttle. During the National Delegates Conference at Kasarani, in mid-1991, there was complete silence when I moved the motion to repeal Section 2A and Moi finally, albeit reluctantly, agreed to repeal the Section. I guess many others in the forum would have liked to be in my place but they were afraid Moi might carry out some arbitrary backlash.

But I had a fairly good idea of the mood of the country and I believed the people really wanted more political parties. After all these years of Moi's disapproval, what could he now do to me? His grip was weakening and he had realised that he could no longer just do whatever he liked. Consequently the delegates approved the motion unanimously, and that was the end of KANU's hegemony in Kenyan politics.

Moi must have been shocked and flabbergasted by this blatant, mass opposition to his own wishes. Kangema MP John Joseph Kamotho's arrogant assertion that KANU would rule for a hundred years now looked ridiculous and ignorant.

Shortly thereafter, FORD was registered as a party. Many people who were in full support of multipartyism did not, however, join this party. I was one of them. When I studied the core structure of FORD, I concluded that it was most likely headed for an acrimonious split since there were many wrangles and power struggles within the body. There were also many bloated egos which were bound to clash sooner or later.

A little later, I was present in Parliament and the voting on a certain motion was in process. Members were lining up to vote on the motion and I was standing aside in a corner of the House waiting for my turn. With me were my two friends Mwai Kibaki and the MP for Kajiado North, John Keen. We were making small talk when I suddenly had an idea.

"Why can't we form our own political party?" I asked Keen.

Keen looked at me like he had suddenly woken up.

"I can form one on the condition that you two join me," he said with a dawning smile.

I explained that with a political party of our own, we could put forward our own political agenda to a better advantage. Kibaki and Keen had never considered this. Apparently they thought that anyone wanting to oppose Moi had to join FORD. I told them there would be no possibility of becoming party leaders in FORD because it was already like a top-heavy, overloaded ship that was bound to sink under the weight in due course. There were many people who were against Moi but they could not fit into the FORD party structure simply because there was insufficient space for them. It was inevitable that more parties would soon be created to cater for all sorts of interests, I argued, and there was nothing to stop us from forming our own.[66]

Kibaki and Keen liked my idea straightaway, and after a few discussions in which the three of us refined the concept, we finally decided to form the Democratic Party of Kenya (DP).

"You are going to be the Chairman," I said to Kibaki. "And you will be the Secretary General," I told Keen. It was Kibaki who I had in mind for the post of Chairman because Kibaki was better educated and more experienced in politics and, if everything went well and DP happened to win the elections, Kibaki would make the better President. I proposed that John Keen should be the Secretary General of the party since he was a founder member. Kibaki accepted my proposal and we decided to make the announcement on 31 December 1991.

We met at Jacaranda Hotel nearly every day while forming the party. I was initially against calling the new party "The Democratic Party" but Kibaki was very much for it. Since many Kenyans are still illiterate, every party also has an easily grasped symbol as their party logo. I wanted a lantern, to symbolise bringing enlightenment, but Kibaki wanted a certain animal which he felt would have greater impact. We finally settled on a lantern and I was pleased because it had always been my symbol in the Kiambaa Parliamentary Elections.

Kibaki announced his resignation from Parliament while in Mombasa, and a few days later he read a statement to the press at Jacaranda Hotel in Nairobi, giving details about the formation of our new party.

We then began to create a secretariat. We knew that a party which claimed to have a national outlook had to have national representation. Party officials had to be people who shared a similar philosophy and views on national goals. Furthermore the party needed representatives from all over the republic. I approached Eliud Mwamunga from the Coast Province and invited him to join DP. Mwamunga and I were

---

66 The Democratic Party (DP) was one of the biggest parties formed after Moi allowed the return of multipartyism. Many people identify DP with Mwai Kibaki, but the fact of the matter is that it was my idea. I even suggested the name of the party and the party's symbol, a lantern, to suggest that it would be bringing light to troubled Kenyans.

long-time friends and our friendship had grown deeper during the time I had served under him as Assistant Minister in the Ministry of Lands and Settlement. From Eastern Province, David Mwiraria and Joseph Munyao were brought on board while Mohamed Ogle was selected to represent North Eastern. The Treasurer's post went to Mwamunga and Mohamed Ogle was chosen as the party's Organizing Secretary. Munyao was picked as the Assistant Secretary. Munyao had actually been poached from FORD where he was Life Member Number 69. A photo of our first full meeting somehow appeared in the newspapers and Jaramogi admonished Munyao for abandoning FORD. I, on my part, occupied the modest post of Chairman of the Board of Trustees which had eight representatives from each Province.

Matiba, who was one of the most prominent personalities in FORD, had been Kibaki's and my friend for years.[67] However, I did not want Matiba to hear that we had formed a party from anyone else but myself. Matiba had fallen sick while in detention and was recuperating in a London hospital at the time. On the day that the formation of DP was announced, I went to John Michuki's house, phoned Matiba's flat in London and spoke to him at length, explaining that the creation of DP was meant in a democratic spirit and that our aim in forming the party was not to create conflict with FORD. Matiba listened to me and then wished us all the best. I also informed Matiba that a few *athuuri* (elders) would be arriving in London that night to visit him and see if he was comfortable and check on his progress. Our delegation consisted of Dr. Frank Njenga, Uhuru Kenyatta, and my son-in-law, James Kahiu.

However, not all of my friends welcomed the new party. Kibaki and I used to frequent Muthaiga Country Club[68] and often met our friends and acquaintances there as we relaxed. One evening, when Kibaki and I revealed the fact that we were forming DP, our friends, who included Charles Rubia, Matere Kereri and Matu Wamae, stated that they were not in favour of the idea of creating a new party. They declared that the wisest option would be for everyone to join forces in FORD in order to ensure that they would have a majority and thereby defeat Moi. However, I maintained that FORD was a passing phenomenon.

---

67 There were rumours that Kibaki and Matiba had fallen out prior to the formation of FORD and that Kibaki was supposed to join Matiba in resigning from Parliament but he developed cold feet. Whatever the case, the relationship was never the same again.

68 Muthaiga Country Club has been one of the most exclusive clubs in Nairobi since colonial times. Its membership consists of the most affluent. Although not as famous as Muthaiga Golf Club next door, it is more selective.

By use of a parable Kibaki and I tried to explain that "DP was a small tree in the forest, and trees in the forest grow together and they do not fight." I added that the tree would need water to grow and that "this small tree could one day be your shelter in times of need."

And my little fable proved to have some truth in it when people like Kereri and Wamae sailed through to Parliament in the 1992 elections after vying on a DP ticket.

Before FORD did actually break up, Matiba made a triumphant entry into Nairobi after his treatment in London. FORD had publicized the homecoming and urged supporters to come out and receive Matiba in style, but what happened far surpassed the party's expectations.

It was a Saturday and most people were not working, so hundreds of thousands of jubilant supporters lined the road leading from the airport into the city. A tourist or a visitor who was not familiar with Kenya's politics might have thought it was the pope who was arriving. The massive crowds that turned up to welcome Matiba home had never been witnessed before and the popular reception could only be compared to the welcome Kenyatta received when he returned from London in 1946.

The reception had the desired effect, which was to chill Moi and KANU to the bone. The massive outpouring of joy on Matiba's arrival proved to sceptics that FORD was firmly on the ground and was unstoppable.[69] However an even more important and unfortunate consequence of the welcome was to hasten the break-up of FORD. There were some members of FORD who had always been in the Jaramogi faction while others had assumed Matiba would be the party's Presidential candidate. Observing the increasingly popular support for Matiba, the Jaramogi faction started drifting away and then attempted to popularize Jaramogi in order to lessen Matiba's influence. Both Jaramogi and Matiba were headstrong and proud, and very soon FORD split into two parties namely FORD Kenya and FORD Asili which endorsed Jaramogi and Matiba respectively.

The first DP rally at Uhuru Park was marked by exceptionally large crowds. Mwai Kibaki was endorsed as the party's flag bearer for the coming Presidential elections. We were pleased with the turnout and were confident that Kibaki would win. Naturally the two other large opposition parties also believed that their candidates would be successful.

---

69 The same trick was used in 2002 when Kibaki made a similar triumphant return to the country after treatment in London after being involved in a road accident. This time round, the opposition trounced KANU. There was a joke going round that to win the Kenya Presidency, one needed to get sick and seek treatment abroad just shortly before the elections.

Each of the parties thought it had the capacity and public support to defeat KANU and Moi. All the parties' meetings saw massive turnouts and the three parties were confident they each had what it takes to win the Presidency. Jaramogi's support was mainly from Nyanza and some parts of Western Kenya. Matiba's support was from Central Province, Western and some sections of Eastern. Kibaki's party had support from similar sections. Each of the three had almost equal support from sections of Nairobi city.

While it is true that the opposition supporters outnumbered KANU's by a ratio of 3 to 1, the opposition still lost. In our conceit and self aggrandizement, our three parties had split the opposition vote so that none of the parties could possibly win on its own. While each leader of the three believed they would be President, Moi cleverly consolidated the little support that remained for KANU into one solid block. He also employed his usual unorthodox and guaranteed method which had never yet failed to win elections for him.

As it turned out, Moi won, Matiba came second, Kibaki third and Jaramogi fourth. The opposition garnered more than twice as many votes as Moi and KANU, but the minority still won.[70] It would be quite some time before the opposition learned to act as a united force.

For the first time since joining Parliament, I lost the elections. The people in Kiambaa voted in Kamau Icharia to replace me. I had taken a risky gamble by standing on a DP ticket and I lost. There was 'Ford Asili' euphoria sweeping over Kiambu and Murang'a (Matiba's home area) and no one standing on any other party survived the onslaught. The only survivor was Paul Muite who won the Kikuyu (now Kabete) Parliamentary seat on a Ford Kenya ticket.

Kiambu voters opted to support Matiba, a fellow Kikuyu from Murang'a, rather than support a person from Nyeri. Ford Asili swept the board in Kiambu and Murang'a, while DP took all the parliamentary seats in Nyeri, Kibaki's home area. Although I lost, I do not regret standing on a DP ticket. I knew I was going to lose. Matiba, and even my constituents, had told me so many times, but I just felt I could not abandon Kibaki.

"We love you very much but we have to vote for Matiba," one elder told me.

---

70 During the next elections in 1997, the opposition still had not learnt their lesson. Matiba did not vie and Kibaki and Jaramogi's son Raila refused to unite, thus Moi easily won the election, with Kibaki coming second. It was only in 2002 that the main opposition united and learnt that there is strength in numbers and managed to end KANU's rule.

Well, what could I say to that?

Ford Kenya and Ford Asili both had thirty one MPs in Parliament, and therefore the problem of which party would become the official opposition arose. DP had twenty two MPs and it was obvious there would have to be some sort of compromise, possibly a merger of two parties, in order to have a solid opposition.

Jaramogi came to my house and urged me to persuade DP leaders to support Ford Kenya. Mwai Kibaki and John Keen were with me, and Jaramogi was accompanied by James Orengo and John Khaminwa, a lawyer. I offered them some liquor but Jaramogi said he preferred something soft, since he did not drink alcohol any more. I also had a goat roasted for them, and Jaramogi nostalgically remembered how I had barbequed goats for him and Kenyatta at my Molo farm almost thirty years previously.

As we got down to the discussion, however, we all agreed that DP would support Ford Kenya, and that Kibaki would write an official letter to the Speaker of Parliament to that effect. I do not know why they chose my house for these negotiations, but I guess it was because it was far from Nairobi and out of the eagle eye of the media. Anyway, as always, I enjoyed hosting them despite the fact that I had lost my Parliamentary seat.

So I found myself out of Parliament for the first time since Kenyatta nominated me MP in 1974. I took stock and decided it was time to relax from the hustle and bustle of politics. Eighteen years in Parliament is quite a long time, and I decided I should devote myself more fully to my businesses, some of which were struggling to survive. I have to say that I returned to business with zeal and enthusiasm, and continued acquiring and developing property. But the 1990s were a trying period for business. Banks were charging interest rates as high as thirty percent, profits were quite low and many businesses were forced to close down. Meanwhile, all during this time, I was still involved in the internal administration and financing of DP, in addition to acting as a key advisor to Kibaki who had now become the official leader of the opposition. I never contemplated abandoning DP at any time despite the fact that it had caused the loss of my Parliamentary seat.

The 1992 General Elections were a turning point for many members of the Kikuyu community. The Kikuyu who had settled outside Central Province became the targets of sporadic attacks. Their farms and businesses were looted and many of them were killed, especially in the

Rift Valley and Coast Provinces. They were accused of being anti-Moi and of being 'foreigners' in those areas and they were told to move back to Central Province. Politicians such as William ole Ntimama and others made inflammatory statements which incited non-Kikuyu, especially in the Rift Valley.[71] This occurred even before the election itself, and Moi's government did little to quell the wave of violence and destruction aimed at the Kikuyu.

When the elections were finally held in December of the same year, Central Province had voted as a block and not a single KANU candidate made it to Parliament from the area. The community, whose leaders had agitated to remove Moi from power, had made their point. However, they were to pay a heavy price. The hatred against the Kikuyu was expressed through even more death, destruction and mayhem in those regions where they were considered outsiders. Kikuyus were killed or displaced and their property either looted or destroyed. Politicians were inflaming the ignorant masses to take revenge on the 'rebellious' Kikuyu in an unprecedented ethnic conflagration never before seen in Kenya.

At that time, I already viewed myself as a Kikuyu elder. I was 63 years old and I was deeply saddened by this outbreak of ethnic violence against members of the community whose only crimes were being enterprising and independent-minded. I decided to initiate peace talks between the Kikuyu and other communities in the Rift Valley, where most of the chaos had occurred. I discussed the matter with Rift Valley leaders and they concurred. Interestingly, my Kikuyu counterparts such as Mwai Kibaki and John Michuki were opposed to the idea, saying that it was the onus of the government to protect its people and control the situation. I told them that this was true, but tried to convince them that all methods should be tried if peace was to be achieved.

"Our people are dying and the government is dragging its feet," I told them. "It is upon us leaders to do something about it."

At any rate, this was the start of the so-called GEMA-Kamatusa talks. GEMA of course stood for the Gikuyu (Kikuyu), Embu, Meru communities from the Mt. Kenya region which had voted against KANU. Kamatusa stood for Kalenjin, Maasai, Turkana and Samburu communities

---

71 Ntimama told the Kikuyu in Narok to "lie low like envelopes" or be forcefully ejected from the area. Many were killed in various sorties carried out against them by the Maasai in areas such as Enoosupukia and Maela. Barngetuny, on the other hand, advised KANU members to chop off the fingers of those who waved the two-finger salute, which was the symbol of the opposing FORD in contrast to the one-finger salute of KANU. Such statements fuelled peasant hatred against Kikuyus, who were wealthier than other communities and who were portrayed as grabbers.

in the Rift Valley which had voted pro-KANU and were now fighting the Kikuyu. The GEMA leaders appointed me to lead their side, by virtue of my having been GEMA chairman and the most visible amongst them. The Kamatusa communities were led by Nicholas Biwott, the powerful Keiyo MP, and the radical William ole Ntimama.

Biwott and I were the co-chairmen of the initiative. There were very many people who were involved, such as Kenya Power and Lighting Company (KPLC) Managing Director Samuel Gichuru, Dagoretti MP Chris Kamuyu and others. The initiative was created specifically to address the situation as it was in 1992. We should have had similar discussions in 1997 and 2002, but there was just no carry-through.

The talks got off to a good start and the first meeting was held at my Highland Hotel in Molo, one of the areas most affected by the election violence. We leaders discussed ways of bringing peace between the warring communities and agreed to do everything possible to achieve this goal. I was pleased by the initial results and vowed to see the efforts to the end. Merely sitting with the powerful Rift Valley leaders was an achievement itself. Moi did not oppose the efforts of the group talks and for some time, we seemed to be making progress.

But this did not last. A by-election for Nyandarua's Kipipiri parliamentary seat came up when the area MP, Laban Muchemi, died. DP and KANU were the main parties contesting the seat and both campaigned seriously. This was the first time that KANU was engaging another party in a by-election and it went full-out to ensure that its candidate won the seat. DP, on the other hand, campaigned for their candidate, Mwangi Githiomi, while criticizing KANU of impoverishing the area with empty promises and rhetoric. At the time, I did not want to take part in the DP campaigns due to the fragile nature of the GEMA-Kamatusa talks and I decided to retreat tactfully to my home in Mombasa.

However, it seemed that my absence in the campaigns was conspicuous and the grassroots leaders in Kipipiri started demanding my participation. DP's top leadership pressed me to join them and I finally accepted. After all, Kipipiri was not among the areas where violence had occurred. Two days before the election, I went for the first campaign meeting at Wanjohi Township in Kipipiri where I found Kibaki addressing the crowd. When I was asked to address the people, the crowd went wild. I guess they saw me as the face of DP. I asked the excited supporters to cease making the KANU salute and respect each other's opinions because, I said, this was a new dawn and no one would stop the people from expressing themselves.

Later, one leader informed me that waving the one finger salute was merely a tactic. Apparently KANU was giving away considerable amounts of money and naturally the people wanted whatever benefits they could get. They therefore attended KANU meetings for the money, not for the love of the party.

Upon my return to Nairobi the following day, the first person to phone me was KPLC's Samwel Gichuru. Gichuru was a powerful and wealthy person in Moi's inner circle and he was one of the untouchables of the regime. Gichuru told me that Moi was extremely upset. Gichuru had informed Moi that I was in Mombasa, and he was disappointed to see me in Kipipiri.

The fact is that on the day I went to campaign in Kipipiri, I was on the road when Moi's motorcade passed me on the way to Nakuru. I had to slouch down in my seat so that I was not seen.

Moi's intelligence sources had reported that all was going well in the Kipipiri campaigns until I had shown up and given my speeches. What could I say? I replied that I had only been serving DP, my party.

DP won the election by a landslide and KANU received a bitter humiliation, the first since multi-party politics had been introduced in 1991.

As an election gimmick, electricity poles had been laid on the roadsides all over Kipipiri Constituency with the promise that the whole area would be supplied with power if the people voted for KANU. When KANU lost, they were all removed. Moi's 'carrot and stick' tactics had flopped hopelessly. This became a subject of jokes and ridicule all over Kenya.

A few days afterwards, Moi and Simeon Nyachae were at Baringo to open an agricultural show and the President spoke bitterly about the Kipipiri loss. That same evening, as I was having a drink at the poolside of Jacaranda Hotel in Nairobi, I was phoned by a reporter and informed that Biwott had dissolved the GEMA-Kamatusa talks. When asked to comment, I told the reporter that the talks did not belong to either Biwott or to me, rather they belonged to the communities involved and thereafter newspapers carried the story of the dissolution the following day.

When I tried to reach Biwott by phone, to discuss the matter, the latter was unreachable. It was as if he had vanished into thin air. I was quite sad about the matter. It was the end of a genuine initiative that might have brought peace among the differing communities. It is even more distressing that more than fifteen years later, this violence is still being repeated after every general election. I strongly believe that the talks saved some lives while they were going on, and that a similar initiative should be created so that the communities involved can talk, get to know one another, and to realize that they all are the losers when violence breaks out.

In 1997, DP endorsed Kibaki to run for the presidency once again. But the opposition, as mentioned before, refused to unite and Moi won the elections. I believe it is quite possible that DP won the elections but there may have been rigging to alter the results. Moi extended the voting for a day and we heard reports from all over the country about strange events happening overnight.

All the same, I won back my Kiambaa seat. The Ford Asili craze of 1992 was over. I won the Kiambaa elections after defeating Stanley Munga Githunguri who seemed to have enjoyed a lot of government backing. Huge sums of money were used in an effort to ensure I did not recapture the Kiambaa Parliamentary seat, but all this came to naught.

Meanwhile since Ford Asili had faded away, Matiba was not even in the running. However, for DP, the loss of the presidency left a bitter taste. This was the second time we had lost to Moi and it was totally obvious that there was something that we were not doing right. Still, I continued supporting DP. I love the party and continue to be a life member. Actually I am a life member of KANU as well!

The next momentous event in my business life was the entry of South African Breweries (SAB) into the Kenyan market. One day, while I was staying at my Indian Ocean Beach Resort in Mombasa, the receptionist phoned me in my cottage and told me there was a visitor who wanted to see me. The visitor's name did not ring a bell. When I went round to receive the visitor, I found that it was a white man I had known some twenty-five years before, a Mr. Glen. The man told me that he was now a business consultant, and he was in Kenya on behalf of SAB. South African Breweries, the biggest in Africa and fourth largest in the world, was interested in increasing its profile in the East African region by building a factory in Kenya and setting up an administration and marketing centre. Previously, the organization's products were being sold in Kenya on franchise basis by Kenya Breweries Limited (KBL). SAB knew that the East African market had enormous potential and that it could increase its profits by setting up a factory in the region. Such a factory would minimize transport costs and the company could carry out a more vigorous marketing strategy.

SAB, therefore, was looking for strategic local investors who knew the local brewing industry well. The consultant wished to engage me as an investor since he was aware that I had been in the beer distribution industry for over thirty-seven years and that I was also financially capable of investing significant amounts in setting up such a factory. It seems that the opinion was that with my business experience in beer, few were better suited to be SAB's strategic investor in Kenya. He explained the facts and figures of the project to me and I in turn informed him that I would examine the various facets of the proposal and communicate my decision after seeking advice from my financial managers.

After investigating the feasibility of the project and receiving advice from experts, I decided it would be prudent and advantageous to make the investment. It would be a challenge, but then I had never feared trying something new. I determined that, since I was going to be made a director of the company, I could put money into the factory and simultaneously increase my fleet of transport lorries so that I could act as a distributor for the company as well. In this respect, I did not intend to stop distributing beer for my old company KBL and I was confident that I would handle both tasks with ease. At the time, I never realised that others might see a conflict of interests in this new move. After all, I reasoned, whereas I was an investor with the new company, I was just one of the transporters (although one of the biggest) of KBL. Unfortunately this opinion of mine was to cause me a great deal of stress in later life.

And so Castle Brewing Kenya Limited was started. I invested hundreds of millions in the project and was made a director of the company. The factory was built in Thika and it employed hundreds of people. The people of Thika town were happy since they knew the new factory would make a great deal of difference to the town's economy. Other than the obvious benefit of creating jobs, businesses and other sectors such as housing would profit significantly. There was excitement at the prospect of Castle penetrating the Kenyan market which heretofore had been virtually monopolized by KBL since it was founded in 1922.

This started my problems with KBL. Castle Brewing entered the market with style, selling beers that rivalled each of KBL's products. A major marketing war started, and for the first time in its history KBL felt the heat of competitive enterprise. Previously, the only competition had come from expensive foreign wines and local illicit brews and even so, competition was negligible. Now here was a well-established and experienced brewery with the resources and quality products to match its own. During that period KBL executives found themselves anxious and stressed. Castle sold its drinks for less than KBL and offered all sorts of freebies to their customers in an effort to popularizing their brands.

After thirty-eight years of distributing KBL products in an arrangement where the two parties had made large profits, my contract as a distributor was cancelled by KBL. In turn, KBL accused me of breach of contract as I was not only a director of a rival business, but apparently my transport of their products was seen as giving aid to their competitor and they could not continue doing business with me. On my part, I felt that I had never breached any part of the contract and that I was just a businessman who had taken advantage of an opportunity. KBL, I felt, was unfairly freezing the beer distributorship contract and I was bound to lose hundreds of millions of shillings. I felt aggrieved, and took KBL to court.

The case attracted widespread media attention especially due to the players and amounts of money involved. Through Kimani Kaihiro and Gatonye Advocates, I sought damages from Kenya Breweries Limited for breach of contract. KBL defended itself through its lawyers, Kaplan and Stratton and wanted the suit thrown out of court for lack of merit. The case was heard in the High Court in Nairobi.

After protracted argument and considerable protestation by both sides, the case was closed. The court found KBL guilty of breach of contract and ordered the company to pay me damages worth 231 million shillings. The ruling made history as the highest amount of money ever awarded for such a case in Kenya. Naturally I was happy with the ruling and many people phoned me to congratulate me on my 'windfall'. But it should be understood that this was no windfall at all. I had demanded a much higher sum which is what I feel I was entitled to following the loss of business.

But I was never to receive the money. KBL promptly sacked Kaplan and Stratton and instructed Mutula Kilonzo and Company advocates to lodge an appeal. The appeal was heard by Justice John Gicheru, Akilano Akiwumi and J.J.A. Lakha and they overruled the lower magistrate's ruling and ruled that I be paid nothing and that I pay the costs of KBL's suit. They argued that I did not deserve the damages awarded to me. In addition I had to pay the cost of the appeal. As you can imagine, I was devastated with this ruling.

I had invested a great deal of money in the distributorship over the years and in the end it cost me the largest financial loss I had ever suffered. I had dozens of trucks to transport beer, premises and beer depots in many areas across Nairobi. As a result, my beloved Nararashi Distributors was no more, and I felt as though I had lost a close relative. This time people called to commiserate with me. My daughter sent me a fax consoling me and telling me to remain strong. She also thought the problem might have political connotations and she advised me, as my daughter, to avoid politics as much as possible.

But I blame my adversaries for the outcome of the appeal. I now know that when I was awarded the 231 million shillings, someone talked to very high-ranking government officials and alleged that some of the millions I received would be used to finance DP and other anti-KANU activities. I know this to be a fact because I even discussed the matter with Presidet Moi over the phone and told him that the allegation was completely false. But I still believe that justice was not done. Although I no longer feel bitter about the case, it nevertheless marked the end of an era for me.

I did land a distributorship contract with Castle Breweries, however, but it was not quite as lucrative as my contract with KBL. Castle Brewing was a relatively new company with new products. After Castle closed down its operations I sold my lorries and other assets related to the beer distribution venture. I had to sell most of my assets at throw-away prices and I had to pay hundreds of employees their terminal dues. This was an enormous loss for me but I still believe that one can learn from mistakes and emerge all the wiser from the experience.

In 2002, another election was on the horizon. Moi finally agreed to retire (this was stipulated by the Constitution, anyway) but he was determined that KANU should continue being the ruling party. By this time, Raila Odinga's National Democratic Party (NDP) had already entered a partnership with KANU and two of its members, Raila himself and Adhu Awiti, were Cabinet Ministers. Moi wanted Uhuru Kenyatta to be the party's Presidential candidate but many members of the partnership were opposed to the idea. They felt that they were more highly qualified, due to their extensive political experience, than the 'green' young son of the founding father, President Jomo Kenyatta. Raila Odinga, George Saitoti, Kalonzo Musyoka and Musalia Mudavadi, among others, felt that they could do a much better job of leading the country. When KANU National Delegates met at Kasarani, ostensibly to decide on the

Presidential candidate, Moi manipulated the circumstances so that Uhuru was selected, much to the consternation of the others. Raila, Saitoti, Musalia Mudavadi and others quit the partnership not long thereafter.

After quitting the partnership, Raila, Kibaki, Charity Ngilu and Simeon Nyachae were the leading opposition candidates. They had twice been beaten by Moi in the elections and they were somewhat wiser this time around. While the opposition parties held frantic meetings to hammer out a power-sharing formula, Moi travelled around the country publicizing his so-called "Project Uhuru."

When the opposition alliance was finally in place, it was named National Rainbow Coalition (NARC). The main motive now holding the opposition together was that they realised Moi could easily be beaten if they could just stay united and select the most suitable candidate for the Presidency. Eventually, they picked Kibaki as the Presidential candidate and Raila coined the famous phrase, "Kibaki *tosha!*" (Kibaki is enough!).

Then I must have surprised and confounded even my closest friends by switching my support from Kibaki to "Project Uhuru". I would like to elucidate this matter because I have been accused of lacking political loyalty by my actions in withdrawing support for my close friend and joining the camp led by Moi, who was my long term adversary. I know I have been accused of having been 'bought' and I would like to clarify that this was not the case at all. I basically have no price tag and no politician can afford me. If I was the 'buying' type, I would do the buying myself.

The decision to support Uhuru was not an easy one for me to make. I had become convinced that the opposition would be unable to maintain a united front and that Moi would be handed victory on a silver platter, as usual. After all, we had had already lost twice with DP in 1992 and 1997 and I was not prepared to lose again. I simply do not have a loser's mentality—I just find it difficult to find myself defeated. For me it was just a case of "If you can't beat them, join them."

I was convinced to support and endorse Uhuru when Mama Ngina Kenyatta visited me at my Cianda Estate. She pleaded with me to support Uhuru for the good of the country.

"It will be Uhuru you are supporting," the former First Lady told me, "not Moi." She reminded me of the relationship I had with Mzee Kenyatta, all the times we had spent together and then concluded by saying that I would act as an elder advisor to Uhuru, should he become president.

So I thought about it and decided that Uhuru had higher chances of succeeding than a disunited opposition. When people asked me whether I joined the Uhuru camp because of the *kamwana* (young man) euphoria that was sweeping Kiambu, I must categorically deny it.

Whatever the case, many in the opposition were outraged and shocked by this decision. I was roundly condemned, and in a rare show of hostility, my close friend Kibaki publicly censured me for joining 'the enemy'. I was angered by Kibaki's criticism, but when contacted by the press over the remarks that had been attributed to Kibaki, I refused to comment and told the press that I would "reveal all" about Kibaki if my friend did not stop harassing me in public. After all we had been friends for so long and, as is always the case with lifelong buddies, we harbour intimate and even embarrassing details about one another.

The clash between the two of us was given a great deal of publicity, and the press attempted to portray me as someone who had deserted his friend in time of need. When it appeared that the disagreement might become more serious and acrimonious and lead to dividing the Kikuyu still more, two 'elders' in the form of Duncan Ndegwa and James Kome were sent to my Cianda House office where they pleaded with me to stop the quarrel since it was "causing a lot of embarrassment". I told them I had no malice, but they should talk to Kibaki about the matter, instead. The 'elders' then talked to Kibaki, and the two of us did not mention one another in bad light in public again. All the while I campaigned for Uhuru, I never derided or criticized Kibaki nor did I portray Moi as a good man.

Uhuru lost and Kibaki won, and I retained my seat on a KANU ticket. When Kibaki formed his coalition government and appointed affiliate party chiefs to important posts in his Cabinet, I was of course absent from the list. My adversaries, of course, laughed at my fate. There I was in a weak opposition, while my former friend Kibaki and others, were now enjoying prestige and power. But I had merely abandoned what I saw as a lost cause and placed my hopes on what I believed was the winning side. Now I was in the opposition again, and it made good cannon fodder for my enemies. I had made a mistake by backing the losing horse but then, everybody makes mistakes.

But I was not affected by the temporary dispute between Kibaki and myself. Although our relationship cooled down for a while during the campaign period and shortly thereafter, the two of us still spoke occasionally, but some people might have looked at our conversations as awkward.

Thus, I sat on the side of KANU, the opposition in Parliament, while my friend occupied the President's chair next to the Speaker on those occasions that he came to Parliament. Life went on as usual for me and I continued running my businesses and attending to the needs of the Kiambaa people. As always, I set aside every Monday to listen to the problems of my constituents. Those with problems concerning school fees, hospital invoices, a pending funeral or other difficulties would be able to visit me on this day, and I would spend time listening to their problems and writing cheques to help offset various bills. On weekends I would attend *harambees,* and on Sunday mornings I would go to church as I had always done since my early days.

One day in 2004 while I was relaxing in Mombasa I received a call. It was from the Head of the Civil Service, Francis Muthaura, who informed me that President Kibaki wanted to see me at State House at 11 am. I told Muthaura that I was in Mombasa but I would take the next available flight and then asked Muthaura to request that the appointment be rescheduled for 1 pm. When I finally arrived and went to State House, Kibaki disclosed that he wanted to include other parties in a 'Government of National Unity' and that he wanted me to join his Cabinet.

I was quite surprised. I was in KANU, as were all the Kiambu MPs apart from Paul Muite who had won his seat on a Safina Party ticket.

All along, speculation had been that Kibaki would select Muite in order to include a Kiambu MP in his Cabinet with an aim to heal the apparent rift between the Kiambu Kikuyu and others members of the community who enjoyed representation in government. A few days earlier, I had spoken to Kibaki's powerful Minister for Internal Security, Dr. Chris Murungaru, who had informed me that Muite was soon to join the Cabinet. At the time, I was quite joyful about Muite's inclusion.[72] The Kiambu people had been alienated from the rest of the Kikuyus after voting for KANU and they would now be included in government.

I really do not know why Kibaki changed his mind and appointed me instead. It seems that Kibaki felt he could rely on me more than Muite, as in "better the devil you know". I had always been loyal to Kibaki and had always supported him, up until the point when I joined Uhuru's camp. I had always campaigned for Kibaki and never prioritized my own ambitions, ever since the times of GEMA and the time I was canvassing for Kibaki to become Vice President. It was me, among others, who

---

72   It may seem odd that I would be happy when someone else from Kiambu was appointed to the Cabinet. I knew my chances of being appointed were slim because I was in KANU. I was happy for the Kiambu people that one of their MPs would be in Cabinet.

convinced Moi and Njonjo to select Kibaki for the Vice Presidential position. Muite, on the other hand, had never warmed to Kibaki and, even when other parties united to form NARC, Safina had chosen to go it alone. By the end of it all, Muite did not get a Cabinet post.[73]

Kibaki and I did not talk about forgiveness because we had never actually been enemies. We had just differed in opinion. So I joined Kibaki's government for the good of the country. I was looking at the appointment from the view of the people of Kiambu, the Kikuyu in general, and the good of Kenya. I felt that I could do more for the people inside government. Others from KANU who got posts were John Koech, William ole Ntimama and Mohammed Maalim. The leader of Ford People, Simeon Nyachae, was also appointed to the Cabinet and Kipkalya Kones of the same party got an Assistant Minister's seat. Kibaki was trying to create a regional balance in the Cabinet in an attempt to stop the bitterness in regions which had not voted for NARC.

I was quite pleased to be given the newly created Ministry for Special Projects.

At the time of my appointment to the Cabinet, there was a major drought in Kenya and many people were faced with starvation. People in places such as Tana River District were actually dying of hunger. As a consequence I took my duties very seriously and engaged in the task of feeding the hungry with zeal, personally visiting as many affected areas as possible. I did not just sit in my office and wait for reports from my officers, like some ministers did. I took an active role, and liaised with the relevant Ministries and humanitarian organizations as much as possible in order to ensure that people did not die of hunger.

When I learned that the people of a particular area were facing starvation, I would ask for a helicopter and go there myself to assess the situation. I even made visits abroad to seek aid from various governments, and I feel that we in the Ministry tried our best to prevent the death of many people.

After serving in the Ministry of Special Programmes for a few months, there was a Cabinet reshuffle in 2005. I was with friends at the Kiambu Club one evening when the reshuffle announcement came up on TV. When the Ministry of Special Projects came on screen, we noticed that the position had been given to John Munyes. I thought I had

---

73 It later emerged that Muite had been offered the post of Assistant Minister which he turned down, feeling that it was a slight against him. After turning down the post, he became a severe critic of Kibaki's government, but his stance did not go down well with his constituents and he was voted out in the 2007 general elections.

been sacked and was somewhat disappointed. I was not traumatized by this development, after all, anything can be expected in politics. I started adjusting to the idea of no longer being in the Cabinet. However, a short time later my name came on the screen and I realized I was now the Minister for Defence. The Defence Ministry had been scrapped by Moi twenty-five years earlier and prior to that, only two people, Dr. Njoroge Mungai and James Gichuru, had ever been Defence Ministers. The Ministry is in charge of the Army, Navy and the Air Force.

Once I was in the new Ministry, I sought to understand the issues affecting the soldiers and attempted to find solutions to difficult situations. After some study I concluded that the soldiers were underpaid and this could affect their morale. I negotiated a massive salary increment, and some six billion shillings was set aside to raise the officers' emoluments. As far as I know, there had never been such a large percentage increase for Armed Forces salaries since Independence and I was happy that I could help the military improve their financial conditions. During my tenure in the Ministry, the Armed Forces were involved in various community projects such as construction of schools, digging dams in places like Pokot and drilling boreholes in North Eastern Province. I cannot claim any credit for these efforts because the Armed Forces are always involved in community programmes during peacetime.

However, I saw to it that the Armed Forces increased their interaction with the people in a bid to improve public relations and as a result the public no longer saw them as idlers who stayed in the barracks and wasted taxpayer's money. Many people misunderstand the role of the Armed Forces and have negative images of the military, which is generally just not true. A country must have an army whether it is at war or not, and one cannot accuse soldiers of idleness when there is no war.

Perhaps it would please some critics to see our Armed Forces at war in this country. I really believe they should think about the matter more seriously.

While in this Ministry, I tried to streamline procurement procedures in order to stamp out corruption which had been rampant in some departments. I believe I did a fairly good job in both the Ministries of Defence and of Special Projects.

During my time in government, my lowest moment came when Kibaki's camp lost the Constitutional Referendum in 2005. There had been a great many disagreements over the draft Constitution which had been drawn up by commissioners from various sectors of society in a forum at the Bomas of Kenya, thus earning it the name 'Bomas

Draft'. Many people did not agree with certain sections of the proposed Constitution and they vehemently urged Kibaki not to assent to the draft until those sections were rectified. Others said that the Constitution was alright as it was and that it should be implemented as it stood. The matter became a circus as Ministers within the same Cabinet tore into each other over the Bomas Draft.

On the one hand there were a number of Ministers led by Raila Odinga, William Ruto, Charity Ngilu and Kalonzo Musyoka, all of whom opposed the draft as it was. On the other hand were those who believed that the document was nearly perfect and that there was no need to delay the unveiling of a new Kenyan Constitution. The Parliamentary discussions became so heated that the issue had to be resolved through a referendum, as is stipulated by law. In such a referendum, the people themselves would vote and decide whether the proposed draft should be made into a new Constitution or not. I feel that the day Parliament voted to hold the referendum was the day Kibaki's government started to lose its footing.

Before the referendum campaigns kicked off, the Electoral Commission announced that those supporting the Draft Constitution would use a banana symbol. Those opposing it, on the other hand, would use an orange as their campaign symbol. As it turned out, the Orange team, led by Raila Amolo Odinga, trounced Mwai Kibaki's banana team in the referendum. Consequently, Kibaki dissolved his cabinet.

When Kibaki named a new Cabinet, members of the Orange team were left out and they quickly dismissed the new line as an illegitimate government. Raila and the others had always harboured ambitions of becoming President, and although there were still two years to go before the next elections, they slowly started campaigning. The Orange team did not plead for seats in the Cabinet. Instead they went round the country agitating for change and trying to convince people that when time for the General Elections came, they should vote in the same manner as they had during the referendum. Raila described the Orange Democratic Movement as a "political tsunami" that would sweep away Kibaki's influence and then take over the government after the elections.

In 2007, the General Elections were due again. The main contenders were Mwai Kibaki, Raila Odinga and Kalonzo Musyoka. This time round I did not abandon Kibaki's camp. I supported the loose coalition of parties under which Kibaki was seeking re-election. This coalition was named the Party of National Unity (PNU) and it was an umbrella for various parties including NARC, which was the coalition that had propelled Kibaki to

State House in 2002. By this time Raila, Kalonzo, Charity Ngilu and others who had previously supported Kibaki, had decamped and formed the Orange Democratic Movement (ODM).

I feel that it was terribly regrettable for the leaders to allow the situation to deteriorate to this level. I blame the Bomas debacle, which had its roots in the Moi regime. The Bomas team had been set up by Moi and I feel that Kibaki should have disbanded it and dismissed its recommendations since Moi had never been sincere in reforming the Constitution. I am sure that had the Bomas forum been dismissed when Kibaki took over, the death and destruction following the 2007 elections could have been avoided. It was the referendum that pulled the people apart and set the stage for the 2007 election fiasco and Kibaki should have had the foresight to rectify the situation before it got so far out of hand. But I do not blame Kibaki alone. I blame myself and other leaders close to Kibaki for not being able to deduce the consequences of the Bomas forum and its recommendations.

This time round, I lost the Kiambaa parliamentary election to Stanley Munga Githunguri by a wide margin. I garnered 15,000 votes to Githunguri's 57,000 votes. I do not know why the people of Kiambaa voted me out after our long relationship, but I am not bitter about it. A change is as good as a rest, and the people of Kiambaa probably wanted change. After all, I had served them for twenty three years as their Member of Parliament and another five years as a nominated MP in Kenyatta's government.

I can now confess and reveal that I was so sure I would be re-elected that I hardly campaigned. I spent most of my time away from the constituency campaigning for Kibaki. In fact, even when voting was in progress, I still had not realized how much the tide had turned against me.

However, I have to say that my stint in politics gave me the opportunity to travel widely and meet interesting people. I have now retired from politics, but I am sure there are people who wonder how final this statement is.

I still receive Cabinet Ministers, MPs, Permanent Secretaries and others in prominent positions in government who consult me on a daily basis, so this keeps me up-to-date.

Looking back, I like to think that I spent a fairly successful life in the political limelight. With the help of many other people, dozens of schools, churches and other facilities have been built for my constituents, and dozens of people have been educated to university level. Naturally everyone has their own opinion, but in general, I feel I have served my country well and I have not yet come to the end of my service. I try to be ready to lend a helping hand when I am needed.

At my age, I am a happy old man living out my sunset years in the company of my charming and lovely wife, Grace Njoki, and my latest son, Emmanuel Karume. I think I will retire from business at the age of 80, but this is questionable, as well. I happen to have a talent for business and like taking a hands-on approach, so it is difficult to imagine retiring at all.

But this is not the end of my story! I must still tell you about my family and, like every old man, my own thoughts and reflections on life.

Chapter 10

A Lucky Family

Earlier on, I narrated how I met my future wife, Maryanne Wariara Wairiri, in Elburgon in 1951. At the time, I used to sell charcoal, fencing poles and timber in Nairobi. Although I was fairly well off for my age, I had not yet made particularly substantial sums. However, Wariara and I worked our way up until we owned one of the largest wholesale and retail shops in Kiambu District. While I was in detention, Wariara continued managing our shop at Raini in Kiambaa and she ran it so efficiently that when I was released, I found the business thriving and considerable sums in the bank.

Earlier, I had also owned one of the few hardware shops operated by Africans but this had been looted and destroyed by colonial agents when I was briefly detained in 1954. My uncle-in-law, Thuo Kigera from Nakuru, had his shop confiscated and given to a government employee after he was detained.

Wariara had been brought up by very hardworking parents and her father's family businesses had made him one of the wealthiest men in Elburgon. I was not intimidated by her father's wealth, and although the old man had first scoffed at my proposal for his daughter's hand in marriage, he eventually relented and we were married.

Although there was the usual attraction based on appearances, what convinced me to marry Wariara was her hard work and discipline. She assisted at her father's shop, which is where I met her. From what she told me, she was attracted to me because I seemed ambitious and was dedicated to my labours. One can say that the two of us shared the same work ethic, a factor that made us quite compatible life partners.

With Wariara's effort, support and encouragement, our businesses grew and we went from village entrepreneurship to a large conglomerate. She put her energy and skills into our businesses and I attribute her support as one of the pillars of my success. She managed several 'small' businesses and later went on to manage larger enterprises and the family estates in Kiambu which created even more wealth for family investments.

When I finally entered the political scene, her campaigning was extremely instrumental in my success. She crisscrossed Kiambaa constituency drumming up support for me. She was my manager for Women's Affairs in the Constituency, and she participated in many projects to help elevate the status of women in Kiambaa. She was also a great hostess, hosting many of Kenya's political and business luminaries of the time. In her lifetime, she hosted all the first three future Presidents before they assumed office.

Wariara welcomed Jomo Kenyatta to our homestead when he was not even an MP, and Mwai Kibaki when he was just a young Chief Executive of KANU. She also received Moi when he was the country's Vice President. Later, she entertained Kenyatta and Moi when they were President, and she would surely have hosted Kibaki if she had not passed away shortly after he was elected President. This was quite demanding given the size of the entourages that generally accompany such prominent people.

Wariara was at my side while the history of Kenya took shape, and she played her part in it actively. From Independence until her death in 2003, she was always at my side. In politics and in business, she was my partner throughout her life, and we both learned a great deal from each other.

Alongside such an exhilarating and heady public life, we also took time to bring up a family. In 1951, we were blessed with a healthy baby girl whom we named Wanjiku. Later in 1955 after my short stint in detention, we had a boy, Joseph Karume. Soon afterwards we were blessed with another girl, Teresia Njeri, and then followed Henry Wairiri, Kennedy Njoroge, Lucy Wanjiru, Jane Mukuhi, Albert Kigera and Samuel Wanjema. Later, of course, after I married Grace Njoki in 2006, Emmanuel Karume came along in 2008.

My chief regret in life was the fact that I did not have the opportunity to get adequate education to prepare me for life, and I vowed that my children would get the best schooling available. Thus it was quite satisfying that all my children had a good start in life.

Wanjiku studied at the University of Nairobi and later in Canada and became a medical doctor; Joseph Karume studied in Germany and is in business; Henry Wairiri studied to be a pilot but now assists me with the family business. Unfortunately my son Kennedy Njoroge passed away in 1997 and we all miss him very much. Lucy Wanjiru is in hotel management and is currently undertaking further studies in Geneva. Jane Mukuhi is also in hotel management. Albert Kigera is managing one of the family businesses, and so is Samuel Wanjema. Until a year ago, Samuel was my last-born but now my last born, Emmanuel Karume, is just over one year old and spends his days playing, eating and sleeping!

I am very pleased to now have the assistance of some of my children in the family businesses. In the past, as my businesses grew and we continued expanding our investments, the workload became too demanding for us to handle by ourselves. I had acquired a considerable amount of property, but my own presence, or that of my wife, always seemed to be required for strict supervision of the enterprises. Managers had been employed to run the businesses but they never seemed to work as efficiently or honestly as they should have.

As a result, I went to my father-in-law, Wairiri, talked to him and informed him of our dilemma. Wairiri suggested that the best alternative would be to marry a second wife. After all, Wairiri himself had three wives and my own father had three. For wealthy men this was the solution to such problems. They would marry additional wives to assist in business and management of property, and naturally for prestige, too.

Initially, Wariara was not very malleable to this decision. However after I married Njeri, she eventually warmed up to the idea. It may sound ridiculous in modern times, but polygamy was the order of the day in Kikuyuland, especially for those endowed with property.

In the olden days, traditionally, sometimes the husband would be the one to tell his wife that he had seen such and such a girl, and give his opinion on her suitability as a co-wife. If, on the other hand, the husband wanted another wife and had not identified a possible choice, the senior wife or wives would recommend a girl to become their co-wife. They did this with careful assessment, making sure that their families grew through the addition of beautiful and hardworking junior wives. Jealousy rarely featured in marriages, and the wives and children coexisted in peace. The primary qualities of a successful polygamous marriage were fairness, firmness and wisdom on the part of the husband.

The more wives and children one had, the more successful one was deemed to be, and the more respect one attracted. Traditionally many wealthy men had a number of wives, with some colonial chiefs having as many as 40 wives.[74] This custom grew unfashionable with the advent of Christianity and westernisation, although many Kikuyu men still took two or three wives if they could afford it.

But nowadays polygamy is viewed as odd and unacceptable to society, even unaffordable, and most Christian churches will not solemnise a marriage to more than one wife.

After my visit to my father-in-law, I identified a likely bride. She was a beautiful girl named Margaret Njeri, the daughter of Muhia, and a niece to my first wife, Wariara. She lived in Ngarariga, Limuru, where her family had relocated from Molo where she was born. I visited and wooed her and she accepted my proposal. Since her father had passed away, I approached her paternal uncle called Giathi and soon plans for the wedding were finalized. The usual Gikuyu ceremonies of *kũracia* (to pay dowry) and *kũguraria*[75] were then carried out.

Initially Njeri ran my second shop in Kiambu, but I later took her to settle on the Molo farm. I was fortunate that Njeri was as hard-working as her co-wife, Wariara. After she had streamlined the farm management and improved on the farming methods, she soon started making considerable profits from the Molo farm. She reared hundreds of cattle, and cultivated maize and potatoes on the farm. She was an extremely dedicated farmer, and entertained many of my business and political colleagues. She also supervised the management of Highland Hotel, another of my properties in Molo. After she passed away in 1990 after a short illness, I never again made any profit from the Molo farm. My managers would tell me it was a good month if we just barely managed to pay all our labourers. In 2006 I sold the farm to the Government for the resettlement of landless people.

---

74 Many colonial chiefs were polygamists, with many of them having over ten wives. This was because, as colonial servants, they had income and benefits and were able to afford the considerable expenses of establishing such extensive families, who each needed their own land and houses. Chief Kareithi of Nyeri, for example, had 22 wives, while his counterparts in Murang'a, Chief Michuki and Karuri wa Gakure, had more than 40 wives each. Kinyanjui wa Gathirimu had the most, with more than 100 wives. Of course some of these wives were mere concubines. Mostly such extensive polygamy was for purposes of status only.

75 *Kũguraria* means, literally, to shed blood. Blood was the symbol of life, but no human blood was involved in this ceremony. The father of the man who wanted to marry would deliver a ram to the home of the girl's father. The ram would be slaughtered to symbolize life through the blood it shed. By witnessing the shedding of blood, the lives of the bride and groom were now one and they could go ahead and create life. In the same ceremony, the shoulder of the ram, which was considered the best joint of meat, would be given to the groom's father by the bride to show that she had accepted his son as her husband. This was known as *gũtinia kiande* (cutting of the shoulder). After this ceremony the couple could go and live as husband and wife.

Over the years, Wariara and Njeri became very close. Their friendship, in fact, surprised everyone they met. Whenever I took a trip to Molo and left Wariara behind in Kiambu, she would complain. Similarly if I went back down to Kiambu, Njeri would be unhappy if she did not get the chance to visit Wariara. They became very close, more like sisters, and they would both attend church, political meetings, public gatherings and even State House functions with me. They would together go for holidays to the family home in Nyali, Mombasa, and exchange ideas and experiences in business and particularly in farming.

Unfortunately Njeri was not blessed with any children, but this did not cause her any loneliness. During school holidays, Wariara's children would occasionally end up in Njeri's house in Molo and stay there with her. They referred to her as their mum, as they still do today. If ever there was a polygamous marriage not marred by petty squabbles and jealousies, it was ours. The marriage prospered. Both wives had a knack for farming and business and gave me overwhelming support when I was forced to divide my time between business and political commitments.

I tried my best to balance my time fairly between Wariara and Njeri and there never was a question about the distribution of wealth because all our businesses were considered to be for the whole family. Both of them worked hard and the family prospered.

In the past polygamous marriages were very strong since the whole family was tied together by cultural bonds and traditions. But the polygamous system was eventually eroded by Christianity and Western 'civilization'. Whereas polygamous men and women were generally a happy lot in the past, polygamous families can, for the most part, barely survive in a modern setting. Apart from the church and other western influences, I believe there is much more materialism and lack of mutual trust nowadays. Hostility is bound to occur.

Even more importantly land was traditionally a central prerequisite to polygamy. Every wife had to have her fair and proper portion of land, and her own home. But these days large holdings are no longer available as they were in the time of my father and grandfather. A large polygamous family increased its wealth by having many hands to take up all the tasks involved in everyday living. There were always family members ready to till the land, weed and harvest (the specialization of women and girls), tend to the livestock (the responsibility of boys), defend the homes (a preserve of young men) and arbitrate, judge and foresee future needs (the preserve of older men, and older women too, although they generally exercised their subtle influence through their husbands).

My friends and I who were polygamous miss those days but then, one must change with the times and adapt. I gained considerable insight on a great many issues from both my wives and I still miss their company to this day. Although Wariara and Njeri both had their weaknesses and strengths, as I do myself, they understood one another and we all managed to live as a closely knit family. The presence of both wives offered our children an excellent home environment because they benefited from advice, good upbringing and an abundance of love from both their 'mothers'.

At that time there were one hundred and forty one women's groups in Kiambaa, and Wariara was the chairperson of many of them. They organised themselves and raised money to buy a hundred acres of land in Kiambu town which was subdivided so that each group got two plots each for commercial development. Wariara was the treasurer of the giant Mugumo Nyakinyua Women's Group, and I helped them to buy five hundred and twenty acres of land in Ruiru. The Mugumo group would usually entertain Kenyatta at his home in Gatundu. The groups also achieved other things, such as buying cattle for their members.

Wariara worked with many women leaders in Kiambaa such as Muthoni Gichane who was the Ndumberi KANU chairperson. Wariara was also my campaign coordinator with women and women groups. I also negotiated for a farm in Matunda, near Moi's Bridge, for the Mugumo group. Together with another group made up of Kalenjin, we bought the farm from a departing *Mzungu* and the women who had very small farms in Kiambu settled there.

In December 1989, Wariara, Njeri and I took our annual holiday in Mombasa. We enjoyed the sea, the beach, the ocean breeze and the break from our children who had been left behind. Wariara and Njeri cooked together or took turns. But after only two days into the holiday, I had to go back to Nairobi. A friend of mine, Simon Mbugua, who had been the Permanent Secretary in the Ministry of Works, had passed away and I went for the funeral. I promised my two wives that I would finish up quickly and be back with them as soon as possible.

Two days later, both Wariara and Njeri fell sick and were airlifted to Nairobi Hospital, where they were diagnosed with acute malaria. Wariara survived, but Njeri did not. On 6 January 1990, she passed away. We buried her at Cianda Estate. The whole family clearly felt the difference without Njeri's presence.

As it is, I lost a companion while Wariara lost her best friend. The children lost one of their mothers. It was a sad time for our family.

In late 1997, Wariara was diagnosed with cancer of the stomach. She was taken to hospital in London where she underwent an operation. She recovered fully, and for the next five years she lived a healthy life although in a state of semi-retirement. Then in 2003 the cancer recurred and this time I took her to a hospital in Washington DC where she passed away on 28 March 2003. Once again our home was enveloped by grief, but I had to accept it as the will of God. However every cloud has a silver lining. On the night before Wariara was buried, my son, Wanjema, and his wife, Mumbi, had a baby girl born at Nairobi Hospital. The girl was named Wariara, to symbolize that Wariara's legacy still lived on even though she had died.

I understand that some people had advised President Kibaki against coming to Wariara's funeral. Perhaps, since I had left DP and was now a KANU MP, there may have been a feeling that I had abandoned Kibaki. All the same, he came for the funeral and spoke very kindly.

During his speech, he revealed that there had been a very close relationship between Wariara, himself and me. He said that politics could not and should not break up a relationship which had lasted over forty years. He recalled the sacrifices Wariara had made for us and many other politicians. He remembered that sometimes she had been awakened in the middle of the night, in order to serve them meals and refreshments and make them comfortable.

Moi, who had been hosted by Wariara many times first as Vice President and then as President, also spoke. He said that Wariara must have been a powerful woman since she had managed to bring him, Kibaki and myself together. Kibaki took this statement generously and said that Moi had provided peaceful leadership in Kenya for twenty four years. This was the first time Kibaki and Daniel arap Moi were meeting after the 2002 general elections.

I thanked those who had come, and said goodbye to President Moi. When I got back to my car, I waited for President Kibaki. His limousine was parked just next to mine and I wanted to say farewell to him, but I was told that Kibaki, with a few members of his entourage, had stayed behind after the funeral and were waiting in the house.

When I got there, I found him in the lounge with Mama Lucy Kibaki. The President said that he had always had a great deal of respect for Wariara and that he felt he could not leave without consoling me personally, after the other people left. I was moved by his sympathy.

However, for some reason, John Matere Keriri, who was State House Comptroller, seemed very uneasy. When the President asked for some juice, Keriri quickly ordered an attendant to bring some juice from one of the President's Escort cars. When the packed juice was placed in front of him, Kibaki looked at it and asked Keriri to return it to the car.

"I have always had fresh juice from Karume's kitchen," he said. "We have often had drinks together in this room, up to midnight and beyond. After all these years with Njenga, I don't think today is the day I shall be poisoned."

It was just like the old days.

I arranged for roast meat to be served to the President and the others who were present. The Kiambaa councillor, a man called Gichuru, brought the crisp and juicy meat on a tray.

But as the guests washed their hands, Keriri interrupted.

"James," he asked me, looking at his watch impatiently, "Do you now want to serve us dinner?"

It had been a difficult day for me, and I was getting irritated.

"Listen here, John," I snapped, "I found all of you in the house. It was not me who invited you in. Understand?"

As we argued, Kibaki told Councillor Gichuru to cut up the meat, starting with the ribs.

"*Wacha wale wafanye kazi ya fitina na sisi tukule nyama,*" (Let those ones continue bickering while we eat the meat) he said.

Looking back over the years, I know that, without the extraordinary dedication of Wariara and Njeri, my strong and honest lifelong companions, I would never have got as far as I have.

Another sad moment in my life, which came some years earlier, in 1997, was when I lost my dear son, Kennedy Njoroge.

After Wariara's death I immersed myself in business and political affairs. I was a KANU MP at the time and President Kibaki had not yet appointed me to the Cabinet, thus I was not very involved in political affairs. Apart from attending Parliament three times a week, I avoided party politics. Many of my former colleagues in the Democratic Party shunned me for having joined KANU, but I ignored their protestations. After all, I had joined the party out of principle and had not been overly influenced by other people's opinions when I made the decision. Although KANU was the official opposition party, I did not involve myself in the party's affairs in Parliament. I have to admit that I did not serve this party with the same vigour and zeal that I had served DP. This is probably because I was a peripheral member and neither an insider nor a stalwart.

Later, after Wariara's death, as I endeavoured to consolidate my businesses, I felt that there was a void inside me. There was a vacuum in my life which persisted despite all the efforts I put into my businesses. I tried to fight the void by immersing myself in my work, but was unsuccessful. I would retire to my farm and enormous house every day at around 7 pm and be greeted by echoes of silence.

My house has dozens of rooms, and it was quite uncomfortable to be alone in such an expansive house. I would sit in the lounge and watch TV although naturally I no longer featured in the news as I had in previous times. My cook, a young man called Wambugu, would bring my supper and by 9:30 pm. I would be in bed. None of my children lived in the house. They were all adults and had moved out, long ago, to their own homes.

In short, I suppose I was a very lonely man. Since 1951, I had always enjoyed the company of Wariara and Njeri. I had loved my wives very much, but I had never contemplated the idea that they would leave me behind so suddenly. I realised that for the first time in five decades I was alone again. It was not a pleasant feeling. All my children were adults with lives of their own, and I could not continually impose on them or interfere. I had no one to talk to particularly in the evenings at home. But I persevered.

In early 2006, I finally decided that I needed a partner and began to make plans to find a wife. The partner I was looking for was someone who, while not young, was not especially elderly. I wanted a mature lady who could understand me and make me feel comfortable, someone who would fit in well with my children. I thought seriously about my requirements and decided that I would like someone who could manage the household and also be actively involved in my life and business. Preferably she should be without children. I required someone who would not be overwhelmed by my wealth and who could assist me in management. Finding such a person would be difficult, I knew, but I believe that with God all things are possible, and it was to God that I turned in my new quest.

As I may have mentioned earlier, I am a staunch Catholic and I am devoted to my church. One Sunday after mass I called aside a few women acquaintances who also attended Cianda Catholic Church and others who were members of the Anglican Church, and explained my predicament to them. I informed them of the qualities I was looking for in a life partner and asked them if they would assist me in finding such a person. I have always been supportive of church activities as any churchgoer in Kiambaa and Kiambu district can confirm. The women were quite touched by my request. I guess they saw me as a lonely man, and they promised to do everything in their power to see that I got a wife. The pastor was also exceptionally helpful and requested the women parishioners to ensure that my wishes be answered speedily.

As it turned out, it was not as difficult as I had envisioned. On the 31 January 2006, the women made an appointment with me at my Jacaranda Hotel in Westlands, Nairobi. They were accompanied by Grace Njoki, a pastor at the Anglican Church of Kenya Cathedral in Kiambu town. This Cathedral is the headquarters of the Church's Mount Kenya South Diocese. Njoki was introduced to me and the women explained that she was a trained pastor, had never been married and did not have any children. She was the woman they thought would best be suited as my partner.

I was surprised. It was all so much easier than I had expected. For one, I already knew Njoki. Wariara, my late wife, had been a close friend of Njoki's mother until her death. The two women had been friends for a long time. Wariara had also often given firewood to the family when they did not have any, and so I knew the family background reasonably well. A friend of mine, Fred Ngugi, was also married to Njoki's sister, Wanjiku. Both couples, the Ngugi's and us, would occasionally visit Njoki's mother and we got to know her very well. Wariara got very close to Njoki's mother and she would sometimes visit her or vice versa. In fact, Njoki's mother used to call me "father" because her father had been initiated in the *Njenga* age group. On the other hand, I called her "Mum". However, I had known Njoki as a young girl and we had hardly ever interacted, due to our disparate lifestyles and ages. She had grown into a charming, self-confident and lovely woman.

After the introductions, the women left the room and Njoki and I started to get acquainted. We talked and I explained why I needed a wife, and assured Njoki that she perfectly fitted my criteria as a partner. However, I was not sure that I would fit in with hers. I knew she would need time to make such an important decision and commitment. We therefore agreed that she would think about the matter and give me her decision in a few days.

Shortly thereafter Njoki rejoined the women and they took their leave.

I was anxious to hear Njoki's decision and waited rather apprehensively. A week later Njoki finally came to a resolution and we met. She informed me that after considerable soul searching, she had decided to become my wife. I was quite happy and pleased with the development, and I was determined to make Njoki happy, too.

I decided to send Fred Ngugi and his wife to Njoki's mother. I called them to my office in Kiambu and told them that I had decided to get married again. They were full of congratulations and they asked me who the lucky lady was. You should have seen the surprise on their faces when I told them that it was Njoki.

"Are you sure Njoki wants to get married?" asked Wanjiku, Njoki's sister. "You see, Njoki is already married to the Church."

"You can call her yourself to confirm it," I assured her.

So they went to Njoki's mother to break the news. When they told the old lady that I was seeking her daughter's hand in marriage, she said that if that was the will of God, then may it be so.

However, she gave one condition for Njoki and one for me. My condition was that although she had no objection to the union, she was insistent that we must have a church wedding. As for Njoki, the condition was that she should not marry me if she was going to cause problems in my homestead and destroy the achievements of her late friend, Wariara.

Neither of us saw anything untoward with the lady's conditions, and so the necessary arrangements went on.

We soon organised a delegation to visit Njeri's home for the purposes of paying the dowry. Bishop Peter Njenga, my cousin J.R. Njenga, my sister, Margaret Nditi and I went to see the elders from Njoki's family. My sister Nditi had been sceptical when I told her I intended to marry Njoki since she knew her to be deeply devoted to the church.

The elder who received our small delegation was my friend, Ex-Senior Chief John Kuria, who was Njoki's cousin. After this customary ceremony, we were granted permission to get married.

Although I was a staunch Catholic while Njoki was an ACK pastor we agreed that neither of us would change our denominations since we were both devoted to our churches. After all we both worshipped the same God.

Immediately thereafter we set about organizing the wedding. We both agreed that it should be a private, low key affair. The wedding was set for 20 February 2006, which was 20 days after we had been introduced at Jacaranda. The media was not invited, nor did I invite any of my Cabinet or Parliamentary colleagues. I did not even invite my friend, President Kibaki, or any of my other very close friends! All I wanted was a small private ceremony. However, a few relatives and few close friends of both families, in addition to all my children, were invited. I phoned all the children on Sunday, a day before the wedding, and they all managed to attend. If you ask me why I left it so late to invite them, I have to say that I really did not want them to start arguing with me. I had made my decision and I wanted them to accept it, and to welcome Njoki as my wife.

When I remember the wedding day I laugh. That same morning, there was a Security Committee meeting scheduled at State House. When the State House Comptroller Hyslop Ipu informed me about the meeting a few days earlier, I had desperately tried to arrange for a postponement.

"Isn't it possible to change the day?" I pleaded. "I have another appointment."

"Well, what is it? Is it something important enough to justify putting off the Committee meeting?"

I was stuck. I did not want to start telling people about the wedding.

"Please, can you at least change the time?" I asked. Can you make it 9 am?"

"Listen," Ipu told me, "all the invitations for the Security Meeting have already been sent out. It will inconvenience many people if we change the time."

He looked at me with a puzzled frown. "What is it? Why do you need to change the time?"

I just shook my head and kept silent. There was nothing else I could do because I really wanted to keep the ceremony private.

So I went to the meeting at 10 o'clock. There I was, as the Minister for Defence. With me was John Michuki, the Minister for Internal Security, P.S. Zacharia Mwaura, PS Internal Security Gituai, the Chief of General Staff, Jeremiah Kianga and the Head of the Civil Service Francis Muthaura

In the meeting, I found I could not concentrate at all. I kept fidgeting and glancing at my watch, and my colleagues might as well have been talking Greek as far as I was concerned. I wondered what people would say about someone who was late for his own wedding. The wedding was scheduled for 11 am and I was counting the minutes.

I wished my colleagues would hurry up and finish their discussions, but they seemed to be intent on dragging the meeting out as long as possible. Finally, the meeting was over at 11 am precisely and I shot out of State House like an arrow. Jumping into my car, I told my driver to step on the accelerator and despite our speed, the journey from Nairobi to Kiambu seemed endless.

In the car I phoned Njoki and assured her that I was on my way. I then phoned Bishop Peter Njenga, who was with Reverend Maina Kigondu of the ACK to let him know I was on my way, and he joked and said he thought I had changed my mind. They were together with Father Michael Mungai and Father Karing'u of the Catholic Church. The wedding was to be officiated over by Ministers from both the Catholic and ACK Churches. Lastly, I had to phone for someone to bring my wedding suit from home to the Kentmere Club in Limuru so I could change before the ceremony. I tried to explain to Wambugu, my cook and generally helpful young man, which suit I intended to wear for the occasion, but he did not quite understand my description and brought the wrong one.

Finally I arrived at the Kentmere Club, about half an hour late, and we proceeded with the ceremony in tents we had put up for the purpose.

At the end of the ceremony Njoki and I signed the marriage certificate in front of the Bishop and were soon pronounced husband and wife. I should explain that our registration certificate had been prepared by Bernice Gachiengo who was Registrar General in the Attorney General's office. She is a family friend, almost like a daughter, and she had insisted that she would come and prepare the document herself.

The only politicians who were present at the wedding were Joseph Munyao and Kuria Kanyingi. Munyao's niece is married to my wife's cousin and so he is a member of the family, while Kanyingi was invited because he is my friend and the Kentmere Club is in Limuru constituency where he was the then MP. As a matter of fact, I had not disclosed to him about my intentions. I merely told him I would be having a cup of tea at the club and wished him to join me. Imagine his surprise when he found a wedding in progress and me as the groom!

The wedding and the reception, at the same venue, were supposed to be top secret but this was not to be. Although the wedding had been uninterrupted by outsiders, and the only photographers invited were privately hired, things changed at the reception.

As the festivities were going on, I noticed what seemed to be press photographers. When inquiries were made, they confirmed that indeed, they were TV journalists. I should have known better. I suppose any wedding involving prominent personalities would be almost impossible to keep under wraps. Someone somewhere had leaked the information. My first instinct was to throw them out, but I knew the damage was already done. Knowing the tactics of the press, I was sure they would write a sensational story about being kicked out of my wedding. We therefore organized a photo session for them before politely dismissing them. The story and pictures appeared in the evening news.

When Cabinet met the following Thursday and the normal business was completed, my colleagues scolded me for not inviting them to the wedding. Michuki wondered how I could have failed to inform them, despite the fact that I had been with them in the same room on the morning in question. A 'vote of disapproval' was jokingly moved by the President and the other members joined in. I told them I had kept it secret because I did not want publicity as the matter was very personal to me. Many of my Parliamentary colleagues, friends and business associates also expressed surprise and disappointment at not being invited. But they congratulated me all the same.

Njoki and I became a happy couple and we soon proceeded for our honeymoon in London. Njoki had never been abroad and I had wanted to treat her to something she had never experienced before, but she found it terribly cold as it was during winter.

After we came back, she asked me, "Why did you take me to London? You should have taken me to Mombasa!" I admire her for being so down-to-earth and I think she was right. The Kenyan coast is definitely better!

My house on Lynton Farm, where I lived before moving to Cianda. In the picture are my two wives and some relatives.

With my two wives during the wedding of my son Joseph Karume.

Joseph Gatuguta, Waira Kamau, myself, Arthur Magugu, an unidentified person, Mbiyu Koinange and Stanley Oloitiptip during a KANU delegates meeting in early 1970s.

Trying out a cattle feed chopping machine with friends during a visit to Germany in 1975. On the extreme left is my son Joseph Karume and on the extreme righ is Kinyanjui Kabibi.

Campaigning in Kiambaa Consitutency during the 1979 General Elections. The lantern was always my symbol, signifying bringing enlightenment to the people. The symbol was later adapted by the Democratic Party. 1979 was the year that I first got into Parliament as an elected MP.

Myself, James Kinyanjui Matonyo, Stanley Githunguri, Charles Njonjo and Edward Kariuki Kimani.

With Stanley Githuguri at a harambee in Elburgon (mid 1970s).

With Ngengi Muigai (centre) and Arthur Magugu during a political function in the early 1980s.

Njeri, one of the children, Wariara, my grandmother and various relatives,
Lynton Farm in 1976.

With John Keen (DP's
Sec. Gen.) during a DP
meeting in 1993

Democratic Party Chairman Mwai Kibaki addresses the first DP rally at Uhuru Park in 1992.

Meeting the head of South African Breweries. On the extreme left is Joe Kibe and on the right is Joseph Wanjau.

With members of a visiting delegation of the British Army, National Defence College.

Meeting visiting former US President Bill Clinton in 2005. Others are Cabinet colleagues Raila Odinga (partly hidden) Charity Ngilu and Raphael Tuju.

Myself and my two wives, 1970s.

Jane Mukuhi Karume after graduating with a Masters Degree in London.

Henry Wairiri Karume on his wedding day.

Joint rally with Peter Gacathi (left), Nginyo Kariuki, Mbiyu Koinange and Mr. Munyui during my first campaign in 1979. I won the Kiambaa Parliamentary seat.

With Muringo Kiereini, a friend, Wariara and Jeremiah Kiereini in Mombasa.

My son Joseph Karume.

My daughter Lucy Wanjiru.

*My daughter Francisca Wanjiku and
her husband James Kahiu.*

*With my two wives and grandmother and a group of visiting relatives and friends on
Lynton Farm, September 1976.*

Wariara and myself exchanging rings during our wedding, 1999.

Visit to Benson Munge and Paul Mwobi, my uncles, 2009.

At my Cianda Estate house, 2009.

Visit to Peter Muhoho (My teacher), 2009. On the left is Mrs Muhoho, and standing behind is Njoki Muhoho.

My house at Cianda Estate.

My daughter Teresia Njeri.

At my Cianda Estate.

My son Albert Kigera Karume.

My son Samuel Wanjema.

Indian Ocean Beach Resort Club.

With Archbishop Ndingi Mwana a'Nzeki.

Wearing a githii at my home in Cianda.

Njoki and myself exchanging rings during our wedding, 2006.

With wife, Njoki, and baby Emmanuel Karume in April 2009.

Emmanuel Karume in October 2009.

Giving a cake to my wife Njoki at our wedding in February 2006.

With my new family in October 2009.

During a visit to Mzee Githua in Mang'u – 2009.

With wife Grace Njoki during her ordination in 2008.

Grace Njoki being ordinated as a full priest of the ACK Church.

A jovial couple after the ordination.

My mother-in-law (seated) and Njoki's relatives and friends after the ordination.

With my mother-in-law (Njoki's mother), Eliza Gachigi, 2008.

*As Defense Minister, inspecting a Guard
of Honour mounted by the Chinese army
in 2006.*

*A thoughtful moment – thinking about
the past . . . and the future.*

With President Mwai Kibaki on a campaign tour, December 2007.

President Kibaki greeting my wife Njoki during the 2007 campaigns.

Addressing a presidential campaign rally during the 2007 campaigns.

In my office at the Jacaranda Hotel, Westlands, 2009.

Chapter 11

Thoughts and Reflections

Just after Kenya attained Independence, society was functioning smoothly. As a senior citizen now looking back over the years, I have to say that, in my opinion, the Civil Service was working well and the private sector was alive with new found energy. Transport and infrastructure was being improved, or put in place, with amazing dedication. Education and other sectors were thriving, and those who did not have land for farming were encouraged to make purchases through use of soft loans offered by the government.

An air of optimism pervaded the land in extreme contrast to the long period of suffering that was experienced hitherto. The philosophy that Jomo Kenyatta and other nationalists believed in was that we were now the masters of our own destiny and anything was possible for those who were willing to work hard. *Wananchi's* expectations of government performance were high, but this was not a problem since the new government took up the challenge of running the country with a great deal of determination and enthusiasm.

The young civil servants (and they were all very young), were full of nationalism. I remember that people like Kenneth Matiba, John Michuki, Tom Mboya, Lawrence Sagini, Peter Shiuka, Job Omino, Kitili Mwendwa, Duncan Ndegwa, Charles Njonjo, Andrew Omanga, Juxton Shako, Mwinga Chokwe, Peter Gachangi, Dr. Njoroge Mungai and others were still in their late 20s or early 30s when they were entrusted with very senior posts, which they handled meticulously. They were full of eagerness and wanted to play a part in making the new nation. Despite the many challenges they encountered in refashioning colonial structures, they put their souls into their efforts. Sloppy work was not condoned, and the culture of god-fathers was virtually non-existent.

Contrary to common belief, Kenyatta did not make allowances for corruption. As mentioned elsewhere in this book, Kenyatta encouraged people to work hard and tried to show Kenyans that nothing is accomplished without sweat. Just after Independence, government offices functioned well and Civil Servants served the people with diligence, with eagerness and the integrity that befitted those offices. But nowadays, some will not even call you back if you phone them with some inquiry.

The existing rot in the Civil Service grew tremendously during Moi's rule and it may take the terms of several Presidents to undo the damage. I feel that this regime ruled by favouritism and it was during this second presidency that a culture of sycophancy took root. Those who toed the line were rewarded while those who truly merited praise were ignored or even punished. However, although there were problems, at least there was peace and stability.

But in those very early days after we gained Independence, corruption was not condoned. People did not pay bribes to be served in government offices. Although there were a few corrupt people in government, dishonesty was not as outright or blatant as it became during the second regime. James Gichuru and Mbiyu Koinange, the two people closest to Kenyatta, hated corruption with a passion.

I believe that most Kenyans, myself included, had a sense of national pride, integrity and moral forthrightness and no one could even imagine the absolutely incredible levels of grand corruption that later came to be associated with the second regime, for example, Goldenberg and Anglo Leasing scandals which nearly caused the collapse of the Treasury.

Another thing that disturbs me is the way President Kibaki's directives are not followed or are ignored altogether. During Kenyatta's and Moi's time, I recall that Presidential orders would be implemented within a day, or within the scheduled period. It pains me to see people ignoring presidential directives whereas the President is supposed to be the Chief Executive of the nation.

The President has the power to rule and should not tolerate sloppiness and indiscipline. I feel that the country needs to have a powerful person in charge. I believe in the Gikuyu saying, "You cannot share power like (you would) a sweet potato."

I am not certain what this apparent indifference can be attributed to, nor do I understand why President Kibaki does things in the way he does, using a hands-off approach. One of the reasons for this attitude might be because Kibaki does not have a real *njama*, a 'Council of Elders', or a think-tank, to help him formulate and implement government policies. A think-tank can help a leader to analyse problems and to provide guidance in times of confusion and crisis. It would not necessarily replace the role of the Cabinet, either. Kenyatta had his council of advisors, and so had Moi. However, Kibaki's style has been different.

Nevertheless, despite these matters, I feel that Kibaki has definitely been the best President Kenya has ever had. He is not corrupt at all, and things are slowly but surely getting done. Little by little, almost imperceptibly, the excesses of the past are being dealt with. Whether Kenyans are too impatient or too patient, is a subject of discussion!

I still believe that Kibaki should assert himself more as the leader of Kenya. I think that a leader must not only lead and inspire, he must know how to, figuratively, use the *bakora* (cane).

But we must remember that, all in all, Kenya's leadership through the Kenyatta, Moi and Kibaki eras has largely been successful compared to that of some neighbouring countries. There has been no war in Kenya since Independence, something which cannot be said about many African countries. Furthermore, there has been no major internal conflicts apart from the politically-induced tribal clashes during general elections, which I consider to be the work of short-sighted and basically ignorant politicians. Kenyans have lived peacefully since independence, and it has the three Presidents to thank for. There has been no coups and the attempts that have been there have not been successful, unlike those in many other countries in Africa where coups have been the order of the day.

I have known each of the three Presidents from before Independence. I was very close to Kenyatta, and Kibaki is a personal friend. Although my relationship with Moi was cold during his early days as President, it later warmed up and the two of us became, if not close friends, at least acquaintances who could tolerate one another. I even served a brief stint as Assistant Minister in Moi's government. To date, the two of us still hold occasional conversations over the phone.

Is it possible, then, that I, like many others, have benefited from my relationships with the three Presidents? In other words, have I benefited from their influence to acquire wealth? I know these are questions that many people ask about me.

The answer to this is a simple "no". I have never used undue influence, nor do I condone corruption. I am convinced corruption is evil and causes harm to society. I have acquired all my wealth through hard work and

I have never collaborated with any politician or civil servant to acquire anything unlawfully.

In order to explain this more fully, I have to tell you about the business philosophy I have developed over the many years of my life.

First, I feel it is necessary to use one's intelligence and the talent God has given one in order to identify opportunities and exploit them. Why did God give us a brain and hands and feet if not to work in the quest for wealth and a stress-free life? I find it interesting and challenging to face what life brings along.

Second, I am strongly convinced that if I mix my genuine enterprises with corruption in any way, it would 'poison' or destroy my businesses. I have always had that belief, and have been more and more convinced of it as the truth. Sometimes I ask myself why people steal. What drives them? Why does this happen in the government or elsewhere? I suppose there may be many different motives, but the end result is the same. One can steal perpetually, but never get satisfied and in the end, greed destroys the person and their family. I have seen it happen over and over again.

From my youth, I worked from sunrise to sunset every day and still do so even now. People should know that I was relatively wealthy long before the country attained Independence, and long before I met any of the three Presidents. As a young man I burned and sold charcoal, then moved on to selling timber, a much more lucrative product, and then ventured into the general business before I was detained and released by the colonial authorities. By the time Kenyatta became President, when I was just 34, I had already made my first million and was the first African to have a shop in the Indian Bazaar of Kiambu Town.

I feel that those who do not like hard work will always remain poor, but those who are willing to roll up their sleeves will be rewarded. Short cuts will merely destroy one and their ambition and later, even their family will be affected. In addition, I must declare that I have never wanted or needed to engage in bribery because I was always focused on what I wanted and I have really struggled to achieve my goals.

Furthermore, I have always been a firm Christian and I believe most implicitly that wealth, or anything acquired corruptly or through devious means, will always attract retribution from God. I have a very strong faith in this principle.

I also feel that people who have grown rich due to corrupt deals do not enjoy it because their conscience continually gnaws at them. They know they are guilty, and their souls and minds cannot rest at peace. I have seen this myself, over many years of experience, and I would not want to live such a life. This is why I have always made sure that my hands are clean. My businesses have always been in the private business sector and hence there is no possibility I have ever taken either advantage, or money, from public coffers. What has helped me build up little by little were the loans I obtained from banks every now and again, and then the gradual repayments which I made. In fact, all my properties have been purchased through loans.

These same principles hold for my political career. I have never requested nor required favours. Kenyatta nominated me to Parliament against my will in 1974. By 1979, when the next elections were held, Kenyatta was dead and I did not need his or anybody's patronage to get elected as MP for Kiambaa, where I served for five terms until my retirement. All through this time, I never depended on anyone's intervention to be successfully elected, which is why I calmly accepted the verdict of Kiambaa people when they ousted me in 2007 and voted in Stanley Munga Githunguri.

A wise man knows when it is time to stop and I feel that I have served my country with diligence and dedication and it was now time to rest and let others carry on with the work. One of the problems with Kenyan politicians is that they never know when to call it quits, struggling stubbornly to hold on to power till they are in their graves. Who knows, I also may have overstayed to some extent!

It is a shame that Kenyan MPs who are among the best-paid legislators in the whole world today, are adamant in refusing to have their allowances taxed. Their excuse—that they have more expenses because they are always donating money in *harambees*—does not hold any water. Even the ordinary person donates money in such fund-raising events. A *harambee* is not a one-person affair. It is not the MP alone who gives money for a project. In fact some private citizens contribute more than many MPs!

Even after the Constituency Development Fund (CDF) was established, MPs continued increasing their salaries. As one of the results, the Koigi Commission looked into the matter. I believe the final opinion was that no Member of Parliament should be a Guest of Honour at *harambee* functions because they were corrupting people.

Harambees are so called because it is an appeal for *all people* to pool together for a common, noble cause. An MP is just one of these people, and there might be thousands of people at such a function. The

MP may give more than other people, because he earns more. But there are business people and senior civil servants who often contribute larger sums than MPs, and they are taxed like everyone else. So it is nonsense for MPs to say that their salaries go into *harambees* and funerals of their constituents. Refusal to pay taxes is is tantamount to blackmailing *wananchi,* pretending that this arrangement will help them contribute generously in *harambees*. Furthermore, if some are daft enough to take on multiple mortgages and loans and then bring home peanuts as a salary, that is their own problem.

As to the reason I and my fellow MPs did not pay taxes when I was in Parliament, the fact is that the issue never came up. This issue of taxation only came up during the 10th Parliament. Most likely this was because it was before Kenyan MPs increased their own salaries to astronomical figures. The pay which MPs took home all through Kenyatta's time and through the earlier years of Moi's rule was meagre, and many of those who left Parliament ended up living in mediocre circumstances. They did not get pensions either and most were poor or middle class. They did not go to Parliament in order to enrich themselves.

There was a time when I was the only MP from the greater Kiambu who was living in my own constituency. All the other MPs were staying in expensive houses in exclusive suburbs of Nairobi. However it was not long before I discovered why they did so.

There are advantages and disadvantages of living at home. One of the biggest problems I encountered, for example, was that every morning, I would find some twenty or thirty people, especially students, waiting at my gate. The students would have been sent home from school because they could not raise school fees. I would ask my driver to stop, talk to them a little and then tell them to come the next day to my office in Kiambu. When they came, they would tell me where they were going to school, and I would write cheques to cover their fees, directly to the schools. I spent a great deal of money helping such students and others in need.

So in Parliament I would joke with my fellow MPs and say, "Ah, now I know why you do not stay at home! You knew it was going to be demanding. You knew the problems!"

However, I have remained there all through these years and enjoyed it immensely. In fact, all my salary, in addition to some of my personal income was going to *harambees* at the time.

In general, I have to say that God has always given me what I have asked of Him, and for that I am very grateful. I have absolutely no regrets about the way I have gone about my life and business. I feel that I have succeeded in most of my business and political ventures and I hope I have also been a good father to my family.

True, there are some few things that I could have wished for, but these desires never came to anything. And perhaps this was for a good reason, because that is life. Life is never planned beforehand and the destiny of man depends on God the creator. In business, for example, my most trying moments were in the Castle Breweries saga.

But I can say that I have always managed to acquire most of the material things I needed through hard work. I have always felt driven, focused on work, and focused on achieving my goals. And I have to thank God that I have received these blessings in abundance.

However, there is one thing that I have never been able to achieve despite my childhood ambitions; I have never been able to acquire sufficient education. Up to this day, I still wonder what I might have become had I gone beyond primary school. Although I consider myself quite well educated for a person born in those early years, I still regret that my father did not have enough money to get me into Mang'u High School.

In my school days, I had two ultimate ambitions—to become a railway station master or a lawyer. The job of a railway station master was a prestigious one in those days. The railway was thriving since road transport was rare because, in general, only whites had cars. Everyone travelling far distances used the train. The station master's position was considered a white collar job and was reserved for Europeans and Indians. Most likely only very educated Africans could get such a job, although, now that I think about it, I never met a black station master. All the same, I dreamed that higher education would enable me to become one, even if I would have been the first African to reach that position. I was willing to give it a try.

As to why I wanted to become a lawyer, I can give two convincing reasons. Firstly, around the late 1940s, my uncle, Samuel Wanjema, was arrested in Nakuru and accused of stealing car tyres. The family hired a Mr. Baker, a black South African lawyer, to represent him. Along with my family members, I attended all the court sessions. I was extraordinarily impressed with the lawyer's tactics and eloquence and the methods he used to counter the prosecutor's arguments. In the end, when my uncle was acquitted, I was awestruck. Despite the fact that the judge and the prosecution lawyers were Europeans, an African had defeated them! From this inspiration, I was convinced that a black man with an education could outdo whites, a thought which had never occurred to me before because all the Africans I had seen were subordinates to Europeans and Indians.

A second legal case arising shortly after my uncle was acquitted caught the attention of the whole country. It was during the Second World War, thus there were many British troops and African conscripts that had to be fed. One day, a colonial District Commissioner who was in charge of procuring food for the troops found a Maasai herder tending his livestock in Narok. As was the habit with senior officers, he pointed out a bull in the herd and demanded that it be captured so it could be slaughtered for the troops. The Maasai herder had no problem with this, since it was a common occurrence. However, the DC had pointed out the prized ceremonial bull of the herd.

It was a big bull, traditionally highly valued, and was used to sire the herd's calves. According to custom such a bull was considered to be very special. The herder explained the matter to the officer and told him to pick even ten other animals from the herd provided he left this bull alone. Nevertheless, the DC insisted that the prize bull be captured. He wanted that particular bull, the one he had selected, and stated that no African was going to contradict his instructions.

At that time the Maasai pastoralists were devoted to their herds, even more than they are today. When the DC's men began to isolate the bull from the rest of the herd in order to capture it, the herder acted swiftly. He took his spear and stabbed the white officer. The spear went right through his his body, killing him instantly.

The subsequent murder case attracted national attention. The white community were outraged that a herdsman could kill one of Her Majesty's District Commissioners because of a mere cow, but the Africans who knew the Maasai attachment to cattle, and the arrogance of the whites, felt that his action was justified. The same South African lawyer who had represented my uncle, Mr. Baker, now represented the herdsman. Although the Maasai herdsman was sentenced to death, this did not lessen my admiration of the lawyer. The extraordinary skill of the lawyer became the stuff of legend, at least for me. After that case, I was even more committed to becoming a lawyer.

In addition, I witnessed many cases where Africans were mistreated by whites on our own land, and this hardened my attitude towards colonialism. Europeans could get away with virtually anything while Africans were whipped, jailed or even killed for the flimsiest of reasons.

Were I to become a lawyer, I would have represented my fellow Africans and tried to stem the injustices that were being committed against them. How unfortunate it was that I never even made it to secondary school due to my inability to raise the school fees! Money was limited in my home, and my father felt that I should give my brothers a chance to at least get a little education, too.

When I was at Riara School in 1941 and 1942, my lifelong friend and, in later years a millionaire businessman in his own right, Mbugua Githere, kept nagging me to leave school and go into business with him. Mbugua had a bicycle repair shop in Gachie village and had dropped out of school after Standard Two. He was doing very well in his business, and his offers of a partnership were tempting, but when I related my dream of becoming a lawyer, Mbugua argued.

"When we've made enough money from business," he would say, "when we are rich, we can afford to hire all the lawyers we want!"

As a matter of fact, Mbugua's prediction later came to be true. Decades later the two of us would laugh over the issue when we were busy making our fortunes.

Nevertheless, I wonder what my life might have become had I furthered my education and become, perhaps, a station master or a lawyer. Would I have been as wealthy as I am today? Would I have managed to hang on to my humility? Would I have served Kenya better? These are questions that will never be answered. However, it must have been God's plan for me to go into business.

Whatever the case, my plans altered dramatically after I dropped out of school in 1949 after sitting the Common Entrance Exam. The rest, as they say, is history. What I did do was become a successful businessman and politician, and the idle imaginings of what I might have become are now the musings of an old man.

Perhaps that is why education occupies such a special place in my heart. Although I never acquired higher education, I have no heart to deny others the chance since I believe that education is the key to prosperity in modern times. I am genuinely convinced that with a good education and a determined character, the possibilities for Kenyans are endless.

I intend to set aside and donate a few dozen acres of land from my Cianda Estate for the construction of a university. These are grand ideas but are not empty promises. I am aware that knowledge is power and that is how much I believe in the power of education.

Alternatively I intend to set up a proposed 'Njenga Karume Foundation' and its main activity would be to educate the destitute and help the poor.

The Foundation would continue the charitable work I started in Kiambaa and hopefully it will be part of my legacy there. Charity begins at home, after all. I would like the Foundation to be an educational centre which will benefit Kiambaa's people and other Kenyans, too. It is a tragedy that there are still some parents who do not educate their children despite the free primary school education offered by the government. Such people are wrecking the future of their children and the poor children are none the wiser. In fact, I believe that the government should enact laws to force such parents to take all their children to school.

In addition, I am saddened by the plight of former freedom fighters. Our first President and his colleagues short-changed members of the Mau Mau by ignoring them after independence was granted. Many of them died paupers despite their sacrifice to the country, yet others grew rich on the fruits of independence despite the fact that they never suffered in the bush or in detention.

As I mentioned earlier, I feel that some land should have been set aside for former freedom fighters who fought in the forests. It would have been impossible to expect them to buy land from departing settlers. They simply did not have the means to purchase it since they had spent many years in the forest or in detention camps. Whatever the first regime's strong points may have been, history will fault the regime for neglecting those sons of the soil who gave their all, some even their lives, for the liberation of their country.

The same goes for the second regime which equally ignored the freedom fighters. Most of those who fought for our freedom died traumatized and bitter people, wondering what it was they had been fighting for. Some came out of the war more impoverished than ever before, since they had lost all their property while fighting for liberation. This perverse reversal of justice saddens me.

Looking back, I wish I would have put this point across to those in power, shortly after Independence. I wish I had discussed it with some of the prominent people I associated with at the time. But I was so much younger than all the rest, and I was not in government. And when I think about it now, no one ever brought it to my attention. It would have been almost impossible to "advise the elders," who merely tolerated my presence, and to be frank, it never seemed to hold much importance to me them, what with all the other exciting things happening at Independence! Hindsight is sometimes a difficult thing to live with.

The government could have easily done something. It could have created scholarships, trusts or educational institutions for recognised freedom fighters, especially those who fought in the forests. It would have cost little and would have demonstrated great goodwill.

I still support GEMA. GEMA is and was a good thing, and many ordinary members benefited from its activities before it was banned by Moi in 1979. It settled many landless people who would otherwise be destitute today. I believe it can still be a beneficial organization even now, as it could help members to invest in various sectors and offer them professional advice on how to go about business. Although I am not an official of the new GEMA that was revived in 2007, (I insisted that it should be led by younger blood), I still support its activities and attend its meetings. I think that the only difference with the new GEMA is that it has changed its outlook to fit with the times. GEMA, I feel, is not tribal. Its intention is to put its own house in order first, before seeking links with other communities.

When I am reminded that I was among those who, together with others like Kihika Kimani, were accused of having favoured Kikuyu during the land-buying exercise of formerly white owned farms during independence, I must flatly deny it. Some members of communities who live and have always lived in the Rift Valley have accused the Kikuyu of being aliens and they have been harassed, chased away and even killed especially in the aftermath of General elections. The communities harassing the the Kikuyu say that the land is not rightfully theirs, and that they only managed to get it because they were favoured by Kenyatta's government.

I am happy that I helped in settling many landless non-Kikuyus in various parts of the country. One such example is at Matunda, which is situated between Kitale and Moi's Bridge, somewhere near Eldoret. A *Mzungu* settler called Hudson and his wife wished to sell their farm to me. It was over five thousand acres. By raising funds through *harambees* and other fund raising activities, I managed to arrange the purchase of the farm for a group of about two thousand GEMA women in Kitale. However, when we were in the process of discussing the purchase, some Kalenjin women also showed interest. Apparently they had been waiting for an opportunity to buy the farm themselves. I agreed to the subdivision and the Kalenjin women and GEMA women split the farm so that each group would get half. Everybody was happy with the arrangement, and both groups still reside on the farm.

There was another farm in Molo called Muchina Farm. A group of Kikuyus wished to buy it, but a group of Kisii people had shown interest much earlier. The government officials dealing with the transfer had originally assigned the farm to the Kikuyu, but I intervened, talked to the officials and helped organise matters so that the Kisii could buy the farm.

I recall there was another case of a Mr. Green, of Kaplan and Straton law firm, who wished to sell his farm to me. Since he wanted to retain the elegant character of the farm, he did not want the farm labourers and other poor people to buy the land. I brought the issue to the government's attention and the matter went as far as President Kenyatta. The President sent Jackson Angaine, the Minister for Lands and Settlement, to discuss the sale with Mr. Green. The European was stubborn, but at the end of the day the farm was sold to the staff.

Kenyatta did not go out of his way or make special conditions in order to give the Kikuyu land. Land in the Rift Valley was dealt with on a willing-buyer, willing-seller basis and anyone could have acquired it if they had the money and the will. The fact is that many other communities just did not take up these opportunities because, unlike the over-crowded Kikuyu of Central Province, they still had enough land available.

At one time, Vice President Daniel arap Moi had the opportunity to buy a farm in Rongai, Nakuru, from a departing white settler. Moi informed Kenyatta about the farm. He asked the President to buy it so that he would have a place to visit when at State House Nakuru, or attending functions in the area. But Kenyatta would not have it. He told Moi that he had many farms, and that it was Moi who did not have any farms to talk about. He advised Moi to buy the farm for himself, and that is how Moi acquired his famous Kabarak Farm. Moi later arranged for Kenyatta to buy another farm in the area which became known as Gicheha Farm.

In fact when Kenyatta saw that most of the farms were being bought by the Kikuyu, he made it a point to encourage other communities to buy, too. There was, for example, the issue of the twenty eight thousand acre Keringet Farm. A group of Kipsigis was interested in buying it, and so was a group of Kikuyus. There was an impending conflict, and the matter was taken to Kenyatta for arbitration. Kenyatta listened to both sides, one that was led by Taita Towett, and the other by Kihika Kimani. In the end Kenyatta decided that the Kipsigis purchase the farm since the Kikuyu had bought many others.

Then there was the 11,000 acre Ngata Farm. Rival groups were interested in purchasing the land and there was the same tug of war.

Kenyatta was again consulted and this time he came up with a different solution. He decided that the farm be shared equally. Five thousand five hundred acres went to the Kalenjin community and the other half was made into an Agricultural Development Corporation (ADC) farm. The Kikuyu were of course very disappointed, but they later got other chances. Unfortunately, after the death of Kenyatta, it was a great pity that the Moi regime sub-divided the ADC farm and dished it out to government officials.

Again, in other areas such as Trans Nzoia and Uasin Gishu, the Kisii and other communities bought land.

Kenyatta aside, people like William ole Ntimama had no problem allocating plots to a few Kikuyu when he was Ol Kejuado County Council Chairman. This was because when they bought land there, the Kikuyu brought investments which developed the area. However, years later, when the local Kikuyu indicated they would not vote Ntimama to Parliament and opted to vote for Justus ole Tipis instead, his hatred for them began. During the clamour for multi-party rule in the early 1990s, Ntimama made his infamous declaration telling the Kikuyu in the Narok area to "lie low like envelopes" or be hounded out. These are the slogans of war mongering politicians and such statements have retarded development and national unity in Kenya.

It is necessary to understand that those communities who persecute others and chase them from their farms do not benefit at all. They cannot possibly take the vacated land for their own use as the true owners and are already known, and they have title deeds to prove ownership. Nothing disturbs me more than seeing people who bought land with their hard earned money, living in deplorable conditions as Internally Displaced Persons (IDPs) after every election.

This is one aspect where Kibaki's government has failed. This matter must be settled and the security of the people must be ensured. These people, both the innocent victims and the aggressors, suffer because of the political bigotry of the politicians, and their own ignorance.

Those people who were chased out of their land after the December 2007 clashes, who were killed and maimed, made only one mistake—they voted for the government which is now in power. So while the current politicians enjoy privilege and benefits, those who voted for them, continue to suffer. This is not fair!

In the course of my life, I have been lucky enough to make many friends all over the world and wherever I travel in Kenya, be it Garissa, Kisumu or Mombasa, I have friends who will invite me to stay. I believe in the adage that one should "make new friends, but keep the old" for one never knows when one will be in need of a good turn. My childhood friends such as Mbugua Githere and Muiruri Laban, later became my business partners and we achieved considerable success together. Other friends I made in the early years, like Brian Hobson of East African Breweries, Jomo Kenyatta, Mbiyu Koinange, Karuga Koinange, and James Gichuru are still in my heart. With those friends who are still alive today, I maintain good relationships and they have supported me in my journey to success as a businessman and a politician.

All the same, there are some friends who occupy a special place in my life. Chief among these is President Mwai Kibaki. The two of us have been close friends ever since we got to know one another in the 1950s. Together with Kibaki and John Keen, we founded the Democratic Party, one of the biggest political parties to emerge after multipartyism was re-introduced in 1991.

Despite the little break in our relationship when I decided to support Uhuru Kenyatta for the Presidency in 2002, the two of us are strong and firm friends. Although I now see less of Kibaki due to his Presidential commitments, the two of us talk and consult on many occasions. Our lives, especially in politics, have been intertwined since the early years of Independence and it is very doubtful that either of us would be where we are without each other.

Kibaki is more of a brother than a friend. He has been an inspiration since I met him. Despite his high level of education, compared to mine, he is never conceited. We have come a long way together as the history of this nation was being made.

Another very close friend and great inspiration in my political career was James Gichuru, who was the country's first Minister for Finance. I had known Gichuru since the 1950s when he was the Chairman of the Kenya African Union. We, and others in KAU, would frequently have drinks together at the Race Course Road—near St Peter's Xavier Catholic Church. I had the money and he had the aura and the charisma.

In addition to his other occupations, Gichuru was also a beer distributor in Nairobi with Kamande Gichira and me. Actually it was Gichuru who introduced me to beer distribution in Nairobi at the time I was supplying beer in Kiambu. We did a great deal of business together in the beer distribution industry under our flagship company, Nararashi.

As I explained earlier, James Gichuru became the President of KANU, which evolved from KAU, and gave up the post for Kenyatta when the latter was released from detention in 1961. I admired Gichuru for this, and for his principles and his courage. Gichuru lived a simple life up to his death, and compared to others, he did not use his position to enrich himself. He was one of Kenyatta's most trusted lieutenants and advisors. He was very loyal to Kenyatta and to the country, and although he was older than me, he was my role model of what a politician should be. I have never known a more selfless nationalist.

I remember one incident just after the State of Emergency was declared in 1952. The colonial government tried its best to stop the Mau Mau but that was proving to be very difficult. The Government called upon African leaders to denounce Mau Mau in public so that people would stop joining the movement. In one such gathering at Kirigiti Stadium in Kiambu, Kenyatta denounced the Mau Mau in front of a crowd estimated to be twenty thousand people. Despite this declaration, he was arrested shortly thereafter and accused of being the brains behind the movement. Another meeting was called in Dagoretti much later after Kenyatta's arrest, and this time James Gichuru as KAU's representative, was invited to condemn the movement. The colonialists had asked him to denounce Kenyatta, Mbiyu, Gatabaki wa Mundati and a few others, in addition to criticising the Mau Mau. I was present at the meeting and actually witnessed the proceedings.

What the organizers of the meeting did not know was that Gichuru had deliberately passed via a bar at Dagoretti Market owned by Kariuki Githuku and his brother Njuguna, and quite intentionally, in order to build up his courage, taken five bottles of beer in quick succession. When he went to the meeting, he shocked the white administrators when, speaking in Gikuyu, he opened the meeting with the words: *"Njĩtagũo Gĩchũrũ wa Gĩtaũ. Arũme nĩ maruaga no niĩ nĩ mũno."* (My name is Gichuru Gitau. Men get circumcised, but I am more than circumcised.)[76] He then stormed out of the meeting.

---

76 What Gichuru meant was that he was a real man and he would not be cowed by the colonialists. In Kikuyu culture, circumcision was a painful experience and if one withstood the pain, it was taken as proof that he was now a real man who was courageous and could carry out the duties entrusted to men.

The DO for Kikuyu area, John Johnston, asked the area chief, Gitau Mirio, to translate Gichuru's statement. Gitau explained that Gichuru had never talked about the Mau Mau at all and translated the statement for him, which left the European hosts shocked and thoroughly embarrassed.

Gichuru was later arrested taken to Kamungu, a place where he had a 'native' bar in partnership with Mathia Muiruri, an Assistant Chief, and was held under a form of house arrest.

The DO then spoke to the DC who in turn went to his superiors in Government, to find out exactly how to handle the matter. Eventually the colonial authorities considered his case and Gichuru was forcibly relocated to Kilimambogo in Ukambani where he spent some time teaching at the institute there.

When some of Kenya's prominent personalities, such as Dr. Munyua Waiyaki returned from America, he was offered a Ministerial post by the colonial government which he accepted. For this, he got a serious tongue lashing from Gichuru and was accused of succumbing to the white man's bribery. The colonial government had started giving posts to Africans to stop the agitation for freedom and the release of Jomo Kenyatta.

One day in 1960, Gichuru was invited to Government House where Governor Malcolm MacDonald proposed that Gichuru would make a better Prime Minister than the jailed Kenyatta. All they wanted in return was for KAU to soften its stance. Gichuru informed the Governor that he would not cut any sort of deal unless Kenyatta was released.

"Is this why you called me here?" Gichuru exclaimed. "We have all agreed that no government will be formed before Kenyatta is free!"

"But you can be the Prime Minister," the Governor said.

Gichuru just looked at him with disdain.

"Once you are the Prime Minister, you can release Kenyatta yourself!" the Governor continued, trying to convince Gichuru. "This will make you incredibly popular!"

"It is not me who detained him," Gichuru said coldly.

Later when Gichuru was explaining the matter to us, he complained that it had been a waste of time.

"I thought he was inviting me for something good!" he said. "I thought there was some good news about Kenyatta!"

I personally relied on the man for advice in politics and business, especially the former. Although Gichuru was involved in business, he was not very much into it and he had little desire to amass wealth. After a long illness, Gichuru died in 1982.

Socially and in business, even now, I have countless friends. It would probably take many volumes of this autobiography to name them all. However let me name a few who have been with me in times of joy and distress and without whose support my life might have turned out differently.

One such friend is Duncan Ndegwa, a former Head of Civil Service and Central Bank Governor. Before Duncan Ndegwa left for Scotland for further studies, we met and became friends at the African Corner Bar. We used go there to drink with my partner Kigwi, Mwai Kibaki, Mbugua Githere and other friends. I recall that Ndegwa had a very classy Volkswagen beetle and we all used to admire it. When he came back from abroad our friendship continued to grow and we have remained close ever since. Other friends are businessmen and politicians, Kenneth Matiba and John Michuki, Joseph Munyao, and many others.

In family circles, one of the closest friends I have is my cousin, James Raymond Njenga Kiguru, a former Commissioner of Lands. We have many businesses together and are very close in terms of social and family relations. When he was alive, Solomon Wairiri Kigera, my father-in-law, had great influence on me as well and gave me lots of advice on life and business.

From my own experience, there are some tips I would like to offer, especially to the youth.

One principle I stand by is that mixing business with family and friends does not work well. In matters of business, business must come first. It is not necessarily bad to do business with friends, but the relationship and any sentimentality should not interfere.

I learned this while I was still a child on Delamere's farm in Elementaita.

One day, I was with my mother on our small farm in Kagaa, the squatter village. She was digging out sweet potatoes for home use. At times, when she had some extra, she would sell them at the market at Ndunyu Buru in order to supplement the family's income. Since I was still very young, I was just playing in the *shamba* as she worked.

Every time she dug out a sweet potato, she would throw it on to a pile near me. I would occasionally take a small sweet potato from the pile, brush off the soil and eat it raw. We never worried about germs then, and my mother had no problem with me eating a little here and there.

However, on this occasion, I took the biggest sweet potato from the pile and chewed it while she worked.

When she was done, she came over and started putting the tubers into her *kiondo* (basket) to take them to the market. She knew that bigger sweet potatoes fetched more money and immediately noticed that the biggest sweet potato she had dug out was missing.

"Njenga, where is the big sweet potato?" she asked me.

I told her I had eaten it and this earned me a spanking, warning me never to do such a thing again. She said that if I was hungry, I should eat the small ones or those with defects. The best ones should be kept for sale.

For me, this was a lesson that business comes first.

In another incident, I was planning to go to Mombasa on business. I phoned my daughter, Lucy Wanjiru (who was then managing my Indian Ocean Beach Resort), to ask her to reserve a room for me. However, it was at the peak of the tourist season and a day before I left Nairobi, the hotel was swarming with visitors.

After booking in a large family of visitors, my daughter realized there was still one family member without a room. She knew that she would have to find a room for the person, otherwise the whole family would leave and look for alternative accommodation. So she booked the guest into the room she had originally reserved for me.

Perhaps she had not thought it through when she did this, but later she realized the significance of what she had done. She had sold my room, in my own hotel, one I had built from scratch, and one in which she was only the manager!

Lucy called me in Nairobi and in a voice full of fear and uncertainty, told me what she had done and apologized profusely. She expected me to scold her. Laughing, I told her she had done very well and then told her the story of my mother's sweet potatoes. Business is business, I told her. It was better that I sleep in another hotel, rather than interfere with her work. And that is just what I did—I was booked in another hotel until a room was available in my own!

Another bit of advice I would like to pass on is that one should not be motivated by greed in one's quest for wealth. Greed, I believe, has a way of making one lose sight of morality, and it becomes too easy to become involved in illegal activities that may interfere with one's life and family. Greed leads to shortcuts, which most likely will eventually lead to trouble. Stolen wealth, in my opinion, leaves one's conscience clouded forever and one might not enjoy the wealth at all. One will not be able to sleep well knowing that tomorrow the evil might be exposed. I would like to advise the youth to learn that greed and ambition are two different things. Ambition, combined with the strength of integrity and the fruits of sweat will always ensure success. Quick money might be enjoyable but the joy does not last for long.

There are many traditional proverbs about greed in all communities around the world. I recall we used to be told a story about a gathering of *wazee*, eating roasted goat as they sat out under the trees. One of them would cut and slice the meat and the others would take up the pieces one at a time. But the greedy man would snatch up as many pieces as he could, stuff his mouth and end up choking.

Such stories were told in order to teach people, especially children, the importance of moderation and respect for others. I wish some of our leaders would seriously think about what kind of example they are setting for the next generation.

During Kenyatta's time, many people close to the President made considerable fortunes by exporting maize. A friend of mine, George Mwicigi, told me that if I went and talked to Kenyatta, I would definitely be given a licence. Mwicigi was not on such friendly terms with Kenyatta as I was. He wanted me to secure the licence which he planned to use, together with me, to make money.

I thought about it and decided to look into the matter more carefully. Not everything about those exports was above board, and for many they were an opportunity to make a killing. How would I feel, I wondered, after making money from the maize exports, if Kenyans started starving? As a result of these reflections I refused to take the advantage, and by the end of this opportunity, I was nevertheless still wealthier than those who had. Easy come, easy go is a saying that I firmly believe in, and the qualities of honesty, dignity and integrity are three virtues that I cherish.

Greed and the desire for quick money destroys the moral fibre of society, creating a situation where people, especially the youth, lose trust in each other and drift apart. I wish the culture of honesty pursued by our forefathers would return.

I also believe in thrift and saving. By living within one's means, a person can always save and later invest in a bigger venture. I started saving during the time I was a charcoal burner and graduated to selling posts and lumber. After that I saved enough to start a small general shop and then a larger one. This is the way it should happen—working hard, building up, meeting challenges and achieving your goals. That said, I have no real formula for creating wealth. My own prosperity comes from the blessings of God and the products of my own determination and hard work.

Never believe that you have reached your limit. Wanting to invest and achieve more is not greed but a sign that you believe in yourself and your ability to achieve whatever you set out to get. Save a little, spend less, and then you will realize your dreams, whatever they may be. The moment you imagine that you have achieved all you can, you will stagnate and life becomes dull and meaningless. That is why I still go to the office or to my farms every day.

Another tip that I can offer to the youth who want to make names for themselves in life is to avoid over-indulgence in alcohol. I have seen alcohol and drugs ruin many young people and I am saddened by the proliferation of cheap and illicit brews and drugs to which many youth have become addicted. Although I have to acknowledge that I made much of my wealth by selling and distributing beer, I must however emphasise, not by overdoing it. As for drugs, they will only make one succeed in destroying oneself.

Today I rarely touch alcoholic drinks, but in my prime I used to enjoy my drink in social circles. However, I always knew where to place the limit. I never let alcohol interfere with my work or my life.

Although I had accumulated plenty of money by my early twenties, I never let it get into my head. I have witnessed many of my colleagues, both in business and politics, fall by the wayside due to alcohol despite their promising future. If one can avoid the pitfalls of alcohol in their youth and build a foundation for the future, then chances of success are very high. I cannot point at one single person who over-indulged in his youth and later became successful. So I advise the youth to save, invest wisely, and never squander their capital.

Alcohol can make a slave of a person and ruin him completely whatever genius he or she might have. It is good in recreational and social situations, but it should not be overdone. Drink with prudence, always.

In addition, I would like to advise people to always be straightforward. Be yourself. Do not discard friends because you have made good. You might need them when you least imagine you will. Being honest and open with friends and partners has helped me reach my current status. Never despise people or put on airs simply because you have more than they have. You might make billions and then look for genuine friends to talk to and get none. Money alone is not enough to make a person happy. Without the love of friends and family, life loses meaning and whatever wealth you may have is worthless in your pursuit for joy and a good life. Furthermore, one should not get drunk on power and become arrogant. I have witnessed some of my colleagues get drunk with power and wealth and end up being detested by other people and die lonely and miserable in later life.

Naturally, life has not always been a bed of roses for me and I have suffered quite a number of setbacks in my personal and business life. The death of my son Njoroge, and my wives, Wariara and Njeri, left me a saddened man, but I accepted it as God's will and have had to live with it. After all, death comes to everyone and no one can escape it.

As I mentioned earlier, the most trying moment in my business life was when Kenya Breweries cancelled my contract for beer distribution and I lost my investment in Castle Breweries. The two events left me with extremely big debts and I had to sell off considerable property to repay them.

However, I managed to save two of my most treasured properties. One was the beach plot by the Indian Ocean where the Indian Ocean Beach Resort stands. Logic dictated that I should dispose of property in Nairobi or elsewhere, but selling a beach plot was selling away something that I might never be able acquire again. After all, there are only so many beach plots along the coast. Another property I managed to save was Gachoroba Estate, a tea farm in Kiambu which I had used as collateral for a loan from Stanbic Bank. Apart from the Castle Breweries case, I think I have weathered other financial predicaments quite well.

Because many people always ask me to tell them the secrets of success in business, let me summarize, in order of priority, ten points I consider the most important elements that bring about this:

1. Honesty and integrity – these elements court trust and reliability;
2. Hard work – work hard every day to advance specific goals;
3. Innovation – think of new ideas to promote your business;
4. Taking risks – which suggest you have confidence to venture;
5. Taking loans – loans invigorate business and force concentration;
6. Partnerships – enter into partnerships with like-minded persons;

7. Avoiding conflicts – as much as possible, avoid employing many relatives in your businesses;
8. Commitment – be committed to whatever you set out to do, and follow your ambitions through;
9. Balancing – maintain the right balance between business, leisure and politics;
10. Resilience – do not give up; problems will always come, they are a challenge.

This, however, should not give the impression that all the ventures that I have gone into have been a bed of roses. To the contrary, I have failed in some businesses because of a variety of reasons but that did not deter me from going on or opening up new ventures. One has to defy fear of failure and fear to take risks.

Apart from the Castle Breweries debacle earlier mentioned, I have tried a few other things that did not work as I had expected. A good example is a flower growing business I tried and failed. This is despite the fact that I had imported a cold storage plant from Holland at a cost of 12 million shillings and installed it at my Cianda Estate. This figure is not inclusive of the technical and accommodation fees I paid the expatriates who flew in from Europe at my expense to assemble and install the plant. The plant now stands desolate just a few metres from my house and I plan to transform it into a milk-cooling plant. But that in the nature of business—sometimes you win, and sometimes you lose. All you need is to minimise your losses.

In my vision, Kenya's prospects for prosperity lie in education, technology and industrialization. The countries that have seriously invested in industrialization, such as the so-called Asian Tigers, have made great steps in the creation of wealth, leaving countries such as Kenya, which did not take industrialization seriously, lagging behind. I put the blame of the reversal of industrialization on Moi's government. The vision of industrialization that existed during Kenyatta's time and the many industries which were built by the state, were unfortunately run down after he died, and many jobs and opportunities were lost. Investors fled the country and the taxpayer lost considerably. However, the situation can be reversed and the industries can be made productive again. This can be verified by the current state of the Kenya Meat Commission and the New Kenya Cooperative Creameries which were revived by the Kibaki government and are now doing very well.

With industrialization and elimination of corruption, Kenya can become an emerging economy within a short time. However, it will take a very strong leader to eliminate corruption. Corruption has almost brought this once promising nation to its knees, and although efforts are now being made to eliminate it, I feel that what is being done is not enough. The country needs a strong anti-corruption authority to fight the vice and those who steal and enrich themselves must be made to return everything they have stolen. The government is not doing its job properly if it is unable to save the resources and wealth of the nation from thieves hiding in positions of power. We did not fight so fiercely for our freedom in the past so that crooks and thieves could rob us in the present.

I keep telling people that I will retire 'soon', but judging by my work ethic, who knows if this is plausible. I tend to be a workaholic of sorts, and I despise laziness. So I am always on the move, either attending political or business meetings. Perhaps I will slow down and delegate more, but total retirement does not seem to be something that I would do. My wife Njoki constantly encourages me to relax, but I seem to be simply unable to do so. I cannot sleep beyond 5 am since I have never done so throughout my adult life. All the same, I can feel age catching up with me and I suppose this will force me to slow down.

Perhaps I shall take up golf, finally, now that I'm over 80 years! After all I had been given a set of golf clubs by my friend Mwai Kibaki in 1972 but never got a chance to use them. I was far too busy, and I gave the set of clubs to one of my sons.

Whether I will actually take up golf or not is open to debate. More believable than that is my goal to spend more time with my cattle. My love for livestock is a partiality inspired by my grandfather. I fondly remember looking after his animals on Delamere's Elementaita Estate, and later at Elburgon, and I still retain some of the old concepts of livestock as wealth. On his death bed, my grandfather stated his wish that I prosper and own large herds of livestock, and I have tried my best to fulfil the old man's dying wishes. I have managed to acquire hundreds of cattle and goats which I enjoy watching as they graze. Despite my tight schedule, I a ways make time to check on them and I have to admit that I can stay with the animals for hours. I really do not need them, but they are simply a necessary part of my life. I know I amuse my guests at my Jacaranda Hotel office when I rush through meetings and then excuse myself, telling them that I have to hurry, because I am seeing my cows in the afternoon.

Then of course there is my wife Grace Njoki and young son, Emmanuel Karume. The two have put a fresh wave of vigour into my life and I look forward to happy days with them. They have added a new joy in my family life and I now have something special to look forward to when I get home. As a couple, we are very compatible and we complement one another in an ideal manner, so I believe that my remaining days promise to be full of bliss. For a boy who was born a squatter in a European settler's farm and started business as a charcoal burner, I feel I have achieved happiness far beyond my wildest expectations.

Epilogue

My name is Grace Njoki and I am the last born in a family of twelve. I was born at home on 6 June 1963 in Ndumberi, Kiambaa constituency, Kiambu. I was supposed to be named Wanjiru after my maternal aunt but my father decided I should be named Njoki, meaning in Kikuyu the "one who had come back". My parents had lost two girls named Njango who passed away one after the other. They were named after my maternal grandmother. The second Njango had been named after the first Wanjiku in the Kikuyu tradition of perpetuating a name when a person dies.[77] I would have been the third Njango, coming back to life, thus I became Njoki.

I received my basic education at Ndumberi Primary School before being admitted to Ting'ang'a High School in the same area. Unfortunately I did not join university because I did not quite make the grades. However, unlike many of my age mates, I did not opt to get married after high school. I stayed at home for a short time mulling over my options in life. For some reason, lofty or ambitious careers like becoming a doctor or a pilot did not really appeal to me. Instead, all my life, I had wanted to do one thing and do it thoroughly, and that was to serve God. I regarded this as a vocation, a calling. I decided to serve the Lord first and other things in life, if so destined, would come later.

Instead of looking for a suitable young man to get married to, therefore, I went to serve the church. I started as an evangelist at ACK St. Peter's Ndumberi Church in 1987. My work involved preaching the gospel to others and persuading them to join the church. I served as an evangelist up to 2002 and was so engrossed in my work that although the thought of marriage may have crossed my mind one time or the other, it was never with any degree of seriousness.

I had never vowed not to get married, but I was uncertain that I could handle the service to the Lord and the duties of making a home. I therefore stayed on as an evangelist up to September 2002 when I

---

77   See Chapter 1

joined Carlile Theological College in Nairobi for a course in Theology. After three years of hard study, I finished the course and was posted as a Church Army Sister to ACK St. Mary's Thindigua Church in July 2005. I was referred to as a trainee Evangelist as I had not met all the requirements and I was not ordained yet.

This posting was a practical part of the college course. I served at this station till October 2005 when I finally graduated from Carlile College and confirmed as a full Church Evangelist. I was 43 at the time and now felt that, if it was not too late, I could give marriage a try after this long period of dedicating my life to God.

Then, of course, something strange and astonishing happened. On 18 January 2006, I met with three women from my home area who had been my friends for a long time. We had gone to a certain home for an unveiling of the cross ceremony when the three called me aside and asked me whether I knew Njenga Karume. Of course I knew him, I replied. I pointed to him since he was at the same ceremony too. They then asked me whether I had ever thought of getting married. I was puzzled by the question because it was so unexpected. I informed them that I often prayed to God to let me marry a good man when and if He wished me to do so. Later I learned that they took my answer to Njenga, although at that time I did not understand what all their questions were about.

Later they revealed that *Mheshimiwa* wanted a new wife since he was lonely after the death of his previous partners and that they had recommended me as a possible replacement. A meeting was then arranged at Jacaranda Hotel, Nairobi, and after brief introductions Njenga and I were left on our own. After talking for a while where we got to know each other, he proposed. I was overwhelmed.

I had been thinking of getting married and I knew Njenga as my representative in Parliament, and also a friend of my parents. I had heard a lot about his warm personality and initially, at the first thrilling moment, I did not see any problem with the arrangement. However Njenga told me to take my time, go home, think seriously on my future and not speak a word to anybody about the matter.

The intervening period was one of the most stressful times in my life. Here I was, simple me, and here was the Minister for Defence asking me if I would marry him. I mean, I could not even talk to anybody about it, since he had asked me not to reveal the matter. There was the issue of his position as Minister, and also the awkwardness of telling anyone that I, a Church Evangelist of long-standing, was thinking about marrying such a prominent person! I even had to see a doctor because I could not sleep. The doctor informed me that the source of my problems was stress and he asked me what was on my mind, but I did not tell him. I was suffering from insomnia, and he gave me some very strong sleeping pills. They did not work. I would pinch myself at night to see whether I was living a dream, and I would feel the pain and know that this was reality. At the end of it all, I informed Njenga that I would like to become his wife.

A few days later, Njenga called me on my cell phone and asked me to tell my mother that he would be coming for a visit to pay the bride price. I said that I just did not have the courage to tell her myself and he said he would send another person then. He contacted my sister and when he told her about our plans to wed, she was shocked, as was my whole family. The whole thing just seemed surreal and out of this world. Needless to say, the dowry was paid and we were married twenty days later. It was just an incredible time in my life.

We soon went for our honeymoon in London, and it was quite an experience. For one, I had never been on a plane before, let alone visiting London. Then there was the cold winter weather. It was a revelation to me, and I thought these were the wonders of God being played out.

When Njenga and I got married we were advised we should attempt to understand one another and be flexible according to our needs. I had lived a simple lifestyle while Njenga was involved in many high profile activities, yet somehow we had to compromise.

In the end, this proved to be very easy since we are both very adaptable. Of course I understood that he had business and public responsibilities to take care of. I had no problem with such things. On my part, I had my Lord to serve, and Njenga said he would support me in all ways on this. As a matter of fact, he told me that I could be the staunchest member of my congregation and that I could preach to him even at home!

All the same my life changed completely. I had lived a simple life serving the church and was not used to the kind of opulence I suddenly found myself in. Also, I had always been single, and it was quite a change to start living with another person as a life partner. However, Njenga is very amiable and charming and made me feel at home in the blink of an eye. As for the sudden wealth, it did not affect me much because, as a spiritual person, I have never been materialistic. I was not overwhelmed by his affluence at all.

I rapidly became adjusted to my new life in Njenga's homestead. He asked me to take up the role of supervising the management of his cows and horticultural products at Cianda Estate where we live, and I enjoy this very much. When I was living at home I used to milk our few cows using my hands, and although our current herd runs into hundreds of heads which are milked by machines, I sometimes milk one or two with my hands just for fun. It is a challenge to manage such a big herd, but I believe I am managing it very well.

I am also in charge of superintending the growing of various horticultural products on the farm, including cabbages, carrots and potatoes. I use irrigation in some areas, and the results have been very good in my opinion. I supply some of the family hotels with foodstuffs, which keeps me on my toes since I have to promptly supply good quality foodstuff, most of which are perishable items.

Faced with these new business challenges, Njenga and I have discussed my skills and come to the decision that I would profit from more expertise in management. In early 2008 we decided that I should enrol for a course in business management, but then I discovered that I was pregnant and so the idea was suspended. However when our child is a little older I will definitely join such a course because proficiency and aptitude are required when running these kinds of enterprises.

One of my happiest moments in my married life and actually in all my life, was when I gave birth to our son Emmanuel Karume at the Aga Khan University Hospital, Nairobi, on 17 July 2008. I felt so full of warmth and delight and could not believe my eyes, holding that little bundle of joy which I had delivered at the unusual age of 45 years, an age doctors consider risky for both mother and baby. The delivery went smoothly, however, and the child's father was the first to see and hold him. The baby was delivered through Caesarean section and I was still recovering from the effects of anaesthesia when *Mzee,* who was waiting at the hospital, was taken to see him.

Another thing that helped me fit into my new life was that I was accepted by Njenga's children wholeheartedly, and they were happy to see their father get a helpmate. This was a point I had not given much thought to, but I was very pleased to notice more and more family support as days went by. They all came to the wedding and gave their blessings. They gave me a traditional stool, a *njūng'wa*, which is a sign of acceptance. Now we are all very close and if they ever have little arguments with their father, they ask me to be the arbitrator.

When our son was born, Njenga's children all came to visit me at the hospital and later came to the house to see their kid brother. Although some of them are older than me, they have no problem with our union and, in turn, their own children call me _cūcū_ (grandmother), which gives me a lot of pleasure. It is a unique experience being called mum and _cūcū_ simultaneously for the first time in my life. I am so grateful for this. I respect his children and they respect me. They include me in their lives and sometimes, because their father is sometimes difficult to access, they leave messages with me to deliver to him.

Good things, as in misfortunes, do not seem to come singly. On 27 July 2008, ten days after the birth of the baby, I was made a full Priest of the ACK. Then, on 12 January 2009 I became a Deacon and was given the robes of a full Minister. I am now attached to St. James Cathedral in Kiambu. As a Minister of the Church I can now perform all church ceremonies such as weddings, Holy Communion, Baptisms and funerals. Previously, when I was a deacon, I could only preach and perform minor chores such as the baptism of babies. This means that my dream of serving the Lord continues to be fulfilled.

I come from a very religious family. My brother is also an ACK Reverend and he graduated shortly after I did. I think we were called to serve the Lord and could not refuse the calling.

My husband has advised me not to accept the salary that the church pays its ministers. He says that we have more than enough to live on and that the money intended for my salary can be better used for other church causes. I could not agree more. This impromptu decision by my husband clearly demonstrates what a spontaneously generous man he is. Now I offer my services for free, what is referred to as a 'Tent Maker' in our church, and I have never been happier. He has influenced me with his own munificence.

I still maintain the same friendships as before my marriage, although some of my friends find it difficult to understand that I am not in a position to do them undue favours. A few of them imagine that my new-found high status will be advantageous to them but I try to explain to those with high expectations that whatever wealth surrounds me is not mine and I cannot afford to splash it out on them. Therefore there are some friends whose relationship towards me has changed. They treat me in a special way, as if I am not the person they knew, and this causes me a lot of distress since I am basically the same person at heart. But it is to be expected, I guess.

As for financial assistance to the Church, if it is for a good cause, I try to convince my husband that some help would be appreciated. The same goes for my family. There is nothing extraordinary that I can do for them unless my husband so wishes. I am married to the man I love;

I am in a married partnership for life and I am not ever going to take advantage of my place. I usually make this clear to those who are seeking favours from me.

I am more than happy with my husband and son. I admire Njenga for his humility, flexibility and sense of humour. He is a very down-to-earth person who likes to help society and those who are in distress. He is not conceited about his achievements, and he makes everyone he meets feel that they are important human beings. He also supports me in my service of the Church, and genuinely so, and I am grateful to him for that. It is difficult to quarrel with someone like him because he genuinely listens to the other person's opinions. It may sound like a cliché, but ours is a marriage made in heaven. Of course I am still trying to understand his rich political and business background, and I am making progress. His history is long and interesting, it fascinates me.

As for the future, I hope that our life together will continue to be as happy as it is now. I will proceed with my farming and my church work, and to assist my husband as best as I can. My wish is that our son will inherit the traits of his father, and that he will become like him. However, for the time being, our child will live as ordinary a life as possible and work as hard, or even harder, than his father. It is all the work of God—that is all I can say.

The three of us live in an extensive house deep inside the Cianda Estate. Although there are bodyguards and workers everywhere, we try to live as normal a life as possible. I have been trying to adapt to life in the limelight where moments of privacy are rare but Njenga does not live an extravagant or demanding lifestyle. He likes eating *ndũma* (arrowroots), *gĩtheri* (boiled maize and beans), *mũkimo* (mashed potatoes with *gĩtheri* and green pumpkin leaves) and such simple, traditional foods, just as he did in his childhood on Delamere's ranch in the Rift Valley. Naturally these are the foods that I myself was brought up on, and I enjoy preparing them for family meals.

As for Njenga, it is business as usual. I can see he is very proud to be a father again, at 80, and he spends as much time as possible with the family. I try to make my indefatigable husband relax and stay at home, but this is sometimes not possible with his busy schedule.

"I have to go to work," he tells me jokingly. "Otherwise what will the two of you eat if I stay at home?"

That personifies the real Njenga, the head of our family.

Index

A

O

P

R

S